W9-BAC-194

BUSINESS WEEK Guide to
The Best
Business Schools

Other BUSINESS WEEK Guides by McGraw-Hill

BUSINESS WEEK's Guide to The Best Executive Education Programs
   by John A. Byrne and Cynthia Green

BUSINESS WEEK's Guide to Mutual Funds
   by Jeffrey M. Laderman

A BUSINESS WEEK Guide: The Quality Imperative
   by The Editors of BUSINESS WEEK with Cynthia Green

BUSINESS WEEK's Guide to Small Business Trends and Entrepreneurship
   by The Editors of BUSINESS WEEK

BUSINESS WEEK Guide to
The Best
Business Schools

Fourth Edition

John A. Byrne

Senior Writer, BUSINESS WEEK

with a team of
BUSINESS WEEK Editors

McGraw-Hill, Inc.

New York   San Francisco   Washington, D.C.   Auckland   Bogotá
Caracas   Lisbon   London   Madrid   Mexico City   Milan
Montreal   New Delhi   San Juan   Singapore
Sydney   Tokyo   Toronto

Library of Congress Cataloging-in-Publication Data

Byrne, John A.
    Business Week guide to the best business schools / John A. Byrne
with a team of Business Week editors.—4th ed.
        p.   cm.
    Previous ed. published under title: A Business Week guide, the
best business schools.
    Includes index.
    ISBN 0-07-009422-5 (pbk. : acid-free paper)
    1. Business schools—United States—Evaluation. 2. College
choice—United States—Handbooks, manuals, etc. 3. Master of
business administration degree—United States—Handbooks, manuals,
etc. I. Business Week. II. Title. III. Title: Business week
guide, the best business schools.
HF1131.B95 1995
650'.071'173—dc20
                                     94-41147
                                         CIP

2 3 4 5 6 7 8 9 0 DOC/DOC 9 0 0 9 8 7 6 5

ISBN 0-07-009422-5 (PBK)

The sponsoring editor for this book was Philip Ruppel, the editing supervisor was
Jane Palmieri, and the production supervisor was Suzanne W. B. Rapcavage. It was set
in Garamond Light by North Market Street Graphics.

Printed and bound by R. R. Donnelley & Sons Company.

McGraw-Hill books are available at special quantity discounts to use as premiums and
sales promotions, or for use in corporate training programs. For more information,
please write to the Director of Special Sales, McGraw-Hill, Inc., 11 West 19th Street,
New York, NY 10011. Or contact your local bookstore.

CONTENTS

Preface / ix

1. WHY GO FOR THE MBA? / 1
The Promise of a B-School Education / **4**
All MBAs Are Not Created Equal / **5**
What to Consider If You Want an MBA / **6**
Favorite Hunting Grounds / **7**

2. DO YOU GET YOUR MONEY'S WORTH? / 11

3. HOW TO GET INTO ONE OF THE BEST B-SCHOOLS / 17
How to Increase Your Score on the GMATs / **18**
How to Score Big on the B-School Essay / **20**
To Interview or Not / **22**
A Caveat on References / **23**
How to Get a School to Foot Part of the Tuition Bill / **23**

4. RANKING THE B-SCHOOLS / 25
BUSINESS WEEK's Top 20 Business Schools / **26**

5. B-SCHOOLS BY THE NUMBERS / 47
GMAT Scores / **48**
B-School Selectivity / **49**
Full-Time Enrollments / **50**
International Enrollments / **51**
Women MBA Enrollments / **52**
Minority Enrollments / **53**

Contents

Pre-MBA Annual Pay / **54**

Starting Pay in 1994 / **55**

Signing Bonuses / **56**

Return on Investment / **57**

Paycuts after Getting an MBA? / **58**

Job Offers at Graduation / **59**

Outstanding MBA Loans / **60**

6. THE TOP TWENTY / 61

1. University of Pennsylvania (Wharton) / **62**
2. Northwestern University (Kellogg) / **70**
3. The University of Chicago / **78**
4. Stanford University / **86**
5. Harvard University / **94**
6. University of Michigan / **102**
7. Indiana University / **110**
8. Columbia University / **118**
9. University of California, Los Angeles (Anderson) / **126**
10. Massachusetts Institute of Technology (Sloan) / **134**
11. Duke University (Fuqua) / **142**
12. University of Virginia (Darden) / **150**
13. Dartmouth College (Amos Tuck) / **158**
14. Carnegie Mellon University / **166**
15. Cornell University (Johnson) / **174**
16. New York University (Stern) / **182**
17. University of Texas at Austin / **190**
18. University of North Carolina at Chapel Hill (Kenan-Flagler) / **198**
19. University of California at Berkeley (Haas) / **206**
20. Purdue University (Krannert) / **214**

7. THE RUNNERS-UP / 222

American Graduate School of International Management (Thunderbird) / **223**

Case Western Reserve University (Weatherhead) / **227**

Emory University (Goizueta) / **231**

Georgetown University / **235**

Michigan State University (Broad) / **239**

Pennsylvania State University (Smeal) / **243**

Southern Methodist University (Cox) / **247**

Tulane University (Freeman) / **251**

University of Illinois at Urbana-Champaign / **255**

University of Iowa / **259**

University of Minnesota (Carlson) / **263**

University of Notre Dame / **267**

University of Pittsburgh (Katz) / **271**

University of Rochester (Simon) / **275**

University of Southern California / **279**

University of Washington / **283**

University of Wisconsin—Madison / **287**

Vanderbilt University (Owen) / **291**

Washington University (Olin) / **295**

Yale University / **299**

8. THE BEST BUSINESS SCHOOLS OUTSIDE THE UNITED STATES / 303

U.S. B-Schools versus European B-Schools / **304**

Things to Consider Before Applying Abroad / **305**

Yet Another Option for an International Experience / **306**

Leading Institutions Offering Exchange Programs with Top 20 B-Schools / **308**

The European Institute of Business Administration (INSEAD) / **309**

International Graduate School of Management (IESE) / **311**

International Institute for Management Development (IMD) / **313**

London Business School / **315**

SDA Bocconi / **317**

Western Business School / **319**

9. MBAs FOR BARGAIN HUNTERS / 321

BUSINESS WEEK's Best Buys / **322**

Arizona State University / **325**

Baruch College / **326**

Brigham Young University (Marriott) / **327**

Georgia Institute of Technology / **328**

Ohio State University (Fisher) / **329**

Rice University (Jones) / **330**

Texas A&M University / **331**

University of Alabama (Manderson) / **332**

Contents

University at Buffalo, State University of New York / **333**
University of Florida / **334**
University of Georgia (Terry) / **335**
University of Kansas at Lawrence / **336**
University of Kentucky / **337**
University of Maryland at College Park / **338**
University of Tennessee at Knoxville / **339**

Appendix / 341
Index / 349

PREFACE

You have in your hands the fourth edition of what has now become something of a bible for all students and observers of the best graduate schools of business. Applicants rely on the guide for its storehouse of straight facts and firsthand knowledge on the top programs. Some B-school administrators view the up-to-date guide as a strategic study of their business. This latest edition is the largest and most comprehensive of them all.

The origins of this project go back to a phenomenally popular BUSINESS WEEK cover story of November 28, 1988, on the nation's best business schools. So taken was the public with the subject of graduate business education and a ranking of schools that the issue became an instant best-seller on the newsstands. Hundreds of letters flowed into the magazine's New York office. Newspapers and magazines worldwide reported the findings of the article.

The response from readers led to the idea that BUSINESS WEEK should significantly expand its coverage of the B-school world with a comprehensive guide to the best schools. The goal was to produce a full-fledged scouting report, something that went beyond merely listing the schools and offering a superficial description of their programs. The project won enthusiastic support within McGraw-Hill, Inc., publisher of BUSINESS WEEK, and the company's Professional Publishing Group agreed to publish the guide.

Six years ago, a key to the cover story's success was a unique rating of the B-schools. BUSINESS WEEK ranked the top B-schools by surveying recent graduates and corporate recruiters. In the past, rankings relied primarily on the opinions of B-school deans, faculty, or top executives who were asked to name the top programs—even though they often had only indirect knowledge of many of the schools.

For this guide, BUSINESS WEEK used its most recent surveys of graduates and corporate recruiters as a starting point. Then the staff interviewed hundreds of students, alumni, recruiters, faculty members, and deans to draw out the strengths and weaknesses of the top schools. An effort was also made to find out how the schools differ in their personalities, cultures, and extracurricular activities.

The result is a guide that reveals in great depth the fascinating findings of our graduate survey of the Class of 1994. Besides the Top 20 schools, BUSINESS WEEK names and profiles nearly 40 other excellent MBA schools that are often overshadowed by the top-tier institutions in the United States. And we add to this mix plenty of invaluable information on how to get into one of these elite schools.

Directing the project was Senior Writer John A. Byrne, who has covered graduate business education on a regular basis for more than 10 years. Author of *The Headhunters* and *The Whiz Kids: Ten Founding Fathers of American Business—and the Legacy They Left Us,* Byrne initiated the original research. He also conceived and wrote much of what you'll read in the guide.

Lori Bongiorno, a BUSINESS WEEK assistant editor, made a major contribution in reporting and writing several of the B-school profiles in the book. She also played a key role in the research for the cover stories. Judi Crowe greatly assisted in analyzing the results of thousands of completed questionnaires from the magazine's polls. Jeffrey D. Glasser helped to report and write portions of this new edition. Lourdes Hernandez proved invaluable at the difficult task of sending out most of the surveys and inputting much of the data into computers. Managing Editor Mark Morrison supervised the project.

WHY GO FOR THE MBA?

The MBA boom is over.

For three decades, would-be executives swarmed graduate business schools in steadily increasing numbers. Applications flowed into admissions offices at record levels. Year after year, schools routinely put through hefty increases in tuition. Universities that had no business to be offering MBAs quickly decided to do so for the extra revenue.

But no trend can forever defy gravity or demography. The first signs of a downturn appeared just after the 1980s came to a close. Since 1990, the number of people willing to endure the grueling four-hour Graduate Management Admission Test (GMAT) has fallen by over 10 percent. Business school observers predict that test takers will decline about 3 percent a year for the next few years.

Does this mean that an MBA isn't a good idea anymore? Not on your life. The demand for top MBAs by employers bottomed out in 1990, when many graduates scrambled for just a single offer—a far cry from the 1980s, when companies couldn't hire enough MBAs. Things began improving in 1992, but many schools reported a jump in opportunities for the Class of 1994 largely because consulting firms and investment banks stepped up hiring. Despite widespread corporate layoffs, the top-tier B-schools were reporting increases in on-campus interviews and job offers. "A lot of companies that held back MBA hiring have holes in their management lineup, and they're playing catchup," says Maury Hanigan, a New York–based staffing consultant. Citicorp planned to hire 410 MBAs worldwide in 1994, up 27 percent from 1992. Consultants Booz-Allen & Hamilton made 609 job offers to MBAs in the United States alone in 1994, up from only 400 a year earlier. Electronic Data Systems' consulting arm plans to hire 250 MBAs in 1995, up from 80 in 1994.

Whatever the job prospects, the promise of a business school education has as much relevance today as ever. Indeed, vast changes in business education in recent years have made the MBA more valuable to its holders. After years of criticism from many companies for turning out narrow, numbers-minded analysts with poor communication skills, one business school after another has radically changed the content and structure of its programs.

Schools are adding more courses on "soft" skills, such as leadership and teamwork, and placing greater emphasis on globalization and quality management. They're also trying to teach business as a whole instead of a set of disparate functions, and they're breaking down the walls that have long separated academia from the real world of business. "I think we're bringing more value to students today than we did in the past because of these changes," says B. Joseph White, dean of the University of Michigan's business school.

Indeed, today may be an advantageous time to attend a top business school because you'll have the opportunity to be both a participant in and a beneficiary of these changes. Besides, the MBA is still the degree to prepare you for life in the corporate or entrepreneurial world, to give you a headstart against the competition, and to somehow make you stand out in the managerial crowd. The payback from your investment may take longer today, but the right MBA can often lead to a more exciting career and a fatter paycheck. It can provide a foundation from which to launch a successful business. It can even be a ticket to a high-powered job running one of the biggest companies.

These are all good reasons why so many people continue to rush off to get an MBA—even though some of the luster has worn off the degree. "Today, the MBA is a good thing if it's a good thing for you," believes Tom Peters, the well-known management guru who got his MBA from Stanford in 1970. "I would argue that the magic and mystique of the degree is gone. Business success or success at brick-laying or anything else in life is all about verve and passion, imagination and flair, and boldness. Had Ted Turner ever taken a decision analysis course or pruned a decision tree in business school, he never would have been on the cover of *Time* as Man of the Year."

Okay. But how many people are as exceptional as Turner, who built Cable News Network into a worldwide television powerhouse? Peters thinks the key question to ask yourself is this: "Is it a worthwhile way to spend two years of the prime of my life?" Notwithstanding Peters' comments, the vast majority of MBAs from top schools answer in the affirmative. Many describe their two years of business study as the high point of their lives: meeting new friends, sharing new experiences, discovering horizons and careers they never knew existed. A good B-school education also imparts a level of confidence and maturity that years of actual work experience could never deliver. "It's like drinking from a fire hydrant," explains one Stanford University graduate. "There is so much intense learning and growing going on, both inside and outside the classroom."

Even in the more volatile 1990s, the MBA remains a modern-day symbol of business success. The education teaches you to think and analyze. The experience fosters enduring friendships and business contacts with exciting, dynamic people. It still opens doors to some of the most admired corporations in America, from Apple Computer to Xerox Corp., and has received far greater status in Europe and Asia. Some graduates gleefully report doubling their salaries after spending two years in a top B-school program. No wonder so much magic and mystery have surrounded what has become the most famous acronym in the vocabulary of business.

Yet because many prospective students don't do their homework, they end up wasting a lot of time and a lot of money. At the outset, they don't find out what an MBA can and can't do for them. They fail to properly evaluate a particular school or program to discover what it can deliver. They don't adequately analyze the costs of going to school against the likely benefits. As a result, many MBAs find the rewards of their degree elusive. Much to their chagrin, it fails to deliver on a better job, a bigger salary, and greater opportunity to ascend the corporate ladder.

In today's less-than-certain world, disappointment is more likely than ever. Just as many of the country's largest corporations were weeding out tens of thousands of middle-management jobs, a record 84,642 MBAs were churned out in 1992, the latest year for which figures are available. In 1980, U.S. B-schools graduated only 49,000 MBAs. It's amazing to think that when President Kennedy took office in 1960, only 4814 people received the degree. Now, there are an estimated 200,000 students studying for the MBA.

The numbers have had B-school deans scratching their heads for years. "It's hard to convince myself that the world needs 70,000 or so MBAs a year," says Robert K. Jaedicke, former dean of Stanford University's B-school. "If you look at the growth rate over the past 25 years, you could come to the conclusion that everybody in the United States will have an MBA degree by the year 2010."

He's only kidding. But you might ask, "What gives?" With visions of big promotions and heady salaries dancing in their heads, hordes of people have gravitated to the B-school world. Many of them felt disadvantaged at work without an MBA. Many others, particularly those with liberal arts backgrounds, felt they needed some business instruction to be successful in Corporate America. Still others, trapped in careers they really didn't enjoy, saw the MBA as the ticket out.

For many, however, the so-called "Passport to the Good Life" became little more than a frustrating dead end. Perhaps they put too much hope and too many expectations on a piece of paper. "An MBA degree is not a magic wand that transforms inexperienced and immature undergraduates into licensed managers," says Arnoud De Meyer, an associate dean at INSEAD, the European Institute of Business Administration in Fontainebleau, France. "I have never met a company recruiter who hires MBAs; they hire people with high potential. An advanced business degree is only part of a total package of education and experience, as well as the motivation to work in a particular industry."

Oftentimes, an MBA doesn't even become part of the package to help people move ahead because too many receive the degree from institutions that lack either national or regional reputations for quality. There were about 370 graduate business schools in 1974. Today, nearly 700 institutions offer the degree in the United States—only a little over a third of which meet even the minimum standards of accreditation set by the American Assembly of Collegiate Schools of Business. Harvard University's B-school dean, John H. McArthur, has gone so far as to say that 97 percent of the schools hand out the degree to "virtually anyone who applies." Besides all the U.S. schools in the business, another 500 institutions grant advanced business degrees abroad.

That's one reason why BUSINESS WEEK published this guide. Not merely a listing of business schools, it's a scouting report on the best of the bunch. For years, as many as 40 schools claimed they were in the Top 20, and at least 100 institutions told prospective applicants they were in the Top 50. To be sure, too many schools jumped on the MBA bandwagon because it became something of a fad to offer the degree. Not only was it the degree to have, it was the degree to have to succeed. It's true that in some professions, especially consulting, banking, and consumer packaging, an MBA can be of critical importance. But its necessity in general business has often been overstated.

When BUSINESS WEEK and Louis Harris & Associates polled senior executives from major corporations, more than half of them said it wasn't important for an executive to have an MBA to get ahead in the company. Despite that belief, however, 56 percent of the executives agreed that when merit and abilities are equal, MBAs often get promoted faster than people without the degree. And when asked whether they would advise a son or daughter planning a career in business to get an MBA, an overwhelming 78 percent said they would.

The Promise of a B-School Education

You remember what MBAs were supposed to be like in the 1980s: narrow-minded people who were overly competitive and out for a buck? Forget the stereotype. If it was ever true, it's certainly not the case today. At the best schools, MBAs are a broad and diverse mix of people. Northwestern's Class of 1994 included someone who was hijacked in the Philippines by rebels, a *Sports Illustrated* reporter, a story editor from Metro-Goldwyn-Mayer, a professional soccer player, a dean of students at a girls' prep school, and a former Seattle Seahawks cheerleader. Among the consultants and engineers in Stanford's Class of 1994 was a former speechwriter for the president of the United States.

Like many MBA candidates, some of these people never really planned a career in business and grew unhappy with what they were doing for a living. Maybe you're a musician, artist, engineer, psychologist, doctor, lawyer, or teacher. Is the MBA a good investment for the career switcher? A degree from a top school can make the transition to the business world a lot easier. It will not only give you a taste of what business is all about, it may also provide the contacts you need to land a viable job when the educational experience is complete. Indeed, some MBA-recruiting companies like the different perspectives that people from law or medicine can bring to business. If you're really tired of what you're doing, a quality MBA can be a pass to this new and different world.

There are other kinds of career switchers, too. These are people who already have good jobs in business, but don't want to stay in the same industry or career for the rest of their lives. An MBA degree is a tougher choice in this case. Don't expect any guarantees that the MBA will allow you to start fresh. If you have had valuable experience in an industry or a company, you'll find an MBA more worthwhile if you intend to build upon that previous experience—not reject it in the hopes of doing something completely different. A chemist for a drug company may well want to return to the pharmaceutical industry in a business management position in finance or marketing. Those who want to divorce themselves from their previous experience face a tougher road.

There is also a new kind of MBA student—the would-be entrepreneur. Many now view the B-school as a useful "boot camp" in which you learn the nuts and bolts of business, make a slew of networking contacts, and get a corporate job where you'll spend your first three to five years before launching your own company. Responding to a growing interest in entrepreneurship, B-schools have launched a bevy of courses that make it possible to do your own thing sooner in life than you ever expected. Widely available courses instruct how to put together a business plan; raise money from venture capitalists and other investors; incorporate your business and produce, market, and sell a product. Some schools, such as UCLA, Babson, Carnegie Mellon, and the University of Southern California, have developed complete programs in entrepreneurship. The upshot? Dozens of businesses have been started by recent MBA graduates, from restaurants and coffee-houses to computer and electronics firms. Obviously, none of these courses confer immediate success. That's all up to you.

All MBAs Are Not Created Equal

Despite the recessionary ups and downs, the MBA degree remains valuable. Anyway you look at it, it's the graduate degree of choice among the corporate elite. Of the chief executives of the top 1000 corporations in 1993, some 267 hold the degree (up from only 225 in 1990). Most brand-name companies consider the MBA to be something of a screen for the best and brightest young people around the world. That's why they recruit so many MBAs and why they so willingly pay them handsome salaries. The combination of a top degree and an employment history with a Procter & Gamble or a Citicorp can make a big difference on a résumé. Executive headhunters say today that their clients often specify that the MBA is a prerequisite for top management positions.

When should you go to business school, then? The succinct and difficult answer is when you can get into one that's good enough to make a meaningful difference to you and your career. With growing recognition that quantity-over-quality thinking has gotten American management into lots of trouble, a better idea has taken hold: The MBA is more crucial, or less, depending on which school confers it. "When people talk about the MBA, they tend to talk about the generic degree," says Thomas F. Keller, dean of Duke University's Fuqua School of Business. "But the MBA is not a standardized product, and a lot of programs don't offer much value."

Little-known institutions with small MBA programs that lack accreditation probably aren't going to give you either a quality business education or a hefty starting salary. "The initials don't mean anything," insists John W. Rosenblum, former dean of the University of Virginia's Darden School. "The sooner we stop writing MBA and start acknowledging it's as meaningless as a BA the better off we'll be. What counts is where did you get it. We have too many people studying for MBA degrees without careful thought as to why, and we have too many schools offering MBAs without careful thought as to why."

If you want a worthwhile MBA, you have to get it from a school with a reputation for quality and/or prestige—whether it's known worldwide, throughout the United States, or only regionally. BUSINESS WEEK customer satisfaction surveys of alumni have found that the greater the reputation of the school, the more likely you are to be more than satisfied with its results. You might even want to ignore the big national schools if your goal is to take over the family business or simply become a kingpin in your home region. An MBA from a state university could turn out to be far more valuable than one from Harvard. Why? Because you'd make more relevant business and government contacts to further your career in the area.

Who exactly goes to business school these days? When you count both full- and part-time programs together, you find that students range in age from 21 to the early 50s, though the biggest single age group is 28 years old. About one-quarter are at least 31 years of age, while only 7 percent are at least 40. Men easily outnumber women: At Columbia University roughly one in three students is a woman; at MIT only one in four. Students are predominantly white. One recent study by the Graduate Management Admission Council found that only 8 percent of MBAs are black, 4 percent are Hispanic, and 5 percent are Asian. At any of the top schools, however, you'll find a lot more ethnic and foreign diversity. At Wharton, 30 percent of the students hail from foreign countries, 15 percent are minorities; at the University of Michigan's B-school, 26 percent of the Class of 1996 is made up of minorities and 18 percent is foreign.

Most of the better schools prefer that MBA candidates have two to three years of full-time work experience under their belts before applying. Your chances of gaining admission to a good program fall significantly without work experience. Many MBAs who lack time in the real world say they regret not having waited before going to B-school. Having already earned a living gives you a reference point to use as you study business. It also makes your comments and insights in the classroom more valuable to a discussion. And work experience is often used by the better schools as an important consideration as to whether you get into the school or not. The better the company and the experience, the more likely it will open the door to a quality MBA program.

What to Consider If You Want an MBA

One thing's for sure: The MBA doesn't come cheap. If you're leaving a good job, you might have to give up $70,000 to $90,000 in salary over the two years you'll commit to most full-time programs. It will shock some to know that the average Harvard MBA quit a job paying about $54,000 a year to attend, and graduated with debts of more than $43,400 to pay for the degree. Those numbers help to put in perspective the starting pay and bonus packages for a Harvard MBA, which averaged $102,600 in 1994. Expect to pay about $20,000 or more in annual tuition and fees at the best private schools that exude MBA prestige. Add a few thousand more for books and other expenses, and the total cost, including lost earnings, can easily approach $150,000. Quite a bit of money for a business education and a piece of parchment. That's why, in fact, so many top MBAs flock to the world of management consulting and investment banking: They pay graduates the highest starting salaries, and that money is often sorely needed to pay off a pile of loans.

If you work the averages, however, a Top 20 degree should have enabled you to land a job that paid a starting salary and bonus of about $73,000 in 1994. Simple calculator math will tell you that it might take a good number of years to recoup your investment in lost earnings and tuition. In fact, some career counselors contend that on this basis it's simply not worth the cost. But those assessments often ignore an important consideration: The economic advantage you initially gain from the MBA is usually maintained throughout your career. And it's more likely to give you a better shot at attaining what most people seek in their first job after B-school: interesting work, good chances for promotions, solid pay, clear responsibilities, friendly coworkers, job security, and challenging problems to work on. Besides, you can't feed into a calculator the increased confidence and psychological comfort an MBA may give you as a business executive or manager. One Harvard grad likened it to a vacation in Europe: "Can you justify its payback? No. But does it broaden your horizons, give you a new perspective on the world? Is it valuable? Of course."

There are also ways to limit the cost of the degree. Students at state schools pay substantially less tuition than those at private schools. If you're a resident of California, for example, you could get a degree from UCLA for little more than $14,000—over two years! That's a mere fraction of what the degree would cost you at Northwestern or Chicago. The same is true at such top schools as the University of Michigan in Ann Arbor or the University of North Carolina at Chapel Hill, arguably the best values in MBA education. At North Carolina, even a nonresident of the state pays only $8300 a year in tuition—less than half of what you'd pay at any top private school. Compare that to neighboring Duke University, where the annual bill is $20,800. And in many cases, nonresidents are eligible to pay resident tuition in their second year of graduate study.

That's a pretty compelling argument in favor of the public university: Few students want to graduate with $40,000 or more debt on their backs. But also remember that the graduates of public universities seldom bring home the highest starting salaries. A Duke graduate, for instance, tends to earn on average a little over $4000 more out of the gate than a counterpart from the University of North Carolina. In 1994, Harvard grads made the most at just over $90,000 in starting salary and bonus—after paying over $24,000 a year in tuition and fees. The University of Texas MBA averaged about $63,000 in starting salary and bonus. Besides the basic salary and signing bonus, the elite MBA grads often get a spate of other perks that range from moving expenses and guaranteed year-end bonuses to new cars and a year's reimbursement of tuition. A degree from Northwestern or Harvard is far more likely to bring these bennies than one from Indiana or Texas.

Cost, then, is certainly one criterion in deciding whether you can go for an MBA and where you should go. That's also why BUSINESS WEEK puts together a list of "value" schools that offer a solid education at the lowest possible cost (see Chapter 9). What are other considerations? While a school's overall standing is critical to the value of its degree, you also should think about what you want to gain from an education. Do you want a job in finance? marketing? manufacturing? human resources? Some schools have reputations for being the absolute best in a particular field. If you're interested in entrepreneurship, for example, it would be hard to beat UCLA's incredible program.

Favorite Hunting Grounds

Within the top tier of business schools, the issue for prospective students is not which school is No. 1 or No. 3, but how well the school's strengths and culture fit the students' needs. Where do corporate recruiters say they find the best graduates for specific skills?

General Management

1. Harvard
2. Northwestern
3. Stanford
4. Michigan
5. Virginia
6. Columbia
7. Wharton
8. North Carolina
9. Indiana
10. Duke

Marketing

1. Northwestern
2. Michigan
3. Harvard
4. North Carolina
5. Virginia

Finance

1. Wharton
2. Chicago
3. Columbia
4. New York
5. Michigan

Accounting

1. Wharton
2. Chicago
3. Michigan
4. Northwestern
5. Indiana

Manufacturing

1. MIT

2. Carnegie Mellon

3. Michigan

4. Northwestern

5. Purdue

Before applying to any school, you really need to do your homework. Go beyond the slick brochures and promises made by the marketing people of these schools. Treat it the way an MBA would in a typical case study. "You should gather all the information about placement, the quality of the school, and do a business analysis of it," suggests Robert L. Virgil, former dean of Washington University's Olin School of Business. "If you're investing two years of your life and a lot of money, I think you should visit the school when it's in session. Attend a class or two, talk to the students, grab a recruiter during a coffee break to find out what he or she thinks the place is like. Then, look at yourself in the mirror and see if you really match up with the school."

Before selecting which schools you might want to attend, chat candidly with recent graduates. If you already have your heart set on becoming a consultant at McKinsey & Co., it would be wise to find a McKinsey staffer who is an alumnus of the school you want to attend. Most alumni and/or admissions departments will help you locate recent graduates. Wharton goes so far as to send all applicants a directory of alumni who have volunteered to share their first-hand knowledge of Wharton by telephone. Applicants can call on Wharton MBAs by location, company, and undergraduate school from Alaska to Venezuela, from American Express to Yoplait, from Albright College to Wellesley College. Remember, however, when speaking to alumni, that graduate schools of business have changed so dramatically in recent years that alums who have been out of the school for five or more years may not have a good feel for the current MBA program. "We're changing so rapidly, they don't know what the school is all about today," says Donald Jacobs, dean of Northwestern's Kellogg School.

Consider, too, how a particular school's method of instruction suits your personality. At Harvard, you could find yourself straining to make your voice heard in classroom discussions that account for most of your grade. If you're not good at scrambling for attention in a class of 90 very competitive students, you'll likely be better off at a school such as Dartmouth's Amos Tuck. There's more emphasis there on how well you work in small teams and on cooperation instead of competition. On the other hand, if you're very aggressive and enjoy the thrill of a contest, you should go to one of the more competitive schools. (See Chapter 2 for BUSINESS WEEK's survey of top graduates and what they say about their schools.)

You won't find large numbers of terribly disappointed people. MBAs from the top schools generally offer positive endorsements of the experience—whether they are freshly minted or have been out for a number of years. Most have little doubt that the time and expense of getting the degree were well worth it. They say they forged friendships and contacts that will endure through a lifetime; they linked up with new jobs that paid better money and offered greater opportunities for advancement than the positions they left. Some consider it the most important and formative decision they've made in their lifetimes.

So what if the boom is over?

DO YOU GET YOUR MONEY'S WORTH?

In 1987, John K. Reagan was a newly minted MBA from Duke University's J.B. Fuqua School of Business. Today, he's a less-than-satisfied customer. For almost two of the past seven years he has been without full-time work, and he now earns less at age 32 than he did in the job he left at 22 to enroll at Fuqua.

The same year that Reagan graduated from Duke, Lisa Lisanti Juliano earned an MBA from Stanford University. She's not the most successful member of her class, but she's doing mighty fine, thank you. Juliano recently celebrated her seventh year with a Johnson & Johnson subsidiary, where 10 people report to her as a regional sales manager. At 34, she can boast of a well-paying job with plenty of growth opportunities. She believes her degree paid off in spades and would pursue it again in a heartbeat.

Reagan and Juliano both quit jobs to obtain a graduate degree that seemed to promise a better job, bigger salary, and greater chance of advancement. Both also graduated in 1987, arguably the best of times for MBAs. Wall Street was hiring thousands of them. Bidding wars for top graduates were not unusual. Reagan racked up 30 on-campus interviews. Juliano had 20.

Just months after they graduated, however, the stock market crashed, corporate downsizings became the rule, and the economy began showing signs of strain. Many of their classmates discovered that the LIFO accounting method taught in every B-school curriculum applied directly to them: last in, first out.

Not surprisingly, the economic downturn in the late 1980s and early 1990s has prompted much concern over the value of an MBA. Was some of the earlier enthusiasm for the degree misplaced? Does an MBA deliver less value than it did a decade ago? Is there a glut of MBAs on the market? If anyone is in a position to know, it's the Class of 1987. So BUSINESS WEEK surveyed 3683 of the Class's members from the nation's Top 20 B-schools. (The magazine actually polled grads from the 21 schools that made the BW Top 20 list in 1988 and/or 1990.) Some 1553 responded. Even in the topsy-turvy economy of 1992, most had few regrets. If they had to do it over again, about 83 percent would still go to business school. Fewer than 3 percent say they wouldn't; 14 percent weren't sure. Typically, the better their school's standing, the more certain its alums were that they would make the same choice—even if they were currently unemployed.

Contrary to some reports, there's also no evidence of mounting employer disaffection for the degree. Even companies that have shed thousands of white-collar workers still feel the need to replenish the young talent in the company for the years ahead.

Indeed, the MBA is now a virtual prerequisite for admission and advancement in many industries. "There are few opportunities in investment banking, consulting, and commercial banking for people without MBAs," says Maury Hanigan, a New York–based consultant who helps companies recruit students more effectively. "And if you want a corporate fast-track career, an MBA is still important."

Yet even the deans of the most prestigious schools concede that the return on this educational investment takes longer than before. An MBA costs much more to obtain—especially for older students who quit well-paying jobs to go back to school. When B. Joseph White, dean of the University of Michigan's B-school, got his MBA in 1971, the ratio of his classmates' average starting salary ($15,000) to their annual tuition ($2500) was 6 to 1, he figures. "Today, our students start at about $58,000, and the nonresident tuition is around $17,000," says White. "So that ratio is now about 3.5 to 1. The payback is slower because it has become a more costly investment."

A stagnant or fast-changing economy can also make it an unpredictable investment. After getting an accounting degree from Georgetown University, John Reagan sensed he wasn't cut out to be an accountant. He spent a year in sales at the Dallas Market Center Co. before going to Duke. The MBA, he thought, would broaden his skills and open new options. "I never expected that attending Duke would guarantee me a high-paying job, nor did I hold the school to some fiduciary duty to get me that kind of job," he says.

Although Fuqua got him plenty of interviews with big-name companies, he had no offers. Returning to Dallas, Reagan eventually landed a marketing job with a startup in the food business. Within four months, the company suspended operations, and he was out. Reagan was no longer a not-yet-hired student; he was just unemployed. "In business school, you have a perceived value to a company. Once you're out on the street, you're just another name in a personnel file."

Unable to connect with another company, Reagan began work on a temporary basis in early 1989 for Foxmeyer Corp., a national drug wholesaler. He was able to turn the post into a permanent job—until it was eliminated in late 1990. Two years later, he was earning just over $21,000 a year as a clerk for Trinity Industries, Inc., a Dallas property-management firm. "It's frustrating and disappointing," he says. "Some people still hold out the MBA as some sort of golden ticket on the flight to the good life. I would tell them to check the boarding pass, because your seat is being oversold by every school in America."

If a top-notch MBA didn't pay off for Reagan, it more than delivered the goods for Lisa Juliano. In the early 1980s, she was working at U.S. Steel as an environmental engineer when the company axed her department. With an undergraduate degree in chemical engineering from Lafayette College, she scrambled to sell herself to another division, finally gaining a job selling industrial plastics. But the experience nudged her toward an MBA and a different industry with greater growth potential. "I was lucky to have gone through that turmoil early in my career, because it convinced me that I wanted to be in an area where there was growth," she says.

Armed with her Stanford MBA, she focused on the booming health care field in 1987, accepting a marketing job with LifeScan Inc., a Johnson & Johnson subsidiary that makes blood-glucose monitors. Within 10 months, she got a promotion to product manager. Other promotions followed: international marketing manager and then domestic marketing manager. Not long after, she made a lateral move into sales, as a regional manager. "The degree enabled me to make a fresh start in an exciting industry," she says. "And it probably helped me through the first promotion or two."

Both Reagan's and Juliano's stories demonstrate that there's no magic in even a Top 20 degree. Juliano's career got a big boost from her MBA, but Reagan's inability to take immediate advantage of his degree put him in a bad position in a weak economy. So if an MBA isn't going to come with a guarantee, is it worth it? "MBAs may well look worse off but be better off than they would have been without the degree," insists Ronald E. Frank, dean of Emory University's B-school. He has a point: In an increasingly competitive job market, everything counts. The person with the MBA is still likely to have an advantage over the person who lacks one, even if the degree isn't the first-class ticket it once seemed to be.

That said, it's still interesting to note what the graduates from the Class of 1987 think about their investment—a full five years after they've ridden the waves of a tough economy. Although the scope of the BUSINESS WEEK survey was limited, the results of the poll provide a pretty good glimpse of what various graduates of the best schools think. Whose graduates are most satisfied with the MBA? Whose graduates earn the most five years out? Whose graduates would be more likely to get an MBA knowing what they now know? The answers are as intriguing as the questions.

School	Without question	Maybe	Never	School	Without question	Maybe	Never
Stanford	93.8%	5.4%	0.9%	UCLA	81.3%	13.2%	5.5%
Dartmouth	92.3	7.7	0.0	Michigan	80.9	17.0	2.1
Harvard	92.2	5.9	2.0	MIT	80.6	19.4	0.0
Virginia	90.6	7.8	1.6	Indiana	80.5	15.6	3.9
North Carolina	87.9	10.3	1.7	Berkeley	78.7	17.0	4.3
Cornell	86.0	12.9	1.1	Carnegie Mellon	76.9	20.5	2.6
Northwestern	84.9	11.8	3.4	Wharton	76.0	19.0	5.0
Yale	84.4	15.6	0.0	Rochester	75.0	25.0	0.0
Texas	84.2	13.2	2.6	Duke	74.7	19.0	6.3
Columbia	84.1	11.6	4.3	NYU	64.3	32.1	3.6
Chicago	82.0	16.2	1.8	Averages	83.0	14.3	2.7

1. Knowing what you now know from working for five years, would you still have gone for an MBA?

As an applicant you're probably weighing the costs versus the benefits of an MBA degree. The fact that so many graduates from the top schools would do it again if they had the chance is pretty convincing evidence that the degree is worth it. And remember, this is the Class of 1987—MBAs who have been out in a truly tough marketplace.

School	Same school	Not sure	Another	School	Same school	Not sure	Another
Stanford	99.1%	0.9%	0.0%	MIT	75.8%	21.0%	3.2%
Dartmouth	92.3	5.8	1.9	Michigan	75.5	20.2	4.3
Harvard	92.2	5.9	2.0	Columbia	75.4	18.8	5.8
North Carolina	91.4	1.7	6.9	Cornell	73.1	18.3	8.6
Northwestern	89.1	9.2	1.7	Texas	69.7	21.1	9.2
Virginia	89.1	9.4	1.6	Indiana	68.8	24.7	6.5
UCLA	85.7	14.6	0.0	Berkeley	66.0	31.9	2.1
Wharton	83.5	14.9	1.7	Rochester	54.5	34.1	11.4
Chicago	78.4	18.0	3.6	NYU	53.6	35.7	10.7
Yale	78.1	15.6	6.3	Carnegie Mellon	46.2	43.6	10.3
Duke	77.2	19.0	3.8	Averages	79.4	16.5	4.1

2. If your answer is yes, would you have attended the same school or another?

Even more interesting than whether the Class of 1987 would still go back for an MBA, is this question. By far, Stanford graduates were the most satisfied and most loyal of the bunch. On the other hand, at least one out of every 10 graduates from Carnegie Mellon, New York University, and the University of Rochester are certain that if they had to do it again, they'd pick another B-school.

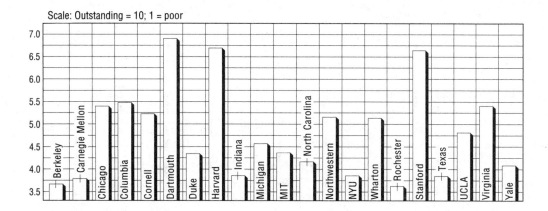

Scale: Outstanding = 10; 1 = poor

3. To what extent has your school's alumni network helped you in your career so far?

There's a wealth of difference in the value attached to alumni networks. Not all that surprisingly, the trio of MBA elites—Dartmouth, Harvard, and Stanford—lead hands down. Alums at Rochester, Berkeley, and Carnegie Mellon have found that their colleagues haven't been very helpful to their career success at all.

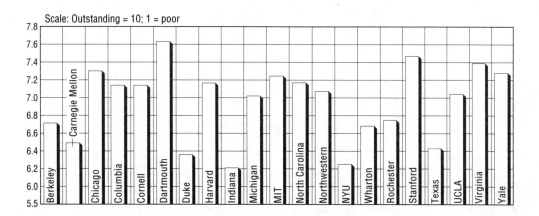

Scale: Outstanding = 10; 1 = poor

4. To what extent has the knowledge you gained in your school's MBA program helped you in your career?

For all the talk from B-school deans about how much the content of their programs differs from one to the other, there's little variance from alumni when it comes to discerning how helpful the knowledge gained in a program has been to their careers. While Dartmouth leads the pack, the spread is so thin that last-place Indiana isn't all that far behind.

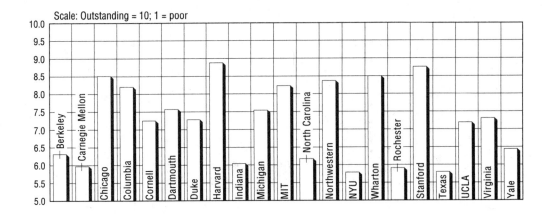

Scale: Outstanding = 10; 1 = poor

5. To what extent has your school's reputation helped you in your career so far?

Reputation still counts for a lot. All those years of pumping MBAs out into the marketplace has helped to solidify Harvard's reputation. That's certainly less so at New York University and the University of Texas.

School	Average pay	School	Average pay
Harvard	$167,740	New York University	$91,070
Stanford	144,540	Carnegie Mellon	85,400
Chicago	127,350	Berkeley	84,880
MIT	122,380	Virginia	83,060
Dartmouth	119,380	North Carolina	77,760
Columbia	119,160	Michigan	77,200
Wharton	113,790	Texas	74,340
Northwestern	100,260	Duke	66,420
Cornell	98,490	Rochester	63,610
UCLA	97,290	Indiana	62,650
Yale	94,400	Average	98,627

6. Five years out: How much money do they make?

These numbers are mere averages, so they hide the big swings in pay five years out. They may also be on the high side, because those who responded to the BUSINESS WEEK survey could be found and therefore may have been more likely to have stable jobs. Still, the numbers immediately tell you one thing: If you're thinking about getting an MBA from a school where the starting pay levels are not all that high, don't expect to zoom to the head of the pack later on. The degrees that promise the most money out of the gate tend to pay back the most in later years as well.

16

HOW TO GET INTO ONE OF
THE BEST B-SCHOOLS

Now that the MBA boom is over, just how hard is it to get into a top-notch business school? The answer: a little bit easier than a few years ago. But it's still tough. The best schools remain flooded with hopeful applicants. Most of the prestige schools have witnessed only a leveling off of the growth or a slight decline in applications. It's still true that many people who already have their MBAs from name schools wouldn't be able to get through the same B-school doors today.

The University of Virginia's Darden School, for example, accepted 43 percent of those who applied for admission in 1985. In putting together the Class of 1996, however, it was considerably choosier, accepting only 28 percent. At Northwestern University's Kellogg School of Business, a record 31,000 prospective students requested literature in 1991. Those early requests resulted in 4400 applications for 530 seats in the Class of 1994. Wharton received 5019 applications for its Class of 1996, up from 4399 a year earlier. Only 23 percent of those who applied were invited to attend. The most selective school in the country remains Stanford University, which accepted roughly 10 percent of the more than 4500 candidates who applied for one of the 350 seats in Stanford's Class of 1996.

How do you get through so narrow and selective a door as that? B-schools generally look at academic factors such as your undergraduate grades and scores on the Graduate Management Admission Test (GMAT). They also consider leadership ability, special talents, background characteristics, motivation, work experience, and career interests. These factors are less tangible, and it's harder to predict how they'll be weighed by admissions committees. But work experience can often tilt a decision in your favor. So could well-written essay answers or a good showing in a personal interview.

Above all, hedge your bets by applying to half a dozen or so schools—and try to apply early if you can. Most schools list their final deadline for admissions between March 1 and June 1. But you can be at a disadvantage if you mail in your application so late in the game. Ideally, you should try to get it in by early January to gain admission for the fall semester or quarter. Duke University's B-school admissions staff begins reading applications on December 1 and continues to admit students until the class is full. Under that system, the earlier you apply the better off you are. "If people waited until our final deadline, they would have virtually no chance of being admitted," says Anne Sandoe-Thorp, director of admissions for Duke. "If you're an average candidate, your chances go down significantly the later you wait."

In contrast, Northwestern's Kellogg School tries to adjust its admittance rate in each of three admission periods. In the earlier periods, the school might admit as much as 10 percent of the pool, even though the admit ratio for the year is 1 out of 8 or 9. So chances are that if you apply early, you'll still be better off.

How to Increase Your Score on the GMATs

No matter how you slice it, your chances of getting into a good school are very dependent on how well you score on the Graduate Management Admission Test (GMAT). Four times a year, in January, March, June, and October, thousands of people sit for four hours with number two pencils in hand, filling in answers that will largely decide what kind of school they can apply to. Every accredited B-school, with the exception of Harvard, which relies more heavily on work experience and essay answers, requires the GMAT as part of the admissions package.

If you manage to eke out only the average score of 494, from a range of 200 to 800, your chances of making it to a top school are pretty slim. You really need to score above 600 to seriously entertain the idea of making it into a Top 20 school. And you need to score no less than 580 to walk through the door of one of BUSINESS WEEK's Runners-Up schools—excellent graduate business institutions that tend to be overshadowed and therefore hidden from view by the frenzy to land a spot in the Top 20. True, Virginia accepted some applicants with GMATs as low as 450, and the University of Michigan as low as 440. But the average at the schools was 643 and 630, respectively.

If your test score doesn't quite measure up, don't surrender just yet. It's possible that you could be rejected from one school based on your GMAT score and be accepted by a Top 20 school with the same score. Why? Some schools, feverishly working to boost their reputations by appearing selective, will simply toss you out of their admit pool. They are using GMAT averages as a marketing tool to attract better candidates. Other schools, already assured of their quality reputation, might pay more attention to other parts of your application—work experience, essays, personal interviews, and undergraduate grades.

Many admission directors, too, look beyond the overall GMAT score to see how well or poorly you did on the quantitative and verbal sections of the test. Yale University's B-school, for instance, accepts students who on average fall within the 94th percentile on the verbal part of the GMAT. Yale's foreign students, however, typically score only in the 70th percentile. But their "quant" scores are so high it doesn't make much of a difference overall. The reverse is often true of American applicants, who don't do nearly so well on the math.

Fewer than 10, out of the more than 269,000 tested, ace the GMAT in any given year. Fewer than 2000 people score 700 or above on this test. A score in the low 500s would put you into the 60th percentile, while a score of 600 would propel you into the 89th percentile. So a difference of 100 points can move you up into elite-school status. That's why it's important to spend some time gaining familiarity with the test before you take it. Most test-takers simply buy a workbook and use the sample tests in it for practice. One in four goes to the trouble of taking a formal preparation class.

Although you can take the test as often as you like, the schools to which you apply will see all your grades. So it's generally not a good policy to take the GMAT itself for practice. You don't send schools the rough drafts of your essay answers, and you don't walk into an interview with jeans and uncombed hair. If you're going to practice for the GMAT, you should do it either in a preparation course or by buying some of the old tests from the Graduate Management Admission Council. This organization also sells *The Official Guide for GMAT Review,* which contains actual tests, for $13.95, and personal computer software to help study for the exam for $59.95. (The address is Graduate Management Admission Test; Educational Testing Service; P.O. Box 6103; Princeton, New Jersey 08541.) At the least, you need to get the *GMAT Bulletin of Information* to register for the test and gain essential information about it. (You can telephone GMAT at 609-771-7330 for the free bulletin.)

The GMAT looks like most other entrance exams. The math is tougher than you found on your old SATs, but the basic format of the test is the same. The verbal sections test your ability to understand and evaluate what is read. The quant sections measure basic math skills as well as your ability to solve quantitative problems and interpret the data in graphs, charts, and tables. Starting in October of 1994, GMAC officials added a pair of essay questions to the test. The grading on this portion of the exam is based on how well you present logical arguments and express ideas that are "correct, concise, and persuasive."

What to expect? In the first essay question, you'll be asked to analyze a given issue. The GMAT will contain a statement followed by a series of questions. Here's an example:

> *"People often complain that products are not made to last. They feel that making products that wear out fairly quickly wastes both natural and human resources. What they fail to see, however, is that such manufacturing practices keep costs down for the consumer and stimulate demand." After reading the statement, you'll be asked the following: "Which do you find more compelling, the complaint about products that do not last, or the response to it? Explain your position, using relevant reasons and/or examples drawn from your own experience, observations, or reading."*

The second essay question requires you to analyze an argument. The GMAT again will provide a statement followed by several queries you have to answer. Example:

> *"The computerized, on-board warning system that will be installed in commercial airliners will virtually solve the problem of midair plane collisions. One plane's warning system can receive signals from another's transponder—a radio set that signals a plane's course—in order to determine the likelihood of a collision and recommend evasion action."*

After reading and digesting this bit of esotericism culled from a magazine, you'll be asked to discuss how logically convincing you find this argument. You'll need to analyze the "line of reasoning and the use of evidence in the argument" and suggest ways to strengthen the argument.

This new essay section will be graded separately from the multiple-choice questions, with scores ranging from zero (unscorable because the writing is illegible, or the test taker failed to write on the assigned topic) to six (outstanding). You're now given a full hour to respond to these two essays, while three hours of the test are devoted to the verbal and quant sections of the exam.

Do you need some advice to up your score? Don't bother with coaching books that contain simulated GMAT exams. Get copies of the real things and practice with them. You need to become "fluent" in test-taking, knowing exactly what to expect when you step into the auditorium to take the exam. That's the goal in most prep courses. A key to this is attaining a level of comfort with the test itself. After a few practice tests, you'll be ready to approach the exam more systematically.

If you can rule out one or more of the five answers on the multiple-choice questions, you generally should guess. But be aware that your odds of guessing the right answer are not necessarily one in four or five. Each section of the GMAT typically flows from the easiest questions to the most difficult. Therefore guessing could be less productive toward the end of a GMAT section.

Is it worth the money to take a prep course? Probably so. One firm claims that its average students increase their GMAT scores by 80 points after taking its six-week review course. (That's the difference between what a student scores on the first diagnostic test and the final one given to them.) But if you do take a course, it makes sense to do it no more than two months before you sit down with the real GMAT. This is the equivalent of training for a race. You don't stop two months before the race.

A class will lighten your wallet to the tune of $700 to $750—but both the Stanley H. Kaplan Educational Center, the nation's largest coaching service that offers a course with 11 sessions, and the Princeton Review, Inc., actually offer financial aid to offset the cost. You'll have to go to the trouble of filling out a financial aid form, but it can be worth it. Kaplan offers unlimited financial help, while the Review discounts its classes an average of $100 to those who prove financial hardship.

Courses often meet in small groups once a week, in the early evenings or on the weekends. Instructors analyze typical mistakes made on actual GMAT tests, then work those areas to death. If you're weak in geometry questions, you'll get drilled on the subject. There also are workshops of six to eight people held on weekends, sometimes on Sunday mornings. Expect to spend about 24 hours in class and another 18 hours in workshops. A one-on-one tutoring service also is available for around $1000. To get more information on the Review courses, call 800-333-0369. To obtain more information on the Kaplan courses, call 800-KAP-TEST.

How to Score Big on the B-School Essay

Many of the best schools don't just evaluate test scores and academic records, they want to get to know the real you. That's why one of the most critical parts of the application process is the section of essay questions.

What can you expect? The University of Michigan's Business School hits you with four mandatory essay questions and gives you the option of responding to a fifth one as well. Here's a sample: "The year is 2010, and the annual edition of *Who's Who* includes your biography. What does it say, beginning from the time when you completed your MBA degree?" Or how about this one: "You are the manager of a product line which has, since its introduction 10 years ago, been extremely popular with consumers and very profitable for your firm. However, your research team has advised you of a long-term study which shows that the product may lead to health problems in consumers 5 to 10 years after they purchase it. Due to increased competition in the rest of your company's industries, the company will be forced to close down a part of its operations, leading to widespread lay-offs, unless it continues to manufacture and market this product. What are the issues facing the company, and how would you approach the situation?"

Those queries are pretty much straightforward. But the admissions directors at some schools almost seem to delight in thinking up unusual questions to ask applicants. One recently asked potential students to write a succinct description of how they handled real-life ethical challenges. Another asked applicants to describe the details of failures in their careers.

Applicants to the University of Pennsylvania's Wharton School found themselves puzzling over one of the more novel essay questions: "Please complete three of the five statements below. Each response should be between one-half page and one page in length. (A) Outside my job, I have demonstrated leadership . . . (B) The area in which I have most tried to improve myself . . . (C) For fun I . . . (D) I have clearly demonstrated my interest in helping others by . . . (E) People describe me as . . ."

How should you answer such questions? Your essays should show how different you are, not how great you are. To stand out among countless applicants who all work capably in their jobs, tell how you have tutored underprivileged children. Discuss your Uncle Scrooge comics collection, or your role as a guitarist in a rock band or a cellist in a classical quartet.

Accomplishments count, but schools also use essays to assess your personal goals and values. So discuss an accomplishment in terms of the obstacles you overcame to achieve it. Too frequent use of the word "I" and too rare use of the word "we" in recording your accomplishments can put off some B-school admissions officers. Sensitive over criticisms that MBAs are too self-centered, many schools today emphasize teamwork and read essays with an eye toward ferreting out the egomaniacs.

Don't plan to knock off the essays in a single evening. Completing a set should take 20 to 40 hours of thinking, organizing, drafting, and polishing. On each essay, stick to the point you want to make. To get some idea of what to emphasize, look over the school's brochures—they often contain clues about what kinds of students are wanted. (Those with managerial potential? diversified skills?) Play up how well you fit their bill.

"Most candidates tend to use a grab-bag approach, hoping they'll hit on something that clicks with us," explains Stephen Christakos, Northwestern's Kellogg School director of admissions. "We don't want people to ramble on." Be succinct and to the point. Figure out the themes you will need to fully answer a question or essay topic, and don't wander or overwrite. Admissions staff, weary from reading through thousands of pages of this stuff, favor quality over quantity. Duke University's Fuqua School of Business was shocked when it received a four-inch-thick package via Federal Express from an overzealous applicant. The application materials were in a three-ring binder that included a table of contents, with charts detailing what the applicant had done so far with his life and where he planned to go. The package drew plenty of chuckles, but no special consideration.

Honesty is vital. "Don't play games," advises Karen Page, who runs a Learning Annex seminar for MBA applicants in New York. "Play up everything you've done for what it's worth, but don't cross the line to lie or cheat." Admissions staff aren't likely to check on your facts, but they've read through so many applications that they can sense when something doesn't quite add up.

If you know a graduate of the school, ask him or her to read your essays before you turn them in. What about attention-getting ploys like writing in crayon or sending a videotape? Some applicants are bold enough to try them. Rather than complete an essay, one UCLA applicant, an avid runner, sent a picture of himself with the headline: "How badly do you want to go to UCLA?" The picture showed him with a victorious smile, completing the New York Marathon in record time. That, too, drew a few laughs around the office. But as a rule, most admissions directors dislike gimmicks.

To Interview or Not

In recent years, a new wrinkle has appeared in the applications process: a personal interview. Northwestern University's Kellogg School was the first B-school to interview every applicant to its full-time program—more than 4300 of them—in one-hour sessions in places as far-flung as Tokyo and Kuala Lumpur. The reason? Kellogg officials don't believe it's possible to assess a person's composure, articulateness, or leadership ability from test scores or past grades. To put the interview into perspective, it's interesting to note that 644 Kellogg applicants for the Class of 1994 scored over 700 on their GMATs. But only 32 percent of them were offered admission. Many observers believe that the reason Northwestern is a favorite among corporate recruiters is because it screens its candidates well, thus bagging the best of them.

Now, other top schools are giving more candidates the once-over. Michigan, Florida, and Chicago claim to interview virtually all MBA applicants. In 1994, for example, Wharton conducted personal interviews with more than 3860 of the 5015 applicants. Duke University's Fuqua School of Business interviewed 76 percent of its applicants in 1994. Some schools allow alumni to interview and file reports on candidates; others prefer that only a select group of admissions staff conduct the questioning.

What should you expect? In general, interviewers want to try to evaluate leadership and communication skills. In foreign applicants, the schools are also looking to evaluate English-speaking proficiency. "I'm most interested in motives," says Steven DeKrey, director of the MBA program at the University of Florida. "I'm after the whys and the decisions that brought the candidate here. Why this school? Why management? I'm looking for the individual who has made his or her own decisions. Someone who isn't aimed at me because of a boss or someone else."

Seek an interview if you think it would be helpful to plead your case in person—especially if you're articulate and think you can demonstrate some leadership qualities. "All we know about you is what you put on paper," reasons Michael Hostetler, a former dean at Duke. "So it's the applicant's best way to make sure we have as accurate a picture of him or her as possible." Conversely, however, it could be the kiss of death. If you're not likely to do well in an interview situation, by all means avoid it. "Anyone who interviews poorly is a fool to do a nonrequired interview," admits DeKrey. A poor performance during an interview can cancel all your hopes for admission to a good school.

A Caveat on References

Most applicants don't give enough attention to the people they ask to recommend them for MBA admission. If you can get a successful alum to write a letter on your behalf, do it. A reference signed by a familiar name is always worth more than one from an unknown person.

If that's not possible, however, make sure that whoever you ask for a reference will give you a good one and will send it in on time. That's not as easy as you might think. Some B-schools ask particularly specific questions of recommenders, and ask that they mail their questionnaires to the schools separately and in private. Harvard, for example, even requires them to rate you on a scale of "Unusually Outstanding/Top 2 percent" to "Poor/Bottom Third" on such characteristics as integrity, intellectual ability, self-confidence, maturity, and your ability to work with others. Make sure that your references have a positive view of your abilities and talents.

How to Get a School to Foot Part of the Tuition Bill

Getting into a good B-school is hard enough. It requires smarts, motivation, and maturity. It also requires money, and lots of it. MIT's Sloan School of Management charges $21,690 for tuition and fees. In 1986, the school's yearly tuition was $11,200. How do most full-time MBAs meet the staggering costs? One study showed that they borrowed half of the cost and squeezed a quarter of it from their parents. Scholarships account for only 11 percent of the total bill for male students, but cover 25 percent of the female MBA's bill. Minorities also are more likely to get a greater proportion of their tuition from scholarship funds.

The best way to get financial help is to ask for it, and ask early. That means your application should arrive as soon as the admissions office begins to accept them. Ask the admissions staff and student aid office about the scholarships offered. Inquire whether work-study or graduate assistantships are available. Most scholarships are based on either merit or need, so you have to prove one or the other—and it's best to provide evidence of both. It's also sometimes possible for a top applicant to gain greater financial aid from a second-tier school than a brand-name one. Why? B-schools that lack Top 20 status may dangle big bucks in front of strong candidates they otherwise might not be able to attract.

Consider Nick Grasberger, who had three years of work experience with USX Corporation and a spinoff company, Aristech Chemical Corporation. Besides the solid work background, he was a dean's list scholar at Notre Dame and scored a 680 on the GMAT.

He was set to go to Wharton after gaining acceptance there, but then the University of Pittsburgh offered him a full tuition scholarship and a $250-a-month stipend even though he hadn't asked for any financial aid at all. Pitt hands out six of these "Associate Fellow" scholarships a year. "I had always had my heart and mind set on Wharton," says Grasberger, "but I may have had to borrow $50,000 to go there." He opted for Pittsburgh, graduating from the 11-month program and joining H. J. Heinz.

New York University's Stern School and many other schools have their version of the Pitt program. Stern, for example, made 30 offers to applicants in 1994 under its Dean's Scholars program, which provides full or partial funding ranging from $5000 to $15,000 a year. "You need to compete in a lot of ways, and we've learned that people are sensitive to price and to the personal attention they get," says George Daly, dean of Stern.

Of the 140 students in Carnegie Mellon's Class of 1996 who applied for financial aid, 120 got scholarships and grants that averaged $5800 each for their first year. At Northwestern's Kellogg School, 20 percent to 25 percent of the class gets some scholarship money. But there are very few full scholarships, and most of those are for minorities. About 68 percent of the MBAs at Duke get financial assistance, 40 percent of them scholarships that average about $7000 a year. If you can't get a scholarship, try for a low-interest loan from the school. Some schools use a central application service such as the Graduate and Professional School Aid Service. If that's required, you can write for a form from GAPSFAS, CN 6660, Princeton, New Jersey 08541. You'll need to complete the form and send it back to Princeton. The service will analyze your resources and send its analysis to the schools of your choice. Check with the admissions or financial aid offices to find out what each requires.

Another option gaining greater attention is the "MBA Loans" program run by the Graduate Management Admission Council. The program ties together federal, need-based loans and private loans in a one-stop-shoppping approach. Students who apply for help under this program are simultaneously considered for all federal loan programs as well as private loans, eliminating the need to fill out numerous applications. GMAC asserts that its single lending source provides low guaranteed fees and low interest rates. For more information, contact GMAC at 800-366-6227.

You might not like the idea of going into hock to pay for your MBA, but if it's the only way to pay the bills, it might be worth it. In most cases, you won't have to worry about repaying the debt until after you graduate and get that lucrative job.

CHAPTER 4

RANKING THE B-SCHOOLS

Rankings of any kind are controversial, whether they rate automobiles or pizzas. Because rankings measure quality and therefore prestige, they tend to arouse great passion and spark much interest. In an increasingly competitive world, reputation counts for a lot. That's why so many people are interested in rankings and why they cause such a stir.

Given all the hoopla over who's first and who's not, it's important for consumers to understand exactly what a ranking measures. In many cases, it simply depends on whose opinions you gather or what statistics you plug into a database to create a ranking. Not surprisingly, the results can sometimes differ dramatically based on the methodology employed.

What's the best graduate business school in the country? The chief executives of America's corporate behemoths say it's Harvard, hands down. The business school deans give the nod to Stanford. Corporate recruiters point to the University of Pennsylvania's Wharton School, while Stanford also gets the highest satisfaction ratings from top MBA graduates.

So who's right? It depends. If your interest is sheer prestige, it's obviously hard to beat a Harvard degree. Indeed, more corporate chief executives hold a Harvard MBA than any other. Some 82 CEOs of the BUSINESS WEEK 1000—U.S. corporations with the highest market value—have MBAs stamped by Harvard, far above Stanford's 14 or Wharton's 17. If you're more concerned with academic research in the mix, you might pick Stanford. Either way, however, you're relying on the image of these two schools by executives and deans, many of whom have limited direct experience with the schools.

Based on an extensive survey of graduates and corporate recruiters, BUSINESS WEEK's ranking of the best schools found that Wharton has the best MBA program in the country. The school captured the top spot in BW's rankings in 1994 by unseating three-time consecutive winner Kellogg School in the customer satisfaction poll. Just behind Wharton are Kellogg, which won in 1988, 1990, and 1992, Chicago, and Stanford, with its best-ever finish in the BW survey. The rest of the findings are in the table on page 26.

Until BUSINESS WEEK began to rate B-schools on customer satisfaction in 1988, most rankings had been based largely on the reputation of the schools' professors and their published work in academic journals. Typically, B-school deans or faculty were asked to list the top schools in order of personal preference. A school's academic prestige usually

BUSINESS WEEK's Top 20 Business Schools

BW overall ranking	Corporate ranking	Graduate ranking	Percentage with offers by graduation	Average number of job offers
1. Pennsylvania (Wharton)	1	3	98.3	3.02
2. Northwestern (Kellogg)	2	5	93.9	2.96
3. Chicago	4	4	97.3	2.92
4. Stanford	5	1	98.7	3.47
5. Harvard	3	17	98.0	3.60
6. Michigan	6	7	92.9	2.68
7. Indiana	8	6	92.8	2.45
8. Columbia	7	10	95.7	2.43
9. UCLA (Anderson)	16	2	97.9	2.74
10. MIT (Sloan)	9	12	97.4	3.25
11. Duke (Fuqua)	14	8	95.8	2.78
12. Virginia (Darden)	15	9	97.6	2.69
13. Dartmouth (Tuck)	12	14	95.2	2.40
14. Carnegie Mellon	18	11	97.4	2.69
15. Cornell (Johnson)	17	13	94.9	2.40
16. NYU (Stern)	13	20	85.7	2.12
17. Texas	11	25	88.0	2.58
18. North Carolina	19	16	94.3	3.09
19. Berkeley (Haas)	21	15	90.3	2.34
20. Purdue (Krannert)	10	33	93.0	2.19

loomed large in such ratings, and the deans and faculty members tended to give lots of weight to a school's reputation for academic research. There's no disputing that research is vital both to a school and to American business. But traditional surveys may not fully reflect a school's teaching excellence, its curriculum, or the value of its graduates to Corporate America.

BUSINESS WEEK adopted a strikingly different approach, surveying both the graduates of top schools and the corporate recruiters who hire them to determine the best business schools. In effect, the survey measures how well the schools are serving their two markets: students and their ultimate employers. The 1994 graduate poll was randomly mailed to more than 6000 MBAs from over 40 of the most prominent schools. MBA grads were asked to assess such characteristics as the quality of the teaching, curriculum, environment, and placement offices at their schools. We received 4608 replies to the 36-question survey, a response rate of 73 percent. The views of the Class of 1994 were then supplemented with those collected by the magazine in 1992 and 1990 to form a graduate ranking. The poll of corporate recruiters was mailed to 354 companies that recruit these graduates off the campuses of the best schools. BW received 254 replies, a 72 percent response rate.

How does this ranking differ from others? A 1994 list by *U.S. News & World Report* found that the best schools were, in order: Stanford, MIT, Harvard, Wharton, Northwestern, Chicago, Dartmouth, Michigan, Duke, UCLA. The next ten? Columbia, Berkeley, Virginia, Carnegie Mellon, Cornell, North Carolina, NYU, Texas at Austin, Yale, and the University of Southern California. What accounts for the differences? The *U.S. News* ranking is largely based on numerical data, such as average GMAT scores, acceptance rates, starting salaries, and the percentage employed at graduation, which was supplied by the schools. However, schools often differ in how they compile and report such numbers. So at one school the average reported GMAT may exclude minority candidates. At another, it could include every matriculated student. Likewise, some schools' reported starting salary numbers may exclude graduates who go into lesser-paying nonprofit or public sector jobs. At others, placement directors may calculate the average by including everyone, regardless of whether they take a nontraditional job or not. *U.S. News* also plugs into its ranking system two separate reputational polls based on simple surveys of B-school deans and chief executives.

Confused? There's more. In 1994, two economics professors from Yale and Columbia universities attempted to rank business schools on the value they add to students' earning power. Embarrassingly, the profs' own schools appeared well back in the pack: Yale was ranked 63rd, or dead last, while Columbia ranked 23rd. Would you believe that Oklahoma State University and the University of New Mexico actually rank higher than MIT and Duke University? They do in this odd and highly controversial ranking. The top ten? Stanford, Harvard, Chicago, Virginia, Wharton, Northwestern, Michigan, Oklahoma State, New Mexico, and Wake Forest University. The latest ranking based on "faculty scholarship," done in 1989 by two University of Maryland professors, had Wharton on top of the heap, followed by Harvard, New York University, Stanford, Columbia, Michigan, Chicago, Northwestern, Texas, and UCLA.

The standing of each of the schools in these polls largely reflects the bias of those who are asked for their opinions or the methodology used by the study's author. Senior executives and CEOs rank the schools based on what they "perceive" to be the best. That's partly a reflection of where they received their own MBAs, as well as how often they read about these institutions in newspapers and magazines. The deans are largely responding on the basis of their perceptions about the quality of the faculty, the academic research, and the articles published in scholarly journals.

How can the applicant use these rankings? Most people, of course, apply to several schools. If you're lucky enough to gain acceptance to a group of the best, don't simply go to the school that's highest up on the list. Instead, try to pick a school where you're most likely to excel. All these top institutions have unique cultures, just as their applicants have unique personalities. Most schools, however, fail to articulate these differences and differentiate themselves from the pack.

Applicants can make the best match by carefully looking over BUSINESS WEEK's graduate survey findings to see how these schools truly differ from one another. Would you thrive in a culture that emphasizes competition, or cooperation? Would you rather have leading-edge professors at the top of their fields in research, or simply the best teachers?

The following tables will give you a clue to these and many other critical factors. Keep in mind, however, that you are looking at the results of what most people believe to be the absolute best B-schools in the nation. Each chart shows the 1994 survey results from 24 schools—the 12 that got the best scores on each question and the 12 that received the worst. If BW were to include a far greater number of more typical business schools, virtually all of the more than 40 institutions polled would look great. As such, each of these top schools is competing against all the others, and that makes for tough competition.

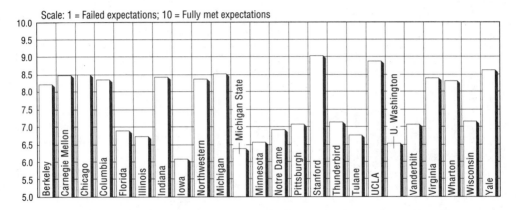

Scale: 1 = Failed expectations; 10 = Fully met expectations

1. To what extent did your MBA experience fulfill or fail to meet your expectations of what a good program should be?

Satisfaction is almost always based on expectations. If you expect a lot, the product or service you buy really has to deliver. That's true of business schools, too. MBA candidates at the top institutions arrive on the campus doorstep with high expectations. As a result, these answers nicely correlate with the quality of the graduates who gain entry into each program. The five at the top? Stanford, UCLA, Yale, Michigan, and Chicago. At the bottom? Iowa, Michigan State, University of Washington, Minnesota, and Illinois.

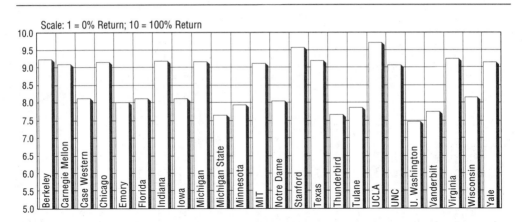

Scale: 1 = 0% Return; 10 = 100% Return

2. Do you believe your MBA was worth its total cost in time, tuition, and lost earnings?

Business school isn't cheap. And most students at these top schools quit jobs paying big bucks to get an MBA. Harvard-bound students left jobs that on average paid nearly $54,000 a year to attend the school at a cost of over $20,000 a year. That makes the degree quite a hefty investment. Grads from public universities—Berkeley, Indiana, Virginia, UCLA, and Texas—think they're getting the best deal. Even though Stanford MBAs have hefty tuition bills, their satisfaction with the degree is as high as that of the graduates of any of the public schools. However, the graduates of the University of Washington, Michigan State, and the American Graduate School of International Management's Thunderbird are less convinced it was worth it.

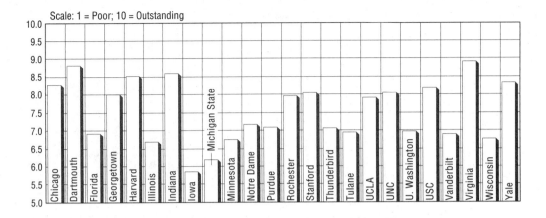

Scale: 1 = Poor; 10 = Outstanding

(Schools: Chicago, Dartmouth, Florida, Georgetown, Harvard, Illinois, Indiana, Iowa, Michigan State, Minnesota, Notre Dame, Purdue, Rochester, Stanford, Thunderbird, Tulane, UCLA, UNC, U. Washington, USC, Vanderbilt, Virginia, Wisconsin, Yale)

3. How would you rate the quality of the teaching in core courses?

What's taught in every MBA core curriculum are the fundamentals: finance, accounting, marketing, organizational behavior, and production 101. Even though these basic skills are critical, many schools put junior profs in these core classes, partly because the veterans prefer to teach higher-level electives. Which schools have been able to get superb teaching in the core? Virginia, Dartmouth, Indiana, and Harvard. On the other hand, Iowa, Michigan State, Illinois, and Minnesota have a lot to learn.

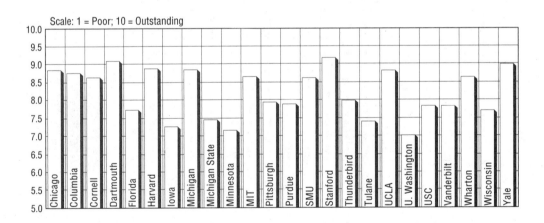

Scale: 1 = Poor; 10 = Outstanding

(Schools: Chicago, Columbia, Cornell, Dartmouth, Florida, Harvard, Iowa, Michigan, Michigan State, Minnesota, MIT, Pittsburgh, Purdue, SMU, Stanford, Thunderbird, Tulane, UCLA, U. Washington, USC, Vanderbilt, Wharton, Wisconsin, Yale)

4. How would you rate the quality of the teaching in elective courses?

After you learn the basics, a school's ability to deliver in-depth knowledge in given areas makes or breaks an MBA education. It's the elective offerings at any school that allow students to custom-design the MBA to their personal career goals. The professors at Stanford, Dartmouth, Harvard, and Michigan earn the best reviews for their teaching in these higher-level courses. The teachers at the University of Washington, Minnesota, Iowa, and Tulane have to try harder.

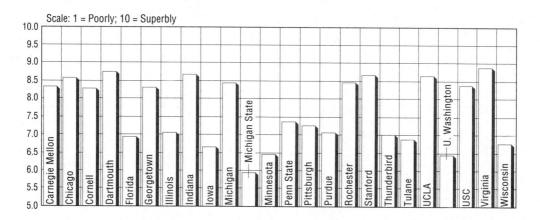

Scale: 1 = Poorly; 10 = Superbly

5. Overall, how did the quality of the teachers compare with others you have had in the past?

There's probably no more sensitive issue on the campus than teaching quality. Even at the best schools, graduates tend to bemoan the uneven quality of teachers. At some top schools, students gripe that they have difficulty understanding the lectures of heavily accented professors from abroad. At others, faculty once granted tenure because of their research can't teach their way out of a paper bag. The best? Virginia's Darden School, Dartmouth, and Stanford. The weakest? Michigan State, University of Washington, and Minnesota.

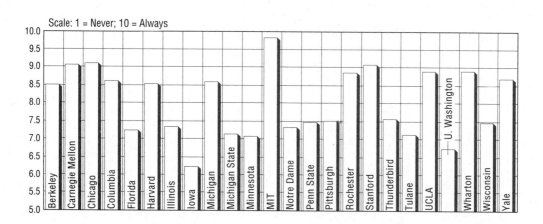

Scale: 1 = Never; 10 = Always

6. Were your teachers at the leading edge of knowledge in their fields?

Schools that rely too heavily on real businesspersons for adjunct faculty run the risk of putting a retired executive in front of a class to tell little more than old war stories. It's not only important to maintain a balance of the theoretical and the practical, it's also critical for a school to boast professors who are at the leading edge of thinking in management, finance, and marketing—people who know their stuff and know it cold. Grads felt this to be particularly true at MIT, Chicago, and Stanford. They were less certain of it at Iowa, University of Washington, and Minnesota.

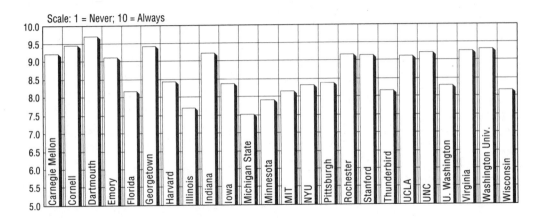

Scale: 1 = Never; 10 = Always

7. Were the faculty available for informal discussion when classes were not in session?

Distinguished professors at B-schools are often in high demand. Corporations want them as consultants. Journal editors want them as writers of articles. Publishers want them as authors of books. And students not only want them in the classroom, they also want time with them after class. Whose faculty seems to be most available to help students outside the scheduled class time? Dartmouth grads thought their profs were best in this department. The teachers at Cornell, Georgetown, Washington University, and Virginia also did extremely well; Michigan State, Illinois, and Minnesota significantly less so.

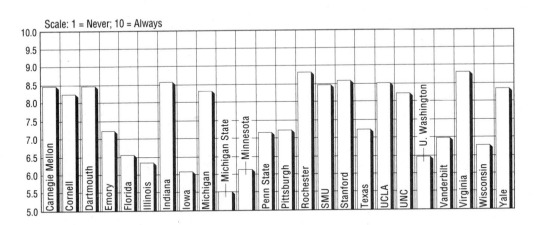

Scale: 1 = Never; 10 = Always

8. To what extent were faculty aware of the material other faculty members would cover?

One of the startling discoveries in all the revisions of MBA programs is how many times key concepts and ideas are taught over and over again. A good MBA program is one that builds upon the knowledge and skill learned in one classroom and constantly moves it forward. That requires integration and coordination among the faculty. Which schools get this right? Smaller institutions such as Rochester, Virginia, and Stanford. On the other end are Michigan State, Iowa, and Minnesota.

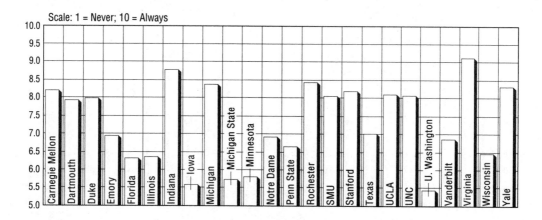

Scale: 1 = Never; 10 = Always

9. To what extent was the coursework integrated as opposed to being taught as a cluster of loosely related topics?

Most business problems have marketing, financial, and operations implications. Yet, most MBA programs look at problems from narrow functional perspectives. That's why so many curriculum makeovers have focused on the need to integrate the basic business disciplines. Who's already doing the best job? Virginia, Indiana, Rochester, and Yale. Graduates at the University of Washington, Iowa, and Michigan State believe their schools don't do nearly so well.

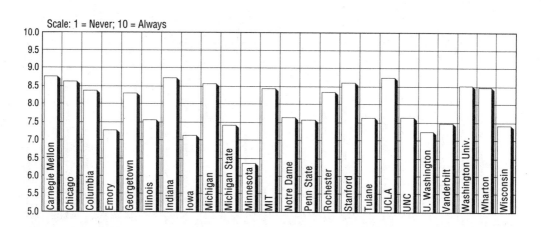

Scale: 1 = Never; 10 = Always

10. How current was the material/research presented in class for discussion and review?

While a lot of the research that goes on in academia is rather esoteric, a good deal of it is vital to a school and to American business. Professors who conduct leading-edge research, however, should be able to transmit some of it to their students in the class. If that research work fails to filter down into the classroom, students can hardly benefit from it. Grads think Carnegie Mellon does the best job of it, with UCLA, Indiana, and Chicago not far behind. Minnesota, Iowa, University of Washington, and Emory bring up the rear.

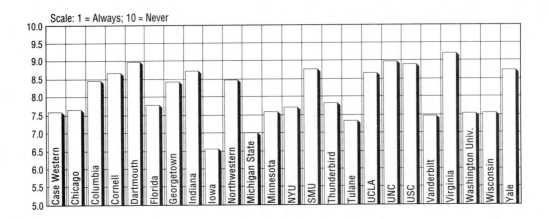

Scale: 1 = Always; 10 = Never

11. Do you believe the faculty compromised teaching in order to pursue their own research?

What drives academia is research. Teachers are largely awarded promotions and tenure on the basis of their own study and publication of it in scholarly journals—much of it, however, is either meaningless or inaccessible to the average businessperson. Few excellent teachers gain tenure if their research doesn't please colleagues; virtually all excellent researchers get tenure even if they can't teach. Grads say profs at Virginia, North Carolina, and Dartmouth are least likely to compromise their teaching in favor of research.

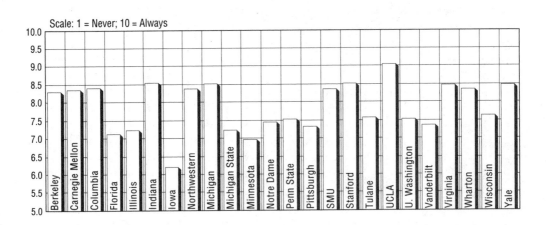

Scale: 1 = Never; 10 = Always

12. Did you receive practical information during the program that will be usable on the job?

For years, many corporate leaders have attacked business schools for teaching too much theory and hardly enough real-world material. These days, more schools are making a concerted effort to provide students with more practical knowledge and skills they can carry with them directly to the job. Who does it best? UCLA, Indiana, Michigan, and Stanford top the list. At the bottom are Iowa, Minnesota, and Florida.

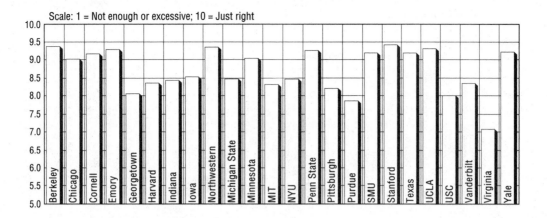

Scale: 1 = Not enough or excessive; 10 = Just right

13. Was the amount of assigned work and reading so excessive that it impeded learning?

Almost everyone who goes to B-school says they never thought it would be as hard as it was—particularly the grueling first year when schools load students up with the required core courses. Some schools, however, throw amazing amounts of work at students, partly because they want them to experience the heavy workload and pressure of life in the real world. Grads felt the "boot camps" that pile on the work are Virginia, Purdue, and Georgetown.

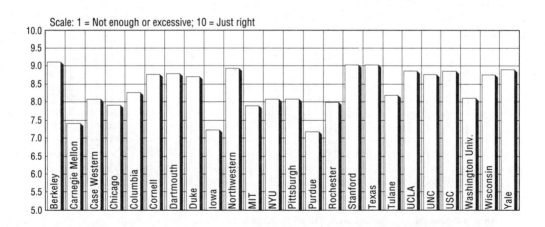

Scale: 1 = Not enough or excessive; 10 = Just right

14. To what extent were analytical skills stressed in the curriculum?

All B-schools rightly attach a great deal of importance to teaching students basic analytical skills. These models and ways of thinking are critical to problem solving and decision making in the real world. But it's possible that a school can put either too little or too much emphasis on this part of the curriculum. Purdue, Iowa, and Carnegie Mellon went a little overboard.

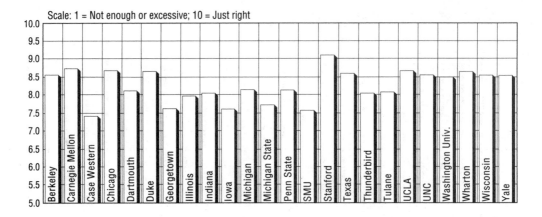

Scale: 1 = Not enough or excessive; 10 = Just right

15. To what extent were interpersonal skills stressed in the curriculum?

When corporate executives are asked their views on MBAs, they typically talk not only about how bright and ambitious they are, but also about how poor their interpersonal skills are. They complain that MBAs lack the sensitivity and personality to be true leaders. In recent years, many B-schools have launched major efforts to hone communication skills and teamwork. Grads at Washington University and Wisconsin would like to see more soft stuff. Georgetown and Case Western MBAs were more likely to think they had more than enough. Overall, however, the differences aren't great.

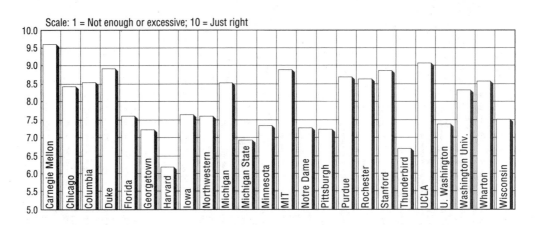

Scale: 1 = Not enough or excessive; 10 = Just right

16. As a result of the program, how would you judge your ability to deal with computers and other analytical tools that affect your ability to manage?

In what many call the "Information Age," managing data has become an important part of business. B-schools have responded to this challenge in different ways, but it's vital to learn how to use computers and other analytical tools to help you become a better manager. Carnegie Mellon grads say they're most comfortable here, followed closely by UCLA, Duke, and MIT. MBAs from Harvard, Thunderbird, and Michigan State are at the other end of this scale.

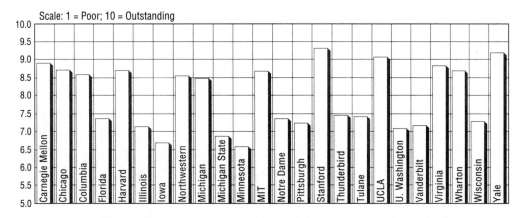

Scale: 1 = Poor; 10 = Outstanding

17. How would you judge the school's performance in providing you with numerous ways of thinking or approaching problems that will serve you well over the long haul?

One of the most important benefits of a good MBA program is learning a systematic way to solve a business problem. When a manager or executive confronts a difficult decision, he or she should have a framework or way of thinking available for weighing the pros and cons. At the very least, B-schools should give you that tool to bring to the real world. Graduates think that Stanford, Yale, and UCLA did the best job in this department. MBAs were less satisfied at Iowa, Minnesota, and Michigan State.

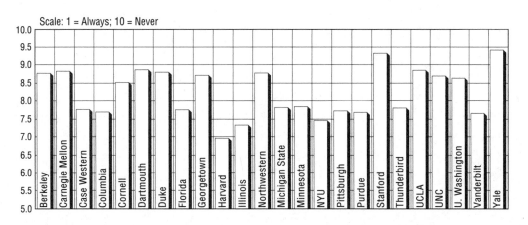

Scale: 1 = Always; 10 = Never

18. Do you feel your classmates emphasized individual achievement at the expense of teamwork?

In *The Big Time,* Ned Dewey of Harvard's famous Class of 1949 said about the recent crop of Harvard MBAs: ". . . I'd as soon take a python to bed as hire one. He'd suck my brains, memorize my Rolodex, and use my telephone to find some other guy who'd pay him twice the money." Despite the obvious hyperbole, it will come as little surprise that Harvard grads rate their school among the most competitive. For cooperation, it's Yale, Stanford, and Dartmouth—schools that foster teamwork, emphasize group projects, and frown on backstabbing.

37

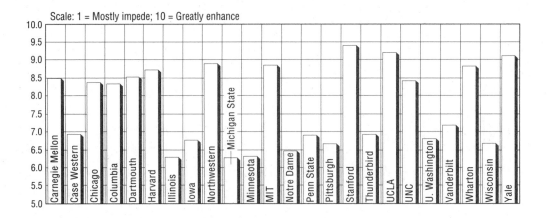

Scale: 1 = Mostly impede; 10 = Greatly enhance

19. Did the caliber of your classmates impede or enhance the learning process?

A funny thing happens when you ask MBA graduates to assess their experience on campus. They often say that they learned as much, if not more, from their fellow classmates as from their professors. The quality and mix of people a school brings into a program are critical to the learning process. Which schools' graduates thought the most of their classmates? Stanford, UCLA, Yale, and Northwestern. The least? Michigan State, Minnesota, and Illinois.

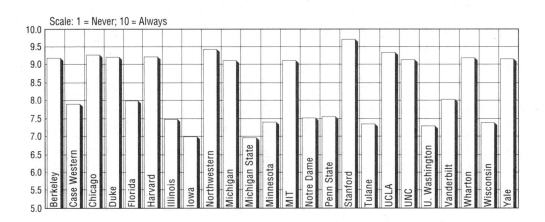

Scale: 1 = Never; 10 = Always

20. Would you urge friends or colleagues to take the same MBA program at the school?

There's no better recommendation than one from a person who is so satisfied with an experience that he or she is willing to urge it on a friend or colleague. The programs which virtually make admissions officers out of their graduates are: Stanford, Northwestern, UCLA, Chicago, and Harvard. MBAs from Michigan State, Iowa, the University of Washington, and Tulane are less sure they would recommend their schools to friends and colleagues.

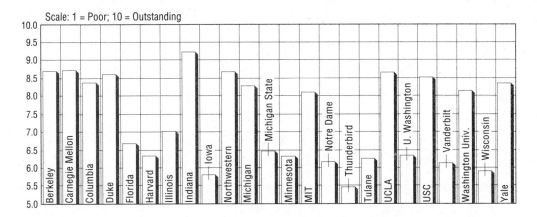

21. How would you judge the responsiveness of the faculty and administration to students' concerns and opinions?

"Customer service" and "total quality" get a good deal of attention in MBA classrooms around the country. But many students have found that these are nearly nonexistent concepts when applied to the schools they attend. Some deans and faculty members go so far as to say that students aren't customers, and they shouldn't try to please them. Who has it right? Indiana, Carnegie Mellon, Berkeley, and Northwestern lead the pack. Deans and faculty from Thunderbird, Iowa, Wisconsin, Vanderbilt, and Notre Dame need to hear a few lectures on customer service.

Scale: 1 = Poor; 10 = Outstanding

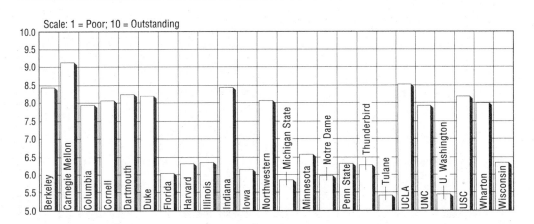

22. How would you assess the responsiveness of the school in meeting the demand for popular electives?

Since you'll only spend two years on campus getting your degree and the first year will typically be tied up with required courses, time to enroll in key electives is limited. Many students complain that courses they looked forward to were oversubscribed. The upshot: They lost out on classes they badly wanted to attend. Which schools do the best job of assuring that such things don't happen? Carnegie Mellon, UCLA, Berkeley, and Indiana. The worst? Tulane, University of Washington, Michigan State, and Notre Dame.

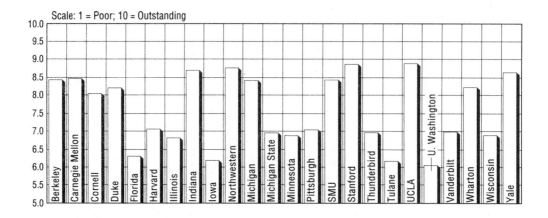

Scale: 1 = Poor; 10 = Outstanding

23. How would you judge the opportunities given to you—either in class or in extracurricular activities—to nurture and improve your skills in leading others?

There are lots of ways to distinguish yourself in a job interview. You can talk about your grades, your work experience, and your internship. Most importantly, however, you'll have to show how you've accumulated experience in leading others. Grads at UCLA, Stanford, Northwestern, and Indiana believe they had the most opportunities to develop leadership skills. At the bottom of the list were University of Washington, Tulane, Iowa, and Florida.

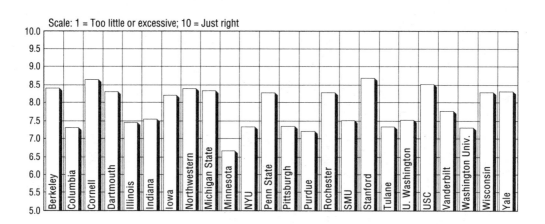

Scale: 1 = Too little or excessive; 10 = Just right

24. How would you appraise your school's efforts to bring you into contact with practicing professionals in the business community?

Because of their locations in major urban centers, some schools can bring extraordinary business talent into classrooms and lecture halls. That's an important advantage for students, who get to rub shoulders with top executives and professionals. Which schools do too little of this? The University of Minnesota in Minneapolis, surprisingly, since many major corporations are headquartered there, and Purdue University.

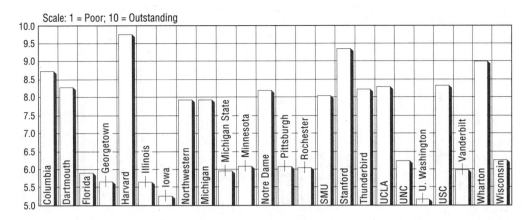

Scale: 1 = Poor; 10 = Outstanding

25. How would you judge the school's network and connections that can help you throughout your career?

MBAs should graduate not only with a degree and a job, but with the contacts that will help them climb the corporate ladder throughout their lifetimes. Though Harvard *students* may be the most competitive, Harvard *graduates* are among the most cooperative. No other school in the nation even comes close to having as large (some 37,000 MBAs) or as elite a network of connections as Harvard. Many chief executives of BUSINESS WEEK's Top 1000 corporations hold Harvard MBAs. University of Washington, Iowa, Illinois, and Georgetown come out on the low end of this scale.

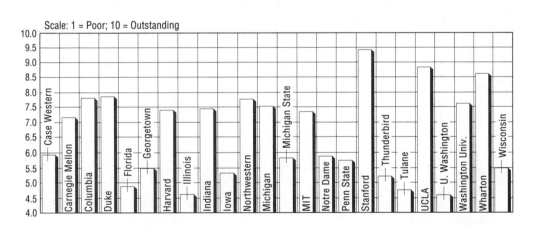

Scale: 1 = Poor; 10 = Outstanding

26. How would you judge the aggressiveness of the school in helping you with summer job placement or a summer internship?

The summer between the traditional two years of an MBA education is an important time. Most MBAs land internships that allow them to sample an industry or a function and gain valuable experience for the final job hunt. This is an opportunity to build the perfect résumé, too. Which schools work the hardest to get their students the most opportunities for summer employment? Stanford, UCLA, Wharton, and Duke. The schools that need to sweat a bit more about this: University of Washington, Illinois, Tulane, and Florida.

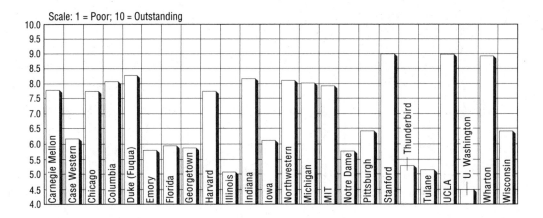

Scale: 1 = Poor; 10 = Outstanding

27. How would you characterize the school's performance in helping you find a job before graduation?

Most of the job-search activity occurs well before you graduate from business school. There are company presentations, interviews for internships, and then interviews for jobs. Landing a position before graduation isn't all that necessary, but it helps take the edge off graduation and provides a clue about which schools work the job market the hardest. The best? Stanford, UCLA, Wharton, and Duke. MBAs were less satisfied at the University of Washington, Illinois, Tulane, and Thunderbird.

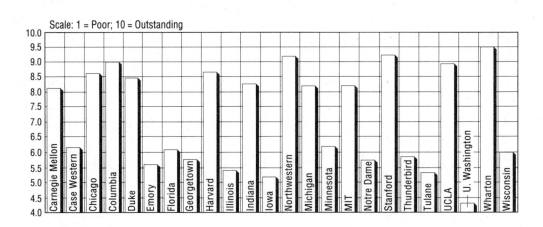

Scale: 1 = Poor; 10 = Outstanding

28. How would you characterize the number and quality of firms recruiting on your campus?

Overall, the Class of 1994 did pretty well in the job market, because of heavy hiring by consulting firms and finance companies. But many industrial recruiters of MBAs have cut back on the number of campuses they regularly visit. Who's doing the best job in attracting a large number of diversified, brand-name companies to campus? Wharton wins hands-down, though Stanford, Northwestern, and Columbia aren't far behind. The worst? The University of Washington, Iowa, Tulane, and Illinois.

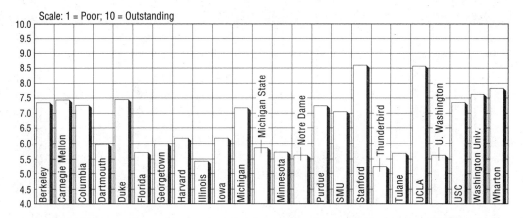

29. If the organizations you targeted for employment did not recruit on campus, how would you assess your school's assistance in supporting your independent search for a job?

Most of the companies that recruit on college campuses are looking for MBAs to fill entry-level jobs. That's especially frustrating to older, more experienced MBAs, who now find themselves overqualified. In general, B-school placement offices have done a poor job of helping these graduates—even though schools are seeking more experience than ever in their applicants. Which schools provide the most help to these grads and others who seek less traditional jobs? Stanford, UCLA, Wharton, and Washington University. The least? Thunderbird, Illinois, Notre Dame, and the University of Washington.

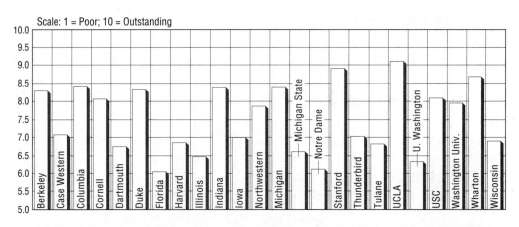

30. How would you appraise the placement office's help with matters such as interview training, negotiating strategy, résumés, etc.?

A school's placement office should do more than just lure company recruiters to the campus. It should help prepare you for the entire process of getting a job. Graduates from even the best schools surprisingly say that landing that first job out of school isn't always as easy as you might think. The B-schools with the best career-planning staffs to help you out are UCLA, Stanford, Wharton, and Columbia. On the other hand, you're likely to be more on your own if you graduate from Florida, Notre Dame, University of Washington, and Illinois.

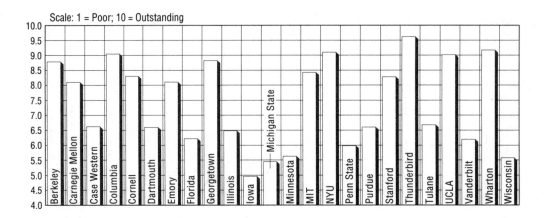

Scale: 1 = Poor; 10 = Outstanding

31. Based on your own personal level of satisfaction, please appraise your school's efforts to include international business topics in the MBA program.

Of all the buzzwords circulating in B-school classrooms these days, global business is way up near the top of the list. Many schools are exposing their students to far more material on how the global business environment impacts local companies. Grads at Thunderbird, Wharton, Columbia, and NYU gave their schools the best grades for satisfying their interests in international business. MBAs at Iowa, Michigan State, Wisconsin, and Minnesota were the least satisfied on this dimension.

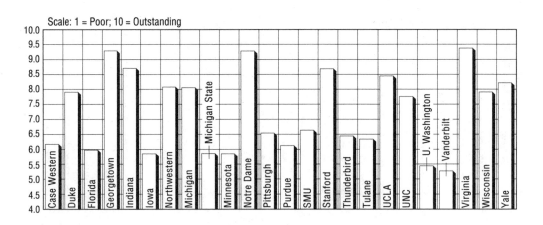

Scale: 1 = Poor; 10 = Outstanding

32. Based on your own personal level of satisfaction, please appraise your school's efforts to include ethics in the MBA program.

Many schools give little more than lip service to ethical business conduct. But the Wall Street scandals of the 1980s have made ethics an important topic at some schools. Not surprisingly, the two school winners in this category are among the very few B-schools that offer mandatory, graded ethics courses: Virginia and Georgetown. The weakest in satisfying grads' appetites for ethics in the program: Vanderbilt and University of Washington.

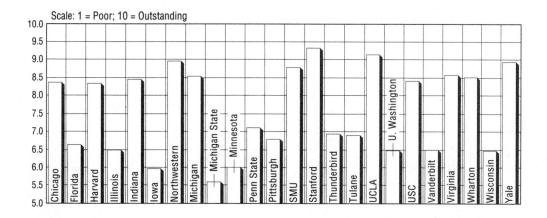

Scale: 1 = Poor; 10 = Outstanding

33. Based on your own personal level of satisfaction, please appraise your school's efforts to include leadership topics in the MBA program.

Perhaps no area has received greater attention in recent years than leadership. One school after another has launched leadership exercises, seminars, and courses in its curriculum. Who leads this fast-changing area? MBAs were most satisfied at Stanford, UCLA, Northwestern, and Yale. Graduates were least satisfied with the attention devoted to leadership at Michigan State, Iowa, and Minnesota.

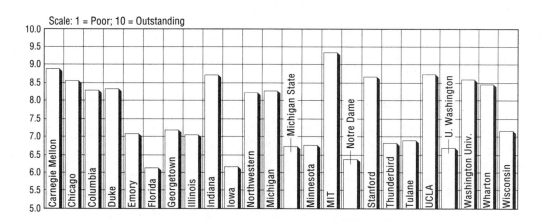

Scale: 1 = Poor; 10 = Outstanding

34. Based on your own personal level of satisfaction, please appraise your school's efforts to include quality concepts in the MBA program.

The most important management development to hit Corporate America in decades is the quality movement once led by the late quality guru, W. Edwards Deming. This is one area where corporations were the pioneers. B-school administrators and faculty have lagged far behind in the interest in quality. Which are the leading B-schools in this area? Grads were most satisfied at MIT, Carnegie Mellon, UCLA, and Indiana. Iowa and Florida would do well to pay more attention to quality.

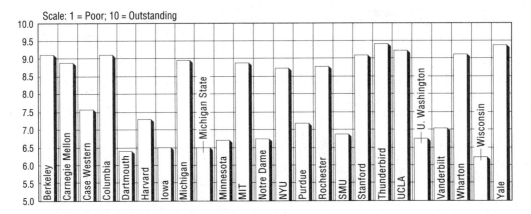

Scale: 1 = Poor; 10 = Outstanding

35. Based on your own personal level of satisfaction, please appraise your school's efforts on diversity.

Some MBA graduates believe that their educational experience was significantly enhanced by the cultural or ethnic diversity of their classmates. If you're likely to think this is an important factor in your education, the graduates who were most satisfied were those at Thunderbird, Yale, and UCLA. Wisconsin, Dartmouth, and Iowa grads were the least satisfied.

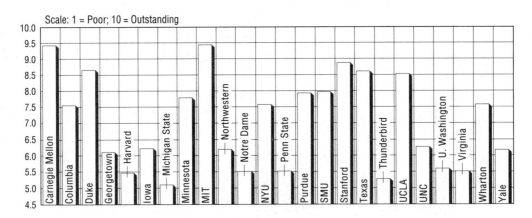

Scale: 1 = Poor; 10 = Outstanding

36. Based on your own personal level of satisfaction, please appraise your school's efforts to include information technology concepts in the MBA program.

Many MBA programs are working hard to integrate computers into their curriculums. The reason: The computer has become an indispensable tool of decision making in today's business world. Which schools do the best job at exposing their MBA candidates to information technology? MIT, Carnegie Mellon, and Stanford. Less successful were Michigan State, Thunderbird, and Harvard.

B-SCHOOLS BY THE NUMBERS

To compile the rankings, BUSINESS WEEK gathers lots of information on both business schools and their graduates. Some of this data is available from the business schools, which routinely publish plenty of their own statistics. But a lot of the information made available here was gathered specifically by BUSINESS WEEK from the latest crop of MBA graduates. Much of the data has never been published before—information on how much MBAs made before they went to top schools or how much debt they graduate with, for instance. And you're not likely to see much of it in the fancy marketing brochures handed out by the schools—especially when it comes to comparative statistics.

Quant jocks—the nickname for MBAs with quantitative backgrounds—will find plenty of numbers to search through and crunch in this section. After all, graduate business schools love numbers. Many of the leading institutions preach business by quantitative analysis and modeling. That may explain their preoccupation with comparative statistics.

The wealth of data crammed into the following tables covers everything from 1994 starting pay packages to applicant selectivity. You'll find which of the top schools boast the highest percentages of international students, women, or minorities. You'll also find out which schools' graduates leave campus with the largest loans hanging over their heads. None of this information constitutes a ranking, nor is any of this data used when BUSINESS WEEK compiles its own rankings of the top schools. But it may help applicants to see how the schools in which they're interested fit into the overall scheme of things. Note that a single asterisk indicates a BUSINESS WEEK estimate.

GMAT Scores

Nearly 300,000 people register to take the Graduate Management Admission Test (GMAT) each year because virtually every business school requires the test's results from applicants. As imperfect as they are, GMAT scores may be the single best indicator of student quality. Generally, average scores for the Top 20 schools continue to climb, with the greatest improvement over the past two years recorded by the University of Virginia. Its average GMAT score for the class entering in 1994 jumped 33 points, to 643. The biggest drop? The University of Texas, where average GMATs have plunged 18 points since 1992, largely because the school is paying more attention to work experience. Other top schools that saw a decline in average GMAT scores: the University of Southern California, which fell 12 points; Duke University, which declined 7 points.

Top 20 school	Average GMAT	Runners-Up school	Average GMAT
Stanford	665*	Yale	656
Dartmouth	660	Emory	625
Harvard	660*	Georgetown	619
Wharton	650	U. Washington	617
Chicago	650	Illinois	615
MIT	650	Rochester	612
Berkeley	647	USC	610
Virginia	643	Vanderbilt	610
Northwestern	640*	Washington U.	608
UCLA	640	Pittsburgh	603
Columbia	640	Wisconsin	603
Carnegie Mellon	640	Tulane	600
Michigan	630	Minnesota	600
Cornell	630	Southern Methodist	600
NYU	630	Michigan State	590*
Texas	625	Case Western	591
Duke	623	Iowa	590
North Carolina	621	Penn State	580*
Indiana	615	Notre Dame	578
Purdue	581	Thunderbird	570

B-School Selectivity

Another sign of a business school's quality is the number of applicants it accepts and rejects. Stanford, partly because of its small size but mostly because of its high standards, leads the pack. It rejects an estimated 90 percent of all applicants. In the past two years, New York University, Duke, and Berkeley have become a little more selective. Indiana University and the University of Texas have become less discriminating. Indiana now accepts 48 percent of all applicants, up from 35 percent in 1992. Texas sends acceptance letters to 35 percent of its applicants, up from 25 percent two years ago.

Top 20 school	Applicants accepted	Runners-Up school	Applicants accepted
Stanford	10%	Penn State	19%
Harvard	16*	USC	33
Dartmouth	17	Thunderbird	35
Northwestern	20	Yale	36
Berkeley	20	Emory	36
North Carolina	22	Iowa	36
Wharton	23	Michigan State	37
UCLA	23	Rochester	38
Columbia	25	Georgetown	40
MIT	25	U. Washington	42
Duke	26	Washington U.	44
Virginia	27	Pittsburgh	47
Purdue	32	Vanderbilt	48
Chicago	33	Minnesota	48
Carnegie Mellon	35	Wisconsin	50
Michigan	35	Case Western	51
Texas	35	Southern Methodist	55
Cornell	37	Tulane	58
NYU	40*	Illinois	62
Indiana	48	Notre Dame	63

Full-Time Enrollments

The size of an MBA program is an important attribute of a school's culture. In the large MBA populations at Harvard, Wharton, and Thunderbird, it's easy to be an anonymous student. That's less true at Purdue University or Dartmouth College, where everyone knows each other by their first names. The Top 20 school with the biggest increase in full-time enrollment? Duke, which has squeezed an extra 54 students into its school since 1992.

Top 20 school	Full-time enrollment	Runners-Up school	Full-time enrollment
Harvard	1619	Thunderbird	1286
Wharton	1522	Illinois	588
Columbia	1375	Wisconsin	544
Northwestern	1160	Yale	445
Chicago	1137	Georgetown	423
NYU	926	Case Western	416
Texas	890	Rochester	400
Michigan	853	Vanderbilt	388
Stanford	726	USC	370
Duke	660	Pittsburgh	369
UCLA	612	U. Washington	300
Indiana	560	Washington U.	299
MIT	500	Minnesota	288
Cornell	490	Notre Dame	283
Virginia	486	Emory	281
Berkeley	427	Tulane	253
Carnegie Mellon	401	Michigan State	250
North Carolina	394	Penn State	240
Dartmouth	363	Southern Methodist	225
Purdue	195	Iowa	219

International Enrollments

With so many schools claiming to boast a global emphasis, this list quickly shows you which institutions have been most receptive to large numbers of non-U.S. students. Rochester leads the runners-up schools with 44 percent; Carnegie Mellon leads the Top 20 with 41 percent. Overall, the percentage of non-U.S. students in elite MBA programs continues to rise. Carnegie Mellon has posted the biggest increase in the past two years, jumping a full 13 points. The University of Chicago and the University of Southern California, meanwhile, fell 5 points each.

Top 20 school	International students	Runners-Up school	International students
Carnegie Mellon	41%	Rochester	44%
MIT	35	Illinois	39
NYU	34	Yale	34
Wharton	30	Penn State	32
Cornell	29	Michigan State	31
Berkeley	29	Thunderbird	30
Purdue	28	Tulane	30
Columbia	27	Pittsburgh	30
Harvard	26	Case Western	29
Northwestern	24	Georgetown	27
Stanford	21	Iowa	26
UCLA	20	Wisconsin	26
Dartmouth	19	Notre Dame	25
Texas	19	Southern Methodist	22
Duke	17	Emory	20
Chicago	16	Minnesota	20
Michigan	15	Vanderbilt	20
Indiana	14	U. Washington	19
Virginia	13	USC	16
North Carolina	12	Washington U.	16

Women MBA Enrollments

In recent years, the deans of several top business schools have expressed concern over the declining enrollment of women in MBA programs. In part, the downturn has been caused by the influx of more international students, a greater proportion of whom are male. But it's also a sign that many women may view law and medicine as more welcoming professions than business. Some schools, however, are having more trouble than others. Georgetown has showed the biggest upturn, rising 12 percentage points since 1992. Among the Top 20, North Carolina led the schools enrolling a larger number of women, rising six percentage points since 1992. The University of Southern California, meanwhile, declined by exactly six points.

Top 20 school	Women students	Runners-Up school	Women students
Berkeley	34%	Georgetown	40%
Columbia	32	Case Western	38
Dartmouth	31	Thunderbird	37
North Carolina	31	Emory	37
Purdue	31	U. Washington	34
Texas	31	Wisconsin	34
Virginia	31	Yale	33
Duke	30	Michigan State	32
Northwestern	30	Penn State	30
Harvard	29	Pittsburgh	30
UCLA	29	Iowa	30
NYU	28	Tulane	28
Stanford	27	Illinois	27
Wharton	27	USC	27
Michigan	27	Vanderbilt	27
Indiana	26	Washington U.	27
MIT	25	Notre Dame	26
Cornell	24	Southern Methodist	25
Carnegie Mellon	20	Minnesota	25
Chicago	20	Rochester	24

Minority Enrollments

With all the talk about cultural diversity in the workforce these days, it's interesting to see how the schools stack up when it comes to enrolling minority students in their programs. The percentages are for black, Hispanic, and American Indian students from the United States. Some business schools, such as Michigan, have aggressive programs to recruit minority students. Only two Top 20 schools are now enrolling fewer minorities than they did in 1992: Stanford, which is down two percentage points, and UCLA, down one point. Most business schools boast considerably improved records on minority enrollment. The biggest jump was a 13-point gain by the University of Chicago, where minority enrollment in 1992 was only 5 percent.

Top 20 school	Minority students	Runners-Up school	Minority students
Michigan	22%	Emory	18%
Texas	19	Wisconsin	17
Chicago	18	USC	15
Harvard	18	Penn State	16
Berkeley	17	Minnesota	13
Virginia	17	Case Western	12
Indiana	15	Rochester	12
Purdue	15	Yale	12
Wharton	15	Washington U.	12
North Carolina	14	Pittsburgh	10
Duke	14	Tulane	10
NYU	14	Michigan State	9
Dartmouth	11	Southern Methodist	9
Northwestern	10	Notre Dame	8
Stanford	10	Georgetown	7
Columbia	9	Illinois	7
UCLA	9	U. Washington	5
Cornell	7	Iowa	5
MIT	6	Vanderbilt	5
Carnegie Mellon	5	Thunderbird	NA

Pre-MBA Annual Pay

Students at top schools quit good-paying jobs to get their MBAs. Indeed, these numbers are a good indication of the quality of students entering business schools. Just how much do people forgo? In almost all cases, the pay that people give up to become students is rising. Two years ago, for example, the average Wharton MBA left a job paying $45,780. For the Class of 1994, the average had climbed to $48,240. Here's what the average graduates of the Class of 1994 gave up to get their degrees:

Top 20 school	Pre-MBA annual pay	Runners-Up school	Pre-MBA annual pay
Harvard	$53,910	Case Western	$48,170
Stanford	49,610	Emory	37,840
Wharton	48,240	Pittsburgh	37,450
Dartmouth	45,300	USC	37,020
UCLA	44,620	Georgetown	36,750
Columbia	44,470	Rochester	35,760
Northwestern	44,000	Southern Methodist	34,880
Berkeley	43,570	U. Washington	34,610
Chicago	42,690	Wisconsin	34,030
MIT	41,820	Notre Dame	33,660
Duke	40,960	Yale	33,510
Cornell	40,740	Vanderbilt	33,430
NYU	38,960	Penn State	32,470
North Carolina	38,690	Washington U.	31,190
Virginia	38,530	Minnesota	30,800
Carnegie Mellon	38,250	Thunderbird	30,080
Texas	36,620	Michigan State	29,930
Michigan	36,050	Tulane	28,870
Indiana	34,320	Illinois	27,620
Purdue	30,600	Iowa	22,050

Starting Pay in 1994

After slogging through a tough MBA program, what can you expect to fetch on the open market? The Class of 1994 from the top schools landed jobs with median starting pay packages of $61,890. And for the first time ever, the average hit six figures at three schools, and the median reached six figures at two: Harvard and Stanford. Thanks largely to heavy recruiting by consulting firms, MBA grads captured more than hefty salaries and sign-on bonuses. Many of them received such bennies and perks as stock options, free cars, interest-free loans, free round-trip airline tickets, relocation and housing allowances, tuition reimbursements up to a full year, and guaranteed year-end bonuses. That's why these numbers tend to be higher than those reported by the schools or the figures in the BW profiles, which include only starting salary and signing bonus.

Top 20 school	Average post-MBA pay	Runners-Up school	Average post-MBA pay
Harvard	$102,630	Yale	$74,030
Stanford	100,800	Georgetown	69,830
Columbia	100,480	Emory	63,830
Dartmouth	95,410	Southern Methodist	60,910
Wharton	89,930	Rochester	60,670
Northwestern	84,640	Case Western	57,200
Chicago	83,210	Vanderbilt	54,310
MIT	80,500	Washington U.	53,400
Virginia	74,280	USC	52,030
UCLA	74,010	Wisconsin	49,700
Berkeley	71,970	Thunderbird	49,660
Cornell	71,970	Notre Dame	49,230
NYU	70,660	Penn State	49,120
Duke	70,490	Minnesota	48,250
Carnegie Mellon	69,890	Illinois	47,130
North Carolina	69,880	Pittsburgh	46,070
Michigan	67,820	U. Washington	44,140
Texas	61,890	Tulane	44,080
Indiana	58,520	Michigan State	41,800
Purdue	54,720	Iowa	41,620

Signing Bonuses

You may have read about the MBA glut, or some other story about how the degree isn't fetching the money and attention it once did in the over-heated 1980s. Forget it. A piece of evidence proving that the degree still delivers is the widespread prevalence of the practice of signing bonuses. At the University of Virginia, 7.5 out of every 10 graduates in the Class of 1994 were each paid a bonus just to accept a job offer from a recruiting company. The highest average signing bonus, however, went to Harvard grads, each of whom received $16,570 just to make a commitment to a company.

Top 20 school	Students getting sign-on bonus	Runners-Up school	Students getting sign-on bonus
Virginia	75%	Georgetown	61%
Chicago	74	Yale	59
Harvard	74	Vanderbilt	49
Wharton	74	Southern Methodist	42
Northwestern	73	Emory	41
Cornell	69	Notre Dame	39
Duke	69	Case Western	37
Stanford	69	U. Washington	35
North Carolina	68	Thunderbird	29
Carnegie Mellon	67	Washington U.	29
Dartmouth	65	Illinois	28
MIT	65	Iowa	25
Columbia	64	USC	25
Michigan	63	Tulane	24
UCLA	57	Wisconsin	23
Purdue	57	Rochester	21
Texas	54	Minnesota	20
Indiana	52	Michigan State	16
NYU	46	Pittsburgh	15
Berkeley	45	Penn State	13

Return on Investment

Not to be mercenary about this, but we know a lot of our readers will be tempted to take out their calculators to figure out which schools' graduates registered the highest percentage increases in pre-MBA pay. To save you the trouble, we crunched the numbers. Yale leads, in part because the school boasts the highest percentage of nonprofit students who go into management consulting or investment banking after getting their degrees. But there are some real surprises here, and the University of Iowa is certainly one of them. On average, its grads earned 89 percent more than they had before they got their MBAs. One sobering footnote to this stat: About 14 percent of Iowa's grads lacked a single job offer at their graduation in 1994.

Top 20 school	Increase over pre-MBA pay	Runners-Up school	Increase over pre-MBA pay
Columbia	126.0%	Yale	120.9%
Dartmouth	110.6	Georgetown	90.0
Stanford	103.2	Iowa	88.7
Chicago	94.9	Southern Methodist	74.6
Virginia	92.8	Washington U.	71.2
MIT	92.5	Illinois	70.6
Northwestern	92.4	Rochester	69.6
Harvard	90.4	Emory	68.7
Michigan	88.1	Thunderbird	65.1
Wharton	86.4	Vanderbilt	62.5
Carnegie Mellon	82.7	Minnesota	56.6
NYU	81.4	Tulane	52.7
North Carolina	80.6	Penn State	51.3
Purdue	78.8	Notre Dame	46.2
Cornell	76.7	Wisconsin	46.0
Duke	72.1	USC	40.5
Indiana	70.5	Michigan State	39.7
UCLA	69.5	U. Washington	27.5
Texas	69.0	Pittsburgh	23.0
Berkeley	65.2	Case Western	18.7

Paycuts after Getting an MBA?

Some graduates of MBA programs actually earn *less* with their degree than they did before going off to school. How is that possible? In many cases, it's by choice—a graduate who prefers to go into nonprofit work or to do a stint with the MBA Enterprise Corps, a Peace Corps–like group devoted to helping newly emerging capitalist countries. Sometimes career switchers will give up lucrative pay and benefits for the chance to do something different. But they may have to take a paycut, because they're no longer leveraging their previous work experience into a new job.

Top 20 school	MBAs who took paycuts	Runners-Up school	MBAs who took paycuts
NYU	0.0%	Yale	0.0%
Carnegie Mellon	0.3	Iowa	0.0
North Carolina	0.6	Southern Methodist	0.0
Indiana	1.1	Tulane	0.9
Texas	2.5	Minnesota	3.0
Michigan	3.1	Georgetown	3.3
MIT	3.1	Thunderbird	3.8
Wharton	3.5	Washington U.	5.3
UCLA	3.9	Rochester	5.4
Purdue	4.3	Emory	5.9
Duke	4.7	USC	6.1
Virginia	5.2	U. Washington	6.9
Dartmouth	6.8	Illinois	7.9
Chicago	6.9	Penn State	8.0
Columbia	7.8	Wisconsin	11.1
Cornell	8.2	Vanderbilt	12.5
Northwestern	9.0	Notre Dame	14.3
Stanford	10.0	Case Western	17.9
Berkeley	10.2	Pittsburgh	20.5
Harvard	12.9	Michigan State	23.5

Job Offers at Graduation

If you graduate without a single job offer, of course, starting salary averages won't offer you much comfort. Fortunately, the Class of 1994 had a relatively easy time getting jobs. Almost all schools showed improved numbers from two years earlier. Indiana University is a good example. In 1992, 79 percent of the graduating class had job offers by commencement. Two years later, thanks to the end of the recession, nearly 93 percent of Indiana's class left with offers in hand. Not surprisingly, the Top 20 schools fared significantly better than the runners-up in gaining job offers for their students. Even so, the vast majority of MBAs who graduate without offers find employment within three to six months of commencement.

Top 20 school	With job offers by graduation	Runners-Up school	With job offers by graduation
Stanford	98.7%	Yale	95.8%
Wharton	98.3	Michigan State	93.1
Harvard	98.0	Minnesota	90.2
UCLA	97.9	Washington U.	88.9
Virginia	97.6	Georgetown	87.8
Carnegie Mellon	97.4	Vanderbilt	87.7
Cornell	97.4	Illinois	86.4
MIT	97.4	Case Western	86.0
Chicago	97.3	Iowa	85.7
Duke	95.8	USC	85.2
Columbia	95.7	Notre Dame	85.1
Dartmouth	95.2	Southern Methodist	84.5
North Carolina	94.3	Emory	83.6
Northwestern	93.9	U. Washington	83.3
Purdue	93.0	Pittsburgh	83.1
Michigan	92.9	Wisconsin	81.5
Indiana	92.8	Tulane	81.4
Berkeley	90.3	Rochester	79.0
Texas	88.0	Penn State	77.5
NYU	85.7	Thunderbird	70.1

Outstanding MBA Loans

Whether or not a member of the Class of 1994 had a job offer by graduation is one thing. Another is how much debt you walk away with once you get your MBA. These are the numbers for those who graduate in hock. Note that the most sizable loans are carried away by graduates at the high-priced elite schools. The leader is no surprise: Harvard MBAs leave with average loans of more than $43,600 each. It's also no surprise that the MBAs with the lightest debt loads are the graduates of the public universities. Among the Top 20 schools, Berkeley grads owe the least, at an average of $16,124—about a third of the debt at Harvard.

Top 20 school	Average outstanding loan	Runners-Up school	Average outstanding loan
Harvard	$43,640	Georgetown	$37,000
Wharton	41,920	Vanderbilt	35,290
Columbia	41,760	Yale	34,400
Chicago	41,710	USC	32,240
Dartmouth	41,060	Emory	30,190
Northwestern	38,910	Tulane	29,210
MIT	33,990	Southern Methodist	29,170
Cornell	33,950	Rochester	28,200
Stanford	32,080	Washington U.	27,990
Duke	31,860	Thunderbird	27,310
Carnegie Mellon	31,640	Notre Dame	26,460
NYU	28,550	Case Western	22,480
Michigan	28,200	Pittsburgh	19,900
Virginia	27,040	U. Washington	19,300
UCLA	24,370	Penn State	17,990
Indiana	21,870	Illinois	16,440
North Carolina	20,140	Minnesota	14,660
Texas	17,180	Iowa	14,470
Berkeley	16,120	Wisconsin	13,530
Purdue	14,800	Michigan State	12,790

CHAPTER 6

THE TOP TWENTY

The schools on BUSINESS WEEK's Top 20 list offer the best MBA education you'll find in the United States, if not the world. But that may be the only common thread that holds these schools together. Like the differing personalities you'd find in any group of people, each institution boasts its own culture and style. Each has strengths and weaknesses. Each promises students vastly different educations and experiences.

Which one is best for you? Read through the profiles to find out. They start with a snapshot view of the school that tells you something about its size, diversity, cost, selectivity, standing in the polls, and how much its graduates command in the marketplace.

There are other interesting statistics here: not only how many applicants are rejected by the school, but how many of those who are accepted reject the school that sent them an invitation. Northwestern, for instance, accepts 20 percent of those who apply, but enrolls just 62 percent of the applicants it agrees to admit. Virtually all of these figures apply to the class that entered in the fall of 1994 and will graduate in 1996.

The average starting pay of a school's MBAs includes sign-on and guaranteed bonuses and is reported for the Class of 1994. BUSINESS WEEK culled this data from its graduate surveys rather than relying on figures from a school's placement office. If you're interested in the average salary—excluding bonuses—provided by the schools, you'll find those numbers in the charts at the ends of the profiles. An asterisk next to any number (or school name in the case of the charts) indicates that the figure is a BUSINESS WEEK estimate. The lists of each school's outstanding professors also are based on the results of the magazine's graduate survey. Professors who received four stars were singled out as a best teacher by 20 percent or more of respondents; three stars, 15–19 percent; two stars, 10–14 percent; one star, under 10 percent.

1. University of Pennsylvania

The Wharton School
102 Vance Hall
Philadelphia, Pennsylvania 19104

Corporate ranking: 1
Enrollment: 1522
Women: 27%
Non-U.S.: 30%
Minority: 15%
Part-time: None
Average age: 27
Applicants accepted: 23%
Median starting pay: $90,000

Graduate ranking: 3
Annual tuition & fees: $21,050
Room and board: $8000
Average GMAT score: 650
GMAT range: 520 to 800
Average GPA: 3.4
GPA range: 2.4 to 4.0
Accepted applicants enrolled: 70%
Average starting pay: $89,930

Teaching methods: Lecture, 55%   Case study, 30%   Simulation, 15%

When Thomas P. Gerrity was a Massachusetts Institute of Technology student in the early 1960s, he was a solidly built wrestler who regularly muscled his way into the New England championships. In 1994, as dean of the University of Pennsylvania's Wharton School, he led his school to a No. 1 finish in BUSINESS WEEK's ranking of the best graduate schools of business.

Gerrity pinned the opposition by boldly pushing the most dramatic curriculum changes at any elite school. Those changes helped Wharton secure the top grade from Corporate America, which singled out the school for having launched the most innovative curriculum in recent years. And by paying far greater attention to student demands for better teaching, Gerrity also gained the third-best marks from Wharton's own graduates.

Wharton's surge from the No. 4 slot in 1992, however, would not have been possible without the radical overhaul of the school's MBA program.

The aim of the makeover has been to turn out what the school hopes will be the business leaders, not just the financiers, of the next century. For years, Wharton's strength in finance has long overshadowed faculty and programs in other departments. Now, the school has placed greater emphasis on "people skills," adding more global perspective and changing the curriculum to foster creativity and innovation. It's also promoting real-world problem solving and examining business issues from the viewpoint of several disciplines. Dean Gerrity calls the changes "bold, dramatic, and revolutionary."

Judged against changes at many other schools, Gerrity is right. The new program was rolled out to all students in the 1993–1994 academic year, after a two-year phase-in. The changes grew out of a 1990 Wharton study on the needs of successful companies and their leaders in the next century. The school consulted business futurists and chief executives and asked leading corporate recruiters to come up with a "wish list." Students, alumni, and faculty met in focus groups. All told, over 3000 executives and alumni provided input and feedback.

What they came up with is one of the most radical departures in business education since the early 1960s, when most schools adopted their current curriculums. For starters, new students now have to report to school in early August, four weeks earlier than usual, for a "pre-entry program" of courses, computer labs, social activities, an Outward Bound–like experience in the Poconos, and speeches. Students strong in math must study art history and sociology—even philosophical lectures on how the sky makes love to the earth. Liberal arts grads get accounting and statistics. This way, it's hoped, the core courses will accomplish more.

The usual two semesters a year have been tossed aside in favor of four 6-week quarters. And courses no longer are solely taught as isolated disciplines. The basic marketing module, for example, overlaps with operations management, finance, microeconomics, and statistics. Up to a third of the course's dozen sessions may be team-taught by "flying squads" of professors from other disciplines.

All this is easier said than done, however. In the first go-round, for example, several MBAs believe that Wharton has been far from successful in meeting its objectives to integrate the differing disciplines of business into a more coherent whole. Students said professors didn't make enough of an effort to accomplish those aims. One exception: a team of Wharton professors from manufacturing, finance, and marketing which began meeting nine months before the start of the school year to create opportunities to teach in teams and focus on links among classes. For a single module on manufacturing, Morris A. Cohen, the manufacturing professor, estimates that the trio spent at least 20 hours planning class sessions. He and the others tallied up another 20 hours sitting in each other's classes. "The coordination took a lot of effort," he says.

At one point, he sat quietly in the back of a classroom of a marketing course taught by David J. Reibstein. The case study under discussion focused on a business decision to accept new orders for a product. Wearing their marketing hats, the students were nearly unanimous in taking on the new business, but they gave little consideration to the company's ability to manufacture enough products to satisfy the demand. At a prearranged point, Cohen shocked students by standing up and shouting at Reibstein: "I have heard enough. This is wrong!" The classroom theatrics helped students gain a better appreciation of the need to consider all aspects of a business decision, and the professors have won praise for their work.

To improve such integrative efforts, Wharton now boasts "clusters" of faculty across departments, which now work closely to coordinate the timing of papers, exams, and field projects, and to chat about what's going on in each class. The school also maintains that faculty are now working together as never before, across Wharton's dozen academic departments, on projects, articles, books, and conferences. It helps, too, that more than 20 percent of Wharton's faculty members hold secondary appointments in other departments within the school or the university.

That cooperation gets quickly tested in the first year of this new program. In the fall, the courses range from the basic Financial and Managerial Accounting to Management of People at Work. A Foundations of Leadership class boasts a "field application project" in which teams of five students each work on real corporate or public policy cases. A new marketing simulation has been moved into the core marketing course. In the spring, your courses will range from Competitive Strategy to Global Strategic Management. Again, there's a field application project to enhance team learning.

At the end of the first year, students can take advantage of an optional Global Immersion Program, with a month-long overseas experience of classes on culture and politics and field trips to the foreign operations of large multinationals. This is no vacation. Before embarking on one of four journeys—MBAs selected from among Russia, China, Japan, and South America in 1994—students engage in six weeks of classroom study and advance work. Of course, this option isn't included in the overall tuition. MBAs who enroll in the program must pay an additional $3500 to $4000 each, though financial aid is available.

By the time the second year begins, you'll be able to sample Wharton's considerable lineup of electives—some 200 in all. The new curriculum demands that every MBA leave the school with "in-depth knowledge" in a given field. You can pursue any one of 26 majors and concentrations, or custom-design your own major. The choice among majors is considerable, from entrepreneurial management to real estate. So you're required to take four electives in a departmental major, along with an advanced study project in your chosen field.

Other changes include a novel series of sessions on leadership and ethics that run during the entire first year. A psychiatrist has been brought in to run group-interaction exercises, and a consulting firm has been hired to do personality tests on students. Test results later appear as video vignettes of character traits. This way, bullies will see themselves in the vignettes of others and listen to analysis from classmates. "It may be humiliating for some, but they're going to see exactly how others perceive them," says Reibstein.

Team learning plays a prominent role in the new program. For an integrative case, Michael Jenkins of the Class of 1993 remembers one instance when a member of his group urged that the team use sophisticated linear programming techniques to explore a business problem. "It led us down the wrong road, forcing all of us to work all day Friday, Saturday, and Sunday on the single project," says Jenkins. "It increased our workload by as many as 100 extra hours. MBA time is measured by pizzas, and we went through five of them."

All these changes have occurred under the deanship of Thomas Gerrity, a former Rhodes Scholar and entrepreneur who succeeded Russell Palmer in the top job in 1990. Gerrity founded Index Group, a hugely successful information technology consulting firm that is now known as CSC Index. By most standards, Palmer was one of the most successful B-school deans of his era. Under him, the school's endowment rose to over $100 million from $21 million. Palmer also oversaw the hiring of more than 120 faculty members.

Among those hires were dozens of top-rated scholars that Palmer personally lured to Wharton to enhance the school's academic reputation. Many of these profs built their own reputations by writing esoteric papers for obscure journals in narrow disciplines. Unfortunately, many of them had difficulty delivering their knowledge in a classroom—making teaching quality a critical issue for Dean Gerrity.

Concerned about the problem, Gerrity recently put a long-time faculty member in charge of an initiative to improve teaching quality and ordered up a host of recommendations. The upshot: Instructors now get student evaluations midway through a course, so that they can attempt to correct some problems before a course is over and done; teaching quality as defined by student evaluations is now a factor in merit pay increases; a panel of the school's best MBA teachers have launched an informal mentorship program for new instructors; and Wharton's vice dean now has some say over which profs teach the core courses.

The annual teaching excellence awards used to be handed out quietly before the students in the pub. "Basically, the rest of the world didn't even know the awards existed," says Bruce Allen, a management professor. "We took it out of the pub and put it on the quad." Now, it's a full-fledged ceremony, with flowing beer, champagne, and food, with Gerrity handing out the honors. "Fellow faculty members applauded, and the students showed up in force."

Those efforts are finally yielding a payoff. For the first time since BUSINESS WEEK began surveying graduates, teaching quality in both the core and elective courses was nicely above average for the 40-plus schools whose graduates were polled by the magazine. Though Wharton still has some way to go before reaching Virginia's approval rating in core classes, or Stanford's high level of satisfaction for the teaching of electives, the school has begun to turn around its once notorious teaching problem.

Wharton, of course, boasts some sensational teachers (the best 10 selected by grads are listed below). It's interesting, however, that only 2 of the 10 teaches in finance, which has long been regarded as Wharton's forte. But then, Wharton is more a business university than just a B-school with tremendous range. Admissions Director Samuel Lundquist, who joined Wharton in 1992 after serving in the same post for five years at Dartmouth's Amos Tuck School, likes to say that he's worked for the two top MBA programs that are "the furthest apart. I came from the smallest MBA school to the second largest; from the most rural to one of the most urban; from a general management curriculum to one that offers functional majors—and the list goes on."

Size, of course, brings lots of variety. Wharton's 180-member tenure-track faculty outnumbers the graduating class of MBAs at such leading business schools as Amos Tuck and Carnegie Mellon. And only Harvard turns out more MBAs each year than Wharton. The options of both academic and social life are bewildering. Wharton offers about 200 courses in the MBA program (more than Harvard, Chicago, or virtually any other graduate B-school in the world). More than 100 different student clubs on campus compete for attention. The school sponsors 23 research centers that study everything from entrepreneurship to real estate. "There are so many goodies," says William Pierskalla, a former Wharton professor and now dean of UCLA's B-school, "that it's hard to choose the best things. The breadth of the place can overwhelm people."

That breadth extends to its international offerings. One of Wharton's most important strengths is the Joseph H. Lauder Institute, which runs one of the most innovative global programs around. A joint venture between the B-school and the university's School of Arts and Sciences, the 24-month program requires a greater commitment than the typical MBA stint. For one thing, the group of 50 students arrives in May instead of August. After spending a month on campus, they're shipped overseas to countries in which their chosen foreign language is spoken (a second language is required for admission into the program). While there, they'll tour the facilities of a dozen corporations and absorb lots of cultural activities, from plays to museums. They return for the start of the school year, only to go back for 12-week internships with both foreign companies and the overseas affiliates of U.S. firms, including Procter & Gamble in Japan. Through school-sponsored trips, one recent graduate went to Southeast Asia, Japan, and India, and spent a summer in France. The graduate also learned to speak fluent Spanish through the bilingual program.

If you're keen on the international business scene yet unwilling to sweat through a 24-month program, Wharton also offers foreign exchange deals with schools in The Netherlands, Brazil, France, Britain, Spain, Italy, Sweden, and Japan (only NYU has a larger exchange program). During each spring break, two group-travel programs take faculty and students to Japan, where they spend a week visiting the Tokyo Stock Exchange, a Nissan auto plant, the headquarters of Normura Securities and Fujitsu, and the Japanese outposts of P&G and Exxon. The trip costs extra, but almost everyone says it is worth the money.

Wharton's considerable breadth in international business and other areas, however, also makes it difficult for students to gain a sense of camaraderie with each other. First-years are divvied up into "cohort" groups of 60 each—with names such as "Killer Bs" or "Special Ks." Each group moves together through the core curriculum, helping to break the place up into smaller subschools.

For a school of this scale and scope, Wharton does a surprisingly good job of holding down nasty competition among its highly ambitious students. Sure, some wags on campus wear Wharton T-shirts depicting two executives shaking hands while holding knives and bats behind their backs. Judging by BUSINESS WEEK's survey results, however, Wharton's culture is merely average in terms of MBA jostling and backstabbing: less competitive than Harvard or Columbia, but not nearly as cooperative as Stanford or Kellogg.

Outside of class, students often tend to scatter, because they live in apartments and homes all around the campus and Philadelphia. Many MBAs live in either Center City, a 10-minute ride by bicycle, or West Philadelphia, an area that has seen better days. Wharton has set aside a dozen floors of Grad Tower B for MBAs alone and dubbed it the "Living Learning Center." About 350 students reside in the on-campus dormitory, making it easy for them to organize in study groups, get advice on courses, or simply find a companion for a late-night snack.

Friendships forged in cohorts often carry through the remainder of the program and into the plethora of Wharton's social activities. Every Thursday at 4:30, it's happy hour at the MBA pub in Steinberg (for Reliance Group chairman and undergrad alum Saul) Conference Center. First-year MBAs tend to prefer Murphy's, a joint with a great jukebox seven blocks west of the campus. A ritualistic fixture of Wharton life is a big celebration once every semester called "Walnut Walk." After mid-terms, MBAs don a combination of formal attire and shorts and begin the bar crawl on Second Street, winding their way through as many as 20 pubs, ending up at a sobering 3 a.m. breakfast.

There's plenty of reason to celebrate during the recruiting season as well. In 1994, only 7 percent of the class failed to have a single job offer by commencement. Some 143 companies recruited on campus in 1994, whizzing through 10,000 interviews for permanent jobs. Another 844 job opportunities were posted by correspondence. Here are the

Top 10 corporate recruiters hauling away the most Wharton grads in 1994: McKinsey (29); Coopers & Lybrand (22); A.T. Kearney (21); Booz Allen & Hamilton (21); Goldman, Sachs (21); Electronic Data Systems (15); Bankers Trust (14); Deloitte & Touche (14); Merrill Lynch (14); and Morgan Stanley (14).

The list above is ample evidence of Wharton's success at placing its top students. But the school does incredibly well in the MBA job sweepstakes overall. In 1994, for example, grads averaged 3 job offers at graduation—better than any school other than Harvard (3.6), Stanford (3.5), MIT (3.3), and UNC (3.1). The jobs those graduates took paid extremely well, because the average salary and bonus in 1994 soared to nearly $90,000 a year. The median starting pay package of exactly $90,000 is the third highest, behind only Harvard and Stanford.

As in most elite schools, the two biggest single groups of students head for jobs in consulting and finance. But then, what would you expect from the school that is considered by corporate recruiters to be the best in finance? Still, Wharton's new program is beginning to alter the focus of future graduates, because it's a far cry from the more theoretical, numbers-crunching curriculum that has formed decades of MBAs at the school.

Contact: Samuel Lundquist, director of admissions, 102 Vance Hall, 3733 Spruce St., 215-898-6183
Final application deadline: April 10

Outstanding Faculty

1. Jeremy J. Siegel (****): "Dr. Macro" is a Wharton institution. An inveterate Wall Street watcher, he begins most classes with a 15- to 20-minute rundown of the day's market information and implications for the economy. He arrived at Wharton in 1976 after teaching stints at MIT, where he earned his Ph.D.; Harvard; and Chicago. Siegel is one of the most quoted B-school economists, appearing frequently on national TV and radio programs. A perennial teaching award winner, he also holds standing-room-only brown bag sessions for students on the outlook for the economy. Has taught macroeconomics analysis and public policy courses to thousands of MBAs since 1986.

2. Peter Knutson (**): Tall and imposing, this accounting maven is one of the few professors on the planet who brings absolute eloquence to even arcane accounting rules. A former Arthur Andersen accountant, he began teaching at Wharton 30 years ago after earning his Ph.D. from Michigan. So formidable is Knutson's knowledge of accounting that he was named to a panel that is currently trying to establish global accounting standards.

3. William C. Tyson (**): A Harvard-educated attorney who brings a combative courtroom demeanor into the classroom, he practiced law for five years before making a quirky transition to B-school prof at Berkeley in 1978. A decade later, he emerged at Wharton as an assistant professor of legal studies and then, of all things, accounting. Tyson has won a pile of awards for his interactive, confrontational style of teaching. Claims expertise in securities regulation, taxation, real estate financing, corporate law, and international business deals.

4. Jamshed K.S. Ghandhi (**):   One of the most feared but respected finance profs at Wharton, his course on Theory and Structure of Capital Markets can be grueling, but most students come away raving. He boasts four degrees, including a bachelor's and master's from Penn, as well as a master's and Ph.D. from Cambridge. This tough-minded prof joined Wharton in 1965. Ever since, he's been winning teaching excellence trophies, including the $15,000 David Hauck Award in 1992. Consults with Citibank and major financial institutions in Turkey, Portugal, and France.

5. Bruce Allen (*):   A few years back, Dean Gerrity assigned Allen the task of spearheading Wharton's initiatives to improve the quality of teaching. He set up midterm student feedbacks, selected top faculty for core courses, and developed a new incentive and reward structure for teaching excellence. Lo and behold, this professor of public policy and management gets high grades himself for his own teaching abilities.

6. Anjani Jain (*):   An expert in operations management, Jain brought down the house as a guest star in the Wharton Follies in 1994, playing Garth in a spoof called "Jain's World." But his performance in the classroom is hardly a spoof. After gaining some of the lowest teaching scores, Jain began two years ago to form quality circles with students and to hold numerous sessions outside of class. Now, he's one of the most popular profs on campus.

Other Best Bets: *Michael Useem* (management), *Franklin Allen* (finance), *Pete Fader* (marketing), and *Erin Anderson* (marketing)

Prominent Alumni: Peter F. O'Malley, president of Los Angeles Dodgers; Charles S. Sanford, Jr., chairman of Bankers Trust; Ronald Perelman, chairman of MacAndrews & Forbes; Lewis Platt, chairman of Hewlett-Packard; James A. Unruh, chairman of Unisys; Alberto Vitale, chairman of Random House; Yataro Kobayashi, chairman of Fuji Xerox; Alain Levy, president of Polygram International; Frank Cahouet, chairman of Mellon Bank; Lawrence Winbach, CEO of Arthur Andersen; Robert Crandall, CEO of American Airlines; James L. Vincent, chairman of Biogen

Wharton MBAs Sound Off

*Many schools boast international curriculums today. At Wharton, almost every study group I was on had people from at least three countries, and on average we as a group spoke three to four languages. You can't beat that for a global education.—**Consultant***

*Wharton deserves high marks for its alumni network, placement capabilities, and strong skills-based emphasis in the curriculum, particularly in the disciplines of finance and accounting. My single greatest complaint is not the teaching quality, as some might suggest. The facilities at Wharton are poor, from many classrooms to the computer labs.—**Investment Banker***

*The administration and faculty were constantly trying to improve the MBA program! They were very open to suggestions from students, who are viewed as customers here. Most professors organized study quality circles to make mid-semester adjustments to improve on their teaching styles and the material covered.—**Investment Banker***

*What distinguishes Wharton from Harvard is its combined focus on case study and theory/research tools. Each class meets twice per week, typically with one focusing on current research and analytical tools and the other a case study where we can immediately apply the theory. This is a much better way to master skills that can be applied later.—**Marketing Manager***

*Overall, Wharton was a good experience. The strengths are clearly its student body, its placement office, and the broad range of electives the school offers. Its weakness: core courses are often taught by tenured faculty with little interest in the students. I also think Wharton is trying to be all things to all people and is falling short.—**Consultant***

*The program is excellent. It provides the basic skills necessary for success after graduation, and the opportunities to get a chance to practice those skills. The cross-disciplinary integration that gets a lot of press is still not a reality, and the goal of teaching leadership remains dubious. But the environment is more collaborative and not nearly as competitive as I had thought.—**Investment Banker***

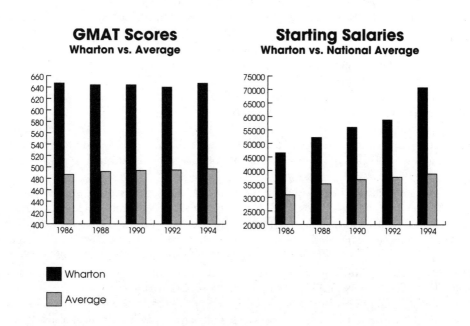

GMAT Scores
Wharton vs. Average

Starting Salaries
Wharton vs. National Average

■ Wharton
▨ Average

2. Northwestern University

J.L. Kellogg School of Management
Leverone Hall
Evanston, Illinois 60208

Corporate ranking: 2
Enrollment: 2510
Women: 30%
Non-U.S.: 24%
Minority: 10%
Part-time: 1350
Average age: 27
Applicants accepted: 20%
Median starting pay: $85,000

Graduate ranking: 5
Annual tuition & fees: $20,634
Room and board: $8670
Average GMAT score: 640*
GMAT range: 600 to 680 (mid 50%)
Average GPA: 3.3
GPA range: 2.4 to 4.0
Accepted applicants enrolled: 62%
Average starting pay: $84,640

Teaching methods: Lecture, 35%   Case study, 55%   Simulation, 10%

After winning three consecutive biennial BUSINESS WEEK polls as the world's best B-school since 1988, Northwestern University's J.L. Kellogg School of Management slipped to second place in 1994. But the fall wasn't the result of any disaffection with the institution or its graduates.

Dean Donald P. Jacobs, arguably the most successful business school dean of this era, established the model of the modern business school in the early 1980s, when such traditional, elite schools as Harvard, Stanford, Chicago, and Wharton were content to ignore market demands for MBAs who could better lead and motivate others. Sure enough, corporate recruiters still praise Kellogg for producing graduates who are best in their ability to work in teams and in their interpersonal skills.

But Jacobs has resisted any pressure to overhaul his program—even as one school after another has torn apart its program to update its curriculum. Wharton nudged out Kellogg as the No. 1 school largely because of strong market approval of its own innovative efforts to rethink management education.

"Our curriculum," Dean Jacobs contends, "is never out of date. Every year it needs tuning, but the program never gets so far out of tune that it needs a grandmaster to do it. If a business school curriculum was that far out of date, why did it push so many students through it? I find it terribly embarrassing."

Self-serving? Maybe. But Jacobs, grandmaster of Kellogg for nearly two decades, can afford the bravado. He has helped the school make the long climb by doing what every dean tries to do: raise money and lure top faculty and staff. Yet the centerpiece of his strategy was distinctive at the time. As a bridge to the real world, Jacobs built one of the nation's largest and most modern executive education centers. The $15 million James L. Allen Center, on the shores of Lake Michigan, hosts more than 3200 executives a year. The result: increased visibility and credibility in the corporate world.

Jacobs didn't slight his students, either. It's no accident that the recruiters believe Kellogg grads demonstrate the best interpersonal skills and show the greatest ability to work as team players. Instead of relying on test scores, past grades, and written essays, Jacobs made Kellogg the first and only business school to interview all its applicants. That gave the school an early edge in attracting articulate students who could work well together.

"It goes back to the input," says Jacobs. "We look for active, bright, caring people. We don't have loners with sharp elbows for students. It's almost counter to what had been produced. And they're being trained by a first-class faculty."

An unassuming academic, Jacobs helps set the mood. On Thanksgiving Day, he skips the traditional family dinner in favor of one with students who can't return home for the holiday, personally carving and serving the turkey. In the early days, Jacobs brought over his own pots, pans, and dishes for the event. At many of the top business schools, students rarely, if ever, see or speak to the dean.

He has also made group work an obsession—so much so that some graduates now complain it's overdone. Jacobs remembers that one rival dean, hearing him speak about the importance of teamwork at Kellogg in the late 1980s, said: "We call that plagiarism, and we kick them out." Now, nearly everyone is encouraging it. Roughly three out of every four classes require significant teamwork. "Turbos"—students who boast strong math skills—and "poets"—those who were liberal arts majors as undergrads—routinely come together in study groups to tackle business problems. It's not always easy. Alberto Gomez, a recent graduate who came to Kellogg from Mexico, recalls a corporate strategy class in which his five-person group was dominated by a student who cracked one joke after another. One shy Japanese member refused to say much of anything. A woman with a consulting background shouldered much of the workload. "I thought that the group was doomed," he says. "We finally had a two-hour session where we got it out into the open. After the talk, you couldn't shut this Japanese guy up. We learned to work as a team."

Indeed, those teams draw upon a richly diverse group of students. Among the Class of 1994, for example, was a story editor from Metro-Goldwyn-Mayer, a professional soccer player, an accomplished concert pianist, a former Seattle Seahawks cheerleader, an aerospace engineer from the former Soviet Union, the former dean of students at a girls' prep school, five Fullbright Scholars, and a *Sports Illustrated* reporter who covered the Olympic Games. Only 16 percent of the students come from the midwest.

Kellogg is rapidly catching up with the traditional elites in attracting the best international students, too. The school received nearly 1100 foreign applications from 67 countries in 1992. A record 22 percent of Kellogg's 1992 entrants boast foreign passports from 38 countries, most of which hail from Asia (47) and Europe (30). Four years earlier, only 13 percent of Kellogg's students were from abroad. Adding to the international mix is the fact that more than 60 percent of the school's American students have lived, studied, or worked overseas.

The team concept brings this diversity to life through an extraordinary display of student entrepreneurship and involvement. A good example of the initiative constantly demonstrated by Kellogg's gung ho students is the preorientation outdoor adventures, a truly unique experience for newcomers. In 1992, second-year students put together 10 different camping trips, from backpacking in Santa Fe to canoeing on the Namekagon River in Wisconsin, from biking in Leelanau, Michigan, to horseback riding in Valle de Bravo, Mexico. Each excursion—which varies in length from four to seven days and costs from

$250 to $900—is led by three or four second-year students. The trips are a great way to meet your classmates and to get the inside scoop on Kellogg.

These voluntary adventures immediately precede CIM (Conceptual Issues in Management) week, a week-long orientation program organized and run entirely by as many as 200 second years. Students begin arriving on a Sunday to walking tours of the campus and downtown Evanston, as well as a reception that evening for those who are married. There's an outdoor field activity, a business simulation game, sessions on cultural diversity, negotiations and team building. There's also a series of intensive math reviews that meet every day for students suffering from math anxiety.

Kellogg classes, which meet twice a week for an hour and 40 minutes, are scheduled on a quarter basis (with three quarters a year). No classes are scheduled on Wednesday, a good day to sleep in, take a swim in the university rec center, or work on group projects. You need 23 courses to graduate. You can waive out of core courses, but must replace them from the more than 200 electives and advanced classes offered. Most Kellogg MMs (instead of the MBA, grads here receive the Master of Management degree) major in 2 or 3 of 17 areas, from marketing to international business. Four courses are required in any given major. If you already own an undergraduate business degree, Kellogg is the only prestige B-school that will hand you a master's in one year. The school's "four-quarter" program welcomes one section of 64 students every June and grads award it extremely high marks.

Kellogg, named after the son of the breakfast cereal founder, built its reputation on marketing. But the school also has an outstanding reputation in general management, manufacturing, and finance. Indeed, some grads think the finance profs represent the single best group of teachers at the school. Surprisingly, given Kellogg's strength in marketing, the finance teachers outnumber the marketing profs by 29 to 24. Behind which subjects has Jacobs assembled the rest of his troops? Managerial economics and decision sciences, the department housing the real quant profs, boasts 23 faculty members. He has 21 people teaching organizational behavior and human resources courses. There are also 18 profs in management and strategy and 17 in accounting and information systems.

Though Jacobs isn't planning any major upheavals in the basic curriculum, he estimates that as much as 10 to 20 percent of the program changes every year. By far the most significant alteration in recent years is the attention paid to international business, entrepreneurship, and manufacturing. Consider the emphasis on global business. Every one of Kellogg's seven academic departments now has at least one course that deals with international issues, and each department has infused global examples throughout all its course offerings. Students also can take not-for-credit language classes taught by university faculty. The courses—in Japanese, French, German, and Spanish—cost an extra $150 each and are held from 5 to 7 p.m. in Leverone Hall after the regularly scheduled business classes.

The most novel idea, however, has been to allow students to create specially designed, two-quarter international independent study courses focusing on a country of their choice. With a faculty sponsor, students arrange the syllabus, assume responsibility for guest speakers, determine research topics, and identify key issues facing industries in their chosen nation. Students complete the coursework in the winter quarter, then travel to the selected country over spring holiday for two-week-long group consulting projects and international study tours. In the spring quarter, students put the finishing touches on their studies and present their findings to faculty and visiting executives. The program began in 1989 with one class of 34 students studying the Soviet Union. In 1994, student teams flew off to Ghana, Costa Rica, China, Mexico, and Japan. As many as 400 students participated in these new courses in 1994.

Broadening interest in new startups also led Jacobs to add a sequence of courses in entrepreneurship as well as a major in the subject in 1992. Besides classes in the basics of new venture formulation, would-be entrepreneurs can dive into such courses as Introduction to New Products and Services and The Entrepreneur and His/Her Social Environment. These days, one of every four students is a member of the school's Entrepreneurship and New Venture Club. Another hot area is quality. Kellogg offers a new three-course sequence in Total Quality Management, including a practicum in which students work with company managers or public school administrators to implement quality efforts.

For those interested in not-for-profit jobs, the school boasts a powerful Public and Nonprofit Management program, with 14 electives, that is as good as or better than the one at Yale. Students, for instance, gain summer stipends if they chose to do internships in lower-paying public or nonprofit positions. And there's a new loan forgiveness program, for graduating students taking jobs in public and nonprofit organizations.

For aspiring gearheads, Kellogg boasts a two-year Master of Manufacturing Management degree, which successfully graduated its first class in 1992. A joint program with the university's Technological Institute, it's an attempt to help restore America's competitive edge. Applicants need an undergraduate degree in engineering or science or three years of work experience in manufacturing. The program's main classroom and lab is at the institute, about two blocks north of the B-school. In 1992, some 57 students entered the program, which includes a guaranteed manufacturing internship in the summer.

What of Jacobs' major challenges? BW's graduate satisfaction surveys show that the quality of teaching at Kellogg is only slightly better than average in either the core or elective classes. To improve, Jacobs has banned new faculty members from core courses in their first quarter at the school. Each new teacher is run through an orientation program that emphasizes teaching issues and is also assigned a mentor from his or her own department for help. For basket cases, an outside evaluator videotapes teachers and provides one-on-one counseling. Jacobs also has set up a system of peer evaluation to assess the teaching skills of both tenured and nontenured professors. The school claims it has recently denied tenure to some profs because of their lackluster teaching records.

Other gripes that may place Kellogg's lead in jeopardy: some grads think that the curriculum lacks rigor and that the institution suffers from grade inflation. Some also argue that despite Jacobs' continuous-improvement argument, the core curriculum needs revision (it contains, for example, not just one but two decision science courses, which many grads consider somewhat redundant). A few grads believe the Kellogg culture is so cooperative that students and faculty are chary of challenging statements and opinions in class, even when disagreement would lead to more productive learning. And several in the Class of 1994 say the school is especially weak in using information technology in the classroom.

That latter complaint may be answered somewhat by the addition in 1994 of Andersen Hall, the former home of the School of Education and Social Policy. Andersen—linked to Leverone Hall next door—brings four new, computer-wired classrooms, 15 group-study rooms, and a computer lab. It also adds a four-story, 3000-square-foot atrium, with a green terrazzo-tiled floor that is already serving as the hub of student life. Kafe Kellogg, a restaurant in the atrium, is a convenient place to grab fresh-baked pizzas, deli sandwiches, and expresso drinks.

It is a welcome addition to an attractive campus setting. Leverone Hall—the primary six-story center of the school—overlooks Deering Meadow, an expanse of grass and oak trees. The university's nearby Deering Library, a Gothic structure that looks as if it has been transplanted from turn-of-the-century England, boasts a management section on the ground floor with its own librarian. Just two blocks away is the Allen Center, which is being expanded by 50 percent. The McManus Living and Learning Center, renovated in the early 1980s, houses a third of the students, who vie for a spot there via a lottery system. Jokingly dubbed the Loving and Lusting Center by students, it has played an integral part in nurturing Kellogg's group culture.

Every Friday afternoon in Leverone's second-floor lounge, a keg gets tapped at 4:45 for the weekly TGIF session. In the spring, the weekly ritual adjourns to the meadow directly in front, where Frisbee flinging remains the sport of choice. At times, the Kellogg experience can resemble a big undergraduate party. Some graduates even complain that the workload isn't tough enough. Concern over grade inflation recently led to an imposed limit on the number of A's handed out by professors (a still-generous maximum of 35 percent for core classes, 45 percent for electives). There are plenty of student clubs, downtown pub crawls, beer and pizza fests, international dinner parties, football games, and museums, too. Evanston is just a cab ride from downtown Chicago. MMs particularly favor Howard Street's Tally Ho and P.M. Club, known for its jukebox loaded with Sinatra tunes. Carmen's on Church Street serves up decent pizza.

Back on campus, most students overbook themselves with extracurricular doings. "Business with a Heart," Kellogg's do-good MBA group, raised more than $50,000 in 1992 for charitable causes. Students built homes for low-income families, staffed homeless shelters, created AIDS awareness programs, and collected and distributed clothing for the less fortunate. All these programs get plenty of coverage in *The Merger,* Kellogg's lively but sometimes amateurish student newspaper.

Given the stormy economic climate, Jacobs is one of a handful of deans who believes that a business school must assume some responsibility for the success of its alumni. To that end, the school boasts a computer service for alums who can dial in for job opportunities, as well as a twice-monthly newsletter with job postings that come in from alumni contacts and executive headhunters. One recent issue listed 44 openings with annual pay that ranged from a low of $35,000 to $350,000. Kellogg also has added a full-time staffer who conducts workshops for alums on networking and career planning and beats the drum in the marketplace for Kellogg grads.

In the future these services will become even more important to Kellogg's 21,000 alumni in 83 countries. The school now recognizes 42 alumni clubs around the world, including chapters in England, France, Germany, Hong Kong, Italy, Japan, Mexico, Singapore, Taiwan, Thailand, and Venezuela. There are 22 U.S. cities, from Atlanta to Washington, D.C., with Kellogg alumni clubs. The doings of alums now occupy 20 or more pages of *Kellogg World,* the alumni magazine published three times a year.

The networking these activities promote is crucial to whatever level of security a degree can offer. More helpful, however, is the fact that few schools do a better job of meeting the needs of Corporate America than Kellogg, which is why the school is ranked second, behind only Wharton, in BW's corporate poll. In 1994, the school claims to have hosted the highest number of on-campus recruiters of any major business school—even higher than Harvard or Wharton. Some 276 companies recruited on campus (versus 143 at Wharton), conducting more than 13,600 interviews. Another 2207 job opportunities were posted by correspondence. Only 6.1 percent of the Class of 1994 failed to have a job offer at graduation. Those that did averaged 2.96 offers each—nicely above the 2.36 average for the top 40-plus schools polled by BW.

Indeed, Kellogg's emergence as a true business school powerhouse has had a major impact on where its graduates now work. In 1994, 35 percent of the class rushed off to work in consulting, and 15 percent gained jobs in corporate finance. Grads who went into product management—long the key to the school's image as a great place for future marketers—fell to only 14 percent, from 21 percent only two years earlier. There's not a single marketer among Kellogg's top ten recruiters in 1994: Booz Allen & Hamilton (21); A.T. Kearney (18); Coopers & Lybrand (16); McKinsey (16); CSC Index (15); Boston Consulting Group (14); Bankers Trust (13); Merrill Lynch (12); CS First Boston (10); and Gemini Consulting (10).

That's also a major reason why Kellogg's average starting salary numbers (see chart at end of profile) have risen 24 percent in the past two years alone. In 1994, grads pulled down average pay-and-bonus packages of $84,640. The only reason Kellogg grads fail to make it into the six-figure average is that more of them (as opposed to the MBAs at Harvard and Stanford) go to work for Corporate America, which pays less than the consulting and investment-banking fields.

Jacobs may look down on his rivals' experimentation with a touch of scorn. But the vast upheaval in the B-school world means that no institution can be complacent. The proof of it is Kellogg's slippage from No. 1 in 1994.

Contact: Stephen Christakos, director of admissions, 708-491-3308
Final application deadlines: March 31

Outstanding Faculty

1. Louis W. Stern (****): This marketing guru doesn't teach, he explodes. His manic energy carries him across a classroom and through the material at a breakneck pace, waving arms and bellowing questions in a weighty baritone. Stern gained his Ph.D. in marketing from Kellogg in 1962 and has taught at the school since 1973. Students regularly gamble 75 percent of their bid points to get into his course on Marketing Channels—an elective that has acquired such caché that even corporate recruiters ask job candidates if they've taken the class with Stern.

2. Martin R. Stoller (**): Just call this newcomer who lectures on organizational behavior "Marty." He came to Kellogg in 1991 with a trio of communications degrees from Northwestern, including a Ph.D. in—of all things—"rhetoric." His teaching mandate: to unleash problem-solving creativity, enhance persuasion skills, boost powers of analysis, and improve presentation skills. Grads say he delivers those goods, and more.

3. Dipak C. Jain (**): This marketing prof first got a taste of teaching business at Gauhati University in India, before joining Kellogg in 1986. Jain deftly teaches courses in marketing research, new products and services, product design and development, and—yes, this is true—multivariate data analysis. He earned his Ph.D. in marketing from the University of Texas at Dallas.

4. Lawrence Revsine (**): Named the 1992 Outstanding Educator by the American Accounting Association. An MBA and a CPA, he has been teaching corporate financial reporting at Kellogg since 1971. Revsine rolls up his sleeves in the classroom, bringing to teaching much insight, creativity, and energy. A prolific author, he has written three books: *Replacement Cost Accounting, Accounting in an Inflationary Environment,* and *Statement on Accounting Theory and Theory Acceptance.* Not exactly Tom Clancy titles, but you wouldn't want Clancy to teach you accounting.

5. Gregory S. Carpenter (*): A consultant for such high-powered companies as General Electric, Citibank, Motorola, and Unilever, Carpenter teaches market planning and strategy. Before arriving at Kellogg in 1990, he taught at Columbia University (where he earned his Ph.D. in 1983), UCLA, and the Yale School of Management. Carpenter gets great student reviews, especially for his teaching of Marketing Policy, an MBA elective, which delves into competitive brand strategy.

6. Phillip A. Braun (*): He gave a soaring, inspirational speech at the graduation ceremonies in 1994, after being elected Outstanding Professor of the Year. Braun even surprised guests by delivering part of his address in Chinese. This finance prof joined Kellogg in 1991, after gaining a Ph.D. from archrival University of Chicago. He's an expert in such areas as investments, international finance, and macroeconomics.

Other Best Bets: *Aharon R. Ofer* (finance), *Arthur Raviv* (finance), *Susan Chapinsky* (finance), and *Robert C. Blattberg* (marketing)

Prominent Alumni: Robert Beeby, CEO of Frito-Lay; Dennis C. Bottorff, CEO of First American; Donald Brinckman, CEO of Safety-Kleen; Donald Clark, CEO of Household International; Howard Dean, CEO of Dean Foods; James H. Keyes, CEO of Johnson Controls; James McManus, chairman of Marketing Corp. of America; Jerry Meyers, CEO of Steelcase; H. Donald Nelson, CEO of US Cellular; Patrick Ryan, CEO of Aon Corp.; William Smithburg, chairman of Quaker Oats Co.

Kellogg MBAs Sound Off

The most interesting and stimulating aspect of the educational experience was the caliber and diversity of my classmates. Every person had a "story to tell" that *was unique and spoke to the class's collective taste for challenge. In addition, the class was incredibly supportive of its members, and the Kellogg environment is very group-oriented—definitely a far cry from the typical business school stereotype!—**Marketing Associate***

*Kellogg functions for the students. It's not perfect, but the fundamental mindset that the students are the customers allows the school to be flexible and progressive. Every single quarter, test courses are run, creating an atmosphere of continuous, incremental change.—**General Manager***

Kellogg's emphasis on learning through group interaction was at times a frustrating and humbling experience. But in hindsight, it was an experience that was exceedingly rewarding and arguably the strongest attribute of the school.
*—**Finance Associate***

*The academic curriculum could definitely have been more rigorous, but in the end the coursework was not the most important part. Kellogg provided a well-balanced experience, with wonderful people. The teaching was either very good or somewhat mediocre. The last two years were right in the middle of major construction, which will vastly improve the facilities and provide much greater access to computers.—**Marketing Analyst***

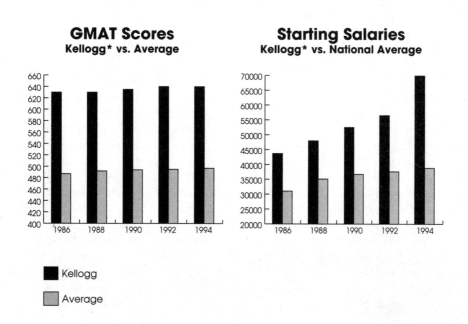

GMAT Scores
Kellogg* vs. Average

Starting Salaries
Kellogg* vs. National Average

■ Kellogg
▨ Average

3. The University of Chicago

Graduate School of Business
1101 East 58th Street
Chicago, Illinois 60637

Corporate ranking: 4
Enrollment: 2362
Women: 20%
Non-U.S.: 16%
Minority: 18%
Part-time: 1225
Average age: 27
Applicants accepted: 33%
Median starting pay: $79,250

Graduate ranking: 4
Annual tuition & fees: $21,656
Room and board: $9054
Average GMAT score: 650
GMAT range: 500 to 770
Average GPA: 3.3
GPA range: 2.5 to 4.0
Accepted applicants enrolled: 50%
Average starting pay: $83,210

Teaching methods: Lecture, 60%   Case study, 25%   Projects, 15%

It's not exactly something you'd expect from the University of Chicago's business school. Shortly after arriving on campus, members of the Class of 1995 were introduced to creative problem-solving and group processes. Immediately, the students were then asked to put those newly learned skills to work during a grueling 24-hour project called the Dean's Challenge.

Has Chicago, long known for its teaching of quantitative methods and macroeconomic decision making, gone soft? Not on your life. The school has not abandoned the traditional academic values that have been the center of its business program. But the problem-solving exercises—added to the school's successful LEAD (Leadership Exploration and Development) program in 1994—reflect a dramatic transformation of the school's approach to management education.

Hailed in the late 1950s when most other business schools were vigorously attacked for being too vocational, Chicago's B-school had long kept true to its academic roots. Until only recently, deans had commonly viewed business schools on a scale, placing case study–based Harvard at one end as representative of the trade school mold and putting Chicago on the other as the lecture-based school that teaches business theory.

Chicago no longer sits on the end of this simple spectrum. The school has rounded out a strong quantitative program with more focus on interpersonal skills. The change is the result of a soul-searching that started in 1988 when students began to challenge the density of the school's curriculum. An internal study came to the sobering conclusion that Chicago underemphasized day-to-day problem-solving as well as the skills needed to manage people.

The school took the unusual step of empowering its own students to create a mandatory, noncredit leadership program that would span its entire first-year curriculum. Corporate sponsors, including Bankers Trust, Merrill Lynch, Leo Burnett, and Pfizer do more than help foot the bill for the program. Managers from these firms are enlisted to participate, run sessions, and critique the numerous workshops and exercises in team building and leadership. The idea: to better balance the academic theory in Chicago's curriculum with "soft" management skills. Some rival deans pooh-pooh the changes because they are outside the school's mainstream curriculum, but Gould wisely chose not to tamper with the basics of the program. If he had, the faculty would have dramatically slowed down the process of change.

Precisely because LEAD is not integrated into the curriculum, it is reinvented every year. The latest version that includes the journal-writing requirement is the result of brainstorming by about 50 Chicago students who were given a $600,000 budget and complete responsibility for designing and implementing the program for the entire incoming class. How does it work? The first-year class is divided into 10 cohort groups of about 50 students. Each group is assigned a faculty adviser and four second-year students who help facilitate classroom discussion and ensure that about a dozen "required activities" run smoothly.

There's a one-day, 10-hour seminar on presentation and communication skills by Beach-Savard consultants, a one-day outward bound program, and a spring retreat to give students the chance to reflect on their first-quarter experience. In one seminar, hypothetical business problems are posed and solved. A business simulation in 1993 required student teams to solve real-world business problems brought to them by sponsors Procter & Gamble and Leo Burnett. One activity even showed the movie classic *Twelve Angry Men* to demonstrate how Henry Fonda convinces fellow jurors that a seemingly guilty defendant may be innocent.

In 1993, the program began with the dean's challenge: Before taking a single class, first-years were divided into 56 teams of 10 students each, and then given 24 hours to come up with a proposal to start a new international business located in at least two countries. Once the business ideas were hatched, they had to be presented to alumni who assumed the role of board directors. After the presentation, each team spent three and one-half hours analyzing how the students worked with each other. The idea? To learn about the strengths and weaknesses of teamwork.

The future direction of the school, however, is less than certain, because the two administrators most responsible for changing Chicago's program left their key positions. After a 10-year stint as dean, John P. Gould stepped down on June 30, 1993. So did his deputy dean, Harry Davis, a soft-spoken innovator who had been LEAD's strongest champion. Robert Homada, a finance professor at the B-school since 1966, took over the helm. Increasing the school's prominence in the International Business arena is one of Homada's major initiatives. His new deputy is Robin Hogarth, another Chicago insider who has taught at Chicago since 1979.

Chicago has already stepped up to the plate in the global arena with the introduction of two new programs. The International Executive MBA program at Barcelona is a part-time program that began in the summer of 1994. While the program is intended for international business executives with at least 10 years of work experience, the experience will still benefit MBAs sitting in Hyde Park classrooms, because Chicago's faculty will gain valuable international experience. In June 1995 the school will launch a new two-year International MBA program, which combines traditional MBA courses with special courses on issues facing companies doing business internationally. MBAs will take courses in culture, history, and politics, and must master at least one foreign language. Students also will be required to spend at least six months studying and living in a foreign country to earn the International MBA degree.

What isn't likely to change is the Chicago environment, a place that reeks tradition and academic excellence. Notwithstanding the program's new touchy-feely aspects, Chicago remains a haven for scholars and intellectuals. Since 1898, the school has turned more than 26,000 MBAs out into the world. They leave an inspiring environment. Spires and gargoyles top the stone-wall buildings. Gothic arches and tree-lined walks mark the stunning campus. It could just as easily be Great Britain's Oxford or Cambridge. "When you come here for the first time," says a student, "you almost get a shiver up your spine."

Along the Midway Plaisance, the grassy expanse of lawn that cuts through the university campus, some students still jokingly refer to themselves as "digit heads"—a reference to the heavily quantitative nature of the Chicago program. You can overhear them in the halls and classrooms talking about the "free market system" and the "capital asset pricing model," ideas and concepts relentlessly drilled into Chicago MBAs.

What does surprise many is the large degree of flexibility built into the program. Chicago is one of the few B-schools that will actually allow you to substitute core courses with higher-level electives if you have mastered the material elsewhere. The only required courses are Business Policy, Management in Organizations, and the LEAD program. To get the MBA, you must complete 21 courses—whether you waive some or not. Most do it over six 11-week quarters spread out through two years. Yet it's possible to complete the program in a year and a half by giving up your shot at an internship and taking classes over the summer. As a full-timer, you can also take evening courses in downtown Chicago with the part-timers in a new $44 million downtown center that opened in March 1994. You can even enter this program in the summer instead of waiting for the fall.

Chicago offers MBAs a "concentration" if they complete three or four courses in one field. You can focus in such basic areas as accounting, business economics, financial management, international business, human resources management, marketing, and statistics. Yet one of the more unusual and pioneering concentrations is quality management, the school's first new area of study in 25 years. Chicago now boasts a sequence of nine courses on Total Quality Management, more than any other major business school, and has a lineup of 13 faculty members who teach quality courses, including one current and one former examiner for the Malcolm Baldrige National Quality Award. A recent survey by *Quality Progress* magazine found Chicago to be the leader among the top 20 B-schools in offering the most quality-related classes and in class time devoted to quality in introductory management courses. So far ahead is Chicago in this field that the school is even developing a Ph.D. in the subject.

If your interests go well beyond business and quality, you also can take up to 6 of the 21 required courses outside the B-school. But the B-school itself offers so many challenging electives that you might not want to stray from the program. One in every five elective courses now consists of various applied field projects or case studies—another change to make Chicago's curriculum more real world. The school has also added a greater number of applied courses in marketing, general management, and finance.

Some of the highly innovative laboratory courses at Chicago certainly disprove the stereotype that Chicago is a hangout for digit heads and Ph.D. scholars. The labs, which allow students to work as consultants to business and government organizations, bridge the gap between the classroom and the marketplace. Consider the school's New Product Laboratory, in which teams of students work on new ideas and products for major corporations, from the Santa Fe Railroad to NutraSweet. In the spring of 1994, Strohs Brewery, US West, and a joint venture of Ameritech and Northern Telecom sponsored new product labs. Yet this course is only one of seven laboratory classes in new product development, quality management, and management processes. "We assign teams to work on the projects and try to maximize diversity on them, so that a French lit major from Wellesley is on a team with an engineer from Cal Tech to generate new ideas for the client," says Davis, former director of the laboratory.

In 1994, 100 students (up from 48 in 1990) enrolled in the six-month course, worth 10 percent of the total MBA workload. Divided into teams of a dozen members, students sign confidentiality statements with clients and then roll up their sleeves. They run consumer research on the idea. They work with prototype developers on the new product and even consult with an advertising agency on communication issues and packaging strategy. At project's end, the teams make full-scale presentations and submit a written business plan, complete with the financials as well as advertising, promotion, and introductory marketing programs.

Sometimes plans hatched by Chicago's MBAs even translate into real products and services. In 1990, for example, Encyclopedia Britannica enlisted the help of a team of 11 students in the new product lab. Their task: to explore new ways to sell the company's products. Dozens of ideas were tossed around, only a couple of which reached the proposal stage. The concept that won approval from the president of Encyclopedia Britannica and her staff was the idea of launching upscale retail stores for the curious family. Students did focus studies, interviewed potential customers at shopping malls, and ran profit and sales projections. The company opened the doors to "The Knowledge Store" in the Woodfield Mall in suburban Chicago in 1991. "If it's successful, I hope we could see hundreds of them across the country," says Patricia A. Wier, president of Encyclopedia Britannica USA. "It's a terrific thing for the students to get some real-world experience, and it's good for the business community because we're able to get some of the brightest people in the country to work on our problems."

About 25 students also participate in the Argonne Chicago Development Corp., in which they're involved in converting scientific discoveries into commercial products and new businesses. ARCH, an extracurricular activity by students, has already given birth to five companies. And recently, two groups of 12 students each have worked with the National Aeronautics Space Administration on the commercialization of products in space.

Chicago, of course, continues to boast outstanding academic researchers. A *Journal of Finance* report ranked the B-school first in the impact of its faculty's research in finance. Three leading academic journals are edited by B-school faculty. Chicago was the first business school to have a Nobel laureate—George Stigler—on its faculty. (Stigler won the prize in 1982 and died in 1991.) Besides Stigler, the business school boasts three other winners of the Nobel Prize in economics: Robert Fogel (1993) and Merton Miller (1990), who both still teach in the MBA program, and Ronald Coase (1991). Not only does Chicago have scholars on its faculty, the Class of 1994 rated the teaching in both core and elective courses as well above the average for the 40-plus schools surveyed by BUSINESS WEEK.

Still, it's worth noting that virtually all of Chicago's top 10 teachers (see below) are in finance, accounting, or economics. None of them is an expert in marketing, production, or organizational behavior, and only one in business policy or management pops up on the "best" list. Some graduates worry that the departure of a few outstanding professors in marketing and general management will harm the school's continued ability to offer a well-rounded MBA program.

Chicago's B-school is a cluster of three classic buildings linked together on the 172-acre university campus in Hyde Park, about 12 minutes from the Loop on the subway. Students flip frisbees or bat softballs around on the outside Midway, which reaches to Lake Michigan from the campus. MBAs tend to hang out at Ida Noyes Hall, a block from the B-school. Many of them live at International House, the university dorm two blocks away, or in apartments or homes in Hyde Park, a troubled yet pricey residential neighborhood that has seen better times. As one male 1992 MBA put it: "I am 5'11", 185 pounds, in great physical shape, and I have never been mugged, but the crime situation here is scary."

Corporate presentations fill the calendar in the fall, when companies arrive for sessions to make their pitch for students and serve snacks and drinks after the presentations. There's also a fall international fest, a winter formal, and the annual Follies in the spring. *Chicago Business,* the student newspaper, keeps everyone well informed of the events—especially of visiting speakers and recruiting companies.

Chicago's reputation for imparting strong analytical and quantitative skills in students still has a dramatic impact on where they go: Some 50 percent of the Class of 1992 headed for jobs in finance (far more than either Harvard or Stanford). About one in five Chicago MBAs became consultants, while 16 percent assumed marketing positions (that's roughly half the number rival Kellogg School sends into marketing jobs). The biggest alumni hang-outs over the years? Some 316 Chicago MBAs are on the payrolls at Amoco, 291 at First National Bank of Chicago, 267 at AT&T, 224 at Arthur Andersen, and 220 at IBM. Other big employers include Motorola (188); Citicorp (173); General Electric (172); Continental Bank (167); and Goldman Sachs (161).

That kind of high-level infiltration of Chicago MBAs certainly helps networking for job possibilities. About 97.3 percent of Chicago MBAs had job offers by graduation in 1994, with an average 2.92 offers each—nicely above the 2.36 average for the 40-plus surveyed schools. Still, in 1994 some 248 companies (50 fewer than in 1990) came to recruit on campus, conducting 10,000 interviews. More than 1500 other job opportunities were posted by correspondence. Leading the pack of enthusiastic recruiters were Booz Allen and Hamilton (24), Goldman Sachs (14), Boston Consulting Group (12), Ernst & Young (10). Cooper's & Lybrand, Deloitte & Touche, J.P. Morgan, and Merrill Lynch plucked 9 grads each.

Quite a group, although nearby rival Northwestern has managed to eke out even slightly better numbers for its 1994 grads, given its No. 2 status in BW polls. Indeed, in recent years, a fierce rivalry has erupted between Chicago and Northwestern, encapsulated by a hot-selling t-shirt: "The Top 10 Reasons Why Kellogg Is For Losers":

10. Masters of Management: fast-food diet for business lightweights.

9. Meet lots of nice people and learn lots of neat stuff.

8. Think Beta is a fraternity.

7. Learn how to eat Corn Flakes in marketing class.

6. Get toy surprise with diploma.

5. Favorite class: Checkbook Accounting.

4. The Rollerblade MBA: Here today, gone tomorrow.

3. Receive complimentary lunches at corporate meetings, and think that they are free.

2. Question: What is a "random walk"? Answer: A dance step?

1. Next Nobel Prize will be their first.

Contact: Donald C. Martin, director of admissions, 312-702-7369
Final application deadline: March 17

Outstanding Faculty

1. Steven N. Kaplan (****):   Kaplan is so young he could easily pass for just another MBA student strolling through the hallways. He joined the faculty in 1988 after earning a trio of degrees from Harvard, including a Ph.D. in business economics. But before taking the professor route, Kaplan toiled in Kidder Peabody's corporate finance department for two years and spent another year as a Booz Allen consultant. He teaches financial management from the perspective of the chief financial officer, deftly employing a case-study approach.

2. Mark Mitchell (***):   He's known for doing off-the-wall things in class, like giving a cash prize to the MBA who scores highest on an exam. Students in Mitchell's corporate finance class quickly learn to come to class prepared, because he does lots of "cold calling." Mitchell joined the faculty in 1990 and just two years later he was selected by MBAs for a teaching award.

3. James Schrager (**):   This senior lecturer has a slew of degrees—M.B.A, J.D., Ph.D.—and he's also a CPA. Schrager divides his time between the front of the classroom and serving as president of Japan Capital Markets, a unit of the Marmon Group. Even though he developed Chicago's course in new venture strategy 13 years ago, he is still enthusiastic about teaching it and business policy. In his spare time, Schrager races his sailboat, does auto repairs, and hits the ski slopes.

4. Eugene Fama (**):   He windsurfs, bikes, is a fan of classical movies, and is one of Chicago's most demanding professors. Fama's finance course is two quarters long and forms the basis for Ph.D. work. MBAs stretch to take Fama's Theory of Financial Decisions, but ultimately many find it rewarding. The finance buff spearheaded the recent push by Chicago's faculty to establish an analytic concentration in finance.

5. Robert W. Vishny (**):   Collects tribal art, loves music and good restaurants. This finance prof got his Ph.D. at MIT in 1985 and came straight to Chicago, where he has excelled in the classroom. It helps that he teaches one of the hottest topics in business today: the battle for corporate control by shareholders. His superb course on corporate finance focuses on the major decisions made by corporate financial managers.

6. Robert A. Bushman (*):   An accounting maven with a CPA from the state of Ohio, Bushman is known for making this dull discipline interesting. He gained his Ph.D. from the University of Minnesota in 1989.

Other Best Bets: *Jennifer Francis* (accounting), *Raffi J. Indejkian* (accounting), *Marvin Zonis* (business administration), and *Richard Leftwich* (accounting and finance)

Prominent Alumni: Robert M. Baughman, CEO of DowBrands; Kenneth G. Fisher, CEO of Encore Computer; David W. Fox, CEO of Northern Trust; Melvin Goodes, CEO of Warner-Lambert; Charles M. Harper, CEO of ConAgra; David H. Jennings, CEO of Stouffer Foods; David W. Johnson, chairman of Campbell Soup; Alfred A. Piergallini, CEO of Gerber Products; Charles R. Shoemate, CEO of CPC International

Chicago MBAs Sound Off

*Many schools offer terrific programs, but in my opinion my experience at Chicago was unique, for no other school offers the flexibility I had in designing my curriculum and few attract such a diverse student body. From the very first quarter, I was able to tailor my schedule to match my career goals, skipping courses in which I had already had exposure or only had a limited interest in without the burden of having to pass qualifying exams. I was given this opportunity because Chicago treats its students like adults. It provides course counseling and information, but the individual makes the final decision.—**Sales and Trading Associate***

*University of Chicago's most unique strength is its laboratory programs. As a participant in the New Product Laboratory, I learned how to research a large topic, synthesize data, write a business plan, run meetings, meet with a real-world client, and present concrete ideas—all within a six-month period. NPL gave me critical experiences that I could discuss in interviews and use on my job. —**Marketing Career Path***

*It is disillusioning when the realization hits that MBA students are in a two-year scramble to find the perfect job. Going in, we thought that we would be getting away from work for an educational sabbatical, and that employers would freely pass out the jobs without our having to roll up our sleeves and leave the ivory tower.—**Sales and Trading Associate***

It may be difficult to believe, but I selected Chicago because I was interest in marketing. Chicago's rigorous curriculum (while remaining flexible) is a nice complement to my Liberal Arts undergraduate experience, and also is highly applicable to brand management. I believe that is why I was able to obtain a *position with a premier consumer products manufacturer and why I am well poised to succeed in the future.—**Assistant Marketing Manager***

*LEAD was a disappointment. Instead of being a laboratory where you could better understand your role in group processes, LEAD was mainly a collection of discussions on trendy topics such as diversity and ethics.—**Consultant***

*This is the most responsive faculty and administration I've ever encountered. I have walked into the Dean's office unannounced and been given extraordinary attention. I've also made suggestions to faculty which were implemented by the following week. Compared to Columbia (my undergrad school), Chicago gets an A+ here. I've gone to school in both Harlem and Hyde Park. Harlem is less racially charged. I was often uncomfortable, and typically went to another area of Chicago (Lincoln Park) to socialize.—**Investment Banking Associate***

*Having a strong international business background, I was disappointed by the breadth and strength of international business course offerings. But I think this should change, with the introduction of the new International Business program at GSB.—**Senior Consultant***

Four Nobel Prize Winners—need we say more? Academically, we are superior.
*—**Investment Banking Associate***

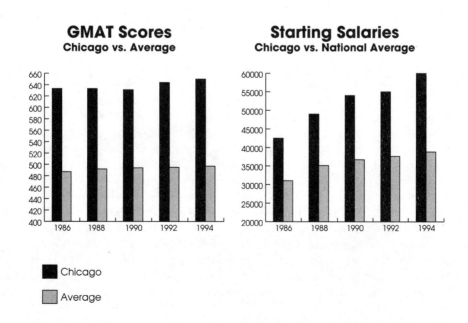

GMAT Scores
Chicago vs. Average

Starting Salaries
Chicago vs. National Average

■ Chicago

▦ Average

4. Stanford University

Graduate School of Business
Stanford, California 94305

Corporate ranking: 5
Enrollment: 726
Women: 27%
Non-U.S.: 21%
Minority: 10%
Part-time: None
Average age: 26.8
Applicants accepted: 10%
Median starting pay: $101,625

Graduate ranking: 1
Annual tuition & fees: $21,189
Room and board: $11,000
Average GMAT score: 665*
GMAT range: 540 to 780*
Average GPA: 3.3*
GPA range: 2.7 to 4.0*
Accepted applicants enrolled: 80%
Average starting pay: $100,800

Teaching methods: Lecture, 50%   Case study, 40%   Group projects, 10%

1987: It was the best of times for the MBA boom, especially for someone with a degree from Stanford, which at the time competed in a nip-and-tuck race with Harvard for preeminence in the business school world. The blue-blooded partnerships on Wall Street battled the best consulting firms for the top of the class, bidding up starting salaries for everyone. Soon after, however, the stock market crashed and corporate downsizings became the rule. New ways of measuring and assessing the quality of a B-school education found that Stanford wasn't nearly as good as it had thought.

Did Stanford's Class of 1987 have any regrets, asked BUSINESS WEEK five years later? Not at all. More than at any other top school, Stanford's graduates were by far the most satisfied with their educational investment. If they could do it over again after being in the world of work for five years, would they? An incredible 94 percent of the Class of 1987 said they still would have gone for an MBA and 99 percent of them unequivocally said they would have returned to their alma mater.

What accounts for such unusual loyalty and commitment? The Stanford Business School is a magisterial institution in a magical setting. The students here are among the most cooperative and least competitive of any top school of business. They are known for their diversity instead of their sameness. Unlike Harvard, there's no grading curve to promote vicious competition. Nor are grades publicly posted or allowed to be disclosed to corporate recruiters. Only at graduation is the top 10 percent of the class announced. The classes are smaller and more intimate, too. And its location in California lends to its different approach. "There's an informality at Stanford," says Jeffrey Pfeffer, one of the most popular professors here. "It's partly the difference between the West and the East. And one of the caps on our enrollment is that our biggest classrooms hold only 70 people."

Students often refer to the campus as the farm—a throwback to when the campus was indeed a farm and racehorse-breeding ranch a century ago. Stanford clearly boasts one of the most handsome campuses in the country. Not far off from the business school looms the university's charming trademark, the Hoover Tower. The B-school is housed in a four-story building in the center of the university's 8200-acre campus. It's a modern anomaly among the campus' arcaded quadrangles of Spanish-style buildings topped by red tile roofs. The three-story Littlefield Center, more in keeping with Stanford's architecture, is home to the school's faculty. These days there's little evidence of the October 1989 earthquake that abruptly disturbed this tranquil setting. Though no one at the school was seriously injured, the B-school suffered millions of dollars in extensive damage. Classes were canceled for two days; the library, heavily damaged, was shut down for the remainder of the school year and a satellite facility was opened in relatively unscathed Littlefield.

Even the earthquake, however, couldn't keep students away. One in five Stanford MBAs turn down Harvard to come here and study amid the redwoods and palm trees. What they find at Stanford is a pure and unadulterated general management program. No single group of faculty overwhelmingly dominates others. With the exception of health care, Stanford has resisted industry-funded centers of research popular at Wharton and other schools partly because they encourage too much specialization. While they attend one of the world's best schools, students quickly find that Stanford lacks the flexibility of many competitors, including Chicago, Kellogg, and Wharton.

That's changing, however, A new core curriculum was launched in 1992. Although the changes are far from dramatic, and come nowhere near the overhaul that has occurred at Wharton, Duke, Indiana, or Michigan, the new curriculum is being well received by students. Stanford says the fine-tuning puts greater emphasis on human resources issues and gives students more flexibility in scheduling their programs. The changes call for reducing the number of core courses to 12 from 13. Stanford is eliminating Macroeconomics and combining Decision Making under Uncertainty and Data Analysis into a single course. It also added a new class in human resources management in 1994 as the twelfth core course. These alternations will trim the course requirements for graduation to 25 from 27. Students may take more electives than the minimum, since the new graduation requirement is considered a floor, not a ceiling.

The slightly lighter workload, Stanford believes, will give first-years the option of taking electives during both the winter and spring terms—an important change, because more and more of the students here are studying foreign languages and are interested in dual degrees. (In 1992 nine students were earning dual degrees in business and education.) Students signed up for 348 quarters of language study in 1992, compared with 108 three years earlier. The redesign also calls for developing a leadership skills program—that sounds a bit like the one Chicago installed back in 1989—composed of noncurricular activities and related elective courses.

Students can waive out of several of the required core courses by taking and passing a proficiency exam before school starts, but they must substitute an elective for any class they avoid. Without a requirement to major or specialize in any given field, they're free to take electives anywhere they want. A few second-year MBA students spend their spring quarter studying at the Center for Technology and Innovation in Japan as part of the university's relatively new academic program in Kyoto. The program involves academic coursework in language, culture, and economic and political systems, and is followed by a summer internship with a Japanese firm (but students must have Japanese language skills before enrolling). Mostly, however, they select from the B-school's own novel array of electives from Creativity in Business and Japanese Marketing to Managing Strategic Alliances and Topics in Philanthropy.

Maybe it's the sun-drenched sandstone buildings, the lush grounds, or the clear, crisp air. Maybe it's just a bit of that Silicon Valley entrepreneurial spirit. But Stanford seems to excel at continually coming up with new ideas and courses. One of the latest: Learning to Lead, a two-quarter course with a summer internship taught by four professors, including Jerry Porras, an associate dean and coauthor of *Built to Last: Successful Habits of Visionary Companies*. The course brings 40 first-year students into the nitty-gritty of leadership, requiring MBAs to read and study business leaders on paper and in action. One evening a week, students meet to engage in leadership exercises and do role-playing. During the summer internship, MBAs go off to "observe leaders at work." A theme of the second quarter coursework is the "leader as change agent"—requiring a major project in which students apply the learning they've gained in the course and internship.

No wonder Stanford is known for innovating some of the most topical course offerings in business—more than half of the 95 or so electives are new every five years, including several of the 21 electives on international topics. Among the more novel additions in recent years is a two-quarter course called Integrated Design for Manufacturing and Marketability, which brings MBAs together with master's engineering students at Stanford. For six months the students spend a good percentage of their time together, getting down and dirty in a machine shop where teams of "suits" and "gearheads" build prototype home can-crushers to sell in a simulated market. Another new elective focuses on the study of restructuring socialist economies.

A good many of these classes percolate from faculty research—in recent years, a rather sensitive subject at Stanford. The school has long sought "balance excellence" in teaching and research. But many grads say that balance is elusive, particularly in the core courses, which can be taught by fairly new Ph.D.s with limited teaching experience. Criticism of the uneven teaching in the core has come up again and again, from BUSINESS WEEK's first surveys in 1988 to its latest in 1992. The pages of the school newspaper, *The Reporter,* have overflowed with complaints about the issue. At times, students have been known to abandon the classrooms of core teachers who were so bad they couldn't clearly communicate their ideas to students.

Dean A. Michael Spence has somehow been able to turn the complaints around. Sure enough, a few graduates still grouse about some of the teachers. But for the first time ever, graduating MBAs in 1994 rated the quality of the teaching in both the core and elective courses at Stanford well above the average of the 40-plus schools in the BUSINESS WEEK sample. Indeed, the absence of serious criticism on the teaching front helped to push Stanford to the number-one ranking among graduates in the 1994 poll. Along with greater support from corporate recruiters, the improvement helped Stanford climb to No. 4 overall in the BUSINESS WEEK ranking—it's highest-ever BW ranking, and much better than the school's disappointing seventh-place finish in 1992.

Indeed, no MBAs in 1994 were more satisfied with their education than those at Stanford. The school topped the customer satisfaction rankings for vastly exceeding graduate expectations, for delivering the best return on investment, for having the most cooperative campus environment, and for attracting students who more than any others truly enhanced the learning process. Dean Spence must get some credit for this turnaround, even though graduates fail to rate the administration or the faculty as being overly responsive to their concerns. Though above-average in this category, Stanford doesn't come near such schools as Indiana, Northwestern, Carnegie Mellon, and UCLA, which have made student satisfaction an important part of the school culture.

An economist and former Rhodes Scholar, the new dean actually taught at Stanford from 1973 to 1975 while his wife earned her own MBA from the school. Before taking on his administrative job at Harvard, he also taught at both the Harvard Business School and at the university's economics department. Spence, who walks and talks like a scholarly academic, has shown he's able to get loose with students as well: He even agreed to get into a dunking tank to help raise funds for Stanford MBAs who shun corporate internships over the summer to work instead for nonprofits and the public sector. No sooner had Spence arrived at Stanford, however, than the university cut the B-school's budget by $1.5 million. The dean was able to offset some of these cutbacks—representing nearly 12 percent of the school's annual budget—with funds from other sources, but he also ended up shaving $400,000 from the school's administration. The funding cut also may have been behind Stanford's decision to increase enrollment of its MBA program to more than 700 from 670 in previous years.

On a more upbeat side, MBAs have good things to say about Stanford's Public Management Program, which in recent years has eclipsed Yale University's well-known efforts in public service. Designed for MBAs interested in the public and nonprofit sectors, the program consistently attracts a significant chunk of students. MBAs seeking a PMP certificate must complete the regular B-school core, plus three public management courses from among 20 electives in the field. About 52 of Stanford's 328 graduates in 1992 got the certificates. The emphasis on public management has another unusual twist: MBAs who land lucrative corporate internships over the summer months often pledge to donate some of their earnings to help subsidize classmates who work for nonprofit groups. There's also a loan-forgiveness program for students who take jobs in the public sector after graduation.

Few students enrolled in the program are headed for permanent jobs with nonprofits, but they want a sense of public policy issues. "This is a business school, after all," says James Thompson, the program's director. "The proof is not what they'll do immediately after getting the MBA. People will go to McKinsey or Hewlett-Packard and after a few years they may go to the nonprofits." In 1992, only 3 percent of the class assumed public service jobs directly out of school.

Stanford launched another certificate program in 1994 for students interested in global business. Developed by four students in the Class of 1994, it awards Global Management Program certificates to those who complete 4 of some 20 electives with an international focus, including two courses beyond those needed for the MBA degree. The program also is a focus for student activities that range from overseas study trips to speeches by leaders of international institutions and governments. About 18 MBAs graduated with the certificate in 1994.

Despite the recent ups and downs of the California economy, Stanford MBAs continue to fare extremely well in the job sweepstakes.

Some 185 companies recruited second-year MBAs at Stanford in 1994, doing about 8200 interviews. Another 900 job opportunities were posted by correspondence. Pretty impressive numbers, for a graduating class of 336 students. That's right: 8200 interviews were conducted here for 336 students! That's why an amazing 98.7 percent of the class had job offers by commencement—the best record of any of the 40-plus schools surveyed by BUSINESS WEEK. And Stanford MBAs were considering 3.47 job offers at graduation—better than any school with the sole exception of Harvard, and well above the 2.36 average for the top schools. The average starting pay-and-bonus packages of $100,800, including perks, were bested only by Harvard grads, who averaged only a couple of thousand dollars more.

Not surprisingly, consulting firms, which typically dangle the big bucks in front of MBAs, are hiring the single biggest chunk of Stanford grads. Nine of Stanford's top 14 employers of the Class of 1994 were from the ranks of the top consultants, who took nearly a third of the graduates (versus only 15 percent for investment banking). The major employers: McKinsey (19); Bain & Co. (18); Boston Consulting Group (15); Booz Allen (12); Goldman Sachs (11); Merrill Lynch (6); CSC Index (6); CS First Boston (5); Montgomery Securities (5); Deloitte & Touche (4); EDS Consulting (4); Gemini Consulting (4); Lehman Brothers (4); and Strategic Decisions Group (4).

In some ways, it's surprising that Stanford doesn't do better than fifth in BUSINESS WEEK's corporate poll. School officials theorize that the small size of the graduating class makes it a more competitive hunting ground for recruiters, who sometimes return to headquarters empty-handed because job offers outnumber Stanford MBAs. They may be particularly bothered because a good chunk of the class accepts jobs with Silicon Valley startups and smaller firms that employ fewer than 1000 workers. Many of these companies are not surveyed by the magazine because they do not hire significant numbers of MBAs and can't compare Stanford's candidates with those from other institutions.

Given Stanford's location, however, technology looms large, and a sizable number of MBAs gain jobs in the computer biz. Many of the visiting speakers also hail from the world of high tech, from NeXT CEO and Apple founder Steve Jobs to Sun Microsystems founder Scott McNearly, who graduated from Stanford. Andrew Grove, chairman of successful chipmaker Intel, now teaches as a lecturer in the fall quarter.

MBAs here engage in a broad range of extracurricular activities, from raising funds for the homeless to competing in every sport from dart throwing to soccer. Compadres is the preferred Mexican restaurant. For a pleasant dinner, especially when a recruiter is picking up the tab, MacArthur Park in downtown Palo Alto is hard to beat. A ritual of MBA life is the Tuesday evening get-together at Old Pro on El Camino Real in Palo Alto. Forsaking many of the yuppie bars of Silicon Valley, Stanford students take over the joint, even calling the place Arjay's after former B-school dean Arjay Miller, who lifted the school to number one in some rankings during his tenure.

You wouldn't ordinarily expect MBAs from the most selective B-school in the country to hang out at The Old Pro. Black-painted plywood covers the windows of the place to protect the glass when the crowd becomes unruly. Neon beer signs light the outside sidewalk, flashing the names Strohs, Michelob, and Miller into the busy street. Silver duct tape seals the gashes in the bar stools. But then, this is Stanford, and that's why its MBAs are so different from the run-of-the-mill products other schools produce.

Contact: Marie M. Mookini, director of admissions, 415-723-2766
Final application deadline: March 15 for fall

Outstanding Faculty

1. James C. Van Horne (****):   This banking and finance guru won Stanford's very first MBA Distinguished Teaching Award in 1982. A decade later, he's as good as ever. Van Horne is a top scholar who enjoys intellectual sparing matches and boasts a rather dry sense of humor in the classroom. He earned his MBA and Ph.D. at Northwestern and taught at Michigan State for one year before arriving at Stanford in 1965. He authored one of *the* textbooks on finance—*Financial Management and Policy*—which is said to be the first to bring modern financial theory and valuation to the teaching of corporate finance. Van Horne's expertise has brought him before Congress on several occasions to testify on proposed changes in banking law.

2. James Collins (****):   When the big earthquake hit on October 17, 1989, Collins was in the midst of teaching a course on small business. The classroom began to move and sway, at first just a little, and then violently. Students groaned a collective "Wohhhh." Collins has had nearly the same impact on his students since he began teaching courses in creativity in business and entrepreneurship at Stanford in 1988. He's young (having earned his Stanford MBA in 1983); he's intellectually sharp (a former McKinsey and Bain consultant); and he's dynamic (having been the runner-up for the distinguished teaching award in his first two years as a prof until finally winning it in 1992).

3. H. Irving Grousbeck (****):   Many grads believe he's the best teacher they've ever had. This Harvard MBA (1960) and cable television entrepreneur teaches Entrepreneurship: Forming New Ventures with great panache. Gushes one admirer: "He personifies the model businessman: He is intelligent, fair, ethical, and practical." He made his fortune as co-founder of Continental Cablevision, the nation's largest privately owned cable company. When the San Francisco Giants went up for sale in 1992, his name was among the first to surface as a possible buyer of the baseball team. Grousbeck, whose remaining 10 percent interest in Continental is said to be worth over $100 million, did the numbers and decided it wasn't a good deal.

4. Edward Paul Lazear (****):   A professor of human resources management and economics, Lazear brings a rigorous approach to a an often soft subject and wins high praise from students for doing so. "Eddie" won the Distinguished Teaching Award in 1994, two years after joining Stanford from the University of Chicago. He also serves on the editorial board of Managerial and Decision Economics.

5. Garth Saloner (***):   Joined the faculty in 1990 after teaching stints at MIT and the Harvard business school, where he worked under strategy guru Michael Porter. An associate dean and the school's director of research, Saloner won the Distinguished Teaching Award in 1993 for winning raves in his strategic management course.

6. Constance Bagley (*): Armed with a Harvard law degree, Bagley worked as a lawyer in New York and San Francisco before deciding that she also felt the urge to teach. A lecturer in business law, "Connie" has been dazzling students at Stanford since 1985. As one admirer put it: "She's absolutely the best. No professor I have ever had knows her subject so well and is completely interested in her students. Interview her, write about her, make her famous before someone else does."

Other Best Bets: *Jack McDonald* (finance), *Robert Burgelman* (entrepreneurship), *Joel Peterson* (real estate), and *David Kreps* (economics)

Prominent Alumni: David S. Tappan, Jr., CEO of Fluor; H. Brewster Atwater, chairman of General Mills; John Young, CEO of Hewlett-Packard; David W. Kemper, CEO of Commerce Bancshares; Daniel C. Ferguson, CEO of Newell; Lloyd P. Johnson, CEO of Norwest; Scott G. McNealy, CEO of Sun Microsystems; James G. Treybig, CEO of Tandem Computers; John B. McCoy, CEO of Banc One; Charles Schwab, CEO of Charles Schwab & Co.; Robert Cohn, founder, Octel

Stanford MBAs Sound Off

Stanford's Graduate School of Business is heaven on earth! As impressive as its academics are, Stanford stresses social interaction just as much—a crucial element to life and business. I have made incredible friendships here. The foundation of Stanford's program is its policy of not discussing grades with recruiters. Not only does it eliminate cutthroat competition and encourage cooperation, but it also encourages you to take courses you might otherwise be too intimidated to take, and to learn rather than just get a good grade.—Finance Associate

I believe in the benefits of Stanford's MBA so strongly that I literally agreed to pay for it twice. My husband will be a graduate of the Stanford MBA Class of '96. Earning my MBA at Stanford was a great experience. I worked hard, gained knowledge, and took advantage of tremendous opportunities.—Consultant

Going to Stanford business school was one of the best experiences of my life. I learned a tremendous amount, both academically and personally. I am sad that I actually have to graduate and leave this wonderful place.—Marketing Career

My MBA experience at Stanford was the best two years of my life. Only here can you have intense case discussions with a group that includes a physicist from Russia, an entrepreneur from Silicon Valley, a Peace Corps volunteer from Asia, and an Army doctor, and then go out for a drink afterwards.—Consultant

Stanford's downplaying of grades is a testament to its conviction that learning should be driven by intellectual curiosity, not fear. That's why Stanford has a very cooperative, noncompetitive environment. Unfortunately, I did find a tendency to slack off in some classes, simply because I knew that I could get away *with it. I can't speak for everyone, but I would have been better served by a high-pressure environment that would have forced me to work harder.—**Marketing Manager***

I was expecting to find a group of "let's do lunch," self-important people here. Instead, my fellow students were extremely talented, diverse, and energetic friends who pushed me to achieve more than I initially thought possible.
*—**Career Path Unknown***

The program was a total disappointment. The relevant parts of an MBA can easily be condensed into a nine-month program. The cases and course content have changed little in 10 years. It's far too outdated. As for computer skills, no more was taught than could be learned by reading an Excel manual for a weekend.
*—**Career Path Unknown***

*After having attended Wharton as an undergraduate, I was delighted with my experience at Stanford. It is hard to imagine spending two years with a more interesting and talented group of classmates. The small size, diversity, and lack of competition ensured that I was able to get to know and learn from them. While there are areas to improve (such as the computer facilities and the retention of talented lecturers), these are the exceptions to the program's many successes.—**Consultant***

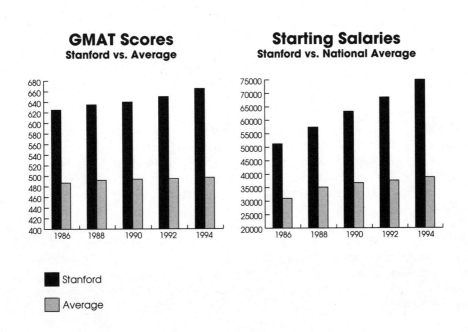

5. Harvard University

Graduate School of Business Administration
Soldiers Field
Boston, Massachusetts 02163

Corporate ranking: 3
Enrollment: 1619
Women: 29%
Non-U.S.: 26%
Minority: 18%
Part-time: None
Average age: 26.4
Applicants accepted: 16%*
Median starting pay: $100,000

Graduate ranking: 17
Annual tuition & fees: $23,984
Room and board: $12,500
Average GMAT score: Not req.
Average GPA: 3.4
GPA range: 2.8 to 4.0
Average years of work exp: 4.0
Accepted applicants enrolled: 85%
Average starting pay: $102,630

Teaching methods: Case study, 100%

Harvard MBA is the entry ticket to the most privileged and invaluable fraternity in business, a pass to an elite network of contacts that span the globe. On its faculty are more super-star professors than work at all the other top B-schools combined. The Harvard business school campus alone contains 27 buildings, including the world's largest business library and a student fitness center with more square footage than most entire B-schools occupy.

So why doesn't Harvard top the BUSINESS WEEK list of the best? Mainly because having a wealth of resources and resting on past success aren't enough anymore, as IBM, Sears Roebuck, and General Motors have discovered. Like GM, say some rival deans, resource-rich Harvard has been arrogant, slow to change, and unresponsive to its primary customers (students). Indeed, for the second consecutive poll, MBAs judged the administration the least responsive to their concerns of any Top 20 program. Harvard graduates, the survey showed, also felt much less confident about their analytical and technical abilities than students at any other Top 20 school. That helps to explain why the school slipped two places in 1994, to fifth overall.

Calling it the GM of business schools, however, would be grossly unfair. Harvard hasn't been on the leading edge of management education for years, but the superb quality of its students and its faculty make the business school one of the best in the world. The diversity and smarts of Harvard MBAs is virtually unmatched. The often-quoted professors are among the most astute and entertaining observers of business anywhere. Too bad that Harvard's administration is so caught up in the institution's past glories.

To more aggressively address its problems, Harvard launched a full-scale review of its MBA program in late 1992. The study—which included faculty team visits to learn what other leading B-schools were doing—led to a series of proposals to remake the MBA program. Among other things, Harvard would reduce class sections to 72 students from 90, and collapse its 11 required first-year courses into four integrated topics to be taught by faculty teams. MBA students would complete up to 25 percent of coursework in group projects outside class.

So far, the school has decided to run a pilot 16-month MBA program beginning in January of 1996. Students would forgo a summer internship to get an MBA quicker. Harvard will use the pilot to test changes to the MBA program.

Tradition, however, isn't easily discarded at Harvard Business School. After all, its rowing crews still paddle the Charles River with oars adorned with dollar signs. So nearly a year after these proposals were made public in November of 1993, little action had been taken on them—though professors are asking students to do more group projects, and in 1994 the school began offering teamwork training to students and began to assign them in eight-person teams for the first year. Still, as one 1994 graduate puts it: "At HBS, change doesn't come very easily, and when it does, it comes in incremental steps." If the faculty approves some or all of the proposals, they will help to address a number of concerns.

Graduates complain that such critical subjects as quality and technology are barely touched upon in the basic MBA curriculum. Many believe that globalization still doesn't get nearly enough attention. Compared to other top schools, Harvard also significantly trails in the number of group exercises and projects assigned students to develop teamwork and leadership skills. "It is as though at HBS revolutionary developments in these areas never occurred, despite the fact that the school has knowledgeable faculty in all these areas," says a 1992 graduate. "Most of the emphasis of the program is still placed on training 27-year-olds how to make CEO-level decisions for the day when that wonderful appointment is realized." The school's management communications segment is also heavily criticized by graduates. It has been taught, some claim, by professors who fail to take the course seriously.

The introspection Harvard is now indulging in may correct many of these deficiencies. It may also dramatically alter the school's highly competitive culture. Harvard is the most Darwinian business school in the world. A nearly traditional symbol of the survival-of-the-fittest culture was the first-morning dash by first-years for the choice seats in the classroom. Students would line up outside classroom buildings before dawn in hopes of capturing the center seats in the so-called skydeck (the top row) where they were more likely to gain "air time" over their colleagues. Because the seat you gain on your first day in class is the one you'll remain in for the rest of the semester, many students would drag themselves out of bed at 4 a.m. to get in line. The worst seats? Those at the wings of the worm deck (the front row). After the pre-dawn competitive rush attracted some bad publicity, Harvard finally ended the practice in 1992 by assigning seats via computer.

Although most students arrive here thinking they'll run into truly savage competition, many are surprised that it's not as cutthroat as they first imagined. Even so, a forced grading curve in which 10 percent of the students receive a "category" grade of 3, the equivalent of a low-pass, sometimes fosters rivalries among students. Non-U.S. students say they especially are at a disadvantage in some first-semester courses. A *Harbus* survey in 1993 showed that international students got 96 percent of the low-pass grades in Marketing. And in 1994, it was shockingly revealed that at least 10 first-years got anonymous hate mail from fellow students. Said one: "Go back to your little miserable country and leave us alone." There's always the danger of, in Harvard MBA parlance, "hitting the screen," or flunking out. If 45 percent of your first-year grades are low-pass, you're effectively put on probation. Roughly 3 percent of first-year students and only 1 percent of second-year students meet this fate.

With classroom participation accounting for 50 percent or more of your grade, there can be a considerable amount of game-playing among the 90 students in a single class. "Chip shots"—short, punchy comments that require little or no preparation but win points at the expense of a classmate—are not uncommon. Yet, there's a playful attitude at work as well. At the end of every week, for example, one section of students began awarding a "Pink Pig" to the student whose comment made the biggest impression. The group also handed out a "Shark Award" to the MBA who made the worst chip shot of the week. Christian C. Johnson, of the Class of 1993, recalls that a student arrived late for class one day on crutches due to a skiing accident. "Someone yelled out from the back row, 'Martin you can give me my crutches back after class.' He won the Shark Award that week."

Still, some students, frantic to distinguish themselves from the crowd, have been known to make remarks geared to fit neatly with a professor's known theory or perspective to gain higher grades. The grading system, while it prevents grade inflation, also can become a demotivating factor because only 10 percent of the students earn the top grade of 1. That means 8 out of 10 students receive a 2 by design. As one graduate put it: "It's easy to get a 2, impossible to get a 1, so why put in extra effort?" Some also complain that their fellow students use Harvard's clubs as little more than résumé-building tools.

Against this competitive backdrop, you'll find the tension mounts with the immediate workload. There's a curious imbalance to the MBA program at Harvard. The first year is hellishly intense—not because it's heavily quantitative or academically rigorous, but because the school loads you up with hundreds of pages of case study reading each week. Virtually all the instruction is via case study, which requires students to analyze and debate brief, problem-oriented company reports or cases in class.

The typical first-year week consists of thirteen 80-minute classes, each requiring the preparation of a case study that might take two to three hours per case. Add in time with your study group and you're apt to work until 1 a.m. or 2 a.m. most weekdays, only to get up the next morning for an 8:30 class. Several grads figure that at least 75 percent of the learning is crammed into those first two semesters. Then, the workload eases up considerably. About 20 percent of the work gets piled into the first semester of your second year, while the remaining 5 percent takes up the last semester. As one grad puts it, "The second year is a good time to do intense job hunting, in-depth work in a chosen field, to relax and enjoy intramurals, or plan an extended summer vacation."

In the first year, Harvard divides the class of 800 into nine sections of about 90 students each. Each section goes through the required first-year courses as a group. There are no waivers and no exceptions. If you're a CPA, you still have to take accounting. In the second year, another required course is Management Policy and Practice, which focuses on vicariously acquiring top management perspective by assuming the role of a decision maker in case studies. You also must take 10 electives out of more than 75 offered at the B-school or a limited number from the university's other graduate schools and departments. There's plenty of freedom to do what you want, because no formal concentration or major is required at Harvard.

Given the competitive atmosphere here, it surprises many newcomers to find that their first class on the very first day of school is Ethics—the result of a $20 million pledge by the late Securities & Exchange Commission Chairman John Shad in 1987. Before the initiative on ethics was launched, it was possible to get a Harvard MBA without any explicit instruction in ethics. Today, the focus begins even before students show up for class. All applicants must write essays on an ethical dilemma, allowing admissions to make the topic a criteria for entrance. Your first class is in a nine-session required "module" dubbed Decision Making and Ethical Values. The nongraded course explores such topics as General Motors' selection of a site for an assembly plant and improper accounting practices at H.J. Heinz Co. unearthed in 1979. "We're not converting sinners, but we're taking young people who have a sense of integrity and trying to get them to connect ethics with business decisions," says Thomas R. Piper, a senior associate dean.

The ethics module is taught by some of Harvard's best professors. Yet, the quality of teaching at Harvard ranges, as one grad described it, from "God-like to God-awful." Overall, however, graduates rate the teaching in both the core and elective courses as well above average. While friction typically exists between research and teaching at most B-schools, at Harvard the faculty's commitment to research is less an issue. A more tangible tension exists between teaching and consulting. There are so many faculty stars here that they are often in high demand as consultants. The upshot: Some students believe the faculty isn't nearly as accessible as they would like.

The same had been true of Dean John H. McArthur, who some students call "the Howard Hughes of B-school deans" because of his low profile. Recently, he has made more of an effort to meet and speak with students. McArthur now has been serving up a breakfast buffet for each incoming section at the dean's house, where he personally greets each student before sitting down at one table to eat.

Many students, however, would not describe McArthur's Harvard as user-friendly. Grads maintain that the administration is nonresponsive and bureaucratic. "They nickel-and-dime you for everything," moans one graduate. Besides the steep tuition, Harvard first-years are expected to arrive at Harvard with a laptop computer, or pay HBS $3200 for one, to pay $2350 for "case materials," and over $1000 for the school's health services and insurance. If you want to avail yourself of the $12 million fitness center, you even have to pay separate fees for towels and lockers. The higher costs don't always guarantee better service, either. Registration for courses can be a disorganized fiasco. And the administration can be heavy-handed: the school summarily banned students from riding bikes on campus in 1992.

Still, this is Harvard. In the red-brick, neo-Georgian buildings on the Charles River in Boston, professors teach in modern, tiered classrooms with state-of-the-art audiovisual equipment. Separated from the rest of the university, the Harvard B-school is a total community unto itself. On the 61-acre campus, you'll find four restaurants, a branch of the Harvard Coop, a post office, and a chapel. Almost everyone eats lunch at Kresge, the main dining hall, or at the on-campus Au Bon Pain—especially on Mondays, Wednesdays, and Fridays, when there's still a 1 p.m. class after lunch. The Pub at Shad is always full on Wednesday nights and Friday afternoons. Off campus, MBAs favor John Harvard's Brew House (a micro-brewery that sells burgers and pizzas); Shay's (wine bar); Border Cafe (Mexican); Miracle of Science (a NYC-like bar).

More than half the first-year students live in the B-school resident halls, which are nicely appointed, like little Sheraton rooms, but so small you can literally lean over your desk chair and fall into bed. Still, you can wake up at 8:20 and make an 8:30 class. Not many consider this an advantage worth the cost, because only 20 percent of second-year students live in the dorms. They prefer to live off-campus in rented homes or apartments, or in the pricey student apartments at Soldiers Field Park, adjacent to the school.

Wherever you stay, you'll never want for things to do at Harvard. First-year sections have regular keg parties or ice cream "study breaks" on Wednesday nights and during exams. There are weekend barbecues at a local beach, ski trips, Red Sox games, and organized trips during vacation, from Florida to China. Besides the more than 50 student clubs on campus, there's a lot of emphasis on sports, from rowing on the Charles to intramural rugby. HBS also is very big on black tie. If you belong to the right clubs, you can end up going to two black-tie dinners or parties a month.

Because over 20 percent of Harvard B-school students are married, there's a very active support group for spouses called Partners. It organizes such things as pot-luck dinners and night classes with spouses' professors. More importantly, the group provides an informal network for couples, who tend to spend more time with each other and less time with sectionmates. After graduation many remain close and their activities are regularly chronicled in the *Harvard Business School Bulletin,* the alumni magazine. Every other month, it's filled with informal reports from the field on how Harvard MBAs are faring in the world of finance and industry.

Rarely will you read of failure. After all, of the top three officers in the 500 largest industrial corporations, 20 percent got their MBAs stamped at Harvard. Twenty-five years out of school, one-third of them boast the title of CEO, managing director, partner, or owner. So Harvard's alumni base is the best in the world.

Harvard's unsurpassed connections make its placement office a formidable operation. In 1994, more than 300 companies sent recruiters to the school to conduct about 9000 on-campus interviews. *The Harbus News,* the best campus newspaper of any B-school, is filled with advertisements and schedules of company presentations and interviews. "I was astounded that at the same time I read of layoffs in the paper every day, my mailbox was filled with announcements of company presentations," recalls Johnson of the Class of 1993. There's also a 30,000-member alumni advisor system, as well as elaborate résumé-creation assistance and services.

No school—not even No. 1-ranked Wharton—beats Harvard when it comes to offering the most recession-proof MBA in the world. Only 2 percent of Harvard's Class of 1994 failed to have a job offer by graduation, a nearly unbeatable record. Moreover, no rival surpassed Harvard when it came to getting its MBAs the most offers in 1994: 3.6 per graduate, way above the 2.36 average for the top 40-plus schools polled by BUSINESS WEEK.

Harvard MBAs pulled down the highest starting-pay packages in 1994—an average of $102,630 in salary, signing and year-end bonuses, and perks. A remarkable 52 percent of graduates earned six-figure deals right out of business school. McKinsey & Co. alone hired nearly 102 of Harvard's graduates, paying top dollars to them all. It's telling, however, that these graduates had quit jobs that had paid them a hefty $53,910 a year. Nice money, if you can get it.

Contact: Jill Fadule, director of admissions, Dillon House, 617-495-6172
Final application deadline: March 1

Outstanding Faculty

1. Andre F. Perold (***):   This dynamic professor racks up some of the best student evaluations anywhere, for his second-year courses in capital markets and investment management. Perold has been teaching at Harvard since 1979, just after earning his Ph.D. in operations research and an M.S. in statistics from Stanford University. He boasts a bachelor's in math and stats, from the University of Witwatersrand in South Africa.

2. William A. Sahlman (***):   Harvard has long had a reputation as the business school for big business. So it may come as a surprise that its No. 1 professor in the classroom is someone who teaches entrepreneurship. Sahlman knows this stuff from the inside out, partly because he's on the boards of several entrepreneurial ventures, including The Butcher Co., Bee Gee Holding Co., and Cottage Software. A Harvard MBA with an undergraduate degree in economics from Princeton, Sahlman joined the B-school as a teacher in 1980. He also gained his Ph.D. in business economics from Harvard. About half the second-year class, some 400 students, typically select his Entrepreneurial Finance elective as their first course choice.

3. Henry B. Reiling (**):   When not in the classroom, super-teacher Reiling is avidly following the sport of basketball, playing a vigorous game of tennis, or running in a marathon. He brings a sport-like intensity to his first-year class in Decision Making and Ethical Values, as well as a second-year elective in Tax Factors in Business Decisions. A former history major from Northwestern, Reiling immersed himself in business by gaining a Harvard MBA and a doctorate in business from Columbia. He joined the Harvard faculty in 1976 after teaching at both Columbia and Stanford.

4. Richard S. Tedlaw (**):   The B-school world's most extraordinary teacher of business history, Tedlaw brings to his classes a compelling philosophy. Like a psychiatrist, his wife Joyce's profession, he says his goal is to make the classroom a safe haven so that students will feel completely free to utter any comment that comes to mind. MBAs agree that this brilliant professor succeeds as few do. Author of a history of consumer product marketing in the U.S., Tedlaw teaches the Business History course, one of Harvard's most popular electives, and has been a consultant to such companies as AT&T, IBM, Intel, and the Royal Bank of Canada.

5. Gary W. Loveman (**):   Harvard's service guru, Loveman has authored case studies on professional service firms, airlines, hotel chains, and not-for-profits. Loveman, who has a bachelor's in economics from Wesleyan and a Ph.D. in economics from MIT, has been studying enterprise reform and small business development in Poland in recent years. But MBAs love him for his Service Management course.

6. Michael C. Jensen (*):   Tall and imposing, he's a firebrand of laissez-faire economics and an unusual Harvard professor. Unlike most, he mainly teaches by lecture, not case study, and his unwavering belief in free-market economics makes him far more conservative than many of his colleagues. "I raise my children by these principles," he says. After high school in Minneapolis he worked as a printer's apprentice, following in his dad's footsteps. An economics course at a nearby college led to his interest in the subject and a Ph.D. at Chicago. He came to Harvard in 1988 from Rochester, where he had first gained attention. Through the 1980s, Jensen riled executives with his defense of takeovers and corporate raiders. His theories—labeled "science fiction" by one CEO—then helped to stop congressional efforts to ban hostile mergers. He's still preaching the same gospel, to good reviews from students.

Other Best Bets: *Timothy Luerhman* (corporate finance), *Elon Kohlberg* (economics), *Jeff Timmons* (entrepreneurial finance), and *Steven C. Wheelwright* (operations)

Prominent Alumni: George J. Sella Jr., CEO of American Cyanamid; Nolan Archibald, CEO of Black & Decker; Daniel B. Burke, CEO of Capital Cities/ABC; James R. Houghton, CEO of Corning; Charles R. Lee, CEO of GTE; Henry B. Schacht, CEO of Cummins Engine; John A. Rollwagen, CEO of Cray Research; Alfred H. Zeien, CEO of Gillette; Richard B. Fisher, Chairman of Morgan Stanley Group; William J. Agee, CEO of Morrison Knudsen; Louis V. Gerstner Jr., CEO of IBM; Melvin J. Gorden, CEO of Tootsie Roll Industries; Drew L. Lewis Jr., CEO of Union Pacific

Harvard MBAs Sound Off

*HBS was both much better and much worse than I expected. The people are great, the facilities are incredible, and the alumni network is excellent. However, the first-year workload is unnecessarily grueling, the course selection process is antiquated (with a high likelihood of not getting your preferred courses), and the school charges you (usually exorbitant amounts) for everything ranging from $2200 for HBS cases to $900 a month for a one-bedroom apartment. We're even charged for inclusion in the résumé book, which is sold to recruiters at a premium.—**Consultant***

*The combination of the case method and the forced curve, while painful at times and capable of creating poor group dynamics, is the best way to motivate students to learn and become leaders. I witnessed very few abuses of this system and do not feel that it impeded real team building.—**Investment Banking Career Path***

*Harvard is only as good as the individual student makes it. I found 20 percent of the students are just there for the name, 60 percent struggle for one-and-a-half years to try to do their best, and 20 percent are truly amazing in their abilities. If you are in (or want to be in) the top 20 percent, then be prepared for long, three-case nights for two years. In the end, you will know it was worth the effort, not because you got a good job (which you do), not because you become a Baker Scholar, but because a lot of your fellow classmates will tell you just how much they wish they had the concentration and drive you showed throughout the two years.—**Consultant***

*HBS completely caters to investment bankers and management consultants, both inside and outside the classroom. You must come to HBS already having learned quantitative-type subjects like Finance and Accounting, because they do not effectively teach these courses. The case method is a flawed teaching methodology for quantitative subjects, and I am graduating unable to read a balance sheet. It is an appalling embarrassment that HBS is graduating people like me. Furthermore, HBS provides no support for students conducting independent job searches—it's investment banking, management consulting, Fortune 500 companies, or nothing. This school is like an archaic dinosaur that needs to take its own advice in terms of what it's teaching in the classroom.—**Career Path Unknown***

*HBS is very good at teaching for the "big picture." I believe I received an excellent education and broad perspective about general management and leadership. However, HBS loses sight of the trees for the forest. It is not a place to go to learn skills that will be useful in that first job. Therefore, it makes it much harder to change industries. Since all first-year courses are required, HBS tends to bore some people and leave others in a state of confusion.—**Manager***

*The outstanding faculty at HBS more than outweighs the aloof and inflexible administration.—**Finance Career Path***

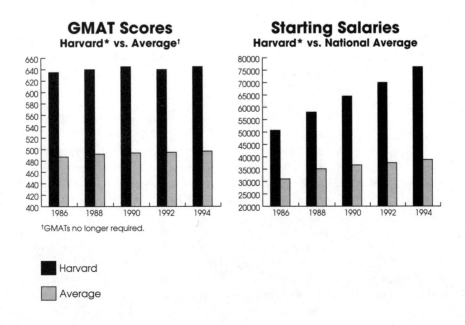

GMAT Scores
Harvard* vs. Average†

†GMATs no longer required.

Starting Salaries
Harvard* vs. National Average

■ Harvard

▨ Average

101

6. University of Michigan

School of Business Administration
Ann Arbor, Michigan 48109

Corporate ranking: 6
Enrollment: 1862
Women: 27%
Non-U.S.: 15%
Minority: 22%
Part-time: 1009
Average age: 27
Applicants accepted: 35%
Median starting pay: $66,000

Graduate ranking: 7
Annual tuition: nonresident—$20,960
  resident—$14,310
Average GMAT score: 630
GMAT range: 440 to 770
Average GPA: 3.2
GPA range: 2.1 to 4.0
Accepted applicants enrolled: 47%
Average starting pay: $67,820

Teaching methods: Lecture, 40%   Case study, 40%   Field projects, 20%

When Michigan's incoming class of MBAs arrives after Labor Day, it skips the tour of the library. Instead, the students engage in team-building exercises and watch a film of Reverend Martin Luther King Jr.'s "I have a dream" speech. Then they board buses for Detroit to clean up abandoned lots and paint dilapidated houses.

Yes, the times they are a-changing. The eighties stereotype of the hard-driving, money-grubbing MBA is going the way of conspicuous consumption. Talk of global citizenship, community involvement, and corporate responsibility fills the halls of many B-schools these days. But at Michigan, the community-service requirement is a small yet critical part of a curriculum overhaul designed three years ago, to put the school on the leading edge of management education.

Why? For years, Michigan has had something of an image problem that has made it difficult to differentiate the school in the marketplace. Northwestern originally built its reputation by being the best school in marketing. Harvard did the same in general management, just as Wharton cultivated an image as the top school in finance. B. Joseph White, who took over as dean in mid-1991, has established Michigan as the leader in curriculum innovation. Corporate recruiters gave Michigan the highest marks for showing the most improvements. Michigan was singled out for having the most innovative curriculum with the exception of Wharton.

A central feature of Michigan's program is a six-week apprenticeship in which student teams work hand-in-hand with corporate managers to solve business problems. Executives from such companies as Boston Consulting Group, Federal Express, Motorola, and Xerox helped to design the unique program. White thinks of the apprenticeship, called the Multidisciplinary Action Project (MAP), as the business equivalent of a medical residency—a period of real-world training under close supervision.

"It goes right to the heart of the weaknesses of MBA programs," believes White, a former Cummins Engine executive. "Typically, schools don't do a good job on cross-functional stuff which is so vital in business. We also have neglected the area of operational effectiveness: How do you achieve increases in productivity, time cycles, etc. And third, we haven't helped students transfer knowledge into action. MAP addresses all three areas."

MAP is a key part of the first-year core curriculum—even though some students groused that they didn't come to school to go back to work. At North American Philips Corp., a student team mapped out and examined the company's relationships with its suppliers. The team's recommendations lowered costs, sped up orders, and improved relations with vendors. Says Michael J. Kearney, a Philips senior vice president, "The advantage to us is that these are bright young people, and they bring with them good insights and new ideas." Unlike the usual summer internships MBAs use to help pay their tuition bills, these apprenticeships are geared to specific projects and supervised by faculty and a committed team of corporate managers. In 1993, the dean had to line up 60 companies to sponsor projects for this facet of the program. "We wouldn't dream of medical school without making rounds, internships, and residencies," says White. "By the end of the decade, I believe there won't be a business school that doesn't add this."

Besides adding medical school–style residencies, White also tore into the basic structure of Michigan's program. He broke the 14-week term in half, forcing professors to pare their course material down to essentials. The new structure also allows the school to react more quickly to business conditions, giving the administration and faculty more room in which to innovate new courses. The shorter format, for example, allowed the school to launch 30 new seven-week electives in topics they wouldn't have wanted to devote 14 weeks to, such as consumer satisfaction and environmental policy. He also added an optional 30 hours of Executive Education–style leadership modules in such topics as creativity, managing influence, negotiations, and team building.

Whether White can sustain the notion that Michigan is the B-school world's innovator is another matter. Many schools are moving to adopt new ideas and concepts. Still, he's encouraging lots of creative changes in what already is one of the best graduate educational experiences in the country. The school is housed in a handsome seven-building complex that features modern classrooms and lecture halls as well as a state-of-the-art computing center and business library.

There's one other surprise: Michigan is attempting to be at the leading edge for training managers to deal with Workforce 2000, the buzzword these days for managing cultural and racial diversity in the workforce. The reason: Nearly one of every four students is a minority. No other Top 20 B-school even approaches that level of commitment. At Carnegie Mellon, minorities account for a mere 5 percent of the students. More typically, the number hovers in the 6 to 9 percent range at such schools as MIT, Columbia, and UCLA. In a recent survey, the *Journal of Blacks in Higher Education* said Michigan appeared to be the best business school for blacks. According to the *Journal,* the B-school boasts a double-digit percentage of African-Americans and turns out more black MBAs than any other American business school.

What's more, the B-school is by no means separate from the university's vibrant academic community. Some people decide to get their MBA from Michigan simply because they want to be in Ann Arbor, which rivals Cambridge as one of the nation's leading college towns. As long as you don't mind cold weather, it's hard to beat Ann Arbor's combination of big-city culture and small-town charm. Its collegial atmosphere has made it a popular place for entrepreneurs and retirees to settle—so much so that the monthly rents can be steep because construction of new housing hasn't kept pace with demand. Michigan does provide limited housing for MBAs, but space fills up quickly. Some students spend nearly as much as New Yorkers for apartment space, up to $800 a month for rent. Parking is a major hassle, too.

Ann Arbor's quaint, village-like atmosphere is far removed from Detroit's gritty, urban character, but in 1994, 15 percent of the graduating class drove off into a career with the auto industry. The organization charts at Ford, General Motors, and Chrysler are heavily salted with Michigan grads. Former Chairman Roger Smith was one of nearly 9000 MBAs at GM. Allan D. Gilmour, vice chairman of Ford, is also a Michigan alum. The school's faculty even boasts an auto historian, David L. Lewis, who is working on a commissioned biography of Ford. In 1988, students launched an Automotive Industry Club to mix engineering and business students with a penchant for Motor City. Articles on the car business are sprinkled through the pages of *The Monroe Street Journal,* the student-run weekly.

A Michigan MBA may be the ticket for future auto industry executives, but the B-school downplays its ties to Detroit for fear of being branded a regional program. That, it is not. If you come to Michigan, you'll find that the faculty uses a wide variety of teaching methods from case study to lecture and group projects. No wonder a popular joke among MBAs asks, "How do they teach business at Harvard? Drop you into the ocean and watch you [pure case]. How do they do it at Chicago? Take you to a foggy field and tell you to flap your wings like a bird [pure theory]. How do they teach business at the U of M? A combination of the two."

Neither does Michigan, an advocate of a generalist approach to management, force its students to major in any given discipline. If they want, students can specialize in areas such as accounting, finance, marketing, and organizational behavior, but it's hardly a requirement. The upshot: "No single group of faculty or methodology owns the school," says White. A dozen of the B-school's professors have joint appointments with the university's departments of psychology, sociology, economics, or law. Michigan also offers 17 joint master's programs in areas as varied as music and engineering. The school recently began offering The Michigan Joint Manufacturing Initiative, which was developed by both the business and engineering schools. The Corporate Environmental Management Program is another joint-degree newcomer. MBAs are free to take up to 10 hours of credit in other schools of the university such as the Program in Hospital Administration, the Institute of Public Policy Studies, or the School of Social Work. White also abandoned Michigan's letter grading system, replacing it with words: Excellent, Good, Pass, Low Pass, and Fail. The reason: to encourage more teamwork and discourage competition among individuals.

You'll start your first year off, however, with an introductory lab that assesses students' strengths and weaknesses. Then, you'll be shipped off to nitty-gritty Detroit or places like the high-unemployment city of Benton Harbor for the two days of orientation devoted to "Global Citizenship." Whether these efforts are nothing more than field trips into the inner city or the incubator for a generation of socially conscious executives, it's hard to say. To some advocates at Michigan, it doesn't make a difference. They argue that it's crucial to move students off sheltered campuses and expose them to real social problems. "This is not do-goodism," says Noel Tichy, a Michigan professor who championed the emphasis on citizenship. "It's enlightened self-interest." He argues that companies are now demanding executives who are sensitive to society's needs and have experience in meeting them.

Michigan has gotten plenty of corporate support for its emphasis on community service. As part of their orientation, MBAs hear speeches from top corporate execs such as Merck Chairman Roy Vagelos and Whirlpool Chairman David R. Whitwam, who challenge them to retain a commitment to society after they graduate. Executives from AT&T, Exxon, Ford, General Electric, General Motors, and Upjohn also joined the students on their trips into the community. After the day spent with paintbrushes and brooms, teams of students launch year-long consulting projects for nonprofit groups, including Joy of Jesus, an interdominational religious group that is revitalizing the Ravendale section of Detroit, and People in Faith United, a coalition of inner-city churches working to revive Detroit's east side. Students create business plans, install accounting systems, and target potential donors for fund-raising.

The first term of the core curriculum focuses on the basics: business economics, financial accounting, marketing, statistics, and corporate strategy. The second term takes the first three of these subjects and requires students to apply the basics to business problems, while adding courses in international business and finance. Once the new year begins, MAP falls into place, accounting for 25 percent of the core curriculum. Faculty from four areas—accounting, operations, human resources, and information systems—team-teach four courses in their fields for seven weeks. Then, there's one week's worth of preparation before the internships begin with companies. The week is treated as if it were an executive education seminar. Students get a 3-inch-thick notebook of readings, exercises, and cases on operational improvement and process analysis. Some executives come into the classroom to teach it. As White puts it, "The internship is sleeves rolled up. It is sweaty. The students work in teams to produce real results. So it brings to bear all the stuff we're trying to help them learn in the first year: teamwork, analytical ability, leadership skills." Throughout all this activity, you're still working on your community action project and attending executive skills workshops.

In the second year, you'll get to choose from more than 130 elective classes—both 7- and 14-week courses. A 7-week course in either ethics or law is the only required elective. A final requirement of the core is Corporate Strategy II. Besides the more typical array of B-school offerings, there are also field project courses and business language classes in French, Spanish, and Japanese. There's also the opportunity to go abroad. A student-initiated "MBA Corps" program allows students to hook up with Eastern European organizations over the summer after participating in a 3-week cram course on a country's culture, language, and economics. The Africa Corps sends teams of MBAs to South Africa, Uganda, and Ghana. There also are exchange programs with eight European business schools, from the University of St. Gallen in Switzerland to Britain's London Business School. Second-year MBAs also get to hook up with Professor Noel Tichy's Global Leadership Program, a 5-week executive education stint that includes trips to the former Soviet Union, India, China, or Brazil.

When you're in Ann Arbor, you can avail yourself of an active social life. Semesters often kick off with a party at Charlie's, a favorite bar, where B-school students will try to consume as much beer and pizza as possible. Michigan does not hold classes on Fridays, which students consider to be an advantage over Northwestern's Kellogg School, which gives students Wednesdays off. At the U of M, the weekend starts Thursday night with beers at Rick's, where a pitcher can be had for only two bucks. Also popular are O'Sullivans and Scorekeepers. Pizzeria Uno on South Michigan is famous for its deep-dish pizza, and the Brown Jug is the place to go in the wee hours of the morning.

The area also goes a bit wild over the Michigan Wolverines, making sports something of a constant obsession. The B-school association purchases blocks of tickets so that students can sit together at football and basketball games, and it sponsors pregame tailgate parties. Intramural sports, including touch football, team racquetball, soccer, and inner-tube water polo, are also popular.

Unlike other Top 20 schools such as Wharton, Columbia, and NYU, you won't find a well-worn path between Ann Arbor and Wall Street. Many of the school's grads with an interest in finance are more keen to work in the field at Kraft, General Foods, or Ford than at Morgan Stanley or Goldman Sachs. The percentage of Michigan MBAs who found jobs in investment banking in 1994 was only 7 percent. (At the peak in 1987 the field only lured 11 percent of the graduates.) To increase its visibility there, however, Dean White traveled to New York with students.

Some 276 companies recruited on campus in 1994, conducting about 9000 interviews with students. Another 892 job opportunities were posted via correspondence. About 7 percent of the Class of 1994 lacked job offers at graduation. Those who had offers in hand averaged about 2.7 each, still higher than the 2.36 average for the 40-plus schools surveyed.

Ford Motor led the list of Michigan's biggest recruiters in 1994, with 19 hires alone. Ford was followed by Coopers & Lybrand (14); General Motors (12); Allied Signal (10); Deloitte & Touche (9); Merrill Lynch (8); Citibank (6); Ernst & Young (6); Booz Allen & Hamilton, First Empire State, Kraft General Foods, and Procter & Gamble (5 each).

Contact: Jane Lieberthal, associate director of admissions, 313-763-5796
Final application deadline: March 1 for fall

Outstanding Faculty

1. C.K. Prahalad (****): Witty, provocative, and animated, this famous guru on global competitiveness is one of the best B-school professors anywhere. Prahalad paces the floor of a classroom as if it were a stage, climbing steps, calling students by name, and challenging them with questions. A first-rate scholar, he thinks of himself as a "sheepdog" teacher: "You never bite, you always lead from behind, but you always know where the flock should be." Born in India, where his father was a judge, he has an uncle and one brother who are teachers as well. As a Ph.D. student at Harvard in the mid-1970s, he began to combine strategy, international business, and technology management—an idea that led him to become one of the foremost authorities on global competitiveness. Prahalad consults with Philips, Colgate-Palmolive, and other major corporations. Teaching philosophy: "If you strongly believe that your goal is not to teach what you know but to enable students to discover for themselves how good they can be, the rest is simple."

2. Aneel Karnani (**): He thinks corporate strategy is "fun" and tries to pass that sentiment on to MBAs. Karnani's classes tend to be high-energy affairs, with a rapid pace of discussion that keeps students engaged. This confrontational prof plays the role of devil's advocate, to force students to defend a point of view and to show them that there is no one easy answer. His teaching style provokes constant debates in class. Arnani earned his Ph.D. at Harvard in 1981, before he arrived at Michigan.

3. Charles Klemstine (**): Relating material to real-world situations is an important component of his accounting classes. Klempstine draws on students' work experience to demonstrate accounting's relevance and usefulness. His classes often start by applying accounting principles to stories in the press. Klemstine has made accounting a popular elective at Michigan; over 25 percent of the MBA class typically takes his classes in Advanced Management Accounting and Cost Management Systems. He won Michigan's 1993 Student Award for Teaching Excellence, and has previously taught at Notre Dame's business School and the University of Virginia's School of Commerce.

4. Rajeev Batra (**): This marketing professor teaches courses on advertising management, marketing research, and brand equity. Batra arrived at Michigan in 1989 after teaching at Columbia Business School. He picked up his marketing Ph.D. from Stanford in 1984. Batra brings real world experience with him to the classroom—prior to beginning his academic career, Batra was a brand manager in India with Chesebrough-Pond's. He has also served as "visiting faculty" with Young and Rubicam and Citbank Consumer Services.

5. Charles Lee (**): His course on financial statement analysis is so demanding that even Lee has gone a night or two without sleep to keep up the pace of evaluating one company a week. His research is closely aligned with the course's subject matter, so he is on top of what is happening in the field. Lee also gets high marks for being responsive to students. At the end of each class, he collects feedback forms that ask the students to note the most important and the muddiest point of the day. Lee arrived at Michigan in 1991, after getting an M.S. and a Ph.D. at Cornell.

6. Victor Bernard (*): He considers a class successful when students control the agenda. One of the reasons students like him so much is that he is truly interested in what they have to say. Bernard is known for his open-door policy, and he even keeps in touch with students after they have left Michigan. His financial statement analysis course is filled with cases, and while Bernard places a premium on making the class as practical as possible, he is still faithful to theory.

Other Best Bets: *Michael Bradley* (finance), *Wayne DeSarbo* (marketing), *M. P. Narayanan* (finance), and *David Wright* (accounting)

Prominent Alumni: Roger Smith, former chairman of General Motors Corp.; Roger Fridholm, president of The Stroh Brewery Co.; Philip L. Smith, former president of General Foods Corp.; Thomas F. Keller, dean of the Fuqua School of Business, Duke University; L. William Seidman, chairman of the Federal Deposit Insurance Corp.; Martha R. Seger, member of the Board of Governors of the Federal Reserve System; L.D. Thomas, president of Amoco Oil Co.

Michigan MBAs Sound Off

*I felt the school put an extraordinary amount of pressure from the start on students to get the "right" internship and job. From the first day of class the school is emphasizing the job search more than the education. I cannot complain (since I did get an advantage on my job search because of the school) but I felt many times that the goal was to get the "right" job rather than to graduate.—**Senior Financial Analyst***

*Michigan's reputation is far above its actual quality. The fact still remains that we have average students at best, and an average set of professors teaching the intro courses. Additionally, the culture downplays hard work and motivation, two essential needs for students in a top program. Finally, the program is heavily weighted toward the "softer" issues such as Organizational Behavior and Corporate Strategy, which come at the expense of analytical/qualitative emphases.—**Associate***

*I am graduating with an MBA/MA in Southeast Asian Studies. While I could have pursued this degree on an ad hoc basis at other schools, Michigan stands head and shoulders above the rest in allowing and encouraging interdisciplinary projects. At how many other schools can MBAs study Bahasa Indonesia, do internships in Poland and Indonesia, and interact with top executives doing business in these countries (in the classroom)—all in one year? Because of my involvement in the Southeast Asia business program and the William Davidson Institute, I accomplished all of this and more!—**Career Path Undecided***

*One problem is the teacher allocation between the executive education and regular MBA programs. In order to attain the number-one position in executive education, the B-School compromises the quality of the MBA program.—**Senior Financial Analyst***

*Dean Joe White is my idol. He is a tremendous leader. He is constantly reevaluating the MBA program and making improvements to make the program better. He is very approachable and is always interacting with students.—**Senior Consultant***

*Michigan's greatest weakness is its faculty. While Michigan has some of the top faculty in the fields of Corporate Strategy, Finance, and Marketing, it also has some of the worst teachers I have ever had—particularly in the fields that are not known as Michigan's strengths (examples include C/S, Communications, Operations Management).—**Consulting Career Path***

*The administration and recruiting companies preach creativity and fresh thinking. Yet they reward only those "in the box." Diversity is a joke—just look in the Lounge during lunchtime. And they say segregation is dead!—**Career Path Unknown***

*I have been consistently amazed at the innovativeness of the University of Michigan's MBA programs. In particular, the faculty is very responsive to student needs, and is willing to take any necessary steps to see that each student receives a superior education. For example, when students requested a course to learn more about fighting private-label brands, the marketing department responded immediately by offering a seminar on Brand Equity. This responsiveness and innovation is what separates Michigan from "the rest of the pack."—**Marketing Consultant**

*Michigan's first-year residency program was the most valuable learning experience for me. It brought everything together into an intense seven-week multidisciplinary project. Many students did not enjoy this aspect of the program while they were in it. I believe this is because of their expectation of being away from employment while in the MBA program. But the MAP residency is not just a job. It is an orchestrated, stressful, thought-provoking dose of reality, just when you need it most.—**Entrepreneurial Career Path**

*My biggest disappointment with my MBA experience was the narrowmindedness of the students. Although there was racial diversity and diversity of backgrounds at Michigan, there was no diversity of interests. Everyone was going into the same finance and marketing positions. No one seemed to care much about quality-of-life issues, just getting a high-paying job.—**Career Path Unknown**

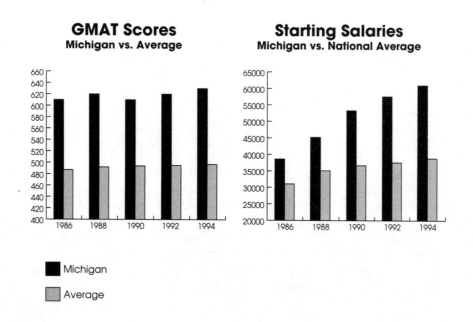

GMAT Scores
Michigan vs. Average

Starting Salaries
Michigan vs. National Average

■ Michigan
▨ Average

7. Indiana University

Graduate School of Business
10th and Fee Lane
Bloomington, Indiana 47405

Corporate ranking: 8
Enrollment: 560
Women: 26%
Non-U.S.: 14%
Minority: 15%
Part-time: None
Average age: 27
Average years of work exp: 4.4
Applicants accepted: 48%
Median starting pay: $58,300

Graduate ranking: 6
Annual tuition & fees: resident—$7196
                                  nonresident—$14,036
Room and board: $4484
Average GMAT score: 615
GMAT range: 400 to 760
Average GPA: 3.2
GPA range: 2.1 to 4.0
Accepted applicants enrolled: 42%
Average starting pay: $58,520

Teaching methods: Lecture, 33% Case study, 33% Group projects, 33%

Have you heard the joke about the student who put up a sign next to the hot-air dryer in one of the school's bathrooms? It read: "Push Button for a Message from the Dean." These days, a lot of B-school deans are blowing excess hot air about the revolutionary changes they've pioneered in management education. In many cases, there's a lot more rhetoric than reality to such boasts. Not at Indiana University's Graduate School of Business. The school has gone to the extremes in reinventing what had once been a basic, no-frills MBA program at one of the better public universities in the United States.

Just how radical? Consider this: In the first year, MBAs only receive two grades—one for each semester. Instead of the usual lineup of functional courses, the first semester's work is more highly integrated in what the school calls a Foundations Core taught by a faculty team of four professors. It's followed in the second semester by a Functional Core taught by a team of five faculty.

There's much more to this overhaul, but what makes it all the more surprising is that it's being accomplished at a school tucked away in southern Indiana—far from the hustle and bustle of Corporate America or the pioneering entrepreneurs of either Silicon Valley or Route 128. The nearest city to rather isolated Bloomington is Indianapolis, about 45 minutes away, and it's hardly a mecca for MBAs. So what propelled Indiana to move so boldly ahead with such dramatic changes in its curriculum?

The school had come in for some heavy criticism from MBAs in BUSINESS WEEK's 1990 poll when IU failed to rank in the Top 20 in the magazine's graduate survey. Overall the school was fifteenth, thanks to a fairly strong ninth-place finish among corporate recruiters. The school took the criticism to heart, speeding a process of change that had begun in 1989 with the appointment of a committee to recommend the future direction of the MBA program. The panel sought the views of students, alumni, industry representatives, leading business execs, and B-school officials.

The effort led to interviews with more than 140 corporate managers and executives. Joseph A. Pica, director of the MBA program, recalls the comments of one CEO of a top company who said he was struggling with having too many managers who are specialists. "He's got marketing people, finance people, information systems people, and his production people," says Pica. "They're all extremely good at what they do, yet what makes the business really work is when you bring the sum together."

That's exactly what Indiana attempts in this new program which was launched in the fall of 1992. To meet the needs of incoming students who require extra startup help in accounting, statistics, and computing, the school now offers short "jump start" courses during the summer. The "preparatory summer" is supposed to provide a more level playing field for all students. A 10-day orientation program kicks off the first year with the typical array of activities, from a team-building exercise that teaches group problem-solving in a wilderness setting at Bradford Woods in Southern Indiana to sessions that promote better awareness of cultural differences and sensitivities as well as their impact on managing the workforce. All students are required to have their own PCs. They get hands-on experience with both mainframes and PCs during orientation week when they take a crash course in spreadsheet analysis and word processing. Through Indiana's computer network, students send messages to classmates and professors by electronic mail. They also can access several databases to help them complete classwork.

To promote more teamwork and cooperation, the school has downsized the entering classes to about 250 from 320. First-year students are grouped into four cohorts of 60 to 65 students. For each two cohorts, a faculty team of four professors will then run the groups through the semester-long Foundations Core—covering accounting, managerial economics, quant methods, and human resources management. Just more of the same under a new label? Not. Faculty teams work with students to aggressively integrate topics, cases, and assignments that span these traditional disciplines. During the first semester, you'll also get "modules" on Power and Negotiation and Applied Business Ethics.

Before the second semester begins, IU deliberately shakes up the cohort groups so you'll meet more of your student colleagues. Then, your group will be assigned a different faculty team of five members to bring you through the Functional Core—designed to explore the relationships among accounting, finance, marketing, operations management, and management information systems. By the end of the first year, you'll have only two grades—one for each semester. There are no waivers and no breaks for anyone, regardless of their previous experience.

MBAs are enthusiastic about the first-year curriculum changes; however, many are disappointed with the second-year experience. Students say the transition isn't smooth enough—many felt the two halves of the MBA program were separate experiences. There were also complaints about redundancy in the second year. One graduate said he thought a one-year program would have been a better value, since there was so much duplication of basic material. Bringing the second year up to par is a major challenge facing John Rau, who became dean in July 1993. The former president and CEO of the LaSalle National Bank in Chicago succeeds Jack Wentworth, who retired after a decade-long stint at the helm of the B-school. Wentworth engineered the radical first-year changes, and now its up to Rau to address these new issues. "The second year doesn't have to be a completely novel approach, but we have to bring it up to the same level of intensity of the first year," says Rau.

IU students can choose from 85 electives. Among the offerings are Bruce Resnick's popular year-long course, Applied Investment Analysis and Portfolio Management. Students manage a portfolio of $200,000. They screen stocks, study companies, and monitor current events in the fall semester. By January, they put their money where their mouths, rather minds, are, making buy recommendations that they present to the class and an advisory board of IU alums working in the investment business. Finance is the overwhelming major of choice, with 52 percent of students pursuing a concentration in that field. Throughout the program, the three major themes of the curriculum are global, technological, and ethical.

Over the summer months, IU is encouraging students to get involved in "professional development activities," from the more traditional summer internships with corporations to a Washington Campus Program that will give students an opportunity to see the Clinton Administration at work. The university also has well-known foreign language and culture institutes on campus for those bound for careers in international business. Among other things, there are summer internships in Germany, Finland, and Slovenia.

In year two, IU now lets students tailor the MBA to their own interests. You can select a major—requiring four courses in a single discipline—or a double major. You can do a major and a minor, or even design your own concentration of advanced study with a faculty advisor, taking courses outside the B-school. There are only three required courses in the second year: The Legal Environment, Macroeconomics, and Strategic Management. An interdisciplinary major in international business includes language and culture requirements.

All of this experimentation is occurring in an attractive, if isolated, environment. With its rolling green hills and broad-branched trees, the campus could easily be the backdrop for a movie about collegiate life. The university, in fact, was the setting for the hit film *Breaking Away* about the Little 500 bicycle race, an annual fixture of Bloomington life. It's what you'd expect of a quaint town in Indiana with a courthouse square, whose population swells by 36,000 students when the university is in session. Many of the school's ivy-covered buildings were constructed at the turn of the century using Indiana limestone.

There are plenty of grassy areas for spreading out your books and studying on a sunny day. "This is a wonderful place to live," says Michael B. Metzger, one of the B-school's top teachers. "I can go to a dinner and a play on Friday night for chicken feed, go to a football game on Saturday afternoon, and go to the opera Saturday night. And the odds of getting mugged are really small. It's great." A few years ago, Metzger turned down an endowed chair at another university that would have made him the highest-paid professor in business law in the country because he's so smitten by the quality of life here.

Business students call home a seven-story, nondescript limestone building that houses administration, faculty, and classrooms. The B-school also contains the placement office, an MBA lounge, and eight computer-equipped labs. The adjoining business library also serves the School of Public and Environmental Affairs. On a nice day, students brown-bag it to the second-floor patio outside. Some first-year MBAs reside at Eigenmann

Hall, a high-rise dorm for graduate students two blocks from the B-school. Because demand outstrips supply, however, most grads move into their own apartments around town. Married students sometimes commute from the south side of Indianapolis because it's difficult for spouses to find work in Bloomington, which has a population of 60,000. IU does hire spouses of some MBAs, but often the work is routine or clerical.

Asked to describe their MBA education, most grads eventually come around to using the word "fun." That's because extracurricular activities assume a large role in student life. The school views its MBA program not as a set of courses, but as a total experience, encompassing both academic and personal development. Almost all of the students join the MBA Association, the umbrella group for 14 special interest groups. Students pay $150 for a two-year MBAA membership. Some of these, such as the Investment Club, help students network by planning field trips and bringing industry speakers to campus. Others handle the MBA newsletter, social events, a teaching evaluation report, and public relations. There are club meetings and functions at the B-school every night. "This building is jammed in the evening with a variety of activities," says Wentworth. "It's one of the advantages of being in a small town with not a whole heck of a lot to do."

One thing they do is congregate every Thursday night at a "designated bar" chosen by the MBAA. Students try to close such popular spots as The Crazy Horse, the Irish Lion, and J. Arthur's. Not to worry. There are no classes on Friday. On other evenings, the association may sponsor theme parties where grads dress up as beach bums, Elvis impersonators, or natives of Wisconsin (for this latter event, MBAs don flannel shirts and Brewers' caps, chatter about bowling, and swill Leinenkugel beer). The best pizza in town can be had at Nick's English Hut, 10 blocks from the B-school. It's a dark and dingy place, stuffed with basketball memorabilia. Autographed pictures of successful IU alums are hung along the painted dark-brown paneling.

The quality of teaching at Indiana has vastly improved since 1992, when IU scored below average for core teaching in BUSINESS WEEK's customer satisfaction polls. Two years later, Indiana received the second highest score for its core teaching in BW's 1994 survey of 40-plus schools—only Virginia scored higher. That's quite an improvement. The faculty-team concept is a major reason for the upswing, because professors don't want to embarrass themselves in front of their peers. The school has also tied salary increases for faculty to teaching quality. "So far we have managed to make teaching in the MBA program, and the core in particular, an honor," says Rau. "The challenge is going to be keeping it that way."

Indiana continues to boast a remarkable placement operation, which is why Indiana does so well on BUSINESS WEEK's corporate rankings. However, the latest crop of MBAs are beginning to complain about a lack of geographically diverse recruiters. Students say its hard for them to find jobs outside of the Midwest.

That's not to say that Indiana doesn't run a first-class placement office. At Indiana, the search for a job begins before the first class. During orientation week, new MBA students explore career options, polish up their résumé on a personal computer, and learn how to find a summer internship. Plenty of schools have an assistant dean for alumni relations, but how many have an assistant dean for company relations? At Indiana, that position is held by C. Randall (Randy) Powell. For years, he has made the MBA program here unique—something that has now obviously changed due to the new curriculum.

When corporate recruiters and speakers come to IU, they stay in the Indiana Memorial Union, a stately limestone building that serves as a hotel and conference center. They often have lunch or dinner with faculty members, who tip them off about promising students. Choice football tickets are part of the VIP treatment recruiters get at Indiana. "We treat recruiters like they are customers," Powell says. "You have to provide good service if you want customers to come back year after year."

Last year, Powell and the 15 full-time employees in IU's business placement office brought 223 companies to Bloomington for recruiting. He helps nearly three-fourths of the school's 296 MBA students find summer internships, and more than 85 percent find a job after graduation. Powell's so aggressive that some grads grouse that his office encourages MBAs to forgo salary negotiations with recruiters and to immediately accept any offer—a reason why MBA starting salaries here are not as high as those of other leading business schools. At least, that's what some of Indiana's MBAs maintain.

In any case, the job search is taken very seriously here. After a student types up his résumé on a computer during orientation, it is immediately entered into the school's database. Student résumés are made available to employers in both book form and on floppy disk. Like other major B-schools, Indiana students are allotted points that they "bid" to interview with a particular company. The typical MBA here has between 15 and 20 interviews in the second year. These are held in one of 40 interviewing rooms in a $2 million complex built in the early 1980s and dubbed "Powell's Placement Palace."

Only about 7 percent of the Class of 1994 failed to have a single job offer by graduation—a rate higher than only three other schools in the Top 20: Berkeley, Texas, and NYU. Those with offers averaged about 2.45 each—roughly the average for the 40-plus schools whose graduates were surveyed by BUSINESS WEEK.

Indiana may not be known for its placing power on Wall Street, but alums working there are willing to spend time with IU MBAs. In the 1993–1994 academic year, the Investment Club visited trading rooms and met with partners at major securities firms. Goldman, Sachs & Co., Salomon Brothers Inc., Kidder Peabody, and Merrill Lynch Capital Markets recruit on campus. They were among the 223 companies that recruited on campus in 1994, conducting 3100 interviews with Indiana students. Ford Motor hauled away the most Indiana MBAs in 1994, hiring 11 grads. Andersen Consulting, Continental Bank, Deloitte & Touche, Furon, Intel, Procter & Gamble, and Whirlpool hired four grads each. Seven more companies each signed up three members of the Class of 1994. They were: Eli Lilly, Federal Express, General Motors, Inland Mortgage, Tandem Computers, and Worthington Industries.

Now, IU has a program that matches the intensity and quality of Powell's incredible placement machine.

Contact: Joseph A. Pica, assistant dean and director, MBA program, Room 254, 812-855-8006
Final application deadline: March 1 for fall

Outstanding Faculty

1. John A. Boquist (****):   His reputation as one of the hardest graders in the MBA program failed to dampen any enthusiasm among students for this superb finance prof. Boquist, who has won teaching awards at both IU and INSEAD, loves to teach. He believes teaching is the core activity of a college professor, and thinks the most important attribute of a good teacher is enthusiasm. Boquist frequently testifies in utility rate cases and legal trials. Indeed, he tries to do one legal case a year because "testifying is the ultimate in teaching." Preparing for a trial, distilling material to its essence, and anticipating tough questions from an opposing attorney is the height of intellectual preparation, he says.

2. P. Ronald Stephenson (***): It's obvious that Stephenson is an avid fisherman as soon as you walk into his office—the walls feature dozens of pictures of himself, family, and friends holding up fish. He's gets as excited about marketing classes as he does about fish. Stephenson is constantly pushing students, and gets impatient with overanalysis or what he calls "mushy" responses. "Ron" operates on a first-name basis with students and boasts substantial consulting experience. He picked up his MBA and Ph.D. at Ohio State University.

3. Wayne L. Winston (***): He realized his lifelong ambition in 1992 when he appeared on the famous *Jeopardy* game show as a contestant. How did this teacher of information systems measure up? He won two rounds before Alex Trebeck bid him farewell. As Winston puts it, "I was beaten by the third highest money winner ever, so I don't feel bad about it!" Son of a college professor, Winston wanted to teach math from the seventh grade on. He eventually got his B.S. in the subject from MIT, but later switched to computer studies because Winston believes it has more practical applications than pure mathematics. After earning a Ph.D. in operations research from Yale, he ended up teaching at IU. In his 17 years here, Winston has been voted the best teacher by the school's MBAs on three separate occasions (including 1991 and 1992). One more thing. He bakes a cake for his class whenever he gives them a test. Something about the test not being a piece of cake . . .

4. Jamie H. Pratt (**): This prof says he likes to teach accounting because students come in with such low expectations—"They're expecting a nerd who isn't much fun." MBAs are in for a surprise with Pratt. He's anything but a geek. After class he can be found playing pickup basketball or baseball with MBAs. Pratt also invites students home to meet his family and see him as a human being. Students still like him, even though he has a reputation for being a difficult teacher—his test scores have the lowest mean in the program. Pratt picked up his Ph.D. at Indiana and then spent a dozen years teaching at the University of Washington before he came back to teach at his alma matter in 1989.

5. Scott B. Smart (**): He makes finance easy to understand by using games, such as buying and selling certificates in NFL teams to illustrate how markets work and change. Because Smart teaches in the integrated core, his goal is to break down complicated concepts so nonfinance majors can understand the subject. Smart joined the IU faculty in 1990 after earning his Ph.D. from Stanford. When Smart is not in the classroom he likes to hike, fish, and bird-watch. At night he plays tapes of owl songs to bring them in closer, and he and a colleague are building a tree house so that they can observe bird behavior up close.

6. Peter K. Mills (**): He shows little patience for long-winded, mindless answers in class, but Mills makes the grade by forcing students to see links between concepts and ideas in management. Born in Jamaica, Mills shows a bit of British reserve in the classroom. He uses surnames and believes in maintaining what he calls "detached concern" from his students. He boasts a pile of degrees: a B.S. and MBA from California State, and two Ph.D.s, one from the University of Stockholm and another from California at Irvine in organization theory. He joined IU in 1989.

Other Best Bets: *Michael B. Metzger* (business law), *Thomas P. Hustad* (marketing), *Sreenivas Kamma* (finance), and *Dan Dalton* (management)

Prominent Alumni: Edward G. Boehne, president, Federal Reserve Bank of Philadelphia; Richard L. Lesher, president, U.S. Chamber of Commerce; Frank E. McKinney, Jr., chairman and CEO, Banc One Indiana Corp.; Harold A. Poling, vice chairman, Ford Motor Co.; Frank P. Popoff, CEO, Dow Chemical Co.; James Lipate, CEO of Pennzoil Co.

Indiana MBAs Sound Off

The type of people who come to Indiana are the type you hope to work with after you complete your degree. They all have a genuine interest in each other, in doing well academically, and in having a good time. The entire experience—the friends I have made, the classroom instruction, two years in Bloomington, being a Hoosier fan, and learning more about myself—has been extremely rewarding.
—Finance Career Path

*Although the placement office still does an excellent job, they have become somewhat complacent. Often they are more concerned with "covering their butt" than they are with developing innovative new programs.—**Marketing Career Path***

*Indiana has been one of the pioneers among business schools in applying business concepts to its MBA program. Cross-functional integration is strived for in all courses, core and electives alike. Quality management is implemented through continuous communication between students and faculty, and we (students) believe we can impact decisions that are important to us. Outside organizations are very much involved in courses and activities, and help bring the classroom closer to the real world. A weakness of Indiana is its lack of a real international focus. Many members of the faculty are uncomfortable debating international issues, and international business is not completely integrated into the curriculum.—**Manufacturing Manager***

*The administration is very receptive to student comments, but has trouble figuring out problems by themselves. For example, we had three Ph.D. students teaching in the Operations Management program. Students complained, and the administration gave us assurances that it wouldn't happen again, but at the expense of our class receiving inferior instruction.—**Financial Analyst***

*Indiana's MBA gives a lot of "bang for the buck." For me cost was a consideration, and very few programs offer the value that Indiana does.—**Derivatives Career Path***

*As with all MBA programs, there are a few areas that could be improved at IU. The school is currently addressing some of the deficiencies, such as increasing the number of presentations by students and giving students a formal presentations grade. They're also improving the level of integration within the first year of the program. However, the second year of the program also requires the same level of integration but has been mostly ignored by the administration. In addition, the selection and quality of international business classes offered should be dramatically restructured, to put it on par with the other functions (finance, marketing, etc.).—**Financial Analyst***

*IU's move to the cohort structure with established study groups was outstanding. It developed interpersonal and teamwork skills in a hands-on way, and emulated well what we are likely to encounter in the working world. The second year of the program needs attention, however, particularly in the areas of scheduling and integration. More attention also needs to be given to maintaining an effective alumni database for each year's class.—**Manufacturing Career Path***

The first year of the program, that was recently restructured, is a significant step forward for IU. The school made a commitment to really improve and it has done it. However, the second year now needs to be restructured. It was somewhat of a letdown to have such a superior first year and just a decent second year.
*—**Financial Analyst***

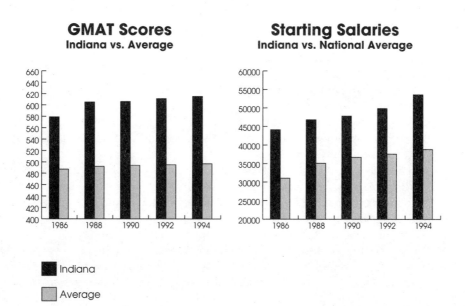

GMAT Scores
Indiana vs. Average

Starting Salaries
Indiana vs. National Average

■ Indiana
▨ Average

8. Columbia University

Columbia Business School
Uris Hall
New York, NY 10027

Corporate ranking: 7
Enrollment: 1375
Women: 32%
Non-U.S.: 27%
Minority: 9%
Part-time: None
Average age: 27
Applicants accepted: 25%
Median starting pay: $75,000

Graduate ranking: 10
Annual tuition & fees: $21,400
Room and board: $12,600
Average GMAT score: 640
GMAT range: 570 to 710
Average GPA: 3.3
GPA range: 2.8 to 4.0
Accepted applicants enrolled: 58%
Average starting pay: $100,480

Teaching methods: Lecture, 30%   Case study, 30%   Group projects, 40%

First, the good news. After years of lobbying and cajoling, Dean Meyer Feldberg finally won approval in 1994 to build a new, state-of-the-art business school building.

Now, the not-so-good news. It might very well take until the end of the century before the multi-storied structure, to be shared with the university's law school, is completed.

Why the big deal about a building? Mainly because Uris Hall, the business school's home, is among the worst facilities of any top B-school. A prototype of what good architecture isn't, the gray concrete building is outmoded and too small. The classrooms are often too hot or too cold. The elevators are notoriously slow. Cockroaches scamper across the bathroom floors and walls. And many students find it a mission impossible to locate an empty room for group meetings.

What is going on in the building, however, is even more impressive. Feldberg, who left as president of the Illinois Institute of Technology to become dean in mid-1989, has led Columbia through a dramatic transformation. He has raised some $68 million in endowment money and put an end to a dozen years of budget deficits. He has launched a new MBA program immodestly dubbed "The Curriculum for the 21st Century," while carving out a niche for Columbia as an international business school. And it looks like he will finally get not only a new building, but a renovation to Uris Hall and a new residence hall for students and faculty as well.

Not surprisingly, then, student satisfaction at the school is way up—helping Columbia climb to 10th place in BW's graduate poll from 18th in 1990. Overall, the school moved up a notch to gain an eighth-place finish in 1994, its best ranking ever, and well above a low of 14th back in 1988.

For Feldberg, a native South African who speaks with a slight British accent, it has hardly been a smooth ride. It took years, including threats that he might move the school out of Manhattan, before he finally secured approval to gain his new building. Meantime, he had to make as many improvements as possible at Uris, expanding a crowded computer center and creating more space for group meetings. In 1994, Columbia was accepting nearly half of those who applied for admission—far more than schools such as Indiana, Texas, or Penn State. The admissions office turned this near-crisis around, so that Columbia now admits only one of four applicants.

Besides the news about the business school's new building, the big news is the revamping of Columbia's MBA program. Entering students are required to own notebook computers, so that each of them becomes computer-literate in business applications and databases. More than 300 data jacks can be found in all study areas, conference rooms, and classrooms, even in the deli and library, so that MBAs can connect to the school's network. Finance exams are now done on computers and turned in via the network. The school hopes to have students register for classes on computer over the next year. Columbia says its computer initiative has been so successful that such schools as Kellogg and MIT are considering similar programs.

The new curriculum, moreover, is the result of intensive study and survey work. In early 1990, a pair of committees composed of senior faculty, administrators, and students began to seek the views of the school's various constituents to help redefine its mission. The groups gathered data from 2000 alumni, 100 recruiting companies, nearly 1000 current students, and 100 of its own faculty, as well as faculty from other schools. They also ran focus groups of managers, meeting with executives from such firms as American Express, Bankers Trust, General Electric, and Merck.

The result of the effort—the first comprehensive review of the Columbia's program since the early 1960s—was a new curriculum, which made its debut in the fall of 1992. The new program puts more emphasis on managing and less on crunching numbers. "Pre-term work" requires incoming students to learn communications, quantitative, and computer skills before beginning the program. In year one, every MBA has three seminars on presentation skills, team building, and writing proficiency. Projects and seminars form a key part of the experience. Before Feldberg's arrival, it was possible to go through the first and sometimes the second semester without being part of a team or having to deliver a presentation.

More importantly, the new program integrates into the first-year core curriculum four key themes: globalization, total quality, ethics, and human resources management. The goal is for each theme to absorb at least 12 class sessions, with slightly more for international issues. In a few cases, a single case study is being simultaneously taught over three separate classes, so that MBAs can see how finance, marketing, and management fit together. An integrative group project at the end of the first term allows students to see how the disciplines play a role in any business decision. "The students always had a good, detailed understanding of the disciplines, but these topics had not been well integrated in the curriculum," explains John B. Donaldson, a popular economics professor. "Although we had a business policy course to bring it together, the feeling was we couldn't rely on just one or two courses to do it."

The new curriculum forced faculty to work together to redesign their core courses. For years, Columbia's basic finance course taught the capital asset pricing model as if it were a religious tenet—even though it has little to do with the nuts and bolts of corporate finance. The revamped class spends more time with cash flow analysis, combining case studies and lectures with an applied group project. The macroeconomics course, which once dealt with the management of the domestic business cycle, now focuses on growth, trade, and international economics. The operations management course, once crammed with mathematical models but few case studies, has been overhauled to encourage more class discussion and integrative material.

These welcome changes impose new demands on Columbia's faculty. They are requiring narrowly trained professors to view business problems more broadly and to work together across disciplines on teams. They also are forcing professors to alter their teaching methods to a more engaging, Socratic style as more case studies and group projects are dumped into the core. That transition can't be easy, because Feldberg is in many ways still struggling with an antiquated culture, one in which academic intellectualism has long assumed greater importance than the business of learning. But Feldberg has been trying to improve the situation. Stringent hiring procedures now pay more attention to teaching, professor evaluations have been redesigned, and faculty are more closely monitored. Outstanding teachers are recognized by newly established teaching awards. Perhaps the single most important move to improve teaching has been Feldberg's appointment of Safwan M. Masri as vice dean for the MBA program. A masterful teacher who ranked among the top three Columbia profs in BW's 1990 poll, Masri says improving faculty teaching is his number-one priority. He has even gotten students involved in faculty hiring. And Masri says the school is thinking of reducing the MBA population so as to lessen the pressure on its better faculty.

In any case, Columbia seems more sensitive to criticism about the quality of teaching. As Robert Glenn Hubbard, a senior vice dean, puts it: "We've come a long way, in the sense that everybody realizes teaching is important, and they're trying to improve to varying extents." After student complaints, says a 1994 graduate, the school recalled a senior professor from sabbatical to replace a poorly performing teacher in a key seminar. Sure enough, the Class of 1994 rated the quality of teaching in both the core and elective offerings as being above average—for the first time!

Those numbers are considerably enhanced by Columbia's rather sizable contingent of adjunct professors, who bring real-time experience into the classroom. A First Boston analyst, one of the top three covering the computer industry, teaches a security analysis class. An elective on leverage buyouts is taught by Bill Comfort, head of Citibank's venture capital unit. Jim Rogers, who originally started the Quantum Fund with George Soros, teaches an advanced security analysis course. One of the most popular courses—Value Investing—brought to Uris such financial luminaries as super investor Warren Buffett, Robert Bruce of Bruce Management, and Mario Gabelli of The Gabelli Group.

Ask a student or faculty member what the best thing is about Columbia, and the answer will be: New York City. Ask what the worst thing is and you'll get the same reply. Like the Big Apple, Columbia offers glamour and excitement, but it is not for the thin-skinned or the faint-hearted. Only at Columbia can you attend a finance class taught by a corporate raider, lunch with a visiting Wall Street banker, and take in a Broadway show on the same day. But in the course of your travels you'll likely encounter a vibrant, though loud, city, suffering from neglect and crime.

It's hard to overstate the wealth of opportunities available to MBAs thanks to the school's location in the leading cultural and financial center. Columbia is the kind of place where you can pick up *The New York Times* and read about the latest deal of someone who spoke to your class the day before. Just a short subway—or limo—ride away from Wall Street, the school is able to tap leading financiers and corporate executives to lecture in class. In the 1993–94 academic year, Columbia lured the chief executives or senior officers of such companies as J.P. Morgan; Nynex; Estee Lauder; Kohlberg, Kravis & Roberts; The Body Shop; Boston Consulting Group; and the Central Bank of China. As one of Columbia's most outstanding professors, John O. Whitney, puts it: "People would crawl through broken beer bottles to hear some of these people." Indeed, each year, 200 CEOs and senior executives come to campus to speak with students. Their tales from the front lines of dealmaking provide a sharp contrast to the strong theoretical and research bent of the 110 full-time faculty.

Another big advantage is the flexibility Columbia offers students. The school allows MBAs to begin its program in any one of three terms each year. It is possible to complete the degree in 16 months, but most students use the summer term for an internship. You also can exempt out of selected core classes by exam. They don't have to be replaced with other electives. With nine full courses and two half-courses, the integrated core comprises half of the workload for the degree. Clusters of 50 students each travel through the entire core together. In year two, students choose from among 150 electives as well as graduate courses offered at other schools at Columbia University. As you might expect, for every elective in production or operations management, the B-school offers five in accounting and finance. The numbers' slant even shows up in *The Bottom Line,* the weekly MBA newspaper in which students often use quant skills to make one point or another.

MBAs can major in any 1 of 12 areas of study, from accounting to media management. You can even focus on "investment management" under a finance concentration or "management consulting" under a management of organizations concentration. These days, up to 60 percent of the class takes on two majors. The school also offers mini-courses in more than 50 languages, including French, German, Italian, Spanish, Chinese, English, and Japanese. The goal of the courses, which limit class size to eight students, is to bring students up to conversational fluency. The classes aren't cheap: They cost between $330 and $355 for three-hour Friday sessions.

The availability of foreign language instruction—even though it's without academic credit—will help Feldberg reconstruct Columbia into one of the premier schools for international business. His biggest coup, however, came in 1991 when he got Jerome A. Chazen, a founding partner of Liz Claiborne Inc. and a 1950 alum, to donate $10 million for an Institute of International Business. This center is tying together all of the school's efforts to globalize, publishing an expanded journal of world business, insuring that the core courses boast a hefty international component, and expanding exchange programs with non-U.S. business schools (there are now 14 such programs and 8 international study trips).

Closer to home, Columbia itself has all the amenities of an Ivy League school, including a grassy quad surrounded by temples of learning, but it is just west of Harlem. Many Columbia B-school students live in roomy apartments on the Upper West Side, a neighborhood filled with trendy restaurants and bars catering to young, upwardly mobile professionals. By all means, avoid the dormitory allocated to the B-school. As one 1994 graduate who barely survived Columbia's dorm living explains: "During the first semester, the shower was broken for two weeks, the oven was inoperable for three weeks, and the heater occasionally emitted ill-smelling fumes. In other apartments, faulty wiring gave electric shocks to those who touched bathroom appliances, and repairs were not made until the students threatened a lawsuit." Columbia MBAs will often share a cab to campus in the morning, although a few hardier souls will take the IRT Local to 116th St.

A typical week at Columbia ends in the first-floor Uris Deli, where a weekly happy hour is held every Thursday night. After a few beers, students will break up into groups and go their separate ways, some heading down the West Side, others to the Village or Little Italy. Some MBAs hang out at the West End Gate at 113th and Broadway, where beat writer Jack Kerouac once carved his name in a table. Since there are no classes on Fridays, students use the three-day weekends to escape from the city or to work part-time. The highlight of Columbia's social season is the annual spring ball, an MBA version of the senior prom—replete with designer evening gowns, stretch limos, and ritzy dinners. The locale for the event changes annually and has included such historic landmarks as the New York Public Library, Federal Hall, the Puck Building, and Tavern on the Green.

Just a cursory glance at Columbia's hefty alumni directory underscores its strong reputation in finance. For years, the school has been a factory for the big league commercial banks and giants of the financial service world. Some 400 of the school's alums draw their paychecks from mighty Citicorp alone. Chase Manhattan Bank employs 160, while Chemical Bank has 163 Columbia MBAs on its payroll. Other major employers of alums: American Express (150); Merrill Lynch (163); Goldman Sachs (150); Bankers Trust (185); Morgan Stanley (120); Shearson Lehman (130); First Boston (115); and Manufacturers Hanover Trust (63). The single biggest exception to this lineup of financial powerhouses is IBM, where some 245 Columbia grads work.

The school's career services office gets generally good reviews for helping students connect with the job market. Some may fault the office for not attracting non-American companies with international jobs. But that's asking an awful lot, even from an institution trying to distinguish itself from the pack as an international business school. After all, 249 companies recruited on campus in 1994, doing 6261 interviews with second-year students. Another 2019 job opportunities came into the office through the mail. Pretty impressive stats.

Wall Street's revival had a big impact at Columbia, with more than 55 percent of the 1994 graduating class going into finance jobs. No wonder Columbia was one of only three schools whose graduates won starting pay packages that averaged in the six figures. That's an incredible $100,480 when you toss in year-end bonuses and other perks. Only Harvard and Stanford graduates earned more in 1994, although the median package was $75,000. Columbia MBAs also averaged 2.43 job offers at commencement, just a bit above the average for the top 40-plus schools surveyed by BW.

Citibank and Morgan Stanley led the pack in recruiting the most '94 MBAs, with 20 hires each. Not far behind were Booz Allen & Hamilton (15); Bankers Trust (14); Coopers & Lybrand (13); Merrill Lynch (12); J.P. Morgan (12); McKinsey (11); Smith Barney Shearson (11); Goldman Sachs (10); Lehman Brothers (10).

That impressive lineup of committed recruiters has much to do with Columbia's reputation. But Feldberg, a master networker, must get some of the credit. Every year, he hosts about 10 cocktail parties for students, alums, and executives from the school's Board of Overseers. He also conjured up a "Take-a-Student-to-Lunch" program to link working alumni with students. In 1994, the school matched 200 alumni with 600 MBAs.

Clearly, Dean Feldberg's improvements are finally beginning to pay off.

Contact: Ethan Hanabury, assistant dean of admissions, 212-854-1961
Final application deadlines: November 1 for January; February 1 for May; April 20 for September

Outstanding Faculty

1. Bruce C.N. Greenwald (****): When he was 12, he started reading balance sheets and losing money on U.S. Steel stock. Greenwald's insights into the financial markets have improved since then. He commonly uses metaphors, coin flips, personal experience, and a modulating voice to make finance palatable. He's taught at the best—Harvard, Stanford, Tuck, and Chicago—and joined Columbia in 1991. His wife is circulation director of *The Village Voice*. Can be tough: "MBAs say such stupid things with so much confidence that I can't help but be mean sometimes."

2. Larry Selden (****): As a former foreign exchange trader and a special assistant to the national director of consulting at Arthur Young & Co., this finance prof has brought plenty of pragmatic instruction into the classroom ever since his arrival in 1976. A 1964 graduate of Washington University, he earned both his MBA and Ph.D. degrees from Wharton.

3. John O. Whitney (****): With his chiseled face, shock of wavy white hair, and piercing blue eyes, Oklahoma-born Whitney looks like a character out of an old Western movie. No wonder he's dubbed the "Cash Flow Cowboy" by MBAs who endlessly rave about his Managing Turnarounds elective. He teaches it twice a term to sections of 55 students each. Lacking both an MBA and a Ph.D., he's an unconventional Columbia prof. The former CEO of Pathmark Supermarkets grew up in a family of teachers, so it's no surprise that he's Columbia's best. Whitney works hard at it: He spent 240 hours reading student papers alone last year. A disciple of quality guru W. Edwards Deming, he also directs the school's Deming Center for Quality Management.

4. Robert N. Bontempo (**): Nobody at Columbia does it better than Bob Bontempo, when it comes to teaching the core Management of Organizations course. His compelling insights into how managements around the world differ from each other bring added value into the course. Bontempo, who joined the faculty in 1989, boasts a trio of degrees: a B.S. from Notre Dame, a B.A. from Indiana University, and a Ph.D. from the University of Illinois.

5. James M. Hulbert (**): A marketing whiz, "Mac" Hulbert has brought superb teaching to Columbia ever since joining the faculty in 1969. The Oklahoma State MBA consults with several large corporations and the federal government on planning and strategy issues.

6. David O. Beim (*):   Former managing director of Dillon Read & Co., Beim got a taste for the teaching life as an adjunct finance professor in 1989–90. The Oxford-educated businessman apparently loved it, for he joined the faculty on a more permanent basis in 1991.

Other Best Bets: *Suresh M. Sundaresan* (finance and economics), *Ronald Schramm* (finance and economics), *Michael L. Tushman* (management), and *John B. Donaldson* (finance and economics)

Prominent Alumni: Warren Buffett, chairman of Berkshire Hathaway; Max C. Chapman, Jr., co-chairman, Nomura Securities International; Jerome A. Chazen, chairman of Liz Claiborne Inc.; William Dillard, chairman of Dillard Department Stores Inc.; Lionel I. Pincus, chairman of E.M. Warburg, Pincus & Co. Inc.; Henry Kravis, partner, Kohlberg, Kravis & Roberts; Mario Gabelli, chairman, The Gabelli Group; Benjamin Rosen, chairman, Compaq Computer Corp.; Joseph Vittoria, chairman, Avis Corp.; Peter Woo, chairman, The Wharf Holdings Ltd.; Philip Geier, chairman, Interpublic Group of Cos.; John Ross, CEO, Deutsche Bank, North America

Columbia MBAs Sound Off

*The most negative thing about Columbia is the facilities. Uris Hall should be razed and replaced by a building with appropriate capacity and services to support an otherwise outstanding school.—**Consultant***

*Columbia often gets a bad rap from students who have trouble adjusting to New York City, which is a roller-coaster ride that you either love passionately or loathe. The bottom line is that no business school has the access in this city that Columbia has. The Columbia name and proximity to Wall Street have enabled me to network into my dream job at double my previous salary.—**Financial Associate***

*My overall Columbia experience was a good one, but several basic problem areas still need to be addressed by the school. The building is much too small for the demands placed on it. Columbia is working on the situation, but needs to speed up its efforts. The computer network is dated and entirely inadequate. Perhaps most importantly, nearly all recruiting at Columbia focuses on finance, brand management/marketing, and consulting positions. Columbia must make a gargantuan effort to overhaul its career development department to bring a more diverse group of recruiters to the school.—**Career Field Unknown***

*I loved the school. There was no spoon-feeding or hand-holding. Just lots of good, healthy, and occasionally, hardcore competition.—**Consultant***

In many ways, Columbia reflects New York City. It is intense, aggressive, fast-paced, diverse, and definitely not for the weak of heart. When you combine this

*environment with top-notch academics, you get MBAs that are not only extremely well prepared, but survivors who are ready to hit the ground running and to face the harsh realities of business life.—**Manager***

*Greed is alive and well at Columbia. People stampede toward investment banking like lemmings, despite a complete lack of understanding of the realities of life as a grunt associate at I-Banks. Given the current Wall Street boom, this attitude is understandable. My classmates' greed is exceeded only by their passion for a good bitch session.—**Consultant***

*While at Columbia, I was shocked to find poor housing conditions, inadequate facilities, and many rude and inefficient administrators. Worse, I found the majority of my professors did not have a global perspective, lacked practical work experience, were inept at working with a diverse student body, and did not offer quality teaching.—**Consultant***

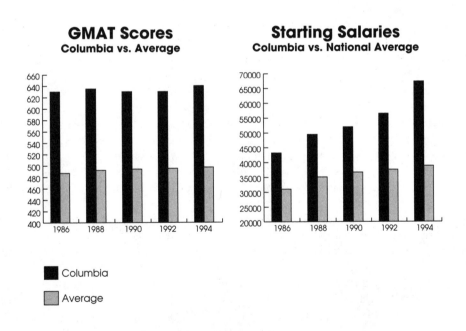

9. University of California, Los Angeles

John E. Anderson Graduate School of Management
405 Hilgard Avenue
Los Angeles, California 90024

Corporate ranking: 16
Enrollment: 1046
Women: 29%
Non-U.S.: 20%
Minority: 9%
Part-time: 434
Average age: 27.2
Average years of work exp.: 4.3
Applicants accepted: 23%
Median starting pay: $70,000

Graduate ranking: 2
Annual tuition & fees: resident—$6797
                              nonresident—$14,496
Room and board: $7925
Average GMAT score: 640
GMAT range: 500 to 700
Average GPA: 3.5
GPA range: 3.1 to 3.85
Accepted applicants enrolled: 54%
Average starting pay: $74,010

Teaching methods: Lecture, 35%   Case study, 55%   Group projects, 10%

Ah, the Golden State. The land of milk and honey—and nuts—with a history unrivaled for its trend-setting peculiarities. Hot tubs, Governor Moonbeam, and pierced navels. Plop into the middle of all those images a top business school not far from Malibu Beach, and you get UCLA's John E. Anderson Graduate School of Management. It's a school that combines the popular mythology of California with the sometimes bewildering quantitative models of the business school world. Though just a short drive from the sandy beach, MBAs here are more likely to carry *The Wall Street Journal* under an arm than a surfboard.

There are probably as many students at Anderson who ache to be investment bankers as there are at Harvard or Wharton. But there surely are many more these days interested in entrepreneurship—the hottest growth area at the B-school since the 1987 crash and the fall of junk bond king Mike Milken, who ruled his empire from Drexel Burnham Lambert's Beverly Hills office. In that short time, UCLA has carved out a distinctive niche in entrepreneurship to supplement its longtime strength in finance.

The innovative changes won recognition in 1991 when Anderson's entrepreneurship curriculum was named the best in the nation by the Association of Collegiate Entrepreneurs—even though UCLA didn't know it was up for the award. No matter. It was well deserved. The B-school now offers at least a dozen electives in entrepreneurship, up from only a pair of courses when Milken was going strong. "Student interest in entrepreneurship classes has exploded," says Alfred E. Osborne, who directs Anderson's Entrepreneurial Studies Center.

Smitten by the entrepreneurial bug, many students have launched their own businesses—including over 7 percent of the class of 1992, more than any other Top 20 school. After studying Small Business Management and writing a business plan, Christine Fang, a 1992 alum, opened a coffeehouse in west Los Angeles with another classmate, Marc Junkunc of the Class of 1993. "In Berkeley, where we met as undergraduates, the coffeehouse culture is part of academic life," says Fang. The pair saw a need for a coffeehouse catering to university students.

At Fang's twoPart, students now sip coffee and often debate not Tolstoy or Lenin but which small business classes to get under their belts. A pair of 1994 grads launched Buzz Records, an independent record label. In Entrepreneurship and Venture Initiation, students start out with a case study involving a trio of MBA students who open up a gelato shop in Florida—a case that explores everything from how to hit people up for money to exactly where to locate your business. The midterm assignment requires an interview with an entrepreneur. Financing an Emerging Enterprise, taught by UCLA's most outstanding professor, William Cockrum, delves into the different financing concepts an owner can employ for a small business.

All these courses and more, however, are just a starting point for the entrepreneurial center, which offers a steady stream of practical programs for students outside the classroom. Through a mentor program, students can meet with successful entrepreneurs on a regular basis. There are also internships with venture capitalists. Each spring, the Anderson School holds a contest where student proposals for new enterprises are judged by a panel of venture capitalists. The winners even take home cash prizes—generally not enough to start a business, but perhaps enough to get your surfboard waxed.

The winners of the top $3000 award in 1992 were Rebecca Brand and Steven Terui, who hatched a business plan for a company that would aggressively export California wine to international markets. A year earlier, the winning MBA student came up with a business to make marine accessories. The business is now up and running in Gardena, California. Osborne intends to carry this experiment much further, however. He's now negotiating with several donors to start a fund to finance the business plans of MBA students. To encourage more ambitious ventures, the school hopes to be able to provide up to $250,000 in seed money to MBA graduates.

With nearly 450 members, the school's Entrepreneur Association is Anderson's most popular student group (40 percent of its members say they want their own businesses within five years). The club brings guest entrepreneurs and venture capitalists to campus for presentations and sponsors an annual conference on new business startups. A small business consulting service sends students out to give management help to entrepreneurs, while a ventures program funds small business ideas developed by students.

Entrepreneurship, of course, isn't for everyone. And even would-be business owners feel the need to get their feet wet in more established companies before embarking on their own. That's why finance remains strong at the school, which continues to hold a spate of events to allow students to mix with local finance leaders and alumni. Besides, if that's not your bag, the Anderson School also is a great jumping-off point for a career in entertainment. Where else could you attend class in the morning and drive over to Hollywood to knock on doors in the afternoon?

It's not unusual for students to follow the same path as Elizabeth Wills, who graduated from Anderson in 1989. After earning an undergraduate degree at Harvard, Wills worked on Wall Street for three years before deciding she was ready for a change. When she came to UCLA, Wills knew she wanted to do something entrepreneurial that involved finance, but she wasn't sure exactly what. The Anderson School helped her find a summer internship at a small leveraged buyout firm in Los Angeles, where she went to work full-time after getting her MBA. At first, Wills was slightly apprehensive about attending UCLA because she "had the impression it was a party school, especially when I read about the beer busts every Thursday night. But I was mistaken. I've worked harder here than I have anyplace else, including Harvard and Goldman, Sachs." Like Wills, many students are surprised that a B-school surrounded by palm trees offers such a challenging MBA program. And the Anderson School does. But the main attractions are quality of life and price. UCLA is located in the California foothills in Brentwood and borders Bel Air, an exclusive neighborhood whose denizens now include Ronald and Nancy Reagan. The atmosphere here is relaxed and friendly. Students catch some rays on the B-school patio while studying or plugging numbers into a spreadsheet on a laptop computer. Even outsiders end up singing Randy Newman's "I Love L.A." by the time they graduate.

Another reason to love this school is its still-low tuition rates. Out-of-state residents pay only $14,496 in their first year, and most of them can qualify as state residents for the second year of the program. That still makes it one of the few real bargains left at a top business program. These bargain rates, however, won't be in effect much longer. Anderson has suffered a more than 20 percent cut in public funding over the past four years.

The upshot: Dean William P. Pierskalla, a former Wharton deputy dean who joined Anderson in mid-1993, is trying to "privatize" the school by hiking tuition fees and getting more alumni and corporate contributions to fund operations. Annual tuition and fees for residents has nearly doubled in two years, and will continue to rise so that it approaches the tuition levels of the University of Michigan's business school. The new dean hopes to increase private funding of the school to as much as 80 percent of its budget by 1998, up from less than 50 percent in 1994.

Even though Pierskalla is hiking tuition rates here, he has quickly won the support and admiration of the students. Raves one fan: "Bill Pierskalla has brought vision, energy, and tremendous management skills to the dean's office." He has expanded the school's board of visitors, making it more than a ceremonial body to tap for fundraising. Pierskalla is getting the outside executives on the board to become more involved in the school and its students. He's also encouraging the faculty to produce research that truly advances management practice.

Like Los Angeles, the Anderson School's population is diverse, with a high percentage of women, international students, and minorities. More than 38 percent of Anderson's students are from California, and a total of 60 percent are from the West. But one-quarter of the school's applications come from New York. "The Easterners have a sense of adventure," says Eric Mokover, assistant director of the MBA program. "It takes guts to go to UCLA when all your friends are going to Wharton." Anderson doesn't place as much importance on GMAT scores as other B-schools, so mention on your application how you opened your first lemonade stand when you were six years old.

Along with sister school Berkeley, UCLA is a popular destination for the Japanese. Anderson receives tremendous support from current and former Japanese students. The bookstore does a healthy business in UCLA sweatshirts, which are status symbols in Japan along with Louis Vuitton handbags and Gucci loafers. The Tokyo alumni club regularly sponsors a reception for students accepted by the Anderson School. These students also received a 40-page guide in Japanese explaining the mysteries of Southern California life—how to open a checking account, find an apartment, and buy a car—penned by a group of second-year Japanese students who sent off a group picture of themselves donning UCLA sweatshirts.

Not every student admitted to UCLA gets this kind of VIP treatment, but the school competes with the best of them by adopting a personalized approach. Everyone accepted here receives a telephone call if they're in the United States and a letter in their native language if they're overseas. Student volunteers handle these hospitalities, helping to tout the school's image and organize activities. One reason: As part of a state university, Anderson doesn't have the resources available to private schools to promote the MBA program to prospective students, alumni, and corporations.

Student participation, both in and out of the classroom, is a hallmark of the place. "Students are the most important part of the school," says J. Clayburn La Force, the former dean. Participation will only be enhanced with the completion in 1995 of a new $75 million management center, to be constructed on the northwestern portion of UCLA's campus near the Sunset Boulevard/Westwood Plaza entrance. The seven buildings in the complex will be tied together by patios, walkways, and courtyards. La Force has been planning the new building for five years because the school's existing facilities are cramped. The B-school has no plans to increase MBA enrollment when the new building opens, but intends to expand its Executive Education offerings.

Students also organize most of the B-school's interaction with the local business community. The Association of Students and Business (ASB) sponsors lectures by prominent executives; career nights drawing dozens of firms in a particular industry such as finance, entertainment, or real estate; and "days on the job," where students turn company employees for a day. ASB's main event is an annual dinner that draws high-level managers from local companies, students, and faculty. The 1991–1992 lineup included Masaaki Morita, Sony Corp. of America's chairman; David Murddock, the self-made billionaire who is chairman of Dole Foods; and Michael R. Hallman, former chairman of Microsoft.

At Anderson, teamwork is king—the result of a redesigned curriculum to foster greater group cooperation among students and faculty. All first-year students now take the same courses at the same time. Under the old system, students were essentially free to take the classes they wanted. Anderson divides the academic year into three quarters—fall, winter, and spring—instead of two semesters. At the beginning of each quarter, the class of 375 students is split up into sections of between 60 and 65 students. Students take all required core courses for that quarter with their section.

Half of the 24 courses required for an MBA are core courses. Eight cover areas such as finance, accounting, organizational behavior, marketing, statistics, and economics. To complete the core, students choose from one of two courses concerned with managing people—either Human Resources Management or Managing People in Organizations—and two of three courses covering technical areas such as information systems, macroeconomics and forecasting, and managerial model building.

Students must take at least 8 of the 11 electives within the Anderson School. Three "free" electives can be taken in other UCLA departments. In taking electives, students can choose from traditional disciplines such as finance, marketing, and management sciences—generally regarded as the Anderson School's three strongest areas—or from interdisciplinary areas such as entrepreneurial studies, international business, arts management, entertainment management, real estate, and not-for-profit/public management.

Teaching has not been a consistent strength of the Anderson School, and the structured first-year program has made disparities in teaching ability more obvious than ever. Dominique "Mike" Hanssens, head of the faculty, says the B-school has responded to student dissatisfaction by removing professors from first-year core courses if they fail to measure up. And BUSINESS WEEK's 1994 surveys show that graduates rate the quality of the teaching in the core above the average, for the 40-plus schools polled. The same is true for the school's varied elective offerings—some 125 choices ranging from Management and Business Applications in Laptop Computing to The Morality of Capitalism.

The culmination of the program is a group consulting project that stretches over two quarters. After visiting a business to study a problem, a team of three to five students develops an analysis, writes it up, and then makes an oral presentation to company executives. The final task is a written document to the professor of record. Students sometimes gripe that the field study project can distract from their all-important job search, but it is crucial in helping students integrate knowledge acquired in the core courses. Moreover, the consulting arm of the accounting firm of Deloitte & Touche began in 1992 to ante up $3000 in award money for the field study team that "best demonstrates exemplary leadership, teamwork, innovative thinking, and strategic creativity." Deloitte—one-third of whose consultants in downtown L.A. are Anderson grads—is also sponsoring workshops and a management hotline so that students can tap the expertise of the firm's consultants during their field study projects.

These projects, however, may undergo a major overhaul in future years. In a pilot move in 1994, some 60 students—or one-fifth of the class—were divided into groups of 20 each to work on corporate strategy issues for three telecommunication companies: Falcon Cable, Technicolor, and Hughes Space and Communications. Five-person teams within each group of 20 are expected to do written reports, oral presentations, and also case studies to leave behind for future students. This effort follows a coordinated pair of strategy and organization classes in the first year, designed to better prepare students for the second-year assignment. The chief executives and their top officers of all three companies came to class on four different occasions to brief students. "We call this the Living Case Study Program," says David Lewin, vice dean for the MBA program. "We want to ratchet up the field study program and increase the school's presence in key industries." Other possibilities: organizing projects with corporate sponsors in the health care business, professional sports, and the hospitality industry.

Besides all the interest in entrepreneurship here, another interdisciplinary area on the rise at the Anderson School is international management. The school has hired Jose de la Torre, who spent 13 years with INSEAD (the famous Institut Européen d'Administration des Affaires) in France, to develop the international character of its program. Rather than creating a separate international management department, de la Torre wants to boost the international content of each functional area. "Our long-run goal is to have no international program, because *everything* will be international," he says. A key part of UCLA's international strategy is an MBA in international management that includes intensive language and culture study. UCLA launched in 1990 a 24-month International Management Fellow program that includes 9 months of study and work in a foreign country. During their time abroad, MBAs will attend a foreign university and do an internship with a local company. The program is being initially limited to 20 students who want to study Spanish or Chinese, but it will eventually include as much as 10 percent of the incoming class as well as French and Japanese educational and work experiences.

Given California's economic difficulties of late, many more students may want to avail themselves of the school's programs in international business and entrepreneurship. The recession has ravaged southern California far worse than many other regions of the country, as aerospace and electronics firms shed hundreds of thousands of workers. Even so, the school did exceptionally well in placing its Class of 1994, winning its Career Center head, Kathryn Van Ness, praise from graduates. Only 2 percent of the class failed to have a job offer by commencement, and a few of those launched their own businesses. Anderson grads averaged 2.74 job offers each—better than the 2.36 average for the 40-plus schools surveyed by BW. Some 123 companies came to recruit on campus, and 1634 job opportunities were posted via correspondence. The major recruiters: Deloitte & Touche (9), Citibank (7), Goldman Sachs (6), Hewlett-Packard (6), J.P. Morgan (5), Clorox (5), Morgan Stanley (5), Bankers Trust (4), EDS Management Consulting (4), Intel (4), Merrill Lynch (4), and Smith Barney Shearson (4).

If Hollywood isn't all that apparent in the school's top employers, the influence of the film capital of the world is apparent in Anderson's annual Cabaret, a talent show featuring three hours of performances by faculty and students. The school's location has a big influence on students' extracurricular activities. Since the weather is warm year-round, many social events take place outside, including the Thursday night beer busts held on the school patio. If Anderson MBAs don't feel like going to the beach to surf, swim, and sunbathe, they can hike and camp in a nearby national forest. In the winter, weekend ski trips are sponsored by You See L.A., a club that helps students visit tourist attractions such as Disneyland, Universal Studios, and the Norton Simon museum. Like other Los Angeles natives, Anderson MBAs have problems finding an affordable place to live and a parking spot. UCLA has a limited amount of graduate student housing. Most MBAs live in Brentwood and Santa Monica, beautiful but expensive neighborhoods. You need a car to survive in L.A., but many UCLA students take the bus to school because of the paucity of campus parking. Other students car-pool, and a few have been known to arrive on skateboards and roller blades. After all, this *is* L.A.

Contact: Linda Baldwin, director of admissions, Suite 3371, 310-825-6944
Final application deadlines: April 1 for fall

Outstanding Faculty

1. William M. Cockrum (****): It's noteworthy that UCLA's best faculty member is merely an "adjunct," lacking the prestige and pay of the full professors here but teaching the professorial types more than a thing or two about the primary calling of their profession. Cockrum took his place at the front of the classroom at UCLA in 1985, just after compiling 24 years of experience in investment banking at Becker Paribas Inc. where he rose to vice chairman. The 1961 Harvard MBA immediately proved he was as good a teacher as an investment banker. His Harvard-style teaching, heavily interactive and based on case studies, also features group grades. Cockrum's courses on Financing the Emerging Enterprise and Business Ethics are among the most popular offerings at the school. When Cockrum isn't the No. 1 winner of the outstanding teacher award at Anderson, an honor he has captured in 1986, 1989, and 1992, he's always among the top five finalists.

2. Jose de la Torre (****): Every other Friday, he teaches an immensely popular class called International Negotiations, which meets from 8:30 a.m. to 4:30 p.m. The marathon sessions find the tireless and engaging teacher in great form. He recently came to UCLA after spending 13 years at the prestigious INSEAD in France. He boasts degrees in aerospace engineering and business from Penn State, and a doctorate from Harvard Business School. De la Torre is a true internationalist: Born and raised in Havana, Cuba, he has lived and worked in Europe, Asia, and Latin America. He's also consulted with such global firms as British Petroleum, British Aerospace, Montedison, GKN, Heineken, Akzo, and Hughes Aircraft. And he's the author of over 40 books and articles on international trade and investment.

3. Ronald C. Goodstein (****): Former retailer-turned-academic, he joined UCLA in mid-1989 as a marketing expert. His classroom lectures include plenty of tales from his days at The Broadway when Goodstein was a divisional group manager responsible for the $2 million-a-year domestics department. He actually started out as a group manager with R. H. Macy Corp. after graduating from the University of Virginia in 1982 with a bachelor's in business. He earned his Ph.D. in marketing at Duke University in 1990. He was a finalist for Anderson's Professor of the Year in both 1991 and 1992.

4. George S. Yip (***): Neat and dapper, this British, Harvard-trained adjunct professor is wowing students with his knowhow of business strategy. He earned his doctorate in policy and organization in 1980, from that east coast business school of some reknown.

5. S. William Yost (***): Yet another of UCLA's super adjunct profs, Yost is one of the school's top case-study teachers. An expert in operations and production, he displays an uncanny ability to explain the most technical of issues with ease. Yost, who earned his doctorate at Harvard in 1968, also exudes a memorable persona, with a Rollie Fingers–like mustache that is waxed and curled up at the ends.

6. George T. Geis (**): Voted the Outstanding Teacher of the Year in 1987 and 1990, Geis teaches management science, informations systems, and accounting. His course, Using Microcomputers for Strategic Information, focuses on financial modeling and business planning. He boasts a trio of degrees: a B.S. from Purdue, an MBA from UCLA, and a Ph.D. from the University of Southern California.

Other Best Bets: *Richard W. Roll* (finance), *Dominique M. Hanssens* (marketing), *J. Fred Weston* (finance), and *Randolph E. Bucklin* (marketing)

Prominent Alumni: Howard W. Davis, president of Tracy-Locke Advertising; Laurence D. Fink, chairman and chief executive of Blackstone Financial Management; Lester B. Korn, former chairman of Korn/Ferry International; Joan W. Robertson Spogli, managing director of Merrill Lynch Capital Markets

Anderson MBAs Sound Off

*What makes Anderson so unique is that we crunch numbers in paradise. Sure, you have to wipe the sand off your "HP" once in awhile, but we get great tans and a great education. All of my friends had multiple offers from top Wall Street firms such as Goldman Sachs, Morgan Stanley, Salomon Brothers, and CS First Boston. I have no regrets.—**Finance Associate***

*Almost everything about Anderson exceeded my expectations. The two major shortcomings were substandard facilities and state funding/budget problems— both of which are being solved as we speak. I'm certain I would not be trying to start my own business without the support and confidence of the Anderson entrepreneurial program. From talking to my friends at other top business schools, it seems to me that no one else has anything like it.—**Entrepreneur***

*This was a rigorous and demanding program. You were having so much fun, though, that it didn't ever feel like a grind. The business community really embraces and supports the program.—**Consultant***

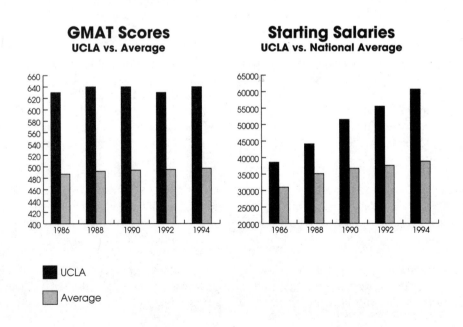

GMAT Scores
UCLA vs. Average

Starting Salaries
UCLA vs. National Average

■ UCLA

▨ Average

10. Massachusetts Institute of Technology

Sloan School of Management
50 Memorial Drive
Cambridge, Massachusetts 02142

Corporate ranking: 9	*Graduate ranking:* 12
Enrollment: 500	*Annual tuition & fees:* $21,690
Women: 25%	*Room and board:* $15,000
Non-U.S.: 35%	*Average GMAT score:* 650
Minority: 6%	*GMAT range:* 480 to 780
Part-time: None	*Average GPA:* 3.5
Average age: 28	*GPA range:* 2.8 to 4.0
Applicants accepted: 25%	*Accepted applicants enrolled:* 75%
Median starting pay: $76,750	*Average starting pay:* $80,500

Teaching methods: Lecture, 33%   Case study, 33%   Group projects, 33%

Think of MIT's Sloan School of Management and a series of images quickly spring to mind: Lester Thurow. Quant jocks. Technology. A rigid curriculum heavily flavored with finance and economic courses. A master's thesis.

Forget it. Thurow, a popular economist and prolific writer, is no longer dean of the Sloan School. Even liberal arts majors can move with ease through the new, highly flexible curriculum. It's now possible to get your master's here without taking a single course in technology. And for the first time in the school's 42-year history, Sloan allowed students in 1994 to skip a once-required thesis for its M.S. in management and instead gain an MBA degree.

The changes come under Glen Urban, who has been at Sloan since 1966 and quietly served behind Thurow as deputy dean from 1987 to 1991. Like the globe-trotting Thurow, Urban is something of a Renaissance man himself. He has sailed his yacht along the East Coast from Novia Scotia to the Caribbean, helicopter-skied in the Bugaboos, explored out-of-the-way places like Easter Island, and sculpted steel, marble, and stone structures. And like Thurow, he articulates a compelling mission for the school: to provide "innovation-driven companies with people who are analytic and technical, who are team builders and know how to lead."

Thurow, of course, brought much attention to Sloan. He hired faculty experts in other cultures and countries, lured a greater percentage of non-U.S. students to the school, and focused the school's efforts around the themes of technology and global business. His single greatest accomplishment as dean is MIT's highly regarded Leaders in Manufacturing program, an intense, 24-month experience allowing students to earn master's degrees in both manufacturing and engineering. The centerpiece of the program is a six-month management internship at one of 13 sponsoring U.S. manufacturers, including Alcoa, Boeing, Chrysler, Eastman Kodak, and Motorola. The program's mission: to help the U.S. recapture world leadership in manufacturing, long a neglected area of study at most business schools. In 1994, only 46 of the 250 people who applied for Leaders in Manufacturing were enrolled.

Urban, who took over the deanship in mid-1993, was an immediate beneficiary of Thurow's hard work. Just nine months after he succeeded Thurow, Urban saw *U.S. News & World Report* rank the school No. 2, behind only Stanford. It was Sloan's best ranking ever in a national survey (largely because its students boast high GMAT scores and because of the school's stellar placement stats). "I inherited a school in good shape," says Urban. "So I will do my best along with the faculty, staff, and students to move us ahead."

To that end, Urban has rolled out a new, innovative curriculum that emphasizes integration and leaves more room for electives. In the fall term, the core consists of a half-dozen "interlocked subjects." Translation: faculty meet regularly to plan the integration of the subjects and ensure balance in the program. In your first term, you'll take a trio of "perspectives" courses: Economic Analysis for Business Decisions teaches students key microeconomics principles for business and industry analysis; Data, Models, and Decisions introduces students to techniques in using data for decisions; and Organizational Processes focuses on the organization of the future. The other three remaining subjects are basic B-school fare: financial and managerial accounting, communications, and strategy.

Students move through the first-semester basics in cohorts, which include faculty mentors who maintain regular links with the group. Class projects are assigned to teams formed during the two-week orientation that work together throughout the semester. Integration is critical to the success of these changes. So far, grads give the school good marks for trying to integrate the core courses with each other. But they are mixed about how well the school has delivered on this promise. A 1994 satisfaction survey by Sloan, for example, discovered that one of five first-year students believe the core was not well integrated, and nearly a third were simply ambivalent about it.

In the spring term, students can design their own program or enroll in one of four career-focused management tracks. The self-managed program, however, requires that you choose four half-semester subjects from a set of six that range from intro to marketing to a course on information systems. Then you're free to sample any of Sloan's 125 electives or three courses in other MIT departments, or even at Harvard University. Sloan even gives you full credit for language and political science courses. If you take the management track route, you're required a minimum of 90 units of class credit in your chosen area over the three remaining semesters. An average full-semester subject earns 9 units of credit, and a typical load ranges from 54 to 60-plus units per term. So even the "management track" leaves time for additional electives—even as early as your second semester.

For Tracksters, there's also a professional seminar, called the ProSeminar, where cohorts of faculty, students, and outside managers meet together over a two-semester period to share experiences and expertise. Each includes summer internships that reinforce and implement classroom learning. The four tracks: Strategic Global Management for the Consulting Industry; Financial Engineering; Financial Management, and Product Development and Management.

These are fairly innovative changes at an already superb business school. So why doesn't Sloan rank higher in BUSINESS WEEK surveys? For years, Sloan graduates griped about the quality of the teaching—a critical component of BW's rankings. Under Thurow, a Committee on Teaching launched efforts to improve in this area. Our 1994 survey turned up the first real evidence of improvement. In both the core and elective offerings, the quality of teaching was for the first time judged above average, among the top 40-plus schools in the sample.

No school, moreover, scored better than Sloan in having faculty who are thought to be at the leading edge of knowledge in their fields. Graduates ranked the faculty an amazing 9.9 out of 10 in this area. Yet the school still lags in one key teaching dimension: the availability of faculty outside of class. The BW poll shows that Sloan is among the true laggards in this category (only 3 of 41 schools ranked lower). And even Sloan's own internal satisfaction survey found that fully a third of the students believe they do not have enough access to professors beyond the classroom. Sloan profs clearly are valued and well compensated as outside consultants, but Urban needs to make sure the faculty spends more time with students.

MIT's quantitative/technical image still can be intimidating to liberal arts types, so prospective students should visit the campus, attend a few classes, and seek out grads to talk to them about their experiences. "A lot of people believe Sloan is for people who want to get into the nitty-gritty of technology, but when you visit the school you see the emphasis is on management," says Scott Beardsley, an alum who now works as a consultant. Sloan holds recruiting sessions throughout the United States and in several international locations where potential applicants and alums are brought together. The school also holds an open house after the admissions season, designed to woo students who have been accepted by other top B-schools. More than half of the school's students attended an open house.

The only academic requirement for attending the school—other than an undergraduate degree—is one semester of work each in calculus and economic theory. If you haven't sat through those classes, you should try to take them before arriving on campus. That way, you'll be up to speed with classmates right from the start.

The two-week-long orientation program is run entirely by the students. In one version, organized and run by second-years to greet the Class of 1993, the newcomers were divided into Zoo Groups—blue cheetahs and green zebras, who were managed by second-year Zookeepers. They played Outward Bound-like games, conducted a treasure hunt, feasted on barbeque, and stumbled along a pub crawl to some of the best watering holes in Boston. There was also a Citicorp ethics exercise, breakfasts and case discussions with faculty, a workshop on diversity, and a dessert party at the Copley Plaza Hotel, where music and dancing went on into the early hours.

It was a good way to ease into a tough program in which the work borders on the excessive. In fact, incoming students are told the most important thing they'll learn is "the art of selective neglect"—meaning figuring out what is critically important and what you can ignore. MIT's theoretical emphasis has traditionally contrasted with the all-case method of Harvard, though lately the programs have been moving closer together. MIT's prejudice against competition between individuals is demonstrated by its policy of not posting grades.

The school's long-standing emphasis on the quantitative still scares away some prospective students and helps to attract a lot of engineering undergraduates who account for 40 percent of the students. But not everyone who attends Sloan has a plastic pen holder in the pocket and a calculator attached to the belt. Sloanies are a diverse, eclectic group with an entrepreneurial bent. Management classes are also open to students from other MIT schools, allowing a wide range of viewpoints in class. At least half of the grads in each Sloan class plan to start their own businesses. One student group, New Ventures Association, boasts a 10K competition, awarding prizes of up to $10,000 to students for top-flight business plans.

Of all the major business schools, none can claim a higher foreign enrollment. Roughly one in three Sloan students comes from outside the U.S., the greatest number from the Far East, where a degree from MIT is considered a status symbol. Sloan receives about 200 applications from Japanese nationals each year, and narrows these down to about 45 semifinalists. An associate dean travels to Japan to interview the semifinalists personally, particularly looking for those with outgoing personalities. To ease the entry of non-U.S. students, Sloan offers a two-week workshop for international students, held prior to orientation. And to continually remind everyone of how global the school has become, some 55 full-size country flags hang in Sloan's main lobby, reflecting the different nationalities attending the school. "You can't ignore that when you're walking to class," says David A. Weber, director of the MBA program.

Regardless of where you're from, virtually all Sloanies end up in an international learning experience. In the spring of 1994, for example, the school fielded five separate study tours that brought students to such countries as Japan, Korea, China, Hong Kong, Taiwan, Mexico, Russia, and Hungary. These tours are organized by the students, who also sponsor pre-trip, month- to semester-long seminars on the countries they plan to visit. Typically, two faculty go with each student group during spring break.

There are many signs of MIT's science/math culture. A graduate of the program doesn't receive an MBA but rather a master's of science in management (MS). Buildings are numbered instead of named. Along with MIT's economics and political science departments, the Sloan school is housed in six buildings on MIT's East Campus along the Charles River. Many buildings at MIT have been recently renovated, including the Sloan Building. One large room in the complex has been redesigned for students, and a new building going up next door will increase the number of available classrooms.

Many students arrive at MIT via the Boston subway system's Red Line. The MIT subway stop at Kendall Square has been refurbished as part of a $250 million redevelopment project that includes a new Marriott Hotel and Legal Seafood, a favorite Boston restaurant. Erratic service on the Red Line is a pet peeve of Sloanies and recently inspired a team of students to undertake a systematic analysis of the line for a class project. The team's conclusion: Red Line trains are more prompt than other color-coded Boston trains, but Red Line riders are more critical.

Team projects and study groups are a way of life at MIT. Even when not required to work in teams, students form study groups and divide reading among themselves. The small size of the management school helps create a friendly and cooperative atmosphere.

"When you know the person sitting next to you, you're less likely to trounce him," says Jeffrey Barks, associate dean. Students are on a first-name basis with faculty and administration members. Teacher/student interaction can at times be strong. In one instance, an Ecuadorian student's paper sparked the interest of Nobel Laureate Franco Modigliani, who traveled to Ecuador to defend the proposal before the government. In another case, two profs joined with a pair of students to travel to Estonia to research investment opportunities.

Most of MIT's social whirl is coordinated by the student-run Graduate Management Society, which sponsors boat cruises on the Charles, ski trips, barbecues, and a weekly "Consumption Function." Several times each semester, groups of students from the more than 40 countries represented at Sloan highlight the food, drink, and music of their region of the world. Such events inevitably include a karaoke night, where students croon golden oldies through a microphone, usually after several rounds of dry beer, or a Latin American fiesta. Over 25 student clubs and athletic teams offer a range of activities from letting off steam in intramural contests to taking field trips to a Nissan or Saturn plant, the latter being sponsored by the Sloan Auto Industries Club.

Sloanies unwind at the Muddy Charles, a bar a couple of minutes from the management school. Since there aren't a lot of residential areas near MIT, students will often go over the bridge into Beacon Hill for drinks or dinner. The lack of off-campus housing near MIT and the school's proximity to the Red Line means that students are scattered all around Cambridge and Boston. As a result, they frequently socialize in their own neighborhoods. School-sponsored parties, above and beyond the calendar of events planned by clubs, bring the whole school together four or five times a year.

Some of the biggest parties are likely to occur near graduation, because Sloanies are among the highest-paid MBAs in the world. The Class of 1994 landed median starting packages of $76,750. Toss in other compensation, such as tuition reimbursement and year-end bonuses, and the average reaches over $80,000. By commencement, an extraordinary 97.4 percent of the class had job offers in hand. On average, each of those graduates was entertaining 3.3 offers—better than any B-school rival with the exception of Stanford and Harvard. Thanks to the Leaders in Manufacturing program, an impressive 16 percent of the class went off into jobs in operations and manufacturing. But management consulting is the most popular destination for Sloanies, attracting 35 percent of the graduates. That's a major reason why the average pay packages are so high, and why the school has a management track for consulting.

Though consumer packaging companies are in short supply here, Sloan attracted 184 recruiting firms to its campus in 1994. They conducted an amazing 2800 interviews for a graduating class of fewer than 250 students. Another 500 job offers were posted by correspondence. The big hires: McKinsey (9); A.T. Kearney (8); General Motors (5); Hewlett-Packard (5); Intel (5); American Management Systems (4); Bain & Co. (4); Merrill Lynch (4); and Monitor Co. (4).

Dean Urban can be comfortably assured by the success of his students.

Contact: Marilyn Mendel Han, director of admissions, 617-253-3730
Final application deadline: February 3 for fall

Outstanding Faculty

1. Paul Asquith (****): His thought-provoking course on Mergers and Acquisitions is always oversubscribed. A scholar as well as a super finance teacher, Asquith loves the details. "I engage in very data-intensive work," he says. "You find out things other people don't see when you look at the details." He holds a trio of degrees in economics, a bachelor's from Michigan State, and a master's and Ph.D. from Chicago. Asquith came to Sloan as a visiting professor in 1989 after teaching at the Harvard Business School. That was the same year he won an award for the best article—an analysis of junk bonds—published in the *Journal of Finance.* Then, in 1990, he was voted the best teacher by the Sloan master's students for his teaching in a number of finance courses, notably Capital Investment Decisions and Corporate Financial Management.

2. Rebecca Henderson (***): Former McKinsey & Co. analyst, Henderson is a young, sharp management professor who has carved out a niche in studying why corporate giants have so much trouble innovating new products. She holds a B.S. degree in mechanical engineering from MIT and a doctorate of philosophy in business economics from Harvard University. Henderson joined Sloan's faculty in 1988.

3. Jeremy C. Stein (**): This popular management professor won kudos from students at the 1994 annual Faculty Appreciation Day held on the last day of classes. Stein was recognized for his ability to make finance understandable and relevant, and for his concern with the advancement of his students. Raved one: "Not even once did we wonder about the relevance of anything he taught!"

4. John D. Sterman (**): An expert in management systems, Associate Professor Sterman is director of MIT's System Dynamics Group. He is a classroom pleaser, even though a very serious scholar. Topic of a recent research study authored by Sterman: "Mode Locking and Entrainment of Endogenous Economic Cycles." Really!

5. Stephan Schrader (**): A fun-loving prof who brings much energy and enthusiasm to the classroom, Schrader is an assistant professor of management. Sloanies honored him in 1994 for "a teaching style which combines wisdom, wit, concern for his students, and excellent presentation and classroom discussion skills."

6. John R. Hauser (**): He teaches introductory subjects in marketing and wins praise for his "excellent combination of theory and practical applications of marketing theory. Grads say Hauser is especially effective in getting less vocal international students involved in case debates. Co-author with Dean Urban of Design and Marketing of New Products, he's also co-director of Sloan's International Center for Research on the Management of Technology.

Other Best Bets: *Alfredo M. Hofman* (management), *Edgar H. Schein* (management), *Arnold Barnett* (statistics), and *Mary P. Rowe* (management)

Prominent Alumni: John Reed, chairman of Citicorp; Richard Ayers, chairman of The Stanley Works; Sandra Helton, treasurer of Corning Inc.; Judy C. Lewent, senior vice president, Merck & Co.

Sloan MBAs Sound Off

Sloan is making the necessary changes to become a world-class business school. In the past, the administration lost sight of the fact that the student is the customer. With the ascension of Glen Urban as dean, this school is improving greatly—and breaking commonly held stereotypes.—**Career Path Unknown**

Master's students remain second-class citizens at this research institution. The faculty varies widely in its willingness to spend time with students. Ethics courses and leadership courses are nonexistent.—**Career Path Unknown**

Sloan offers a unique opportunity to business students—the thesis. It's a chance to explore a topic more in-depth, or as I did, to conduct a study for an organization. I did a market research study for Plimoth Plantation, a living history museum in Plymouth, MA. Sloan offers a combination of lecture and case-study classes that really gives students the opportunity to take a high-level approach as well as learn how to actually do a problem, not just supervise someone doing it.
—**Market Research Analyst**

Sloan is an excellent place for learning and making long-lasting friendships. I have had a blast during my two years here. The faculty, administration, and students are friendly and down-to-earth. We are internally competitive, but never at the expense of other students. What a difference from my undergraduate days at Wharton, where I studied with a bunch of pretentious grade-grubbers. Sloan doesn't offer a full breadth of classes to meet everyone's needs. But for focused people, those interested in innovation and leadership in finance, operations management, information technology, and high-tech marketing, this place is great!—**Securities Analyst**

The only shortcoming is the facility. The classrooms are often too small, and there is insufficient space for group meetings. This shortcoming, however, is being eliminated with the new Tang Center. I especially appreciated the collegial and cooperative atmosphere and environment created and nurtured by students. Everyone is willing to spend time to explain a confusing concept or provide advice on your job search, or even to trade contacts.—**Consultant**

Sloan needs to incorporate more international cases into the curriculum and get international students to speak more in class. I believe that more courses should be taught cross-functionally and that there should be more discussion concerning the ethical implications of decisions. All in all, however, I was very happy with my experience. Not having a quantitative background, I thought Sloan would be far more difficult.—**Consultant**

Sloan is a small, highly supportive educational environment. The stress is on education, and one learns the newest management philosophies. Occasionally this is at the expense of more practical business skills. Sloan is currently not up to par with another local business school (Harvard) in networking and more aggressive business-survival tactics. The benefit to Sloan's approach is that it offers a flexible environment, more conducive to diversity and individuality.
—Consultant

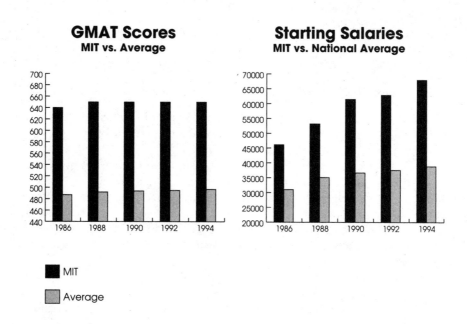

11. Duke University

The Fuqua School of Business
Durham, North Carolina 27708

Corporate ranking: 14
Enrollment: 660
Women: 30%
Non-U.S.: 17%
Minority: 14%
Part-time: None
Average age: 26.8
Applicants accepted: 26%
Median starting pay: $67,500

Graduate ranking: 8
Annual tuition & fees: $21,910
Room and board: $9300
Average GMAT score: 623
GMAT range: 360 to 770
Average GPA: 3.31
GPA range: 2.0 to 4.0
Accepted applicants enrolled: 57%
Average starting pay: $70,490

Teaching methods: Lecture, 33%   Case study, 33%   Simulations, 34%

Listen to Dean Thomas F. Keller describe the Fuqua School of Business: "It's innovative, vital, collegial, team-oriented, a real community. People are pushing and shoving and wanting to go places. It's an ambitious place."

Keller should know. A shrewd promoter, he pushed and shoved Fuqua from relative obscurity to the top tier of the business school world in little more than a decade. He took over the job in 1974—only two years after the school graduated its first class of MBAs—and made all the right moves to establish Duke as a force to be reckoned with. It would be hard to imagine the school without the former accounting professor at its helm. But all good things must come to an end. Keller will retire in 1995, after more than 20 years as dean. He's leaving Fuqua with a new curriculum set in place.

Yet, in 1991, his name surfaced as one of four finalists for the deanship at the University of Michigan's business school. It was enough to cause chest pains for university administrators, who hurriedly signed him to a new contract. If Keller was getting tired or antsy enough to consider a change of venue, he now displays no signs of it.

In 1992 he oversaw a complete revamping of the MBA program to, in his words, "graduate the CEOs of the twenty-first century." As far as curriculum changes go, Duke's new program stacks up with the likes of Wharton and Michigan as among the most dramatic. Every course in the school's catalog, from the building-block classes in the core to all the electives, underwent major revisions. Each of the four semesters now begin with an intensive week-long "integrative learning experience." First-years are thrown into a "personal development program" that takes a year of coursework in business communications and managerial computing. Students can select 12 or more electives during the two-year program, up from only 8 before. The upshot: The number of "contact hours" between students and faculty has increased by a third.

The most visible alteration is the one-week learning experiences that kick off each semester. From the start, the incoming class is divided into four groups and thrown into Team Building and Leadership Development. After a day in class exploring leadership and teamwork, newcomers are shepherded to an outdoors ropes course half an hour south of

Durham for team-building exercises. The week features personal assessment exercises, a community service project, and personal career planning. The idea: to get you to focus on what you want to achieve in your lifetime.

The second semester opens with a one-week computer simulation on the airline industry in which eight teams of 40 students compete against each other as they gain greater insight into Competitive Business Strategy. Team members assume the jobs of managers in finance, marketing, employee relations, operations, and strategy. The exercise is designed to give students the opportunity to apply what they learned in the first-year core courses. Jump-starting the second year is a series of programs cobbled together under the theme of Competitive Advantage Through People and Processes. The week is dedicated to examining how managing people effectively is increasingly tied to competitive success. Multiculturalism and diversity also are explored in depth. The last semester begins with a week-long experience on Complex Management Problems, in which MBAs examine a major controversial issue currently facing a firm or an industry. Teams prepare position papers on the topic and debate the issue, which could range from defense spending to product dumping. In 1993, student teams looked into how technology is changing the way people work and the issues being confronted by executives. Teams developed position papers for 40 projects sponsored by such companies as AT&T, Corning, Federal Express, Ford, IBM, Hewlett-Packard, MCI, and Microsoft.

The most compelling changes in the curriculum, however, are more subtle. In the old format, each course required two classes a week for an hour and 20 minutes each over 14 weeks. Classes still meet twice a week under the new format, but they last for 2 hours and 15 minutes each in seven-week terms. The result: contact hours per course fell to 27 hours from 35 hours. This change alone forced faculty to reexamine the content of their classes, making professors discard older, less relevant material in favor of more topical, critical information. That's a coup because many professors, not wanting to exert too much effort, teach the same course the same way for years on end.

The longer class format also required faculty to rethink the way they teach. After all, a two-hour-plus lecture in every class is likely to work better than Sominex in putting students to sleep. So professors have no choice except to alter their teaching styles. Consider the core course in Organizational Behavior, now dubbed Managerial Effectiveness. "Instead of having a bunch of lectures, a few case studies, and a mid-term and final, it's completely different," says Wesley Magat, a senior associate dean. There are more case studies; assignments are due each day of class; much of the work is performed in preselected teams that do class presentations, and the midterm has been dumped in favor of spot quizzes. The course doesn't even have a textbook, but rather a 3-inch-thick batch of readings that focus on six major themes from motivation to workplace diversity. Only two years earlier, the offering was little more than a textbook-based survey course on how organizations work. "It has changed from a lecture course to one in which students are responsible for much of what goes on in class," adds Magat.

The downside to these changes is that Dean Keller will be asking professors who aren't especially good teachers to make some demanding adjustments in their teaching styles. The school has a reputation for having young, inexperienced, and overly theoretical instructors teach the basic courses. Not surprisingly, the quality of teaching in the core is below average for a top school—based on BUSINESS WEEK's survey of the graduating class of 1994 at 41 schools. It didn't help that four years ago Fuqua hired as many as 10 new instructors and immediately put them in the classrooms to teach. In elective offerings, however, the school's professors did slightly better than average—though graduates complain that too many of the better teachers have been siphoned off by Fuqua's executive education efforts.

Even so, Keller aims to please. To enhance teaching quality, he makes public the student evaluations of teachers. Again and again, he has proven to be one of the most customer-responsive deans in the game. Keller recently ditched a deal with AT&T to offer their managers a short-cut MBA when students objected. In the spring of 1992, when a popular course failed to appear on the schedule to the chagrin of one student, he juggled teaching loads so that it could be offered. No wonder that in BUSINESS WEEK's 1994 survey, Fuqua scored among the highest in responsiveness to student concerns and opinions of the 41 schools polled. Keller has applied Total Quality Management concepts to the school to ensure that everything it does is performed to the best standards possible. The result: The dean has created one of the most user-friendly environments anywhere—an excellent business library, superb computer facilities, clean and modern classrooms.

Indeed, it's hard for a visiting applicant not to be impressed by Duke and the Research Triangle Park area. Duke is one of four major universities in the triangle of Durham, Chapel Hill, and Raleigh. The mild climate, the rural yet progressive environment, and the modern-looking Fuqua School have powers to charm. The concrete and glass B-school building on the edge of the west campus of the university boasts an airy mall-like environment with trees, horseshoe-shaped classrooms, and a 500-seat auditorium. A new executive education facility—linked to the school by a bridge across a ravine—opened in May of 1989. It's a 10-minute walk to the Gothic-looking Duke Chapel, the heart of the university campus.

Once a student, however, you won't have too much time to wander around. Under Keller's revamped curriculum, most students get to select their first 2 electives in the fourth term of the second semester. Then, you can pick up another 9 or 10 in the second year, when there is only one required course in international business. The school doesn't require formal concentrations in any subject, so students are free to choose from among any of the 70 electives offered in an academic year. Fuqua, however, formally lists two concentrations: one in accounting, the other in health services management. The latter major resulted when the university's Department of Health Administration was transferred to the Fuqua School in 1993. Keller expects about 15 to 20 graduates a year with the HSM concentration. You can also take up to four courses in other schools or departments at Duke University, including two foreign language classes.

Like most other B-schools, Duke draws heavily upon Corporate America for guest speakers and lecturers. The 1993–1994 lineup of distinguished speakers featured Norman Augustine, chairman of Martin Marietta Corp.; Lawrence Bossidy, chairman of Allied-Signal, Inc.; John Akers, former chairman of IBM; and William Reilly, chairman of K-III Communications. The school also boasts three full-time executives in residence: William A. Sax, a former vice president of Unocal Corp.; Robert M. Price, retired chairman and CEO, Control Data Corporation; and Alex McMahon, former chairman of the university's

Department of Health Administration. McMahon has toted up a number of years in the health care business, with Blue Cross and Blue Shield of North Carolina and with the American Hospital Association. Whether dispensing career advice or telling war stories, these executives provide a real-world perspective on business issues.

What Keller doesn't want to change is the "Team Fuqua" culture that sets the school apart from many other B-schools with similar resources. Students play an active role in the school's affairs. They sit on the curriculum committee, the MBA programs advisory committee, the admissions committee, the placement committee and the committee to select a new dean. Students have even introduced mid-semester class evaluations which they administer, compile, and return to the professors so that they can improve their teaching skills before the course is over. "There is something unique and special here, a true spirit," says one alum. "The underlying foundation is teamwork: Every class I've taken, with the exception of only one or two, has required me to work in a group."

Fuquons and Fuquites, as Duke students call themselves, have an unusual degree of latitude to do their own thing. They run and manage The Kiosk, Fuqua's snack bar and store. They arrange numerous trips abroad, including a two-week business tour of 14 leading companies in Japan. They sponsor several major conferences each year on such topics as entrepreneurship, marketing, and international business, as well as a series of wacky games to benefit Special Olympics. In 1994, the Fuqua-MBA Games raised $50,000 for the cause. MBAs from 10 different schools competed in such things as a corporate swimsuit relay and a briefcase throw. A new tradition was begun in 1990 with the first of what has become an annual Pig Pickin'. MBAs sponsor the open-pit pig roast on a Saturday in April and invite the entire university to the party.

These events and many more are reported in full in *Over the Counter,* the school's monthly newspaper. Between classes, they scurry to Brightleaf Square at Lakewood Shopping Center, a five-minute drive from campus, where MBAs meet for drinks at Satisfaction or T.J. Hoops, the ultimate sports bar. At Hoops, grads gather to watch the university's basketball team on large-screen TVs and play pool on one of 15 tables. When the Duke Blue Devils are on the road, an alternate cheerleader often comes down to lead the crowd. Every Friday at 5 p.m., MBAs also get together in the atrium of the B-school or in the student lounge for beer and snacks. The new R. David Thomas Center for Executive Education offers a delicious all-you-can-eat buffet featuring three gourmet entrees a day for $7.25.

Ever since the popular movie *Bull Durham,* Fuquons have been trekking downtown to hoot and holler for the Durham Bulls, the professional baseball team upon which the movie was based. Blue-collars and Ph.D.s converge at the stadium where the school sometimes rents a tent where it serves beer and hamburgers. Like just about everything else in Durham, it's no more than a 15-minute ride away. Most MBAs live off-campus in privately owned apartments just a walk or bike ride away. Duke also boasts a complex of Town House Apartments with a swimming pool for graduate students located about three blocks from the main East-West Campus bus line. About 15 percent of Fuqua students live in university-owned housing. If you have to drive to school, you'll be familiar with 751, the nickname for the Fuqua parking lot, about a three-minute walk from school. The lot is so named because it's just off Route 751.

As a relatively young program, Fuqua lacks a large and older alumni network of contacts. The school has graduated over 4500 MBAs since 1972, when it turned out its first class of just a dozen graduates. Keller has been working hard to nurture his alumni base into a viable support network. The school has established alumni clubs in Atlanta, Boston, Chicago, Dallas, Houston, Los Angeles, New York, the Research Triangle, Indianapolis, Washington, D.C., Western Europe, and Japan. An attractive alumni magazine, *Exchange,* keeps alums informed of the latest campus happenings three times a year. In 1992, the school also began to pair up first-year MBA students with 125 alumni who volunteered to serve as career mentors.

The program will make alumni even more loyal to the school. Not that Fuqua's alums haven't already displayed a great deal of loyalty. Each of the last six graduating classes has donated $100,000 or more to the school by commencement. In 1992, the parting gift went to fund permanent recycling stations and an endowment to continue language instruction in German and Japanese for MBAs. The for-credit courses meet four times a week, from 6 to 7:30 p.m., for three terms.

Where do Fuqua alums tend to settle? The school's latest count, in 1994, lists 133 alums at IBM—by far the largest single employer of Fuqua grads; 60 at Northern Telecom; 41 at Procter & Gamble; 40 at General Electric Corp.; 39 at AT&T; 38 at Chase Manhattan; 32 at Merrill Lynch; and 30 at American Airlines. Some 20 or more alums draw their paychecks from the likes of Carolina Power & Light, Burroughs Wellcome, Coca-Cola, General Motors, Sara Lee, and Philip Morris-Kraft—a pretty impressive list of blue chips. The directory lists 19 Fuqua grads at McKinsey & Co.

About 95.8 percent of the Class of 1994 had job offers at graduation, and they averaged 2.78 job offers each versus the 2.36 average for the 40-plus schools surveyed. In 1994, some 166 companies arrived on campus to interview Fuqua grads. All told, they conducted 5592 interviews. Another 1360 job opportunities were posted via correspondence. Who carted away the most MBAs from Fuqua? American Airlines led the race with 11 hires, followed by Deloitte & Touche (9); Merrill Lynch (7); Coopers & Lybrand (7); Goldman Sachs (6); Morgan Stanley (6); General Motors (5); and EDS Management Consulting (5). McKinsey, Chase Manhattan, Smith Barney Shearson, J.P. Morgan, Arthur Andersen, and NationsBank hired four grads each. Now *that's* a lineup that Keller can justifiably crow about.

Contact: Anne Sandoe-Thorp, director of admissions, 919-660-7705
Application deadline: Rolling admissions

Outstanding Faculty

1. S. Viswanthan (****): "Vish" believes that every MBA student must master corporate finance, and he expects them to work hard at it. "My courses are not easy, and I expect every student who takes my class to be motivated to give his personal best. In return I endeavor to deliver the best corporate finance course in the country." Apparently he's keeping up his end of the bargain—the class of 1994 voted him Teacher of the Year. This Kellogg Ph.D., who came to Fuqua in 1986, received tenure in 1994.

2. William Boulding (****): He's known for his humor, confidence, and enthusiasm, but students don't dismiss this laid-back marketing professor as a pushover. Boulding challenges his students' questions and opinions, and they wouldn't want to come to his class unprepared because even though he's funny, the prof runs a tight ship. He has won Duke's outstanding teaching award in the past. Boulding draws on extensive experience from work with the likes of IBM, AT&T, Bank of America, Sears, Northern Telecom, Eli Lilly, and Ford. He came to Duke in 1984, after earning a Ph.D. at Wharton. Tall, slender, and athletic, Boulding was the center of the faculty intramural basketball team.

3. Simon Johnson (****): This English native speaks fluent Russian with a British accent. Johnson runs Fuqua's Business Center for Manager Development in St. Petersburg, and his research focuses on Russia, Ukraine, and Poland. This young, dynamic, prof brings his real-world research into his international economics course, and received a teaching award last year. Johnson came to Fuqua armed with a Ph.D. from MIT.

4. Campbell Harvey (***): In his investment analysis course, MBAs design their own asset-management software package. This project has helped some students to land jobs, and now some companies actually look for MBAs who took his course. He's also known for teaching classes outside in nice weather. This productive, intense finance professor can be found working on evenings and weekends. Harvey arrived at Fuqua in 1986 after earning his Ph.D. from Chicago. He is a consultant to the World Bank and has also consulted for Salomon Brothers, Morgan Stanley, and Kidder Peabody.

5. James E. Smith (***): This youthful and cerebral prof joined Fuqua in 1990, after earning his Ph.D. at Stanford, where he also toted up a pair of degrees in electrical engineering. Would you believe he's a top vote-getter for teaching an introductory probability and statistics course, and an elective in decision analysis? You know he's *got* to be good!

6. Harris Sondak (**): Negotiations and business ethics are his classroom specialties. Students from his negotiations class immediately apply what they learn to the job search, and one student says he used Sondak's techniques to get a good deal on a car. Sondak tries to practice what he preaches, so there are no set rules in his class. In the last class, Sondak shows an episode of *Star Trek* in which a professional negotiator manipulates his opponents, and then the class dissects this character's techniques. Sondak successfully redesigned Fuqua's ethics course. MBAs read original versions of Hobbes, Plato, Martin Luther King, Jr., and others.

Other Best Bets: *Robert E. Whaley* (finance), *Joseph B. Mazzola* (operations management), *Kevin F. McCardle* (decision studies), and *Panagiotis Kouvelis* (operations management)

Prominent Alumni: Benjamin W. Hill, president of Broyhill Furniture, Inc.; J.F. Harrison, vice chairman of Coca-Cola Bottling Co.; John D. Kearney, president of Robinson-Humphrey Co.; John A. Allison, president of Branch Banking & Trust; Kevin M. Twomey, senior vice president, of Mcorp.; Thomas B. Roller, CEO and president of Fruehauf Trailer Corp.

Fuqua MBAs Sound Off

Fuqua is a very hands-on environment and provides extensive resources for students to make what they want of the program. Those who succeed are focused but open-minded, extremely team-oriented but strong individuals as well, and driven not only to build an impressive career but to further their personal maturity and development as global citizens. **—Career Path Unknown**

The biggest problem the school has is consistency in teaching quality. I have had some truly fantastic teachers who know everything about their fields, and some who are complete idiots. Many of the poor teachers, particularly in core courses, are either very young, new teachers, or stodgy old ones who have lost touch with the field. The teachers who are active in business as consultants (or who were until recently) have the most useful information. Some of the best professors are the visiting teachers. **—Marketing Career Path**

"Team Fuqua" is not a buzzword at Fuqua. The team-based achievement mentality of Fuqua was the defining reason I chose the school. Any success in the business world is predicated on working well and productively with peers, superiors, and subordinates. Beyond the outstanding team mentality of my classmates, the administration, placement officials, admissions officers, and faculty all believe in and promote Team Fuqua. The best example of this is the feedback cards teachers pass around the class after the third or fourth class session, to ask for ideas for improvement or criticism of the class to date. All of these suggestions are addressed in class. Consistent themes are acted upon, and changes are initiated. **—Equity Research Career Path**

Everything is "Team Fuqua." I think I would enjoy working by myself for a while. **—Marketing Career Path**

I was very disappointed with the quality of teaching. I only had a small percentage of teachers I would consider excellent instructors. There were many more poor and mediocre instructors than there were good ones. **—Marketing Career Path**

The Fuqua network is currently smaller than that of other B-schools, because the school is so young. We are just now seeing a large number of alums attaining senior management positions. **—Management Associate**

The new MBA curriculum was challenging to faculty, students, and the administration. It was something new that everyone had to adjust to. And yes, there were definite glitches and unexpected problems. But I have never seen a faculty and administration so willing to change and adjust and fix it, as the first year went on. They all listened to the students, and acted quickly for us. The flexibility of the school enables it to move strong and proud into the nineties, giving a solid business education to all of its students. **—Finance Career Path**

To be "diverse," Duke has bent admission requirements, and many students do not belong here. It seems to be getting better, at least since two years ago. I believe that many of Fuqua's problems are at every other business school—too much political correctness, and not enough quality in teaching and students.
—Technical Marketing Career Path

The students have an active voice, to which the administration is quite willing to respond. During my tenure at Fuqua, student comments resulted in a mini-overhaul of computing power (all 386 machines replaced), a significant change in the Career Placement Office, and major structural changes to the Individual Effectiveness class (first-year core). Finally, the degree to which second-year students are involved in the admissions process I find fantastic. They interview, evaluate written applications, and vote on the acceptance of candidates.
—Finance Career Path

I think the next challenge for Fuqua is to take a look at the course offerings and identify what skills the students receive. In the marketing area, there is a great deal of overlap among classes. I'd like the professors to sit down, identify the skills that a marketer should possess, and then identify in which course the skill will be taught. Fuqua can be rather catty/gossipy, given the small class size and the lack of outside activities in the Durham area. It would be healthier if Fuqua students socialized more outside the Fuqua community.—Financial Analyst

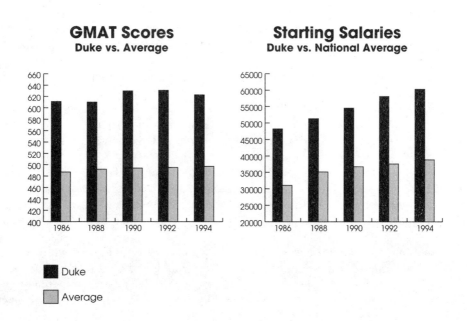

12. University of Virginia

Darden Graduate School of Business Administration
P.O. Box 6550
Charlottesville, Virginia 22906

Corporate ranking: 15
Enrollment: 486
Women: 31%
Non-U.S.: 13%
Minority: 17%
Part-time: None
Average age: 27
Average years of work exp.: 5.0
Applicants accepted: 27%
Median starting pay: $72,250

Graduate ranking: 9
Annual tuition & fees: resident—$9385
nonresident—$17,839
Room and board: $9875
Average GMAT score: 643
GMAT range: 450 to 780
Average GPA: 3.2
GPA range: 2.3 to 4.0
Accepted applicants enrolled: 47%
Average starting pay: $74,280

Teaching methods: Lecture, 5%   Case study, 70%   Group projects & other, 25%

Some fans of the University of Virginia's Darden School of Business liken the MBA program to the more famous one up north at the Harvard business school. Like Harvard, it's a school that boasts superb teaching from professors who generate sometimes heated discussions in their classrooms through the case-study method. The similarities end there, however. Virginia also is cheaper, harder, smaller, and more cooperative.

As it turns out, those are powerful differences that new Dean Leo I. Higdon, Jr., is likely to leverage over the next few years. To do so, Higdon sent Darden officials racing across the country to other business schools soon after arriving here in October of 1993. Why? Higdon, a Chicago MBA, wanted his staff to "benchmark," or compare and analyze, virtually everything Darden does against the best of its B-school rivals to see how it can become better.

Exactly what changes may result from these visits isn't yet certain, but Higdon seems to be taking a business person's approach at Darden. That would seem to be within character. He succeeds Dean John W. Rosenblum, who now teaches Concepts of Strategy and Leading Strategic Change, after a 20-year career at Salomon Brothers where he rose to become co-head of the firm's global investment banking department. On his very first day of school, Higdon received a parking ticket.

Hopefully, it's not a harbinger of things to come. After all, Darden has seen enough turmoil in recent years. In early 1992, for example, an outside committee concluded that the business school was a "hostile climate" for women faculty, and an anonymous group of black students also alleged that Darden was none too friendly an environment for minorities.

Rosenblum and Higdon have moved swiftly and effectively to deal with these complaints, though some MBAs think the school has gone overboard to be what they call "politically correct." Seven of Darden's last 10 faculty hires have been women, and two of the 10 are minorities. In 1993, the school hired its first woman to hold an endowed chair,

Professor Patricia H. Werhane, an ethics scholar. The Graduate Women in Business Network, a support group for women graduate B-school grads, recently voted to establish its permanent headquarters at Darden. And the school is one of ten business schools in a consortium created to increase the enrollment of minority students. Some 17 percent of the Class of 1996 is composed of minorities, up a full 10 points from only 7 percent two years earlier.

Despite the earlier controversy, however, the school has always remained a first-rate institution with a dynamic, caring faculty and bright, hard-working students. The quality of teaching here is among the best in the world, as good as or even better than Dartmouth and Harvard, North Carolina and Cornell. Indeed, BUSINESS WEEK's surveys—from 1990 to 1994—show Virginia to be the school with the highest satisfaction on teaching of any institution measured by BW. That's true in both the elective and core offerings, as well as on such things as faculty accessibility outside the classroom.

How can Virginia be so good? It's because excellence in teaching has long been the sine qua non for tenure and promotion at Darden. Most other schools are happy just to promote and reward scholars—not teachers. As Sherwood C. Frey, one of Darden's best professors, puts it: "You could be the best researcher in the world, but you can't get tenure here if you aren't a good teacher." Hopefully, this is an area Higdon will not change.

Like Harvard, Darden is a "case-study" school that offers graduates a general management education. Many of the professors here, including Rosenblum, are Harvard Business School expatriates who prefer the casual informality and intimacy of Darden over their alma mater in Boston. The differences are evident at the start of every weekday morning, when at 9:30 faculty and students gather in the lobby of the B-school for coffee and talk. When you attend one of the core courses, you'll find yourself in a class with 60 students—a full one-third smaller than Harvard's classes. So students get more "air time" to voice their opinions in class. They're also more likely to know each other, and the faculty is far more inclined to know them. With class discussion accounting for 50 percent of your grade, that's a critical consideration.

When you're in a class of 240, instead of roughly 800 as at Harvard, you're also less likely to feel so fiercely competitive. At Darden, students are not as prone to be victims of "chip shots"—the cutting remarks made by classmates at Harvard and other schools to score points with a professor. "When it happens, you'll see someone swinging an imaginary golf club to make it clear to everyone that it was a chip shot," says Richard M. Paschal, a Darden alumnus. Without Harvard's forced grading curve, there's no disadvantage in contributing to the learning of a classmate. People actually speak of a "Darden community"—a highly supportive environment where students pull each other along.

This cultural advantage occurs in an academic village in an environment as quaint and rich as the Charlottesville area. Looming in the background are the foothills of the Blue Ridge Mountains and the Shenandoah Valley—land idyllic enough to attract a slew of Beautiful People, from Jessica Lange to Sissy Spacek. Darden's MBAs take advantage of the area's beauty by going to The Barracks, a popular stable about five miles from the grounds, for horseback riding in the mountains and to Wintergreen for skiing.

Within view of the campus is Thomas Jefferson's Monticello, an architectural masterpiece that greatly influenced the look of most of the university buildings. Within this classic environment is the Darden School—a rectangular three-story building that some say looks like a modern textile mill. Across a tree-lined courtyard sits the university's law school. A new Jeffersonian-inspired home for the business school is expected to be completed by 1994.

More differences between Harvard and Darden exist in the innovative, integrated curriculum. Each teacher in the first year belongs to one of four groups of profs who all teach the same section of 60 students. There's a programmed feel to the curriculum. As former dean Rosenblum puts it, "Our courses go for three weeks, stop, come back for another three weeks. It's more of an integrated, shuffled-deck kind of experience. There's a flow of learning that goes through the core curriculum."

In the dreaded quant course, for example, you'll cover decision analysis, discounted cash flows, and probability in September. The next month, there are no classes in quantitative analysis. Instead, you'll pick up the start of your courses in operations and finance. Come November, quant classes begin again just as classes in accounting, marketing, and business and the political economy take a breather.

With such an intricately linked schedule, no one can waive out of any of the core courses. CPAs must sit through accounting; former plant supervisors must attend the first-level operations course. All told, the first year contains nine required courses, including what is the only graded, 20-session class in ethics at a major school. There's also a course in Analysis and Communication in which students must make five speeches to small groups, write five business memos and reports, and learn group presentation skills.

While most B-schools, including Harvard, are still grappling with how to incorporate ethics into their programs, Darden is clearly a pioneer in the field. In addition to the required course in ethics for MBAs, the school blends the subject into courses in accounting, marketing, and operations. A 20-year-old Olsson Center for the Study of Applied Ethics also creates teaching materials, tracks scholarships in business ethics, and sponsors seminars in the subject for executives. R. Edward Freeman, who heads up these efforts, is widely regarded as one of the preeminent scholars in business ethics.

Your second year begins with one of two new required 1.5-credit courses, Concepts of Strategy, intending to integrate the concepts and perspectives of the first-year courses. Then there's Leading Strategic Change, a course designed to help students develop leadership skills and attitudes.

Another less controversial requirement in the second year is a "directed study" that allows students to take one of six different options from international field projects in consulting with corporate sponsors such as PepsiCo, British Petroleum, and General Motors to researching and writing a case study for inclusion in Darden's curriculum. About 40 percent of MBAs here ace the program to study abroad. You'll round out the year with a series of required and voluntary electives that can be chosen from a catalog of about 60 courses. They range from Leslie E. Grayson's Management of International Business to Thomas C. MacAvoy's Innovation and Technology Management.

Expect to work hard in these and all the courses at Darden, which throws far more work at students than Northwestern, Chicago, Harvard, or Stanford. "The first year was hell," says Richard A. Longstaff, who graduated in 1992. "It's the only time in my life I worked 16 hours a day." Through the years, graduates have rated the school's program among the toughest of them all in the BW survey. So intense is the experience in the first year that 65 to 80 hours of study per week is the norm. You'll have to study and dissect 14 cases a week. Students who routinely got As as undergraduates find it difficult to ace their courses at Darden. "The workload reaches a point at which students are unable to give any more due to exhaustion and burnout," says a Darden alum. "At the overload point, the relationship between effort and learning breaks down and students are merely going through the motions." The school maintains that the hellish work pace forces students to learn to better manage their time.

In the late 1980s, one Darden student compared the grueling first year to a fraternity hazing. He had a point: Up to 8 percent of those who enrolled in the program failed to complete it. Sensitive to complaints that he was running an academic "boot camp," then-Dean Rosenblum made several alterations. First-year students now prepare 25 fewer cases than earlier due to a deliberate reduction in the number of classes. And they don't have to endure Saturday exams or Saturday deadlines for papers for the required communications course. Not too many years ago, Darden actually held classes on Saturdays, as well. Although Darden schedules more classroom hours than any other leading business school, an effort has been made to make the workload more manageable. Often the school now has only two classes on Wednesdays for first-years, more travel days for second-year students, and day-long program events on a specific issue for first-years. Now, 98 percent of those who enroll at Darden complete the program.

It's still hardly a cakewalk. But students get help—and lots of it. When candidates are admitted to the school, the admissions staff often suggests an accounting or statistics course over the summer. On day one, second-years guide group discussions of case studies to show the newcomers how it is done. On the first weekend, all students and faculty gather for a schoolwide picnic to get to know one another. The dean hosts students at a series of eight receptions during the first month of school. And every Darden student is assigned a faculty advisor and a big brother or sister.

Among several joint-degree programs, Darden boasts a unique MBA/M.A. in Asian Studies that can be earned in three years. The program features customized foreign language courses and six months of independent study in either Japan or a Chinese-speaking country. One major caveat: The third year adds another $30,000 to the cost of the regular MBA program. Darden hopes to launch similar programs in Europe and Latin America over the next couple of years.

When these joint-program MBAs return to campus, they're likely to bemoan the quality of the food in the cafeteria in the B-school, jokingly dubbed "Cafe Death." All the more reason, MBAs say, to order out from Pizza Hut in Charlottesville. When MBAs here work up a thirst, they're apt to stroll down to Sloan's, a popular bar only a three-minute walk from school, or the Biltmore Grill.

Most MBAs live in private housing within walking distance of the university because Darden lacks sufficient dormitory facilities. In Charlottesville, you can still rent a spacious two-bedroom apartment for little more than $500 a month. As many as half of Darden's students end up in Ivy Gardens, a seven-minute stroll from the B-school and the site of the first-years' "100 case party" celebrating the 100th case of the first semester. These apartments, however, became the subject of a highly critical story in the campus newspaper in 1991. The article reported student complaints about everything from rental rates to the treatment of security deposits. Some MBAs even live out in the country in cottages during their second year. Students' working spouses, however, may find it rough to get a job in town. You just don't have anywhere near the professional opportunities that would exist in New York, Boston, Chicago, or L.A.

Even so, there has long been a greater sense of camaraderie among students, spouses, and faculty than is possible at a large urban school. Professors and students team up to play pick-up basketball games. Every Friday at 5 p.m., MBAs trek to the Graduate Happy Hour that brings together 300 to 500 graduate students from all over the university. There's an annual Chili Cook-Off, an occasion that may cause some indigestion but remains one of the school's most popular events. The Birdwood Picnics, the Foxfield Races, the International Food Festival, and the Darden Follies offer a bit of distraction and relief from the heavy workload. The social event of the second semester is clearly the Spring Ball.

In 1994, 173 companies recruited second-year students on campus, conducting 2400 interviews—or roughly 10 job interviews per graduate. Another 429 job opportunities were posted by correspondence. The result: Only 2.4 percent of the Class of 1994 failed to have a single job offer by commencement. That's a better record than any other school, with the exception of Stanford, Harvard, Wharton, INSEAD, and UCLA.

Darden MBAs had in hand an average 2.7 offers at graduation. About 9.3 percent of the class landed jobs with starting-pay packages in the six figures. That compares with 53.7 percent at Stanford, 52.1 percent at Harvard, 39.2 percent at Dartmouth, and 33.3 percent at Wharton.

The primary reason Darden grads fail to land more of the $100,000-plus pay packages is because the highest-paying employers of MBAs tend to nibble instead of bite into Darden's MBA population. McKinsey & Co., the prestigious consulting firm which took nearly 10 percent of Harvard's Class of 1994, hired only four Darden MBAs. The other top employers of the Class of 1994? Coopers & Lybrand's consulting arm hired 14 MBAs here, far ahead of Gemini Consulting (6); AT&T (5); Raymond James & Associates (5); American Airlines (4); Arthur Andersen (4); Ernst & Young (4); Merrill Lynch (4); and the U.S. Navy (4).

Still, these are all strong companies that highly value Darden graduates and their track records of previous hires inside their organization. Not surprisingly, Dean Higdon has already singled out the placement area for major improvement. With his contacts on Wall Street and in Corporate America, Higdon should be able to significantly expand opportunities for future graduates of this mini-Harvard of the South.

Contact: Jon Megibow, director of admissions, 800-UVA-MBA1 or 804-924-7281
Final application deadline: March 15 for fall

Outstanding Faculty

1. Robert F. Bruner (****): Would you believe he used to be a loan officer at First National Bank of Chicago? This dynamic corporate finance prof has won outstanding teaching awards at both Darden and INSEAD. Bruner, who got his master's and doctoral degrees from Harvard, believes failure is an important foundation for learning, and that the teacher must find a "voice" with which to explore and even celebrate failure.

2. E. Richard Brownlee, II (****):   Students were so taken with Bruner and Brownlee that both were elected by MBAs to serve as faculty marshalls for the Class of 1994's graduation ceremonies. Brownlee, an MBA from Ohio University who gained his Ph.D. from Georgia State, is an accounting maven who teaches the first-year accounting course. He brings clarity, perspective, energy, and passion to a subject that most would consider dull.

3. Mark R. Eaker (***):   He cut his teaching teeth at Duke, Southern Methodist, and North Carolina before coming to Darden where he obviously got it right. Eaker, who boasts a Stanford Ph.D., is the course head for first-years' Business and Political Economy. His expertise is in international finance and capital markets. Known for delivering the big picture, he also makes evident why all the details of a case are important. A noontime jogger, he won the outstanding faculty award given for the first time by the Darden Student Association for "excellence in teaching, concern for students, and significant contributions to the Darden community."

4. R. Edward Freeman (**):   Down-to-earth, funny, and provocative, Freeman may very well be the most outstanding teacher of business ethics at any business school. Freeman, who has taught at University of Minnesota and Wharton, teaches the first-year ethics course as well as a popular elective called Business Ethics Through Literature. Along with Frey, he teamed up to cook and cater a dinner for eight for the Business Women's Forum charity auction.

5. Paul W. Farris (**):   A former product manager for Unilever, marketing prof Farris wins high marks for challenging established opinions and making his students think more deeply about topics they may have accepted as conventional wisdom. He boasts an MBA from the University of Washington and a doctoral degree from Harvard, where he briefly taught as an assistant professor.

6. Sherwood C. Frey (*):   Intense, excited, and animated—that's how students describe this statistics professor who drives around in a 1949 Ford Coupe. Frey has a pair of degrees from Berkeley and a Ph.D. from John Hopkins University. The former Harvard Business School faculty member instructs first-years in quantitative analysis, using the subject to teach them the ins and outs of management. Frey, active in community affairs, has also worked as a management consultant.

Other Best Bets: *Robert L. Carraway* (management science), *Dana R. Clyman* (quantitative analysis), *Andrea Larson* (entrepreneurship), and *Allen Beckenstein* (quantitative analysis)

Prominent Alumni: E. Thayer Bigelow, Jr., president and CEO of Time-Warner Cable Programming; George David, president of United Technologies Corp.; Steven S. Reinemund, CEO of Frito-Lay Inc.; Linwood A. Lacey, Jr., chairman of Micro D Inc.; Betty Sue Peabody, director for administration of Mellon Bank Corp.; John G. MacFarlane III, managing director and treasurer of Salomon Brothers, Inc.; H. Eugene Lockhart, Jr., CEO of Mastercard International; Henri A. Termeer, chairman of Genzyme Corp.

Darden MBAs Sound Off

*The Darden experience is not a casual exercise; rather, it is a revolution of intellect and identity. The program is more challenging, mentally and physically, than military boot camp or college football. The workload is obscene, indescribable. But it's also more rewarding. One would be hard-pressed to find a place where so many people learn so much in so little time.—**Consultant***

*Darden is known as "the boot camp." The work load is excessive the first year—but for a strong educational reason: to learn how to creatively solve problems and depend on study group members/classmates for solving problems. I also can boast of the camraderie and friendship developed at Darden. Quite often, I would travel for job interviews with classmates and become friends with them as we shared and hoped for the best rather than ignored and competed for jobs. A very conducive, supportive environment exists at Darden. Between my study group and peers, I know people I can depend on and can grow with through my career.—**Strategic Planner***

While no graduate program can expect to wholly transform the intellectual, spiritual, and professional core of its students, such a credo surely guides Darden in its program. The rigor of the first year, and the Herculean effort required to survive the ordeal, are legendary—and all true. But what is less recognized is the sense of devotion to student learning and student life by our faculty—and the commitment to each other shown by students. I love what Darden has given me.
*—**Investment Banking Career Path***

*In general, I feel Darden has an outstanding MBA program, but it is not suitable for everyone who is looking to go to graduate school. It's a student-centered learning environment, and not everyone can learn and perform well in that kind of atmosphere.—**Operations Career Path***

My only gripe about the school is the high level of secrecy that revolves around key aspects of student life, such as the first-year awards and the second-year scholarship process. In addition, too much power at the school resides with the Office of Student Affairs, which often acts as an impediment to student initiative.
*—**Marketing Career Path***

Unfortunately, Darden falls well short of the mark educationally. Over the past few years Darden has pushed to increase the diversity of individuals attending the institution. Recently these efforts have gone way too far, and the administra-

tion has seriously jeopardized the academic integrity of the program by allowing students with diverse backgrounds to matriculate who do not meet the academic standards of a first-rate program. Consequently, instead of having a normal distribution of academic qualification around the mean, Darden has a "barbell" (i.e., a handful of bright students, and a handful of not-so-bright students, with few in between). This makes teaching and learning extremely difficult. What's worse is the fact that the school then goes on to promote diversity of individuals and to suppress diversity of ideas. Darden universally preaches the politically correct way of acting, yet refuses to acknowledge voices which are farther to the right or left.—Finance Career Path

The Darden experience taught me more about myself than anything else. I am convinced it is the most intensive and rigorous MBA program in the nation. I wouldn't recommend it for the faint-hearted. And even though the first-year boot camp made it seem as though I was trying to drink water from a fire hydrant, it made attaining the degree all the more rewarding. The intensity and demands (mostly on time—unlike most B-schools, Darden has classes every day of the week and the attendance is mandatory) are comparable to investment banking houses, and in a way a good prep for this type of career.—Investment Banking Associate

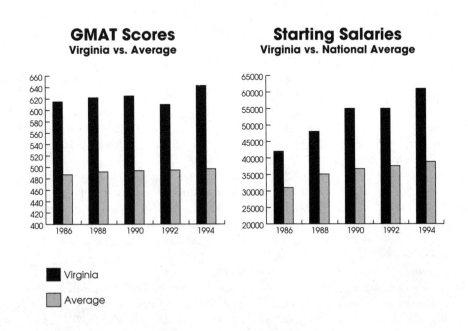

13. Dartmouth College

The Amos Tuck School
Hanover, New Hampshire 03755

Corporate ranking: 12	*Graduate ranking:* 14
Enrollment: 363	*Annual tuition & fees:* $21,225
Women: 31%	*Room and board:* $8375
Non-U.S.: 19%	*Average GMAT score:* 660
Minority: 11%	*GMAT range:* 500 to 780
Part-time: None	*Average GPA:* 3.38
Average age: 26.9	*GPA range:* 2.3 to 4.0
Applicants accepted: 17%	*Accepted applicants enrolled:* 50%
Median starting pay: $87,250	*Average starting pay:* $95,410

Teaching methods: Lecture, 40%   Case study, 40%   Projects, 20%

Imagine a small, though quaint, New England town. Main street is a collection of brick-facade shops, cozy restaurants, and colonial homes. There's no crime and no congestion. Wherever you go, you're immediately recognized with a welcome smile. People are universally smart, open, and friendly. And everyone is known by his or her first name. If this picture is your version of Nirvana, you can't do any better than Dartmouth's Amos Tuck School.

The school's remote locale in a small New Hampshire town and its small size nurture an esprit de corps you'll rarely find at major business schools. Those are key reasons why no school scores better than Tuck in satisfying discerning graduates. A caring faculty, bright students, and devoted alumni have historically placed the school in the top ranks of BUSINESS WEEK's graduate rankings.

That's no surprise to anyone who knows anything about Tuck's unusual culture. On the opening day of classes, professors hand over their personal phone numbers and invite students to call if necessary. Second-years host dozens of welcome parties for new students. They even get up early on Saturday mornings to serve their new brethren breakfast in the mess hall before exams. One professor tells of how his students sent his wife flowers and a restaurant gift certificate because he had to work weekends to accommodate an overload of students in a popular class.

Whoever said that a good B-school encourages cutthroat competition didn't have Dartmouth's Tuck in mind. "Teamwork comes naturally here, either by self-selection or simply because it's expected," says Michael McGinn, a 1992 alum. "We're all genuinely interested in each other's welfare. During the first year, a former investment banker roamed the halls of the dormitory on nights before quantitative exams, offering help to anyone struggling with the material."

Frankly, it sounds almost too good to be true. Sure enough, the school's all-friendly image was somewhat tarnished in 1994, when Edward A. Fox, Tuck's first non-academic dean, was denied a second four-year term. His abrupt departure exposed students to petty politics by a few outspoken faculty who disliked Fox and wrote critical letters about him to the university president. The result: graduate dissatisfaction caused this superb school to plunge to thirteenth from sixth in 1992. Although Fox wasn't an especially dynamic or innovative leader, he successfully led a $27 million capital campaign, created a new international center, and began to lure more diversified faculty and students to Tuck. Minority students now total 11 percent in the Class of 1996, for example, well above 4 percent just two years earlier. Colin Blaydon, a long-time management professor and former dean, is now serving as acting dean.

Nonetheless, Tuck has scored consistently high over the years in having one of the most cooperative campuses of any top business school. For one thing, Tuck is small and compact—each class of about 170 students is less than half the size of one at UCLA and a mere fifth of Harvard. The full-time faculty numbers only 40, fewer than the tenure-track profs in Wharton's finance department alone. "Occasionally, there is a fishbowl feeling," says Bill McNamara, who graduated in 1990. "It is tough to hide here. At a school with very large classes, it's easy to sulk in the back. If you're in the back row here, you're only 20 feet from the professor." Virtually everyone knows each other by name, and one 1992 graduate noted that then-Dean Fox even mentioned the name of his dog at investiture.

For another, it's pretty isolated. Only prop planes can fly into the tiny airport in West Lebanon, six miles south of Hanover. When the weather turns bad, you face a white-knuckle flight onto the short landing strip that's carved into a mountainside. Boston is a two-hour drive away. Sleepy Hanover rolls up the sidewalks fairly early. The only time people are out late is when they're coming out of the Nugget Theatre on the main street or attending something at the Hop, the college's impressive performing arts center.

The B-school sits on the edge of the Dartmouth campus, bordering the Connecticut River. The cluster of five brick Georgian buildings and two contemporary structures that make up the school is like a private 13-acre encampment at the end of a private road appropriately named Tuck Drive. Byrne Hall, the first new building in 20 years—with more classroom space, breakout rooms, and dining areas—opened in 1993. Underground tunnels and glass-enclosed halls—dubbed Habitrails—connect all the buildings so students needn't venture outside to attend class during the bitterly cold winter months. You could trek from your Woodbury House dorm room to a class at columned Tuck Hall in your slippers. The snow-covered campus makes for a pastoral setting. Students can hear the bronze bells of Baker Tower sound off each hour with such ditties as "Heigh Ho, Heigh Ho" and "Yellow Submarine."

Tradition abounds. Founded in 1900, Tuck is the world's first graduate school of management. Mr. Chips would feel particularly welcome in Stell Hall, the newly renovated student commons, with its cathedral ceiling and carved heavy oak interior. Over the fireplace hangs a fading, formal portrait of old man Tuck, a lawyer and Congressman for whom the school was named.

Tuckies tend to be outdoorsy, exceptionally self-assured, and somewhat preppy. The Dartmouth Skiway, a small ski resort some 20 minutes away in Lyme, is the downhill run of choice. There's ice skating on nearby Occom Pond. There's also hiking on Mount Moosilauke on the edge of the White Mountains National Forest, rowing and canoeing on the Connecticut River, or a slew of intramural sports from ice hockey and rugby to basketball and squash. The college also runs a golf course, boathouse, and riding stable available to Tuck students. In winter, both an MBA Hockey Tournament and a three-day Alpine ski racing event draw rival B-school teams from leading schools in the United States and Canada.

That incredibly wide range of outdoor activity isn't equalled in the MBA course offerings. Tuck offers a general management program, with the emphasis on how different functional areas come together. People who are looking for hard-core functional or theoretical experiences probably want to avoid the school, which discourages overspecialization. That also means there are far fewer electives from which to choose. Tuck is the only prestige B-school without a Ph.D. program in business, a fact that leads some academics to pooh-pooh the intellectual rigor of the place. Truth is, it discourages narrow thinking and cultivates a commitment to teaching that is nearly unrivaled.

While many B-schools have been unraveling their programs of late, Tuck is not undertaking any significant changes. The first week features sessions on business ethics, small-group dynamics, an outdoor exercise in teamwork, honor code issues, and discussions on career assessment. Then, the welcome party ends quickly with the first of a trio of 10-week quarters a year in the fall, winter, and spring. During the first year, Tuckies take a set of 13 required courses that cover the business basics. The core classes meet in three sections of about 60 students each, with new student class sections rearranged each term. Classes meet twice a week for an hour and a half each session. Every term has an "integrative learning exercise" in the first year, including a three-day business simulation exercise and an integrated business theme module.

Unlike other schools, Tuck discourages students from waiving out of the core courses that make up the heart of the program. The reason? Like Harvard and Stanford, the school believes that nonaccounting types can benefit from having CPAs in the same classroom. Additionally, more of the work in these courses is applied, rather than theoretical. It's also not easy to take nonbusiness classes at Dartmouth College because it's on a different class schedule than Tuck, which offers more than 50 electives a year.

These days, teamwork has become an overused buzzword on B-school campuses. With the exception of Northwestern, however, few really immerse their students in it like Tuck. A huge amount of the classwork here is done in groups. In the first quarter alone, MBAs do four major team projects in Managerial Economics, Management Communication, Marketing, and Decision Analysis. Virtually all first-year students live together in Woodbury House and Buchanan Hall, so non-U.S. students, who now make up 20 percent of the enrollment, can't gather in subcultures here as they might in other places.

Besides, Tuck makes it almost impossible for that to occur. The capstone event for first-year MBAs is the major consulting project that begins in late November. Teams of students are assigned real clients with real problems, mostly small businesses, town governments, and school districts. They have to meet with the client, study his or her problem or opportunity, and produce a report of recommendations as part of the Managerial Economics course. They then present the final results of their work in an oral presentation to clients, outside consultants, and Tuck faculty as part of the Management Communication course. In the past, Tuckies have tackled marketing and distribution for Catamount Brewery, a local microbrewery; completed a feasibility study to help Plymouth, Massachusetts, lure new business to town; and worked on a report for Vermont Yankee's nuclear facility.

In the first year, a major event is the Tycoon Game. Part folly, part learning experience, the contest is played out by students each spring. Tycoon, a management simulation exercise, is the capstone that allows teams of students to run their own companies and learn from their success and failures in a risk-free environment. There are six teams to each "industry," and they compete against each other for industry dominance. Students select their own strategies, then choose tactics to battle the competition over 10–14 "quarters."

Even though you play with funny money, this is hardly Monopoly. No one wants to go "belly-up," so everyone works hard to make their company the top performer in the game. Students devise strategies, trying to make savvy investment, production, and marketing decisions that will make their companies the most profitable. A typical decision: whether to sell your clocks abroad. If few companies invest in the foreign market, you could make a killing overseas. But if everyone else jumps into the export business, the competition could cost you your shirt. Advertisements that hail the virtues of the different clock companies in the game—the industry of choice—inundate the campus.

For those longing for an international adventure, Tuck launched in 1988 a management program with the International University of Japan. As a Tuck MBA, you could spend a second-year term enrolled in the school as an exchange student. Or you could get into another formal exchange program with the London Business School or Escuela Superior de Administracion in Barcelona, Spain. There's also the possibility of doing a quarter at INSEAD in Fontainebleau, France, arguably the best non-U.S. business school in the world.

Even if, like most students, you stay at Tuck, you'll get a good amount of international exposure. The school claims that more than a third of all course content is international. It has a stash fund for faculty who want to travel abroad to do research on international business issues. Tuck has put more global executives on its advisory board, and is adding more international offerings as electives. The faculty, meantime, is attempting to use more of its own case studies, weeding out as many Harvard cases as possible.

One thing Tuck doesn't have to worry about is the instruction. The quality of teaching here is exceptional—far better than Northwestern, Stanford, or Chicago. The teaching in both the core and the electives offerings is among the best any business school in the world can offer. The plain reason: For years, the school has awarded professors with pay increases, promotions, and tenure on the basis of their ability to teach in the classroom. Teaching is not compromised for research endeavors. Few major business schools have paid as much attention to teaching quality as Tuck. Even the school's advertisements for faculty in academic publications stress this required commitment: "Teaching at the Tuck School is demanding, and demonstrated teaching competence is desirable."

No wonder the faculty wins plaudits from students for its accessibility, enthusiasm, and overall quality. The low student-to-faculty ratio encourages frequent interaction with profs. Learning often continues outside the classroom during informal chats at "Tuck Tails"—regular mixers with faculty and students. When courses are oversubscribed at other schools, students are typically told: "Tough luck. Try next time." At Tuck, teachers with popular courses are often expected to add to their workload by offering extra sessions if the students want them. One 1992 graduate noted that one professor agreed to teach an extra section of a popular course even though he had to schedule it to start before 8 a.m. "Student interests usually take precedence over the faculty," says one Tuck professor. "The first-year program is set up so that students can take all their classes in the morning and go skiing in the afternoon. If you have a 7:40 a.m. class, you might have to get up at 4 a.m. to prepare for it and get to school. The bottom line is that the students prefer that schedule, so it won't be disturbed."

That rare level of commitment from the faculty extends beyond graduation. Graduates routinely mention that they often call on professors to discuss business problems months and even years after they leave the campus. Second-year students often host dinners in their apartments for professors. When grads return to campus, they frequently stay at the homes of faculty members.

The administration is just as accommodating. When one student gave birth to a child during the fall of her second year, she was allowed to attend school part time. The school also invited her to the 1992 graduation ceremony so she could be there with classmates, even though she would not fulfill all the requirements for graduation until December of 1992. "I highlight this not only to show Tuck's interest in students, but to show that the school is trying to practice what it teaches in terms of developing a more flexible workplace to accommodate and encourage a changing and increasingly diverse workforce," she says.

The school also boasts an unusual Visiting Executive program that welcomes more than 30 business leaders each year. They have a two-room office suite in Chase House, attend classes, eat lunch and dinner with students, and participate in discussion groups at night. Recent visitors have included: Procter & Gamble President John Pepper, Champion International Corp. Chairman Andrew C. Sigler, and Disney's Michael Eisner. Some of them will even wander down to swill a beer and catch some grub with students at Cafe Buon Gustaio and Murphy's Tavern—the popular MBA hangouts on the main drag in town.

So what's the downside? The number of elective offerings you can choose from is limited by the school's size. Travel for job interviews is tough. And the diversity and number of companies which recruit at Tuck is limited by its small pool of applicants. Indeed, that's a major reason why Tuck doesn't fare as well as other top schools in BUSINESS WEEK's survey of corporate recruiters.

In 1994, only 88 companies recruited on campus and about 370 job opportunities were posted via correspondence. About 4.8 percent of the Class of 1994 failed to have a job offer by graduation. Tuck MBAs with offers had just 2.4 job offers at commencement, merely average among the top 40 schools and well below the 3.6 high at Harvard. Nonetheless, those offers were among the most lucrative you will find. The Class of 1994 pulled down average salary-and-bonus packages approaching $83,000. Add in other compensation, such as tuition reimbursements, year-end bonuses, relocation expenses, and other perks, and the total starting pay balloons to $95,410.

Not surprisingly given the huge sums, the largest share of the class was recruited by consulting firms and investment banks. Hiring the most Tuck MBAs were: Goldman Sachs (10); Merrill Lynch (9); Booz Allen & Hamilton (7); Coopers & Lybrand (7); Salomon Brothers (7); Bain & Co. (5); CSC Index (5); Wellington Management (5); Andersen Consulting (4); and PepsiCo (4). That's an impressive lineup of big-league recruiters who aren't shy about paying big money for talent.

One reason for this success is Tuck's alumni network. Even though the school has fewer than 6600 living alumni, they are amazingly supportive. About 64 percent of Tuck's alums give money to the school every year—the highest participation rate of any graduate B-school. The school publishes an alumni magazine twice a year and asserts that the "Class Notes" section of it boasts more pages of notes per graduate than any other MBA program in the United States.

Tuck alums, when surveyed by BUSINESS WEEK five years after graduation, give the school the highest grades of any for the strength of its alumni network, rating the value of its connections even higher than Harvard and Stanford. But then, that's the kind of loyalty that only a small town atmosphere can bring about. That's why Tuck's fall in the rankings is likely to be a temporary phenomenon.

Contact: Henry F. Malin, director of admissions, 603-646-3162
Final application deadline: April 18

Outstanding Faculty

1. John K. Shank (****):   He's popularly known as the Rev. Shank, because of the almost Southern Baptist fervor he brings to accounting. It's rumored that when Tuck first built its horseshoe-shaped classrooms, Shank was the first prof down in the bowels testing out the echo from his booming voice. Irreverent and electric, he is probably too wild for Harvard where he once taught. Says a colleague, "Shank has the fastest mouth and mind of anyone on the faculty." If you're in his class on your birthday, watch out: Your present from him will be a series of cold calls.

2. Clyde P. Stickney (****):   The ultimate white-haired statesman, his Southern-accented lectures on accounting are thoughtful, penetrating, and entertaining. He co-wrote one of the top financial accounting textbooks and has been at Tuck since 1977, after teaching stints at Chicago and North Carolina. Raves one grad: "Professor Stickney has no equal. As a CPA I have struggled to understand the 'why' behind many complex financial statements for years, yet Stickney has the knack for getting to the logic of these issues in a simple, understandable sentence."

3. Scott A. Neslin (****):   With pens protruding from his shirt pocket and hair out of place, New York-bred Neslin is considered something of a nebbish nerd by MBAs. A family man who drives both a station wagon and a motorcycle, he has taught statistics at Tuck for 15 years. He still spends inordinate amounts of time preparing for every class. His dedication obviously pays off.

4. Vijay Govindrajan (**):   No matter what he teaches, whether it's basic cost accounting or a newly minted course, it's unusual for "V.G." not to score a straight 5.0 (the highest possible) on student evaluation forms. Yet on his first day as a Harvard Business School student, he was on the end of the very first cold call from, of all people, John Shank. He didn't do all that well, but the Indian-born V.G. later became a Shank protegé and a superb case-study teacher himself.

5. Rohit Deshpande (**): Enigmatic and urbane, this youthful teacher brings an engaging flair to his courses on marketing. He boasts the deep voice of a radio broadcaster and is unusually well-read, especially for a biz prof.

6. David F. Pyke (**): This former high school math teacher wins raves both for his core course in operations and his second-year elective in the strategy of operations. Friendly and warm, Pyke just gained tenure at Tuck in the 1993–1994 school year.

Other Best Bets: *Frederick E. Webster* (marketing), *Phil Anderson* (technology), *Robert Hansen* (marketing), and *James Seward* (finance)

Prominent Alumni: John W. Amerman, chairman of Mattel Inc.; Lisa A. Conte, CEO of Shaman Pharmaceuticals Inc.; Nancy C. Cooper, general partner at Lazard Freres & Co.; John H. Foster, chairman of NovaCare; Frank C. Herringer, president of Transamerica Corp.; Andrew C. Sigler, chairman of Champion International; George R. Trumbull III, CEO of Australian Mutual Provident Society

Tuck MBAs Sound Off

I've seen some aspects of the school, particularly faculty politics here, that don't jibe with Tuck's glowing image. However, these things are mild negatives that add a touch of reality to an otherwise utopian place. My natural cynicism aside, Tuck faculty are the most dedicated and available professionals of any kind I've seen in 15 years of work and college. They really do bend over backwards to help students, even as they argue among themselves.—Communications Career Field

Tuck is absolutely outstanding if someone wants to spend two years learning business concepts and tools from great teachers, with supporting students and friends, in a wonderful place away from city stress and distractions. The level of commitment of the school to its students is truly special. These have been two years in a magic place where the Tuck Honor Code is not as empty phrase. I shall miss it.—Finance Vice President

Tuck exceeded my high expectations. The curriculum, the classmates, the professors made for a perfect package. The school's reputation for collegiality is well deserved. For the team player, I do not believe there is a better MBA program in the world. For those concerned about Tuck's alleged lack of quantitative rigor, I have worked with and spoken to the quant jocks from other top-tier programs, and they possess no analytical advantage over the students I have met at Tuck.
—Investment Banker

If you are mainstream, American, and under 30, there's no better business school in the world. Tuck is a special place, but the cliques in our class hurt unity and disenfranchised many of the international students, creative types, *and other cool people. On balance, however, I loved the school, but wonder how the high schoolishness could be better kept in check.—**Consultant***

*After expensive trips and lengthy interviews at Harvard, Wharton, Chicago, and Northwestern, I sent only one application—to Tuck. Had I not been admitted, I would have just waited another year and tried again. It was the best decision I have ever made.—**Nonprofit Career Path***

*At Tuck I developed an unbounded business perspective, made lifelong friends among my classmates and the faculty, and examined numerous career paths. My experience has provided me with the professional and personal repertoire to be successful for the rest of my life.—**Consultant***

*More than anything else, Tuck is a community. My wife and I were expecting our first child before attending Tuck. We didn't want to go to a school without a strong family community. Tuck is great in that respect. Most married students live in Sachem Village, where there are playgroups for children and the most organized "Partners' Club" you'll ever see. They have reading clubs, professional groups, gourmet clubs, intramural teams—you name it and they do it. This school makes the entire student family a part of its community. Tuck even had a week-long orientation for spouses!—**Consultant***

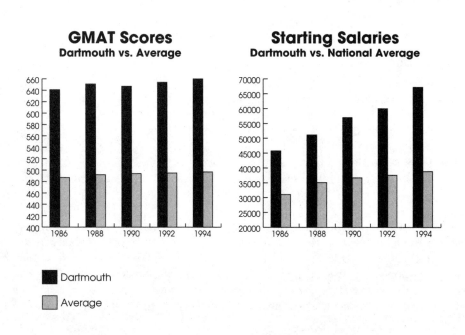

14. Carnegie Mellon University

Graduate School of Industrial Administration
Schenley Park
Pittsburgh, Pennsylvania 15213

Corporate ranking: 18
Enrollment: 540
Women: 20%
Non-U.S.: 41%
Minority: 5%
Part-time: 139
Average age: 26
Applicants accepted: 35%
Median starting pay: $67,500

Graduate ranking: 11
Annual tuition & fees: $20,600
Room and board: $6050
Average GMAT score: 635
GMAT range: 490 to 760
Average GPA: 3.2
GPA range: 2.2 to 4.0
Accepted applicants enrolled: 52%
Average starting pay: $69,890

Teaching methods: Lecture, 60%   Case study, 20%   Group projects, 20%

When Robert S. Sullivan arrived as the new dean of Carnegie Mellon's business school in mid-1991, he must have felt he was in the middle of a wicked storm. Students griped about being squeezed out of popular classes, being forced to take courses out of sequence, and a placement office that was, in the words of one graduate, "uncaring, unresponsive, and ineffective." The nearly universal complaints plunged the business school from 9th to 17th in BUSINESS WEEK's 1992 ranking.

But Sullivan, formerly an associate dean at the University of Texas at Austin, has since engineered a major turnaround at the school. The latest crop of GSIA (Graduate School of Industrial Administration) grads offer high praise to the mild-mannered dean for being extremely responsive to their concerns. Sullivan not only maintains an open-door policy at his office, he's holding regular brown bag luncheons with students in the cafeteria and sponsoring monthly student dinners at his home. Sullivan has placed pervasive emphasis on student satisfaction, quality, and continuous improvement, even sending most of his administrative staff to Total Quality Management training.

Not surprisingly, then, Carnegie's graduate ranking jumped to 12th in 1992, from a dismal 23rd two years earlier. Problem was, the school's corporate ranking took a slight fall this time around—largely because some perceive the school's highly quantitative approach as out of fashion and because of the lag effect of the earlier ranking drop. The bottom line: Carnegie Mellon began its climb back up, rising three places to 14th in 1994.

Sullivan deserves plaudits for vastly improving the internal workings of the school. Besides being far more user-friendly, GSIA has given students more flexibility in scheduling required courses and has dramatically improved its ability to meet student demands for the most popular courses, claiming that 98 percent of all course demand is now met. He has launched new collaborative and joint master's programs in computational science, manufacturing management, environmental engineering, and software engineering and management.

More change is likely. "Nothing is sacred," Sullivan declares. "We're looking at every opportunity to deliver a better intellectual experience." The school also is in the midst of a curriculum review by an innovations committee. To encourage more interaction between faculty and students, Sullivan began an advising program in which every faculty member has 8 to 10 MBA candidates assigned to him or her from the first-year class, along with a second-year student mentor.

By nearly all accounts, first-year students badly need the help. The school dumps so much work on them that sheer survival often seems more important than learning. MBAs routinely describe the experience as grueling and agonizing. Some describe it as an "academic hazing." When they finally graduate, some MBAs say the first year is little more than a blur. Retorts Sullivan, rather defensively: "We're not a party school. We don't bond. But our students are close to each other because they work so hard together."

There's certainly some truth in that. Teamwork is fostered as a means of making it through this boot camp. The quick and daunting pace teaches at least one critical lesson: the interdependence of the group and the need to prioritize everything. It would be tough enough if Carnegie Mellon weren't a "quant" school, but its emphasis on mathematics and quantitative methods makes the workload even more staggering. The school's own research shows that it requires more than five times the amount of class time on quantitative subjects than Harvard and twice as much as Stanford or Columbia. Even courses that are not usually laden with lots of quant work, such as microeconomics, have a heavily mathematical bent at Carnegie Mellon. It's a major reason why only 20 percent of the students here are women, the lowest percentage of any Top 20 school, and why 41 percent are from outside the United States, the highest percentage of international students for a Top 20 school.

The upshot: Sullivan's arrival occurred at a time when business school education and Carnegie Mellon are at a crossroads. Should the school put more emphasis on leadership and less on linear programs and regressions? Should Sullivan lighten the workload? These are difficult issues for the new dean, as he works to improve what still remains a strong MBA program at one of the best business schools in the world.

Yet, it is also a school of many contradictions: Despite its reputation for being something of a haven for quant jocks, the school turns out far more well-rounded MBAs than it is given credit for. The rigor of its program is often mistaken for rigidity. In fact, Carnegie Mellon has long been one of the more innovative B-schools over the years, pioneering truly creative courses taught by an eclectic faculty. And though the school is considered a B-school leader in manufacturing, its efforts in both finance and entrepreneurship are significantly stronger.

A major result of these contradictions is that corporate recruiters come to the school with fairly narrow expectations of its graduates. Many MBAs believe the school severely suffers from this image problem: Too many companies don't know the program well enough, and those that do believe it produces, as one grad put it, "a bunch of muscle-brained quant jocks." To better market the place and sharpen its image, Sullivan has hired a new public relations director who was the former manager of public communications for Heinz USA. Her efforts were enhanced recently when the school officially moved to a new, modern building, twice the size of the old, three-story, yellow brick structure that had been home to the business school for 40 years. The $14 million project boasts excellent high-tech classrooms, computing facilities, a comfy student lounge, and social activity areas.

All of Carnegie's courses fit into an unusual "mini-semester" that is about seven and one-half weeks long—a format that many other B-schools are only now adopting as they revise their curriculums. The eight minis over the two years allow students to take as many as 18 electives without overloading their schedules. That's almost as many electives as some schools require in total courses to graduate. Five courses a mini total 40 courses over the length of this program. Of course, these classes are compressed to fit the mini-semester format, so a few of them extend over two mini-semesters.

On the other hand, within three and one-half weeks of your arrival here, you'll already be sitting down for midterm exams. Study groups convene until 2 or 3 a.m. Students without quant backgrounds often panic because Carnegie profs pack an incredible amount of work in a single mini. "I don't think there's a program in the country that works them harder," says one associate dean. "We work their butts off, and that's one of the comforts they have in going out into the real world. They're used to working hard, and no one can work them harder than we do."

Nearly half of the total courses you'll take are required, versus about 40 percent at either Columbia or Northwestern. The centerpiece of the program is The Management Game. Pioneered by Carnegie Mellon in the 1950s, the game is a computer simulation of the soap industry, originally based on Procter & Gamble. Every second-year student is assigned to a six-person team made up of a president and a host of functional vice presidents who guide their companies through a two-year business cycle over a 15-week period. It's another aspect of the experience here that many other B-schools are only now putting into their revamped programs.

Some older students grouse that the game can become overly repetitive and simpleminded, but most students have good things to say about the experience it gives them. Besides, Carnegie recently added a new, creative wrinkle: While its MBAs play the game, it's also being offered simultaneously at business schools in Japan (Aoyama Gakuin), Sweden (Umea), and Mexico (Monterrey Tech) so Carnegie MBAs find themselves in competition with others outside the school. MBAs even have to negotiate a labor agreement with local union leaders from the steel industry. Computers also put together multimedia marketing campaigns that are judged by local advertising agencies. And each team has to overcome and survive a crisis—whether charges of price-fixing, employee discrimination, or the dumping of a toxic waste—by, among other things, meeting with local reporters.

Each of the teams reports to a board of directors that actually meets in one of the plush and well-appointed boardrooms of some of Pittsburgh's leading corporations, from H. J. Heinz to the Mellon Bank. On each board sits a faculty member and a handful of senior corporate executives, from the chief financial officer of Texas Instruments to a Hewlett-Packard vice president. The board can be tough and demanding. "You're desperately trying to please your board," recalls one graduate, who reported to an unusually hard-to-please chairman. "He'd look at every move we made with a microscope, and continually say, 'It hasn't been like this in the past. I'm not sure you're sticking to the strategy. We have to crush the competition.' We had the dominant market share, but he still wasn't satisfied. We nicknamed him Mr. Marketshare."

If the game helps to prepare students for general management assignments, Wall Street–bound students gain invaluable insights into today's global financial markets through the school's unique Financial Analysis and Security Trading (FAST) room. It's a multimillion-dollar facility that replicates the computer workstations, live international data feeds, and sophisticated software of Wall Street's top trading firms. GSIA profs steeped in finance, math, technology, and behavioral science use it as a laboratory to explore key issues in computer trading and financial engineering.

Among elective offerings, you'll get to pick from among 119 courses in any given academic year. The catalog lists some novel choices, from Managing Service and Customer-Driven Business to Total Quality Management for Intellectual Products, as well as French, German, and Japanese language courses for business. A new Business Drama elective is taught by the Fine Arts faculty. By far, the most popular elective is Gerald Meyers' Business Leadership in Changing Times. The former chairman of American Motors Corp. invites top executives to class on a regular basis to discuss the trials and tribulations of leadership. In 1993–1994, students heard Alcoa Chairman Paul O'Neill, Chase Manhattan CEO Thomas Labreque, and Emerson Electric Chairman Charles Knight, among others. Convicted Wall Street trader Dennis Levine once made an appearance in the class to discuss his prison experience for insider trading.

The school also numbers among its faculty Jean-Jacques Servan-Schreiber, former French cabinet minister and best-selling author of *The American Challenge*. In his highly rated course, Strategic Thinking, he draws analogies between military and business wars in teaching about global markets. Grads also have good things to say about John R. Thorne, who directs Carnegie Mellon's Center for Entrepreneurship.

For a school known for its "quant jocks," you'd hardly think there would be much happening on the entrepreneurial side. But GSIA boasts a complete entrepreneurship track taught by experienced business hands, and a recent survey showed that more than 28 percent of the school's total alumni base are engaged with entrepreneurial ventures. There's even a project course that has become the springboard for students to launch their own businesses. In both 1989 and 1990, Carnegie Mellon students beat out teams from other top schools in "Moot Corp.," a national entrepreneurship competition sponsored by the University of Texas. Teams of GSIA students also carried away the top prize in the American Marketing Association's Graduate Case Competition for three years in a row, and in 1992 won the inaugural Graduate Business Conference case competition.

More than most schools, the faculty at Carnegie Mellon is at the leading edge of knowledge in their fields. The emphasis, then, is heavily on research and not on teaching. So the intellectual content of the program is high, but the ability of the professors to communicate that knowledge isn't always up to par. Sullivan, however, turned this situation around as well, so that 1994 grads scored both the core and elective teaching above the average for the top 40-plus schools whose graduates are polled by the magazine. Despite the notable research slant, the school boasts some superb teachers, and the student-faculty ratio of 5.8 to 1 is one of the lowest at the major schools.

The research emphasis also has allowed the school to pioneer several breakthroughs in management theory and practice over the years, from the rational expectations concept in economics to new fields of cognitive psychology and computer science. The difference is also reflected partly by the degree you get. Carnegie grads don't technically earn an MBA; they receive the MSIA, a Master of Science in Industrial Administration. There are neither departments nor required majors or concentration areas because the school emphasizes what it calls "interdisciplinary thinking"—yet another supposed innovation at schools redoing their programs these days.

If you're wondering about life in Pittsburgh, don't. Forget the old polluted and smokestacked image of the place. It's an attractive city of ethnic neighborhoods, the intellectual community of which is Oakland, where the university makes its home. There's no dorm life at the school. Instead, students are scattered around the city in different apartments and houses. It's wise to live within walking or bicycling distance because, as one student complained, "Parking is hell!" Once on campus, however, students tend to stay, spending vast amounts of time in Hunt Library, the university library next to the B-school, or walking and studying in neighboring Schenley Park, Pittsburgh's equivalent of Central Park in New York.

GSIA students tend to gravitate to Doc's in Shadyside and Chiodo's, where Joe tends bar amidst a collection of Pittsburgh memorabilia. Adjacent to the old steel works in Homestead in the eastern part of the city, this gathering hole is where students traditionally congregate for a wild celebration after final exams. The Squirrel Hill Cafe and Silky's, both a 15- to 20-minute walk from campus, are other GSIA hot spots. All three joints are favorite stops for the regular Tuesday night bar crawls (there are no classes on Wednesdays).

Yet another area where Sullivan has made substantial improvements is the school's Career Opportunity Center—heavily criticized in 1992 when 21 percent of the graduating class failed to have a single job offer at commencement. In early 1994, Sullivan hired Jean Eisel, who headed placement at Arizona State, and Ken Keeley, who was director of Ohio State's MBA program, to be the center's executive director and director, respectively.

Even though the school's corporate rankings are weak, this pair has worked miracles for graduating students. Only 2.6 percent of the Class of 1994 graduated without a single job offer, according to the BW survey. Those that had offers averaged 2.69 opportunities by graduation—up from 1.8 two years earlier, and a tad better than the 2.36 average for the top 40-plus schools. About 122 companies recruited second-year students on campus, conducting 2163 interviews. An additional 22 companies recruited at a GSIA-hosted West Coast job forum. More than 600 other job opportunities were posted by correspondence. Hiring the largest batches of GSIA grads in 1994 were Deloitte & Touche (9); Ford Motor (8); Coopers & Lybrand (7); EDS Consulting (6); Ernst & Young (6); International Paper (5); Andersen Consulting (5); Citibank (4); American Management Systems (3); Arthur D. Little (3); Avery Dennison (3); Bankers Trust (3); Federated Investors (3); and Hoffman LaRoche (3).

Judging by this list of companies, Sullivan already has the widespread support to make a huge leap in the next round of corporate rankings. The vast majority of this school's problems are now behind it. Carnegie Mellon is clearly on the comeback trail.

Contact: Susan Motz, admissions director, 412-268-2272
Final application deadline: March 15 for fall

Outstanding Faculty

1. Jeffrey R. Williams (****): He has been involved in seminars with AT&T, Bell Laboratories, and Bristol Myers Squibb to help these companies manage the effects of competitive markets. That real-world experience has come in handy at Carnegie where he teaches competitive strategy. An expert on the airline and steel industries, Williams brings a trio of degrees to Carnegie, including an MBA from the University of Michigan.

2. Robert M. Dammon (***): Would you believe his current research agenda involves the "theoretical analysis of foreign exchange hedging for multinational corporations and a theoretical and empirical analysis of the relative pricing of high-yield debt"? Well, what would you expect from Carnegie Mellon? Despite the academic gobbledygook, Dammon is a professor who can speak rather eloquent English in a classroom. He came to Carnegie to teach corporate finance with a trio of degrees from the University of Wisconsin, including an MBA.

3. Kannan Srinivasan (***): A former Procter & Gamble brand manager in India, Srinivasan joined the marketing faculty at Carnegie Mellon in 1986 after getting his Ph.D. from UCLA. Other than a short visiting stint at the University of Chicago in early 1994, he's been impressing students here with his remarkable teaching skills in such courses as marketing management and new product management. Srinivasan has twice been nominated for the best teaching award at GSIA in 1991 and 1993.

4. Fallaw B. Sowell (**): This North Carolina–born economics teacher won the teaching excellence award in 1992, just four years after joining the school as an assistant professor. Sowell earned a Ph.D. in economics at Duke in 1985, with a thesis on "Fractionally Integrated Vector Time Series," and an M.S. in statistics at North Carolina.

5. Duane J. Seppi (**): Since joining Carnegie in 1986, Seppi has been teaching a variety of finance courses. But he gets his high marks for his electives in Investment Analysis and Options. This Chicago Ph.D. is also advisor to the Portfolio Management Club, and a faculty volunteer for the "I Have a Dream" program to help disadvantaged children.

6. Arjay Kalra (*): Winner of the George Leland Bach Excellence in Teaching Award in 1994, this marketing prof gains kudos for deftly teaching the elective Marketing Communications and Buyer Behavior. Kalra signed on to Carnegie in 1992, after gaining his Ph.D. in marketing from Duke University. He's also known for his frequent appearances at GSIA's weekly happy hour, "Friday Beers."

Other Best Bets: *Gerald C. Meyers* (management), *Sridhar R. Tayur* (manufacturing), *R. Bruce McKern* (international management), and *Michael A. Trick* (operations research)

Prominent Alumni: Paul A. Allaire, CEO of Xerox Corp.; Ray Smith, CEO of Bell Atlantic; William Aylesworth, CFO of Texas Instruments; Thomas E. Frank, CEO of Hickory Farms; J. Thomas Presby, CEO, Europe, of DRT International; Frank A. Risch, corporate vice president of Exxon Chemical Co.; Francois De Carbonnel, CEO of GE Capital, Europe; Keith Gollust, managing director of Gollust, Tierney and Oliver; Therese Myers, president of Quarterdeck Office Systems

Carnegie Mellon MBAs Sound Off

Anyone who believes that GSIA is for quant jocks only is just plain wrong. It's a great program for anybody looking for a rigorous business education that's as broad as it is deep. What really distinguishes the education is the emphasis on critical thinking. Simply memorizing formulas won't get you through this program. You've got to understand when a problem-solving approach is appropriate and when it's not. Teaching here consistently focuses on relevant, forward-looking business practice.—**Marketing Manager**

Students who are not mathematically inclined, have math GMAT scores lower than verbal GMAT scores, or want to study areas other than finance, production/operations, or information systems, should not attend GSIA. This is especially true for nonquantitative thinkers who want to study marketing or general management—even if GSIA is the highest-ranked school to which they are accepted. Students who are not quantitative in both temperament and career focus will not like the program, will not do well, and will have difficulty finding a job upon graduation.—**Career Path Unknown**

The newly expanded facilities are wonderful. The availability of computer resources dedicated to the program, and the required use of computers for many classes, creates a high-level of integration between technology and the curriculum. By graduation, most students are adept at using computers.—**Systems Engineer**

The school's major disadvantages are its small number of students, weak alumni network, and lack of enough publicity.—**Finance Associate**

Because of our mini-semester system, we get to take many electives. I took over 25. And each seven-week course covers nearly as much if not as much as the full-semester courses I've taken elsewhere. The workload is incredible, and students have no choice but to learn how to manage time very well and prioritize tasks. But it is still possible to get it all done.—**Financial Analyst**

One thing that GSIA does exceptionally well is its project classes. They are company-sponsored projects in which students attempt to research and solve a spe-

*cific business problem. I worked on one which examined cycle-time reduction in the technology transfer process. These projects give students the opportunity to get hands-on experience with real business situations.—**Consultant***

The GSIA administration has established a culture that solicits comments and suggestions on everything. Our electronic bulletin board, where nothing is taboo, allows for a free flow of ideas. This is regularly monitored by the administration, and as soon as an issue or idea surfaces they are quick to respond. In fact, they post messages often to stimulate discussions. They are extremely proactive.
*—**Consultant***

*It was a tough two years, but I have never had such a good time working so hard. GSIA is one big, happy family. Everyone knows everyone, from students to faculty to the administration.—**Consultant***

The education I received was technically and analytically superior—but that's a given at Carnegie Mellon. What I was pleasantly surprised by was the emphasis on teamwork, leadership, and communications skills. It was truly first-rate.
*—**Financial Analyst***

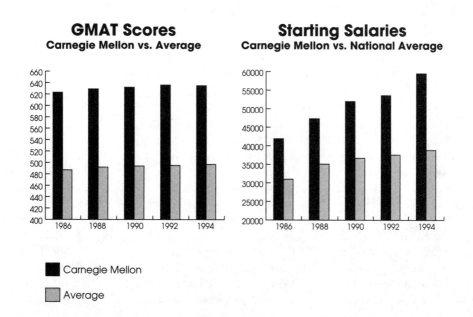

GMAT Scores
Carnegie Mellon vs. Average

Starting Salaries
Carnegie Mellon vs. National Average

■ Carnegie Mellon
▨ Average

15. Cornell University

Johnson Graduate School of Management
Malott Hall
Ithaca, New York 14853

Corporate ranking: 17
Enrollment: 490
Women: 24%
Non-U.S.: 29%
Minority: 7%
Part-time: None
Average age: 27
Applicants accepted: 37%
Median starting pay: $70,000

Graduate ranking: 13
Annual tuition & fees: $20,400
Room and board: $11,400
Average GMAT score: 630
GMAT range: 430 to 760
Average GPA: 3.2
GPA range: 2.2 to 4.0
Accepted applicants enrolled: 42%
Average starting pay: $71,970

Teaching methods: Lecture, 50%   Case study, 30%   Group projects, 20%

At the height of the admissions process, Cornell University's B-School Dean Alan Merten squirrels himself away in the upstairs study of his colonial home and hits the telephone. He begins dialing the hottest MBA candidates who have not yet responded to Cornell's admissions invitations. After dinner, he begins the calls around 8 p.m., reaching as many people on the East Coast and in the Midwest as possible, until he quits at about 11 p.m., when most of the telephoning is to candidates in the West. Sometimes, the sales calls create unusual exchanges between the dean and befuddled applicants on the other end of the line.

"Hello, I'm Alan Merten from Cornell," the dean will say.

"No, you're not."

"Yes, I am," Merten retorts.

"Who is this?"

"I'm the dean of the Johnson School at Cornell."

Finally, there's a dead silence. And then, "Oh, my God!"

Merten laughs as he tells the story that says so much about the place graduates dub "the friendly school." Even months before you get here, there's that special, personal touch. And when you arrive, it's not forgotten. Within the first month, the dean and his wife invite every first-year student to dinner in their home. That's almost 30 students a night, with some faculty, on nine different occasions before covering the 250 students in an average entering class. "I do it because I think it's important, and I like it," says the cordial academic. "Yet, I can't envision anyone five years ago who would do that."

Tucked away in New York's Finger Lakes region in Ithaca, Johnson's small class size fosters unusually close relationships between students and faculty—whether they're climbing mountains, debating an issue in class, or competing against each other in sports. A productive and caring faculty—whose concern with teaching places the professors here in the upper 20th percentile in BUSINESS WEEK's consumer satisfaction surveys—create an intimate and challenging environment. Johnson faculty are among the most approachable and accessible professors in business education. They don't have to post office hours, as one graduate put it, because they are always there.

Indeed, one of the true annual events at the school is the battle between the Frozen Assets, the female MBAs' hockey team, and a group of professors. Faculty and students also compete against each other in the eight-mile Joe Thomas Invitational Run. The Johnson School's high degree of faculty involvement and its flexible curriculum win high marks from students. MBAs who are barely out the door already wax nostalgic about the Cornell experience and the virtues of life in Ithaca, a picturesque village overlooking Cayuga Lake. The school's isolated location fosters a community spirit, and the combination of a small student body and an involved faculty gives Johnson the freedom to be bold and experimental. It often forges links with other Cornell schools to develop unusual programs, encourages team teaching by professors from different disciplines, and creates novel international programs.

Johnson grads are less enthusiastic about the school's facilities and its placement office. Although Cornell's pastoral setting is great for studying and enjoying outdoor sports, it's off the beaten path for college recruiters, although the Johnson School has traditionally attracted a steady stream of recruiters from commercial and investment banks in New York City. MBAs here have high expectations, and they should, considering Cornell's hefty pricetag—$20,400 a year. The B-school, named after Samuel C. Johnson of Johnson's Wax fame, is no bargain when it comes to tuition. You'll get better bang for the buck at the University of North Carolina, Berkeley, or UCLA.

Merten, who became dean in 1989, has since increased the size of career services from four positions to six. He's also worked on building better alumni support for new graduates, bringing out an alumni directory every two or three years instead of every five or six, producing upgraded monthly job listings for MBAs and an executive search manual, and getting Cornell to join a computer job-matching service. He plans to hire a full-time staffer dedicated to nothing but counseling services for alumni, too. Merten also is trying to raise $38 million to renovate Sage Hall, a historic building in the center of campus, to be the new home of the Johnson School. The dean expects to move the B-school from Malott Hall, the current building, to its new home by 1998.

Johnson wants to prepare students to manage in a global, competitive marketplace, and he has just revised the existing MBA curriculum. Johnson will also begin to offer a 12-month MBA program for students who hold a graduate degree in a scientific or technical field. Cornell's strategy appears to keep its mainstream MBA pretty basic and to tap into the strengths of the rest of the university to make the Johnson degree unique. This has partly occurred through the creation of joint degree programs in Asian studies and engineering. Through the Cornell Manufacturing, Engineering, and Productivity Program, students with an undergraduate engineering degree and professional experience can obtain master's degrees in engineering and management in five semesters. The program also allows MBAs who concentrate in manufacturing management to sign up for engineering electives. In the spring of 1994 the school instituted a new 15-unit course semester in manufacturing. An engineer by training, Merten will continue the Johnson School's emphasis on manufacturing.

Preparing students to manage in a world characterized by increasing cultural and ethnic diversity is another issue that Merten sees as a priority. "Many schools are talking about this issue, but we are attempting to address it through a variety of concrete steps," he says. However, students still gripe about the lack of minority students and faculty at the B-school.

The Johnson School has won international recognition for two programs that teach MBAs about Japanese language and culture. The first is a three-year program leading to master's degrees in management and Asian studies. This option includes 12 months of intensive Japanese language classes and often a summer internship in Japan with firms such as Mobil Corp. Japan, Nippon Telegraph and Telephone, and Mitsubishi's chemical unit. The second is a two-year MBA course with a concentration in Japanese business that includes a summer of intensive language classes and Japanese classes throughout the year.

These rigorous Japanese business programs are more than something for Johnson MBAs to put on their résumés or talk about during job interviews. For students with the requisite talent and commitment, they often lead to lucrative management jobs with American companies in Japan. After earning master's degrees in management and Asian studies, Jim Latimer, a Johnson alum, landed a job with Corning Glass's Japanese subsidiary.

Before he came to Cornell, Latimer had never spoken a word of Japanese. After earning an undergraduate degree from Georgia Tech, he had worked for robotics manufacturer Cincinnati Milacron for several years. "If you decide you want to learn Japanese as an adult, Cornell is one of the few places you can take the language for 12 months straight." The FALCON (Full-Year Asian Language Concentration) program is designed for people starting from scratch," he says. Other B-schools such as Michigan, Berkeley, and Wharton allow MBAs to simultaneously earn a master's in Asian studies, but few offer as innovative a program as Cornell's.

In addition to the joint degree programs in Asian studies and engineering, Johnson allows students to earn an MBA and a doctor of law in four years, instead of the five required to earn each degree separately. The B-school also offers a joint degree with Cornell's School of Industrial and Labor Relations. The program targets students with interest in human-resource issues. "What makes us unique among B-schools is how we've taken advantage of other schools at the university," says Curtis Tarr, the former dean. Another unique opportunity at the Johnson School arises because of its ties with the College of Engineering and the School of Industrial and Labor Relations. "Semester in Manufacturing" integrates typically disparate areas such as accounting, marketing, engineering, and quality control into a single 15-credit course. It is the only course taken in the spring semester by students who participate. The course was developed in cooperation with Corning, and features team teaching and extended field trips to manufacturing facilities.

For the run-of-the-mill MBA, there's unusual flexibility and variety, including the choice of 65 electives at the B-school. The greater diversity, however, comes because Johnson MBAs may take more than 15 credits—or about 5 of the 20 courses required for an MBA—in other Cornell top-notch schools, including the College of Architecture, Art and Planning, the School of Hotel Administration, the School of Industrial and Labor Relations, and the College of Human Ecology, which offers courses in health administration. One 1992 grad boasts that he took 6 courses outside the B-school, including a pair at the law school, 2 in the natural resources program, 1 in agricultural economics, and another in government. "I was able to tailor my degree closely to the environmental concerns I have," he says.

To earn an MBA from the Johnson school, you'll need to spend four semesters in Ithaca and earn 60 credits. There are 8 courses equal to 22.5 credits in Johnson's core curriculum, 4 of which are taken in the first semester and 4 in the second semester. These include financial accounting, statistics, microeconomics, marketing, organizational behavior, finance, operations, and strategy.

During the second year, you'll design your own program of elective courses, taking a series of classes as broad or specialized as you like. Johnson provides "road maps" or lists of suggested classes for students pursuing a specific career track, but does not require students to concentrate in any particular area. The choices available to Johnson students through Cornell's Center for International Studies is staggering, including concentrations in international economics and trade, international management, and United States international public policies and issues. If you have a technical or scientific graduate degree, you can opt to complete the MBA in 12 months beginning in 1995. You'll bypass the first-year curriculum and arrive on campus in June with 20 credits of advanced standing. The summer months are dedicated to an intense core program, and then you'll complete your degree with two regular semesters of elective courses.

In addition to the two programs in Japanese business, Cornell offers exchange programs with the London Business School, two universities in Belgium, an institute in France, and schools in Switzerland, Norway, Italy, the Netherlands, Venezuela, Hong Kong, and Australia. However, space in these programs is very limited—only two Johnson students can participate in the program with SDA Bocconi in Milan, for example—and sometimes Johnson cannot satisfy the demand to study abroad.

Like any Ivy League institution, Cornell puts a lot of emphasis on research. But the Johnson school prides itself on good teaching. *Cornell Business,* the feisty MBA-published B-school newspaper, regularly prints student evaluations of faculty to embarrass the laggards into improving their performance. The weak links in teaching, however, are few. BW's surveys show that teaching in both the core and elective courses is above average among the 40-plus schools whose graduates are polled by the magazine. Indeed, Johnson puts some of its best teachers into the basic building-block courses—which the seasoned faculty at many other schools prefer not to teach because they are too elementary.

Among the three most popular electives here are a pair of courses that simply feature the best of the university's professors: World Geopolitical Environment of Business and Regulatory and Legal Environment of Business, both of which require B-school profs to spend 10 percent or less of their time in. Instead, these multidisciplinary offerings feature sociologists, political scientists, and historians such as former President Carter advisor Alfred E. Kahn. The B-school's single most popular elective is David BenDaniel's Entrepreneurship and Enterprise class, which has even spawned a few small businesses, including a limousine service started by one MBA that runs between the Syracuse airport and Ithaca.

Like the Simon School at the University of Rochester, Cornell's Johnson school attracts a good number of finance types who recharge their batteries and beef up their credentials before returning to commercial and investment banking jobs in New York. MBAs don't have to worry about losing touch with the corporate scene while they are up in Ithaca, thanks to visiting executives such as Charles F. Knight of Emerson Electric, Sandy Weill of Primerica, and Lou Noto of Mobil. During breaks in their studies, Johnson MBAs ice skate at the university's rink and play golf on a school course when there's no snow on the ground. Each spring, B-schools from all over the country send teams to Ithaca to participate in an annual Invitational Golf Tournament. Johnson MBAs are dedicated athletes and like to play hockey, lacrosse, and volleyball. There's even a men's hockey team dubbed the Puck Bunnies. You guessed it: Another of the year's big events is the charity matchup pitting the Assets against the Bunnies.

Since many graduates of Cornell's hotel school decide to stay in the area, there is no shortage of excellent restaurants and bars in Ithaca, including the famous Moosewood Restaurant, which has produced several best-selling cookbooks. When it's time to relax, Johnson MBAs often head to Hauncey's for a few beers. Aladdin's has the best pita sandwiches in town and an impressive selection of homemade soups. Coyote Loco and Mexicali Rose are the favored spots for Mexican fare, while the Nines in Collegetown serves a fantastic deep-dish pizza.

While the school's career services office has improved in recent years, students still complain about the quantity and geographical diversity of recruiters. About 94.9 percent of the class had job offers by commencement, averaging 2.4 offers each—about the average of the 40-plus schools surveyed by BUSINESS WEEK.

In 1994, some 104 companies arrived to conduct more than 3800 interviews. Four years earlier, the school attracted about 150 recruiting firms. So Cornell has stepped up efforts to bring students to them, participating in at least half a dozen job fairs across the United States. In 1994, some 593 job opportunities were posted via correspondence. The biggest hires: Citibank (6); Chase Manhattan (6); Deloitte & Touche; Coopers & Lybrand (4); J.P. Morgan (3); Bankers Trust (3); Chemical Bank (3); American Management Systems (3); Procter & Gamble (3); and Goldman Sachs (2).

Dean Merten must now use his personal touch to continue the improvement of the school's recruiting efforts and to make sure he never loses the unusual devotion of his faculty to Johnson's students.

Contact: Anne Coyle, director of admissions, 800-847-2082
Final application deadline: March 15 for fall, January 15 for 12-month program

Outstanding Faculty

1. Warren Bailey (****): An engaging actor and director in his college and graduate school days, Bailey now employs his theatrical skills in the classroom, winning kudos from students for his teaching prowess in International Finance. He puts his expertise in the Pacific Rim markets to the test by trading directly on stock markets in such farflung places as Singapore, Indonesia, and China. This recently tenured prof came to the B-school in 1990 after a four-year stint at Ohio State. Bailey got his Ph.D. from UCLA, his MBA from McGill University, and his bachelor's degree in economics from Cornell. In

1992, Bailey was the first recipient of a new teaching award determined by each graduating class.

2. Alan K. McAdams (****): He's known for his ability to stimulate student interest, his propensity to take controversial positions, and his willingness to "tilt at windmills." McAdams was chief economic consultant and expert witness for the government in United States vs. IBM, testifying for a total of 78 days. Compared to that experience, teaching MBAs is a breeze for him. He holds an MBA and Ph.D. from Stanford. He teaches a strategic consulting course, which features consulting projects.

3. Harold Bierman, Jr. (****): One of Cornell's most durable and enduring professors, Bierman is an veritable institution at Cornell, having taught business strategy here since 1961. Indeed, such former students-turned-CEOs as Emerson Electric's Chuck Knight, Polaroid's MacAllister Booth, and Chevron's Kenneth Derr still speak of the impact "Hal" has had on them as students and throughout their careers. Not surprisingly, he recently won the first teaching award annually selected by the five-year reunion class. The honor was established by an alum whose son is now a first-year student who was particularly excited by Bierman's teaching. When the son told his dad, he said: "The same thing happened to me 30 years ago."

4. Mark Nelson (***): His sense of humor makes this gregarious accounting professor popular with students, even though his courses require MBAs to respond to "cold-calling" about topics in financial accounting and auditing. He's one of the youngest members of the B-school faculty—Nelson received his Ph.D. from Ohio State in 1990.

5. Jerome E. Haas (**): This Johnson School veteran gets rave reviews as a regular blues singer in the Follies, an annual student-faculty event. Haas has been teaching the core finance course for virtually all of his 27 years at the B-school, and he continues to bring enthusiasm into the classroom. He was chief of research for the Federal Energy Regulatory Commission, and a Special Assistant to James Schlesinger in the Carter Administration. Haas picked up an MBA from Wharton and a Ph.D. from Carnegie Mellon.

6. L. Joseph Thomas (**): Thomas left an Eastman Kodak job as a chemical engineer to enter academia and never looked back. He did his graduate work in operations management at Yale and moved to Cornell, where he has been teaching for 26 years—with only slight interruptions as a visiting prof at Stanford and business schools in Switzerland and Belgium. His interactive style of teaching is based on a simple philosophy: "Learning only occurs on the part of the student. I share things I know, but also cause students to think about business problems." Thomas, whose chair has been endowed by a contributor whose surname was Noyes, teaches business logistics and also runs Cornell's executive programs. "My kids love the fact that I'm the Noyes professor," he laughs. "But they spell it the other way, noisy."

Other Best Bets: *Vithala R. Rao* (marketing), *Ronald W. Hilton* (accounting), *Lawrence W. Robinson* (operations management), and *Pradeep K. Chintagunta* (marketing)

Prominent Alumni: Kenneth Derr, CEO of Chevron; Charles F. Knight, chairman of Emerson Electric; I. MacAllister Booth, chairman of Polaroid; Charles Lacy, general manager of Ben and Jerry's Ice Cream; Lou Noto, CEO of Mobil; Karel Vinck, CEO of Bekaerk NY; Robert Dyson, CEO Dyson-Kissner-Doran, Jim Hauslein, chairman, Sunglass

Johnson MBAs Sound Off

Cornell's small student body provides exceptional access to a faculty whose knowledge is surpassed only by their capacity for genuine concern and delight in the progress of their students. A premium is placed on teaching at the Johnson School, promoting spirited dialogue between students and faculty. Such one-on-one attention underscores the differences between knowing and understanding.
—Accounting Associate

There are far too many young students, averaged out by a few much older ones. The trend toward younger students is disturbing, and does not add value to a top-class MBA program.—Technical Career Path

One major benefit offered by the Johnson School is the accessibility to the rest of Cornell University. One can strongly enhance the business school education by taking courses in the Engineering School, the Industrial and Labor Relations School, or the Hotel School, for example. The College of Arts & Sciences offers dozens of language courses, while the Human Ecology College offers courses in health care management. The freedom to take up to 25 percent of your courses outside of the Johnson School becomes a true asset when so much variety is available.—Senior Business Analyst

Because the school is isolated, students study, party, hang out, and sometimes vacation together. Everybody knows everybody. The international students add a lot to the school. Women are very vocal and run many of the clubs. Diversity is a problem among Americans. There are few African-Americans or Hispanics. The program is tough; students are usually in the library.—Career Path Unknown

The worst parts of the JGSM experience are the weather (although the geography and nature is wonderful) and the Career Services Office. The location of Ithaca doesn't help, but the number of companies pales in comparison to even non-top-20 schools. Individuals trying to find jobs in areas other than the northeast are, for the most part, on their own.—Financial Analyst

While some people feel that JGSM's location in Ithaca is a negative, I think it is one of its greatest attributes. Admittedly, it was difficult to "pop" into New York for an interview. However, the advantages far outweighed the disadvantages. The location, combined with JGSM's connection to the greater Cornell campus, allowed for participation in extracurricular activities which are unavailable at *many other top schools. In my two years at JGSM, I took sailing lessons on Lake Cayuga, learned how to rock-climb, and played intramural ice hockey for two seasons.—**Financial Analyst***

*The large international population at the Johnson School added a global perspective to every aspect of the MBA experience. From discussions in class, to living-mates, to the ever-available Japanese golf partners, you could not escape interaction with international students—a situation consistent with business today. The experience is enhanced through the availability of student-run and -led trips to countries such as Japan, India, and Venezuela which combine business and tourism.—**Consultant***

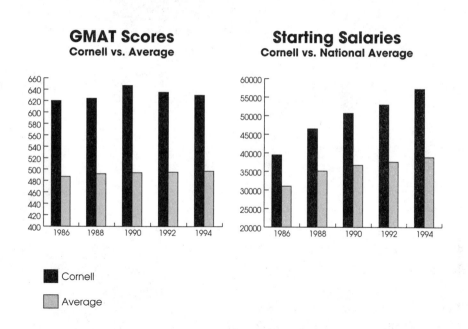

16. New York University

Leonard N. Stern School of Business
Management Education Center
44 West Fourth Street
New York, NY 10012

Corporate ranking: 13
Enrollment: 3201
Women: 28%
Non-U.S.: 34%
Minority: 14%
Part-time: 2275
Average age: 27
Applicants accepted: 40%*
Median starting pay: $70,000

Graduate ranking: 20
Annual tuition & fees: $20,276
Room and board: $9675
Average GMAT score: 630
GMAT range: 550 to 700 (mid-80%)
Average GPA: 3.2
GPA range: 2.7 to 3.7 (mid-80%)
Accepted applicants enrolled: 36%
Average starting pay: $70,660

Teaching methods: Lecture, 50%   Case study, 45%   Group projects, 5%

Taking a cue from David Letterman, the Stern School student nudged up to the onstage mike with her own Top 10 list. The topic: Top 10 Reasons to Go to Stern over Harvard Business School.

10. It's $600 a year cheaper.

9. I'm severely allergic to Ivy.

8. Would be lost with all that grass on that wide campus.

7. Harvard is not on the R line.

6. Wouldn't know what to do with all the money when I graduated.

5. Always hated the Head of the Charles.

4. Networking not all it is cracked up to be.

3. I always wanted to market cat litter for Hartz Mountain Group.

2. Too many on-campus interviews would interfere with my daily schedule.

1. Tired of all those drunken Kennedy parties.

Well, okay, so maybe Letterman wouldn't be all that impressed with the self-depre-cating wit of Stern's MBAs at their recent annual follies show. But now students can add another reason to forgo Harvard: The school has finally moved out of its dingy quarters near Wall Street onto New York University's main campus in Greenwich Village.

The Class of 1994 was the first to arrive at what is called the most expensive building in the history of management education, hearing the wheezing of electric saws and drills as dozens of construction workers rushed about to complete work on the $68 million cen-ter. Layers of fine dust covered nearly everything. The staircases were still taped closed, and only a few elevators were working. At the time, even a joking student might not have wanted to include the building in the Top 10 list.

But the new management education center, with a cobblestone plaza in front, is helping to transform New York University's Stern School into a formidable competitor for top-tier students. The school's 200-strong faculty, once dispersed over 24 floors in 6 separate buildings, is now housed on 3 floors in a single location. For the first time in the school's history, the faculty actually has its own lounge.

Instead of sitting in hard wooden chairs with arm-top desks in flat classrooms, MBAs now boast of the finest, multi-tiered, state-of-the-art classrooms available anywhere. The new environment itself imposes different demands on Stern faculty. Professors standing in front of these classrooms genuinely feel that they are on stage and have to perform—something that will put additional pressure on teaching laggards to upgrade their presentation skills.

No less important, the school has launched major changes in the MBA program, to make the Stern curriculum far more relevant and challenging. The overhaul debuted in 1993, although the school began piloting the new core courses with a group of 65 newcomers in the fall of 1992. "The design of the new program is designed to provide an integrated experience where all the courses 'fit together,' " says Janet R. Marks, associate dean. "We have developed new courses that involve more teamwork, globalization, and communication skills."

The person who engineered these dramatic changes is no longer around to see their result. Dean Richard R. West ended his nine-year stint at the head of NYU's business school in mid-1993. West, formerly dean of Dartmouth's Amos Tuck School, brought in the $30 million naming gift from Hartz Group entrepreneur Leonard N. Stern, and bickered with city-planning officials and contractors in getting the new management center up and running. He also led the curriculum revision effort.

George G. Daly, a former White House economist and long-time dean of the University of Iowa's B-school, took over where West left off. Daly is leading the school through a time of transition. While many things have changed, many of the school's attributes will seem the same. The new school in Washington Square will remain a big, urban, diverse, and eclectic school with one of the best graduate finance programs in the world. Full and part-time students may continue to attend the same elective classes—something that many full-time MBAs enjoy, because part-timers often bring real-life perspective to class discussions. As Mitchell Hecht, an alum, relates, "I found myself taking classes at night to get certain professors, and in the evening classes you get students who are bond traders during the day who question and challenge some of the classroom theory. The level of dialogue and sophistication is pretty high."

Yet the new center is helping Stern to shake its image as a "night school"—the result of its 1916 roots as a satellite campus on Trinity Place for Wall Streeters who walked to class after work. Such students still account for a large part-time enrollment that the school has deliberately shrunk by one-third to 2000 students.

For Stern's incoming full-timers, a three-day orientation featuring among other things an ethics game and an Outward Bound-like experience in Central Park kicked off the

1994 school year right before Labor Day. In the new program, cohort groups of 65 students each travel through 12 core courses together—although you can still waive out of a core offering if you've taken the same course as an undergrad. Many of the remaining eight courses required to graduate will fulfill "major" requirements. Stern students may major in one or more of seven functional areas: accounting, economics, finance, information systems, management, marketing, or statistics and operations research. You can even combine these majors with a further concentration in international business or operations management.

After complaints about the quality of teaching in core courses, teaching effectiveness workshops were required for all new teachers and core courses are supposed to be taught by faculty who have proven themselves to be "effective" teachers. Student evaluations of teachers and classes are made public, so that Stern grads can attempt to avoid the worst of the lot by doing a little research. The latest round of BUSINESS WEEK's customer satisfaction polls show that teaching quality at Stern has improved, though it's rated not much better than average of the 40-plus schools whose graduates are surveyed by the magazine.

It helped that in 1990 West scored a near academic miracle when he got his faculty to pass a promotion and tenure policy that placed as much importance on teaching quality as it did on scholarly research. It was the first time in two decades that the faculty was able to agree on the issue. Eight years earlier, professors here were only one vote shy of approving a policy that would have made research the only criterion for promotion and tenure.

Besides the complaints over teaching, several Stern MBAs maintain that the quality of their classmates isn't always as consistent as it should be, and they say that the large contingent of international students aren't integrated into the school as well as they could be. You'll also hear complaints about the difficulty the placement office has in luring a broader range of corporations to campus to recruit Stern students.

One thing is certain: At Stern, finance is king. A recent study of published research in *Financial Management* ranked Stern's finance department first in the nation ahead of Wharton, UCLA, Chicago, and Columbia. Stern's finance faculty alone outnumbers the entire faculty at many B-schools, including Amos Tuck. Almost 20 percent of the school's 250 courses are in the finance area, from Fixed-Income Securities to Venture Capital to Going Public. And Stern grads—despite their complaints about the teaching—almost universally praise the finance faculty.

While nonfinance types might initially cross Stern off their lists, the school boasts a top-notch program in international business. A peek inside the course catalog fails to tell the whole story, since seemingly non-international courses often include a global aspect. Stern also has a good number of international students. Roughly 35 percent of entering full-time MBAs are not from the U.S.—that's 300 people from more than 60 different countries from Australia to Peru, including what might be the largest single contingent at a U.S. B-school from Japan—nearly 100 Japanese students. The school even publishes a separate guide for international applicants.

Stern also boasts an internationally oriented faculty. Since 1980, more than 60 percent of the teachers hired by Stern didn't have U.S. passports at one time. Sometimes that's a disadvantage, because some students complain that they have had trouble understanding professors with heavy foreign accents. Even so, the Academy of International Business ranked Stern the nation's top school in 1988 for its international program. The centerpiece of the global slant is an exchange program Stern runs with 20 foreign graduate schools in 17 countries, from the Chinese University of Hong Kong to Sweden's Stockholm School of Economics. Each year, about 60 Stern students trek abroad for at least one semester in the fall of their second year.

For the top students who stay in New York, many enroll in an unusual management consulting course in the second year that stretches over both the fall and spring terms of the second year. In the course, students gain a taste for real-world training as they work as consultants for such companies as American Express Co., Digital Equipment Corp., and Sony Corp. At the end of the project, students deliver oral and written reports to high-level executives of each sponsoring company.

Other surprises? Stern boasts a strong program in information systems. From 1980 to 1986, Stern faculty published more articles in the top five management information systems' journals than teachers from any other B-school. Stern's strong showing is largely the result of a highly prolific professor, Henry C. Lucas Jr. At Stern, unlike many other top schools, Information Systems for Management is a required core course, not an elective.

Going to school in New York, of course, can be daunting for some. Stern tries to ease the transition by putting all its first-year students into cohorts of 65 MBAs, each headed by a "Blockhead." Students keep tabs on happenings through the *Stern School Update,* the weekly calendar of lectures, beer blasts, and recruiter visits put out by the office of student affairs. MBAs can also keep abreast of new events through E-mail and Gopher, an on-line info service for Stern-specific news. Student groups range from the Entrepreneurs' Exchange to the Women's Career Forum. MBAs also publish *Opportunity,* the monthly newspaper that attempts to cover the school's ins and outs. It helps that all students are now guaranteed university housing on designated Stern School floors in Alumni Hall on Third Avenue and Tenth Street. About 25 percent of Stern students hole up in university housing.

Stern's new complex is made up of a trio of linked buildings: Virtually all the MBA action occurs in the 11-story Management Education Center (MEC). Then, there's Tisch Hall for the undergraduate program, and the top six newly renovated floors of 100-year-old Shimkin Hall. (The bottom part of the building is occupied by the School of Nursing.) Stern made the absolute most of all the space it could hog. One 200-seat auditorium in the new center boasts a back row higher than the ceiling that gives you the feeling you're in the upper deck at Yankee Stadium. The "Starship Enterprise Lounge"—the modern-looking student lounge on the third and fourth floors of the MEC—has already become a gathering place for all MBAs. Stern no longer has its own library. Instead, the business collection is on the sixth floor of the university's Bobst Library, the red sandstone building adjacent to the B-school complex. Students can do library searches from within the MEC by logging on to Bobcat, the NYU library database. MBAs can find current periodicals in a fifth-floor reading room.

There's no paucity of restaurants and hangouts in Washington Square. Good vegetarian cooking at cheap prices is available at Apple on Waverly. There's Pluck U on West

Third Street for chili, fries, and Buffalo Wings, and Sam's Falafel on Thompson Street for fast food Greek style (with a 15 percent discount to NYU students). Two Boots on Bleeker serves up Cajun-style pizza.

Professors describe Stern students as down-to-earth: not as intellectually probing as those at Wharton or Stanford, but more aggressive and street-smart. And the vast majority of them are into finance, hardly a surprise given the school's proximity to Wall Street. More than half the MBAs pursue finance majors. Neither is it surprising that as Wall Street turns, so does the business school. Stern's recruiting schedules are typically packed with interviewers from the investment banks, brokerage firms, and commercial banks. The revival of the Street enabled the school to bring in about two job offers each to 86 percent of the Class of 1994 by commencement.

In all, 173 companies recruited on campus in 1994 for permanent jobs, conducting more than 5000 interviews. Some 1718 full-time job opportunities came into the school via correspondence. Citicorp took Stern grads by the truckload, hiring 16 members of the Class of 1994. Other big buyers of Stern talent were EDS (8); Andersen Consulting (8); Chemical Bank (7); Smith Barney (6); Merrill Lynch (6); American Express (5); Bankers Trust (5); Coopers & Lybrand (5); and Chase Manhattan (5).

Those recruiters are likely to be impressed with the many changes occurring at this New York City school. With a bit of luck, fewer people will need 10 reasons to pick Stern over other top business schools.

Contact: Hallie Kuiper, associate director of admissions, 212-998-0600
Final application deadlines: April 15 for fall; October 15 for spring

Outstanding Faculty

1. Aswath Damodaran (****): Since arriving at Stern in 1986, this brilliant finance teacher has consistently ranked among the top five—and often No. 1—in the entire faculty. Indian-born Damodaran looks like he's 12 years old, but teaches with the finesse and grace of a seasoned veteran. He's so good in class that in 1990 he became the youngest winner of the university-wide Great Teacher Award. Damodaran might well have been a tennis pro, having been nationally ranked for years. But as an MBA student at UCLA, he found himself in the classroom of Tom Copeland, who now teaches at NYU. Damodaran credits Copeland with changing his life path by making the study of finance fascinating. He went on to earn a Ph.D. from UCLA, becoming a visiting lecturer at Berkeley before moving east to Stern. His devotion is evident: "I love getting up on the days I'm teaching more than on the days I'm not," he says. "I don't think many people are this lucky." Raves one fan: "Wow! He made corporate finance seem easy to a marketing major with no previous finance experience."

2. William Silber (**): This longtime finance prof has kept up ties to the real world. During his 28 years as a Stern professor he has worked as a gold and crude-oil trader, and he is a member of the Commodity Exchange and the New York Cotton Exchange. Silber is known for his sense of humor, accessibility, and his love of teaching (he learns all of his students names, even in evening classes of 200). Alumni say he is one of their most vivid faculty memories. "Professor Silber was so dedicated to his teaching that if you came to his class unprepared, you personally felt like you let him down," notes one alumnus.

3. Michael H. Darling (**):   As a former top executive at Kellogg and Max Factor, London-born Darling brings real-world knowhow to his informative and entertaining lectures on marketing. He keeps his toes in the real world by consulting with the likes of AT&T, Canon, Nabisco, and Sony. Darling, who has an MBA from Concordia University in Montreal, joined Stern in 1986 after being an adjunct prof at Pepperdine University. Lately, he's intrigued with how companies are handling the greening of the American public. Darling includes an environmental module in his core marketing classes as well as his New Product Development course.

4. Richard Freedman (**):   This organizational behavior prof is known for his Socratic style. Freedman loves a good argument as long as it's well supported. And when it comes to case study of management issues, Freedman frames all questions within real-world constraints. "He won't let you get away with just firing half the staff. You have to really work it out," says a student. In 1994, Freedman earned one of four NYU university-wide Distinguished Teaching Awards, based on student and alumni votes and faculty members' service to students and the University.

5. Thomas Copeland (**):   McKinsey and Co. partner by day, and Stern prof by night. Students say Copeland brings a great deal of enthusiasm to his teaching, because he applies what he does all day to his evening classes. The adjunct professor is head of McKinsey's corporate finance practice, and he has also consulted for over 60 companies in two-dozen countries. His academic record is equally impressive. Copeland was a full finance professor and department chairman at UCLA, where he won several awards for teaching. He was a mentor to another top Stern professor, Aswath Damodaran, who studied with him at UCLA.

6. John Czepiel (*):   No one would accuse him of living in an Ivory Tower. A consultant to AT&T's Bell Labs, Union Carbide, and GTE, this marketing prof systematically reads and clips the business press to cite topical examples in his lectures. "I'm shameless," he says. "I'll do anything to keep them interested—stand on a chair, march them around the classroom, or rip up a $20 bill." Czepiel, who earned his master's and Ph.D. from Northwestern, joined Stern in 1972. His courses on Product Strategy and Business-to-Business Marketing are among the most popular at the school, earning him its Excellence in Teaching Award in 1990.

Other Best Bets: *Roy Smith* (finance), *Ingo Walter* (finance), *Edwin Elton* (finance), and *Robert Kavesh* (finance)

Prominent Alumni: Alan Greenspan, chairman of the Federal Reserve Board; Richard J. Kogan, president of Schering-Plough Corp.; Henry Kaufman, president of Henry Kaufman Inc.; Leonard N. Stern, chairman of The Hartz Group; Marion O. Sandler, CEO of Golden West Financial; Tatsuro Toyoda, president of Toyota Motor Co.; Ismail Merchant, film producer; Sherrie Baker, CEO of Halston-Borghese

Stern MBAs Sound Off

For a career on Wall Street or finance in general, there are few better. NYU's reputation, proximity to the street, alumni contacts, and campus recruiting have afforded me the opportunity and the ultimate landing of my ideal job.
—Investment Banking Associate

The part-time program at Stern, which is enormous, I found to be more of a negative for the school rather than a positive, as they would have one believe. In my experience, most of the part-time students were not in any great position to enlighten the full-time students about anything in particular. And in most cases, they were less than enthusiastic about having to sit through one or two 80-minute classes at night after having worked for eight hours that day (can't say as I blamed them, though). This resulted in a "let me get a B and get reimbursed by my employer" attitude.—Finance Career Path

The new building has helped to create a new sense of community. I think that people have focused just on its newness, like the high-tech classrooms and built-in presentation capabilities, but the significance is the change in the ways in which Stern students interact. People stay in the school the way we never did downtown.—Marketing Career Path

Stern's program, in terms of flexibility in course selection to fulfill your major, is too rigid and bureaucratic. A student does not have the freedom to decide what course he or she should take that's best for him or her. Additionally, the emphasis on teamwork here is extreme. Professors would assign a two-page paper to be written by a group of four people.—Career Path Unknown

NYU makes every attempt to help students find means of financial assistance, which was a basis for the decision to choose NYU over other schools, such as Columbia, for myself and many other students.—Marketing Career Path

As a participant in the new curriculum pilot during my first year, I was particularly impressed with the responsiveness of the faculty and administration in their attempt to create a superior MBA program. I believe that this new program offers a progressive and comprehensive view of business and industry.—Marketing Manager

One thing I would like to mention specifically is the diversity. I had a class this semester called Global Perspectives, an economics class that studied the industrialized and newly industrialized powerhouses. No matter what country we studied—Japan, Germany, Korea, India, Brazil, etc.—there was a student from that part of the world to discuss it. It was a thoroughly amazing experience. Being part of the whole Washington Square village campus only adds to the diversity.
—Trading Trainee

*The access to New York City professionals, particularly in finance, was a huge asset. In addition, the abundance of major firms in the area seemed to encourage the professors to teach in a very practical and "real world" manner. I often left class with a clear understanding of how I might apply the day's lesson to a real-world situation.—**Associate***

*As a foreign student, I enjoyed being able to interact with many people from different cultures. Although we as foreign students have to adapt to the American system of education, I felt some instructors did not make enough allowance to our different cultures and sometimes penalized our differences too much (little class participation, for instance).—**Career Path in International Business***

One area of disappointment is the Office of Career Development. This placement office is very focused on traditional finance and marketing jobs. If considering other fields (consulting, for example), OCD doesn't provide good support.
*—**Consultant***

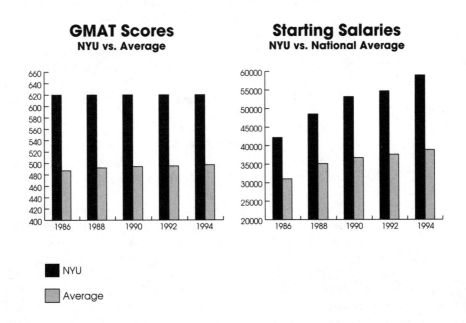

17. University of Texas at Austin

Graduate School of Business
Austin, Texas 78712

Corporate ranking: 11
Enrollment: 890
Women: 31%
Non-U.S.: 19%
Minority: 19%
Part-time: None
Average age: 27
Average years of work exp.: 4
Applicants accepted: 35%
Median starting pay: $59,000

Graduate ranking: 25
Annual tuition: resident—$3630
                  nonresident—$8580
Room and board: $8610
Average GMAT score: 625
GMAT range: 330 to 770
Average GPA: 3.26
GPA range: 1.63 to 4.0
Accepted applicants enrolled: 58%
Average starting pay: $61,890

Teaching methods: Lecture, 30%   Case study, 60%   Group projects, 10%

An old Nike ad once proclaimed, "Image isn't everything." Try telling that to the Texas MBAs. After a two-year introspective look into the program's weaknesses, University of Texas B-school students are on the road to improving the national perception of UT's program. The campaign includes a video aimed at corporate recruiters (the first movie ever filmed for such an audience), and an ambassador program in which MBAs travel around the country to spread the word about the changes that Dean Robert Witt has implemented in Austin. "We were searching for something new and different, and we wanted to show off our strength," says Witt. "So we turned our students loose."

Good thing. For years, Texas has been known for providing great educational value for the money. But the school's reputation in Corporate America just wasn't a match for many of its public or private rivals in the MBA game. The slick video, now being sent to some 2000 corporations, boasts endorsements of Texas MBAs from the likes of Motorola and 3M. And it shows the kind of gung-ho enthusiasm its best students have for the place.

This is more than just an image campaign, however. Texas MBAs are out visiting companies to discuss the sweeping reforms implemented here since a team of McKinsey consultants spent nearly 4000 hours studying the MBA marketplace to devise a plan to move Texas into the top B-school tier. Dean Witt has carried out most of the changes recommended in 1992 by the McKinsey consultants: He has made work experience a virtual requirement for admission (the Class of 1996 averages nearly 4 years of job experience, up from 2.6 four years ago), established and promoted a special information technology program, required applicants to submit multiple essays, placed a greater emphasis on personal interviews in the admissions process, and completely restructured the MBA curriculum to better conform to market demand.

The payoff? Texas zoomed back into BUSINESS WEEK's Top 20 list in 1994 after securing especially strong reviews from the corporate sector. Credit the students' ambassador program for some of the gain. MBAs certainly worked hard to educate the corporate community about the changes, helping the school rank No. 11 with corporate recruiters in 1994. This is the school's highest BUSINESS WEEK ranking ever. Texas MBAs were among the top five for having shown the greatest improvement in recent years, according to corporate recruiters surveyed by BUSINESS WEEK.

Under the new program in place since 1993, students are structured into cohorts, or teams of 60 students who take all of their first-year classes together. Cohorts are further divided into assigned "study teams" of five students. Many of the students from the Class of 1994 seemed happy with the study teams, but even Witt admits that some weren't too keen to be placed in groups. "If you have the misfortune to have more than one person in a group not carrying their weight, then you probably won't like the mandatory nature of the teams," says Witt. Less than 10 percent of the class expressed disapproval of the change.

Students in those first-year study groups have less time to work together, since the school has reduced the first-year core requirements from 36 to 27 hours (9 required courses). The program's total length of 60 hours (allowing for at least 11 electives) has been kept constant, but students now have increased flexibility to explore a "market-driven concentration." Based on the highly successful Information Systems Management program offered to 28 students with the highest GMAT scores, the concentrations allow an MBA to explore his or her area of interest. At Texas there are plenty of options, with 188 different elective courses available in an academic year. Texas has established eight concentrations so far (and plans to start five more by next year) with the help of Corporate Advisory Councils, or groups of executives, who tailor the program toward the business sector's needs. The idea is to improve relations with the corporate community. The areas of concentration include accounting, finance, human resource management, information impact management, information systems management, marketing, natural resources and environmental management strategies, and operations management.

Accounting is a major strength, with nearly one-quarter of the school's tenure-track faculty in the subject. The info systems program is another major asset. A visiting committee for such firms as IBM, Ford Motor, Mobil, and Deloitte & Touche act as top advisors, sponsor internships, and often offer jobs to students. No wonder the program had a 100 percent placement rate in 1994. In recent years the school also has made important inroads in the marketing area, thanks mostly to Leigh McAlister, a genuine dynamo. McAlister wisely linked up with Procter & Gamble, 3M, and Motorola to offer students both coursework and internships in the emerging field of customer business development. The Systemic Business Relationships Program pairs students with participating companies. During the summer MBAs work as interns on interdisciplinary teams solving problems. One MBA worked on a strategy for increasing market share for telephone cross-connect termination blocks for 3M. Another intern at the company prepared a market study for entering the flexible circuit industry. A Procter & Gamble intern created a merchandising strategy for P&G products at Sam's Wholesale Clubs. When students return to campus in the fall, they participate in a symposium with members of the three companies and faculty. The course draws on the summer experience in discussing manufacturer-distributor relationships. It is also an excellent networking opportunity for MBAs, and, like other summer internships, it can open the doors for permanent positions. Each of the three companies takes about five summer interns. The school will try to replicate the successes of its technology and marketing programs when it unveils a Solomon Bros.–type trading room to boost its much-maligned finance department in the fall.

Texas offers a number of extracurricular learning experiences for students. The Quality Management Consortia is sponsored by the Business School and the College of Engineering. The school hosts biweekly seminars for managers of local companies to assist in total quality implementation. About 20 MBAs are hired to work with executives. The companies pay a fee to be included in the program, and MBAs are compensated for their work. MBAs participate in a five-day training session between the fall and spring semesters. "I attribute my successful job search in large part to my considerable efforts and experience gained through QMC," says one recent alum. The school also hosts Moot Corp., an annual event in which teams of MBAs from major schools vie against each other to develop detailed business plans for new companies and to present them to a panel of judges.

Dean Witt has also been active in creating more international opportunities for his MBA students. The school now has student exchange pacts with schools in the Netherlands, Finland, France, Great Britain, Denmark, Germany, Brazil, Australia, Canada, and Mexico. Indeed, the school has spent years cultivating close ties to Mexico's Monterrey Tech, a highly regarded business school in a rapidly growing country that is critical to U.S. trade. Through an unusual partnership agreement, Texas also offers students the chance to gain a double MBA degree with the Lyon Graduate School of Business in France or the Koblenz School of Corporate Management in Germany. In essence, you'd graduate with MBA degrees from both Texas and the partner school.

Students from the Class of 1994 had mixed reactions to the Texas makeover. As one 1994 grad put it, "We have been somewhat caught between the old and new programs." The Class of 1994 referred to itself as the "stepchild class," while the Class of 1995 jokingly refer to themselves as the "guinea pigs." On the 1994 customer satisfaction survey, Texas MBAs' complaints were similar to the ones heard at public schools around the country: improve the placement office; shore up weak departments (finance, in this case); downsize the student population; and find a way to acquire a new state-of-the-art facility.

Dean Witt says he is working on the last complaint, but the Texas Legislature ultimately controls the tuition that the school can charge. Without a major increase in revenue from tuition, Witt has been unable to build a separate facility for the MBA and executive education programs at Texas. On the other hand, this school continues to offer one of the true bargain MBAs available today. You'll find it difficult to get more value for your money, even though Texas's out-of-state tuition has jumped by 58 percent in the past two years, to $8580 a year. That's better than any other Top 20 school, including North Carolina which charges $10,132 a year or UCLA which is now up to $14,496 a year. The charge for Texas residents: a puny $3630 a year. Still, the B-school complex here is in relatively comfortable environs, on the south end of the 300-acre campus in the lively state capital. A modern glass-and-concrete, six-story building, with a mall-like atrium and hallways as wide as those in shopping malls, is home to the graduate school of business.

Austin is a great place to spend two years of your life. Nestled along the Colorado River at the edge of Central Texas Hill Country, it's a lively and dynamic community. You'd never guess that the city boasts a symphony orchestra, 2 ballet troupes, 12 museums, and 11 drama theaters. But with a student population of nearly 50,000, there's plenty of demand for both high culture and pure fun. Many students unwind on Austin's Sixth Street, home to bars and nightclubs that offer everything from live country music to punk and jazz. And while Stanford and UCLA MBAs often boast of their sun-drenched California climate, Austin offers up some pretty lush, temperate environs. The city averages 300 sunny days a year.

That welcoming climate can easily offset some of the other drawbacks of attending a public university for an MBA. Texas could use expanded placement and admissions facilities, although the school has made a huge effort to improve both areas in the last two years. In admissions, Witt's changes have brought a more mature and socially adept student body to campus. But increased application fees and required multiple essays have also caused a drop in applications, forcing Texas to admit 35 percent of its applicants in 1994, up from 25 percent two years earlier, even though MBA enrollment fell by 11 percent during this time frame. The average GMAT score, moreover, fell nearly 20 points, to 625. Witt claims he hasn't lost any sleep over the decline. "We've gotten rid of the people who were not serious about coming to Texas," he says.

The placement operation has also improved since 1992. The school has created an Industry Advisory Council to provide performance feedback and suggestions for changes. Witt also wants faculty members to create links to the corporate world to improve recruitment. For example, several finance profs spent two years working on Wall St. before recently returning to Austin. Witt hopes their expanded contacts will help more finance students to get jobs in New York.

The payoff from these initiatives? Texas managed to lure 39 new companies to recruit at the school in 1994, bringing its total number of on-campus recruiters to a respectable 203 organizations. Members of the Class of 1994 averaged 2.58 job offers each, slightly above the 2.36 average for the 40-plus schools surveyed. Some 88 percent of the class had job offers at graduation. The biggest recruiters: Deloitte & Touche (17); American Airlines (8); McKinsey (7); American Express (7); Andersen Consulting (7); Enron (6); Ford (6); NationsBank (6); EDS (5); and Intel (5).

An impressive lineup. If Witt has his way, this already stellar list of corporate recruiters will look even better in years to come, as his students continue to polish this school's image in the marketplace.

Contact: Fran Forbes, director of admissions, 512-471-1711
Final application deadline: April 15

Outstanding Faculty

1. Keith C. Brown (****): This capital markets maven typically garners close to perfect student evaluations. He joined the faculty at Texas in 1991 after brief teaching stints at San Diego State and Purdue Universities. Brown earned his Ph.D. in financial economics from

Purdue in 1981 with a mind-numbing dissertation called "Estimation of Seemingly Unrelated Regressions with an Incomplete Set of Data." But students aren't yawning in his classes. It's not uncommon for MBA candidates to rate him excellent in every single category on evaluation forms.

2. Robert Parrino (***):   Although he arrived at Texas in 1992, the youthful Parrino has already established himself at one of the school's best professors. A natural curiosity and a keen interest in corporate finance make his courses exceptionally thoughtful and compelling. He cut his teaching teeth at the University of Rochester, where Parrino earned an M.S. in applied economics and a Ph.D. in finance.

3. Shelby H. Carter, Jr. (**):   A former executive of both IBM and Xerox, Carter was born with the gift of insightful gab. Indeed, at one point in his career as a super salesman for Xerox, he was named one of "The Ten Greatest Salespersons" in a book. Besides serving as an adjunct professor at Austin where Carter teaches marketing, he's also the chairman and co-founder of SynOptics Communications, Inc., one of the fastest-growing hi-tech companies in the United States.

4. Jeff D. Sandefer (**):   A 1986 Harvard MBA, lecturer Sandefer teaches a highly popular course on Entrepreneurship and New Ventures. He should know all about that. He's president of two companies: Vanguard Corp., founded to investigate entrepreneurial opportunities in Russia, and Sandefer Offshore Co., which has developed over $500 million in oil and gas reserves in the Gulf of Mexico.

5. Steven R. Salbu (**):   Energetic and dynamic, Salbu loves teaching so much that he becomes oblivious to anything around him other than the interaction between himself and his students. He brings an unusual background to the classroom. Salbu earned an M.A. at Dartmouth in liberal studies and a law degree from the College of William & Mary. His undergraduate degree from Hofstra University in 1977 was in psychology and music. After gaining a master's in applied economics and a Ph.D. in organization and strategy from Wharton, he embarked on a career teaching business ethics and business law. Salbu joined the Texas faculty in 1990.

6. James W. Fredrickson (*):   A masterful discussion leader, he excels in his classes on strategy and leadership. A former faculty member at Columbia University and the University of Pittsburgh, he has served as a consultant to Chase Manhattan Bank, IBM, and Tandy.

Other Best Bets: *D. Eric Hirst* (accounting), *James W. Deitrick* (accounting), *John N. Doggett* (management), and *Leigh M. McAlister* (marketing)

Texas MBAs Sound Off

This program has improved substantially in the past couple of years. First, its students are older and have significantly more work experience than in the recent past. Second, the administration has been truly receptive to students' concerns and has worked hard to improve the career services office, the number and *quality of companies that recruit here, and the computer facilities. These were the three main concerns of our class. The job is far from finished. As a state university with limited resources, UT will face great challenges in the next few years. UT still lacks the strong alumni network of other top-ranked programs. Its MBA program needs to develop more sustainable competitive advantages than low cost and a superb location.—**Finance Career Path***

*UT is a great deal for the tuition, especially if you simply feel like you must have an MBA and are confident in your ability to overcome obstacles in your job search because the degree lacks Ivy League cachet. If you chopped off the bottom half of our class, the remaining students would compare favorably to the students at any top business school. At UT, there are two types of students: the "bargain hunters," and the "last resort" students. If you hang out with the "bargain hunters," you will have an excellent informal educational experience. If you get into case group with the "last resort" types, you'll wish you had never come to UT for an MBA. UT's top-notch programs are in information systems, entrepreneurship, and accounting. The school also has a superior program in marketing, but it's a decidedly mixed bag in finance and management.—**Finance Associate***

*Texas's program is an excellent regional program. The school is "regional" because it seeks to serve mostly Texans, and in fact ends up with a rather "provincial" student body that seems "Texocentric."—**Marketing Associate***

*If you are willing to acknowledge the reduced cost [of a Texas education] will require additional work on your part to secure the job you want, the smaller financial commitment will allow you to go where you want, as opposed to being forced into a position which only serves to pay off your debt. . . . My friends at Wharton and Chicago have one thing I don't: $30,000 to $50,000 more debt!—**Consultant***

*Academically, the program has become much more rigorous, especially with the introduction of cohorts. There are more opportunities here than one could ever hope to take advantage of. Negatives: There's still some complaining about the placement office, but it's vastly improved since I arrived. Few people don't have jobs. The ones who don't have offers are the ones I'd expect not to have them.—**Consultant***

*The Texas MBA program was redesigned last year and is vastly improved. A cohort system has been instituted and more elective courses in place of core classes are allowed. There's a new concentration, information technology applications in finance. And recruitment has been strong. The only problem is that there are not enough jobs in Austin, and nobody wants to move away. It's such a lovely place.—**Finance Analyst***

As with any program, the Texas MBA is what you make of it. If you strategically choose your courses, professors, and outside activities, the experience is hard to beat. The administration is responding to the needs of the business community through the introduction of market-driven concentrations and an increased emphasis on placement. The standardization of the core classes will improve the quality of the elective courses by putting all class members on an equal footing. Quality of life here is definitely a bonus. I met a great group of people, not only in my own class but also from the classes entering before and a year later.
—**Marketing Career Path**

The program has changed dramatically during my class's tenure. I truly feel that the administration, championed by the efforts of the outstanding dean of students, Vic Arnold, has made a comprehensive effort to improve the quality of the program and to respond to the wishes of the students. The administration has made significant strides. And while I am very pleased with my experience, I believe that the class behind me is of higher caliber and is receiving a more rigorous and superior education.—**Sales and Trading Manager**

The only negative associated with the program is that some companies try to low-ball our grads on salary based on impressions of past UT MBAs who often lacked any work experience. That attitude is quickly changing, and I think our starting salaries this year will go up significantly. The students at UT bow to no one. Clearly, the talent level here can be exceeded by only a few schools. Finally, given the fact that I only had to borrow $15,000 to get my MBA at UT, I would make the same decision again.—**Finance Associate**

With few exceptions, the quality of teaching was outstanding. There was a wide array of classes from which to choose. Also, there was a great deal of latitude in crafting a curriculum suited to a student's needs. While career services have typically been a weakness at UT, there has been some improvement there as well.
—**Career Path Unknown**

UT's program is in tune with the changing needs of managers in the business world. This is largely attributable to the close interaction with businesses and executives brought into the classroom. One marketing program brings together 15 student interns and three companies—Procter & Gamble, Motorola, and 3M—to interact and solve real-world problems as well as to provide summer internship employment.—**Sales Account Manager**

UT's career services office has come under criticism over the last several years for its perceived failure to measure up. I have personally witnessed a tremendous drive in my two years for improvement in this and other areas of the school's infrastructure.—**Career Path Unknown**

Realigning electives and concentrations to the needs of the business community is having an immediate effect on UT's reputation with recruiters. Salaries, number of offers, and recruiters are all increasing.—**Consultant**

The most fulfilling aspect of the changes here in the past two years has been that they were led by us, the students. Our class was extremely active in shaping the school, outside the classroom as well as in it. The administration was fabulously supportive.—**Finance Manager**

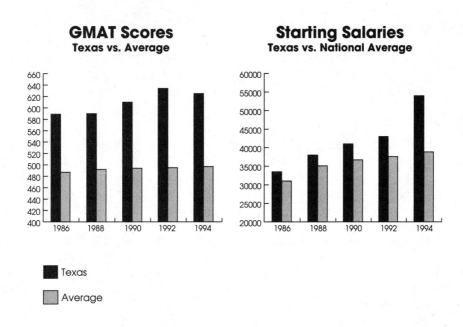

18. University of North Carolina at Chapel Hill

Kenan-Flagler Business School
Campus Box No. 3490
Chapel Hill, North Carolina 27599

Corporate ranking: 19
Enrollment: 394
Women: 31%
Non-U.S.: 13%
Minority: 12%
Part-time: None
Average age: 27.5
Average years of work exp: 4.5
Applicants accepted: 22%
Median starting pay: $64,750

Graduate ranking: 16
Annual tuition & fees: resident—$2648
nonresident—$10,132
Room and board: $6500
Average GMAT score: 621
GMAT range: 450 to 750
Average GPA: 3.2
GPA range: 2.1 to 4.0
Accepted applicants enrolled: 49%
Average starting pay: $69,880

Teaching methods: Lecture, 15% Case study, 75% Field projects, 10%

Affectionately known as the "Southern part of heaven," Chapel Hill is the quintessential college town. For years, it has been known as an intellectual center along the lines of Ann Arbor, Berkeley, Cambridge, or Madison. Its population is dominated by young, bright students who can be overheard chatting about new ideas in the independent book stores, vegetarian restaurants, and coffee houses in and around Franklin Street, the town's main drag.

Less known until recently, however, is that the University of North Carolina has fashioned a bit of heaven in business school terms. On a tree-lined campus boasting brick walkways and Greek revival architecture, the Kenan-Flagler Business School offers the best bargain in MBA education, an up-to-date curriculum taught by caring and devoted faculty who love to teach, small classes of astute students, and a diploma gaining increasing recognition from Corporate America.

The transformation of North Carolina's B-school from a sleepy, top-quality regional to one of the best in the United States was partly accomplished by Dean Paul J. Rizzo, whose five-year reign came to an end in mid-1992. The former vice chairman of IBM, Rizzo unabashedly used his contacts in the corporate world to significantly enhance the national profile of the school. He raised millions of dollars, lured many corporate chieftains to campus for speeches and talks, and convinced prestige recruiters to interview newly minted MBAs. His attention to the external needs of the school perfectly complemented the previous inroads made by former Dean John Evans, who had beefed up the quality of the faculty and curriculum.

The efforts of both deans have helped to make Kenan-Flagler the most selective business school in the country after only Stanford and Harvard. In 1994, UNC accepted a mere 22 percent of those who applied for admission—allowing Kenan-Flagler to pick off some of the best and brightest MBA candidates in the pool. Why so many are competing for so few spots is not surprising. At $10,132 a year in tuition and fees for out-of-state residents, it's one of the best MBA educational values in the world. And an MBA for state residents is an absolute steal at only $2648 a year. Another reason for its success is that despite the bargain-basement price, North Carolina offers students a first-class education. MBAs rave about the teaching abilities of the B-school's professors as well as the genuine interest they show toward their pupils.

At UNC, quality teaching is a valued commodity. Unlike many professors at most B-schools, they fully understand that the primary calling of a teacher is to teach. The effectiveness of instruction in the core is well above average, according to BUSINESS WEEK's customer satisfaction surveys. The magazine's rankings put the overall quality of teaching at UNC in the upper twentieth percentile of the top 40-plus schools. It's not only because of what goes on in the classroom. It's because of the unusual level of commitment shown outside of class. UNC profs regularly participate in brown-bag lunches and coffees with students, always open their doors to MBAs whether they're signed up for their courses or not, and even get involved in the job search process. As one recent graduate put it, "The professors at UNC are unusually dedicated to the students and always have time to help them with questions about everything from coursework to career plans." Adds another: "The faculty is one of the most approachable I have seen. I learned a lot just by walking into many professors' offices for informal chats." Sums up a third, "The teachers here are responsive beyond anyone's expectations!"

It helps that these profs teach in a college town atmosphere that is also conducive to real-world business. Together with Duke University and North Carolina State, UNC is part of Research Triangle, home to R&D and manufacturing facilities operated by IBM, GE, DEC, Mitsubishi, Northern Telecom, Burroughs Wellcome, and Glaxo. MCI recently opened a major new office in nearby Cary, and the highly successful Body Shop, Inc., moved into the area in 1994. The state capital in nearby Raleigh brings government together with academia and business, providing a stimulating, yet pragmatic, environment for a B-school.

UNC has traditionally been recognized for its marketing and finance departments, but its operating management area has been coming on strong the last few years. In addition to reading about new production techniques in a textbook, North Carolina MBA students can see them first-hand at nearby manufacturing plants.

Having major development and manufacturing activities in its backyard and a businessman as its dean (Rizzo has been succeeded by Paul Fulton, former president of Sara Lee) makes North Carolina particularly sensitive to the needs of business. Like many other B-schools, Kenan-Flagler is defining those needs in global terms. One way North Carolina exposes students to international business is through the Kenan Institute of Private Enterprise, which serves as a forum for business, academic, and government leaders. Frank H. Kenan, whose fortune was made in the oil and transportation businesses and whose family built the research center, is an important donor to the B-school. Along with the B-school, the institute cosponsors an international executive lecture series and an executives-in-residence program. Thanks to its connections, 17 percent of first-year internships in 1994 were overseas. It also bankrolls five research centers spanning competitiveness and employment growth, international marketing, manufacturing excellence, human resources, and management and financial services. The institute also administers the MBA Enterprise Corps, a program modeled after the Peace Corps in which MBAs from

Kenan-Flagler and other top schools accept one- to two-year assignments helping entrepreneurs and government officials in Eastern Europe and Southeast Asia to privatize business and start new companies.

Kenan-Flagler, of course, isn't all MBA heaven. As a state-funded institution, the school's ambitions may be somewhat limited by resources and by politics. Though not poor, the school obviously lacks the deep pockets a school like Northwestern, Harvard, or Wharton has to pay for large numbers of staffers in admissions, placement, and alumni offices that give many private schools a substantial edge. Things taken for granted at private schools often require hard-fought battles at public institutions. One example: grads say the computer facilities are lackluster.

Moreover, the school clearly has lost some ground in the last two years because Dean Fulton did not arrive here until January of 1994—about 18 months after Rizzo left. The result: the program's recognition in the corporate sector took a surprising tumble that has cost the school seven places in BUSINESS WEEK's overall rankings in the past two years. Still, the new dean has won great praise from graduates for his enthusiasm and energy. No doubt he will quickly restore the corporate links Rizzo brought to the program, to reestablish this school in the Top 10.

One soon-to-arrive asset in that campaign will be a new building to more comfortably accommodate students and faculty. The school's 376 full-time MBAs currently share space with 700 undergraduate business students in Carroll Hall, about a block away from Old Well, the historical and geographic center of the university. The old Carroll is a classic academic building, in red brick topped by a cupola with white columns in front. The new Carroll, circa 1970s, is a glass-and-stone building with more modern classroom space and faculty offices. Rizzo led a campaign that raised $24 million toward a new B-school home and won a commitment from the state legislature for the remaining loot needed to complete the project. The building—which will be linked to the school's Kenan Center on the extreme south of the 729-acre campus—is expected to open in 1997.

Whether the program is housed in a state-of-the-art facility then or not, North Carolina's MBA curriculum covers all the bases. Prior to your arrival here, an outside consulting group will gather confidential peer and employer assessments of your perceived strengths and weaknesses. Then, during the first-year Managerial Competencies class, the school gives you these evaluations and works with you to identify key areas for growth— even preparing a personal mission statement and career plan. If you're a liberal arts undergrad whose pulse rises at the mere mention of regression analysis, the school puts on an Analytic Skills Workshop over the summer. The intensive program, four weeks' worth of boot-camp drills in accounting, statistics, and economics, goes a long way toward preparing students for the rough and tumble of the first year of rigorous MBA training. An optional program for international students helps them to get a head start on MBA work.

All incoming students move through "Intro Week," a 7-day orientation that gets you acquainted with classmates and faculty through a series of workshops, games, and exercises. Following Intro Week is a new program, dubbed Week in the Life of a General Manager, which marks the first official week of classes and serves as an overview of the entire curriculum. Corporate leaders discuss their roles in the context of each day's lessons.

Right from the start, students are assigned to study groups of five to seven members each, and asked to remain together for the entire first year even when personality conflicts emerge. The idea is to replicate the real world, where people with different levels of knowledge and experience are forced to work together whether they like each other or not. It also goes hand in hand with North Carolina's team approach, which relies heavily on the case-study method and class presentations. "We've emphasized the team concept for more than 20 years," says Bill Bigoness, associate dean of the MBA program. "Our experience has shown the importance of everyone sharing the same challenges, especially throughout the first year, to build team cohesion."

In the first year, everyone is required to take all of the 13 core courses, regardless of previous academic or professional experience. That means that a certified public accountant must take introductory accounting. This prospect may not sound too appealing to those with specialized training, but it guarantees that everyone gets the benefit of each other's knowledge, too. The basic courses in the core—covering accounting to quantitative decision making—meet two or three times per week for 7 or 14 weeks. Underpinning the first-year work and taking over the last three seven-week "modules" is Integrative Management, a course whose purpose is to interweave all the disciplines you've learned into a basis for business decision making.

The second-year curriculum features an integrated full-year, required course, which brings together international business, regulation, and business policy. There's also a practicum or project-based course, requiring that teams apply for projects that companies have submitted for consideration. Sometimes, these courses allow students to create case studies for use in the B-school's curriculum. Midway in the second year, student teams engage in a large-scale computer simulation that finds them managing hypothetical companies in an international environment.

Otherwise, all the electives are now taught in seven-week "modules." You can continue a generalized course of study or concentrate on one or more functional areas, although some graduates complain that North Carolina's list of electives is somewhat limited. Compared to many of the bigger B-schools with greater resources, that's certainly true. In any given year, North Carolina says it offers 79 elective courses. A reciprocal agreement with Duke University's Fuqua School, however, allows students to take classes at Fuqua.

The shorter modules at North Carolina, meantime, allow the school to offer more specialized skills to students as well as cutting-edge topics less deserving of full, lengthy treatment. Some examples: Idalene Kesner, a top-rated teacher, has developed a special consulting class to meet the growing demand among students for information on how to work for themselves or hire their skills to other companies. An environmental management course taught by Mike Berry takes the view that environmental planning is essential to Total Quality Management in any company.

As a public institution in Chapel Hill, the school isn't as well positioned to draw large numbers of foreign students and faculty as some rivals on the East and West Coasts. Only 1 in 8 MBA students here is from abroad—compared to 1 in 4 at Harvard or Columbia or roughly 1 in 3 at MIT or Wharton. Still, the B-school has been committed to boosting the international content of the program. Whenever possible, international cases are being added to the curriculum, and the school is selecting more students who can speak one or more foreign languages. North Carolina also currently boasts exchange programs with schools in Britain, Belgium, France, Canada, Venezuela, and Thailand.

Despite the perception that life in Chapel Hill is laid-back, the MBA program is fairly demanding—especially in the first year. But when students take a break from their studies, they often engage in intramural sports and attend Tar Heels' basketball games. After an evening of slam-dunking, MBAs tend to wend their way to He's Not Here—even though the bar's name fails to acknowledge that women make up 33 percent of North Carolina's enrollment—as well as Spanky's on Franklin Street just two blocks away from the B-school. The Spring Garden Bar and Grill is famous for its cheddar burgers, and the Henderson Street Bar boasts the best jukebox in town.

The school's low tuition, great teachers, and spectacular quality of life win high marks from students. Not quite there, but doing much better than ever, is the school's career services office headed by newcomer Mike Ippolito, who joined Kenan-Flagler in 1993. Ippolito had managed recruitment at three major corporations. In 1994, he brought to campus 97 companies that did 1451 interviews with second-year students. Another 273 job opportunities came over the transom via correspondence. On the face of it those numbers don't appear all that impressive, until you realize that UNC graduates fewer than 200 MBAs a year.

The upshot: only 5.7 percent of the Class of 1994 failed to have a job offer by commencement. Those that did averaged 3.1 offers each, better than any other major business school with the exception of Harvard, Stanford, and MIT. Obviously, UNC grads didn't get anywhere near the starting-pay packages of those elite schools. But they also didn't have to pay outsized tuition bills for their education. Snapping up the most grads in 1994 were Frito Lay (4); Johnson & Johnson (4); Citicorp (3); First Chicago (3); J.P. Morgan (3); NationsBank (3); Northern Telecom (3); and Symmetrix (3). Merrill Lynch and Intel were among 15 other firms that hired a pair of Kenan-Flagler MBAs in 1994. That's a great lineup of quality companies, though noticeably absent are many of the prestige consulting and investment banking firms that hand out the highest starting salaries and bonuses. Even so, one of every four grads in 1994 went to work in investment banking, while 15 percent went into management consulting.

What's more, North Carolina seems to be more broadly distributing its graduates in jobs across the country. In years past, more than half of the school's MBA output stayed in the Southeast—a situation that didn't help the school gain a more prominent national reputation. The number of graduates taking jobs in the Southeast, however, has steadily declined—to 28 percent in 1994 from 35 percent two years earlier. MBAs headed for jobs in the mid-Atlantic and Northeast now outnumber those in the Southeast.

Now Dean Fulton has the tough job of steering the school into Phase Two of the Rizzo plan: developing more corporate contacts, and further emphasizing international business. By some accounts, Fulton knows exactly what to do. Shortly after his arrival as dean, he called on a senior executive friend at First Chicago bank to talk up the quality of the school's graduates. (UNC had fallen off First Chicago's recruiting list a few years before.) The result: First Chicago hired three Kenan-Flagler MBAs in 1994. If Fulton can pull more strings like that as dean, he'll make Kenan-Flagler a genuine "southern part of heaven" all by itself.

Contact: Anne-Marie Summers, director of admissions, CB #3490, Carroll Hall, 919-962-3236
Final application deadline: March 1 for fall

Outstanding Faculty

1. David Ravenscraft (****):   This microeconomics prof is famous for the "prisoner's dilemma game" he springs on students. "I tell them to write down the name of one of the authors of the text. Obviously, this is a no-brainer. Then I tell them the payback-risk (from a dime to a jackpot of quarters) of getting the answer right or wrong. It all depends on how many of their classmates answer correctly or not. In the end, I collect a lot of dimes on those days." A former research economist for the Federal Trade Commission, he earned his Ph.D. from Northwestern. He teaches microeconomics as well as a mergers and acquisitions course. Won the 1991 Teaching Excellence Award.

2. Idalene F. Kesner (****):   She wows students by deftly teaching strategic management and business policy. Armed with an Indiana MBA and Ph.D., "Idie" joined UNC in 1983 and recently spearheaded the MBA second-year curriculum revisions. A devoted teacher, she regularly meets with students outside of class to talk about job opportunities, and she frequently fields calls from grads seeking advice. Hobbies: family, reading, and foreign films.

3. David J. Hartzell (**):   A former Salomon Brothers vice president, he has won teaching awards at both the University of Texas and UNC, where he teaches finance and real estate. He has been known to bring his kids to class and to entertain his students by juggling—especially on course evaluation day. Got his B.S. and M.A. from the University of Delaware and his Ph.D. from UNC. Students describe him as a "pretty laid-back, easygoing, low-stress guy, who has a good feel for the real world."

4. Jay E. Klompmaker (**):   Before entering academia, he got his taste of real business with a large manufacturer of forgings and with an engineering consulting firm. As he puts it: "I was in business before I was in academics. I can identify with practicing managers and executives." Klompmaker, who earned his bachelor's in engineering at the Illinois Institute of Technology, his MBA from Chicago, and his Ph.D. from Michigan, teaches industrial marketing and sales management. He prepares for courses by asking himself a simple question: How would I like students in this class to be different when they leave?

5. James F. Smith (**):   A former Sears, Roebuck manager, Smith obviously found his true calling late in life. He spent two decades in Corporate America before joining the University of Texas at Austin in 1986 as chief economist of its Bureau of Business Research. Smith, author of the school's bimonthly *UNC Business Forecast* newsletter, teaches the core course in macroeconomics. The finance prof won extra plaudits for organizing an MBA trip to Mexico City in August of 1994. Says a Class of 1994 grad: "The fire-and-brimstone conservatism of Jim Smith made learning fast-paced and enjoyable."

6. Ronald T. Pannesi (*):   Founder of the school's Center for Manufacturing Excellence, Pannesi won the 1994 MBA Teaching Award for his courses in operations and manufacturing. A former consultant with Deloitte and Touche, he got his Ph.D. in operations management at Michigan State and quickly joined UNC as a teacher.

Other Best Bets: *Robert A. Connolly* (finance), *James M. Wahlen* (accounting), *Rollie Tillman* (entrepreneurship), and *Gerald D. Bell* (organizational behavior)

Prominent Alumni: Hugh L. McColl, Jr., CEO of NationsBank; Frank H. Kenan, chairman of Kenan Transport Co.; Bill McCoy, vice-chairman of BellSouth; Joseph Clapp, chairman of Roadway Services; John G. Medlin Jr., chairman of First Wachovia; Julian H. Robertson, Jr., president of Tiger Management; Erwin Maddrey, chairman of Delta Woodside Inc.; Frank Dunn, Jr., president of First Union National Bank; Taketo Furuhata, CEO of Itoh & Co.

Kenan-Flagler MBAs Sound Off

*Although career placement has historically been known as a relative weakness of the school, major strides have been taken to improve this area. Under our new dean, career placement will undoubtedly become a strength of the school in the years to come.—**Finance Associate***

It has been the most exciting and enriching experience of my life. I can't imagine any school that could better prepare me for my future in business and life.
*—**Sales Manager***

*Our new dean, Paul Fulton, is outstanding. He has a tremendous amount of connections in the corporate world. He is a doer and very active, having lunch with students weekly. Combine that with our new facility and the quality of life in Chapel Hill, and Kenan-Flagler will soon be among the very best business schools. Chapel Hill can't be beat for a diverse college town.—**Associate Marketing Manager***

*One weakness of the program is its reliance on Harvard business school cases. I found the best classes were those where we were taught tools and concepts that then had to be applied to case situations. I have to question the value of outdated Harvard cases.—**Marketing Associate***

*North Carolina has the advantage of being one of the smallest business schools, yet within the environment of a large, nationally prominent university. I can go from a class of 12 students, in a school where I know every professor personally, to a basketball game where thousands cheer one of the best collegiate teams in the country. I loved the school and the experience.—**Associate Risk Trader***

Overall, this school is a good educational value. However, the low cost is reflected in poor computer facilities and the school's general lack of amenities. The first-year courses were excellent, but the learning curve dropped precipitously in the second year. For the most part, analytical skills were glossed over in most nonfinance courses. The operations department is struggling to put together a cohesive curriculum, and the information technology classes are an embarrassing joke.—**Consultant**

I learned as much in the classroom as I have outside it. The small class size of about 200 students allows this. I am graduating with my dream job. I know that UNC helped to give me the skills and confidence to succeed in my career.
—**Finance Associate**

My experience at Kenan-Flagler was unequivocally positive. I looked at the Top 20 business schools for two years prior to attending. By the time I applied, I had decided that Kenan-Flagler was the only school that met all of my criteria: overall payback on cost versus starting salary; size of program; location; cooperative atmosphere; team focus; and close, friendly relations with faculty and staff. My classmates were the most intelligent, experienced, stimulating group I've ever been associated with.—**Analyst**

I gave up over $300,000 in salary and bonus to attend Kenan-Flagler. Few MBAs can make that statement. Yet overall I am extremely pleased with the program and its results. During my two years here, we really had no dean leading the program. In the past six months, Paul Fulton has entered the dean's position with superb vision, energy, and enthusiasm. I expect wonderful things from him.
—**Entrepreneur**

GMAT Scores
North Carolina vs. Average

Starting Salaries
North Carolina vs. National Average

- ■ North Carolina
- ☐ Average

19. University of California at Berkeley

Walter A. Haas School of Business
350 Barrows Hall
Berkeley, CA 94720

Corporate ranking: 21
Enrollment: 674
Women: 34%
Non-U.S.: 29%
Minority: 17%
Part-time: 247
Average age: 27.6
Average years of work exp.: 4.7
Applicants accepted: 20%
Median starting pay: $70,000

Graduate ranking: 15
Annual tuition & fees: resident—$6662
nonresident—$14,361
Room and board: $11,500
Average GMAT score: 647
GMAT range: 450 to 780
Average GPA: 3.2
GPA range: 2.09 to 4.0
Accepted applicants enrolled: 55%
Average starting pay: $71,970

Teaching methods: Lecture, 35%   Case study, 45%   Group projects, 20%

It was just another one of those hokey pictures in a local newspaper: hard hats atop their heads, four suits awkwardly posing with blue-and-gold shovels at the groundbreaking for a new building. But this ceremonial event—the September 1992 launching of a new $45 million management complex for the Haas School of Business—has been a critical step in a bold plan to gain greater recognition for Berkeley's B-school.

It's about time. The 56,000 square feet the Haas school now occupies in Barrows Hall is the "most overcrowded, outdated, and inflexible space of any major business school in the country." And that's how *CalBusiness,* the school's alumni magazine, describes the downtrodden joint. Berkeley's B-school has been operating with about one-eighth the space per student of Stanford and one-third that of UCLA.

By contrast, the new center, which will open in the spring of 1995, may seem like a palace. Designed by Santa Monica architects Moore Ruble Yudell, the "mini-campus" will consist of three buildings connected by bridges and surrounding a courtyard located at the eastern edge of the Berkeley campus near California Memorial Stadium. The B-school's new home will bring together the school's library, research centers, student computer labs, classrooms, faculty offices, and executive programs.

In addition to putting up a new MBA factory, however, the school is likely to undergo some fairly dramatic changes for the better. An ambitious new dean, the first to hail from the world of business in its 94-year history, has arrived on the scene. William Hasler, former vice chairman of accounting giant KMPG, hopes to prod the faculty at this research-oriented school to offer MBAs a more real-world perspective. Oddly enough, California's budget crunch will give Hasler a unique opportunity to bring in fresh talent. A system-wide early-retirement program pared business faculty by about a fifth, opening the way for new teachers from Columbia, Kellogg, and Cornell.

Hasler, who took over the deanship in mid-1991, is already gaining favorable reviews from students who see him as far more responsive to their concerns. He also appears to have strong support from among Berkeley's alums, who have put up big money to make the new school a reality. The Haas family, which controls jeansmaker Levi Strauss & Co., kicked in $8.75 million for the new management center, bringing their total contribution to $23.75 million, the largest gift in the university's history. The school is named after Walter A. Haas, Sr., a 1910 graduate of the school who was president of Levi from 1928 to 1955.

On the drawing board are efforts to place a greater emphasis on globalization and managing technology. Among other things, Hasler hopes to create a center for international business management like those already in place at Columbia and Wharton. He'd also like to ensure that MBA students get some overseas experience via semester-abroad programs, consulting projects with international companies, and summer internships.

No matter what he tries to accomplish, Hasler will probably have to move slowly. Berkeley is a huge, cumbersome bureaucracy, and nearly everything here causes a protest, a demonstration, or at least a stir. To get moving on the new business complex, for example, he had to fight preservationists who wanted to prevent the school from demolishing a 70-year-old fraternity house. Community leaders were also battling to prevent the dean from tearing down an old hospital at the site. And Hasler himself had to withstand a mind-boggling 200 interviews to win the deanship.

To his credit, he knows how to manage in a partnership where power is dispersed. That's certainly what he had to deal with at Peat Marwick. Moreover, the piece of clay he is sculpting is of high quality already. The school draws an exceptionally diverse population of bright students. It boasts a solid faculty and a fairly strong curriculum.

Though Hasler speaks of putting more focus on global business, he'll find a difficult time making the place more international than it already is. About 30 percent of the MBA students here are from abroad, evenly divided between Europe and Asia. The Class of 1994 included a dozen graduates alone from the University of Tokyo. One of every four tenure-track faculty at Haas can be considered international, at least in origin. The school offers 17 exchange programs with schools outside the United States. An experimental international program saw 15 first-year students take a spring-term class on business in Indonesia. After the course, they traveled to Java to work in teams with Indonesian students on four or five consulting projects for local or American companies. The program was expanded to Malaysia and Russia in 1994, with 30 students.

Above all, Berkeley remains a free and eclectic place. The commitment to equal opportunity that characterized America during the late sixties and early seventies is very much alive at the university, simply dubbed "Cal" by students and faculty. About 34 percent of the students are women and another 17 percent are minorities. You can't beat Berkeley for cultural, ethnic, political, social, and intellectual diversity. About 99 percent of students have work experience, and they seem to know what they want—to make a difference in the world, as corny as that may sound. Failing that, they'll settle for an interesting job with lots of freedom.

Berkeley's cutting-edge finance faculty draws many of Wall Street's future rocket scientists, but quants can afford to be a little weird, especially when they're making the firm millions of dollars a year. Many Berkeley MBAs gravitate toward high-tech companies like Apple Computer, Hewlett-Packard, and Sun Microsystems, where the corporate culture tolerates and sometimes encourages nonconformism. The thinking seems to be that the person who questions why something is done a certain way may come up with a better, more profitable way of doing it. Berkeley grads who don't land jobs in Silicon Valley often go into business for themselves.

Befitting its diverse student population, Berkeley's B-School emphasizes an interdisciplinary approach to graduate business education. That's the way it has been since 1898 when UC Regent Arthur Rodgers, returning from a trip in Asia, maintained that business education should include faculty and courses from across the university. "I don't believe any other B-school has as many programs that are the products of real joint planning with other units on campus," says former Dean Raymond Miles. "Others may talk about it, but we've been doing it for 90 years."

The B-school offers interdisciplinary programs with the schools of engineering, law, public health, environmental design, and Asian studies. The joint MBA/M.A. in Asian studies offers special training in languages, political economy, history, and sociology for students interested in both business and Asia. To be accepted into the three-year program, a student must have a bachelor's degree and at least one year of a relevant Asian language. Curiously enough, B-school founder Rodgers was convinced that California was the gateway to the Pacific Rim and that Berkeley should prepare its students to become "Pacific statesmen."

Being a liberal never went out of fashion in Berkeley. Much about Haas is a reflection of the overriding environment here, from the school's á la carte MBA program to the liberal grading policies of its professors. Like MIT, the university is known for its strong engineering department, and the B-school has traditionally emphasized quantitative skills. In recent years, there has been some movement toward the qualitative, to the chagrin of some students. Berkeley uses a combination of lecture and case study, with a heavy emphasis on group projects and student cooperation.

There are 10 courses in the core requirements covering areas such as finance, accounting, marketing, organizational behavior, economics, statistics, and information systems. Waivers out of some of these courses are possible. Business and Public Policy, a core requirement taught by Robert Harris, David Vogel, and Pablo Spiller, is one of the most popular courses here. Berkeley's strength in this area can be traced back to the sixties, when business and the B-school were under fire from many university students. The protests led to some soul-searching. As a result, the B-school beefed up faculty in the political, legal, and social aspects of business.

No future entrepreneur should go through the Haas School without taking Entrepreneurship, taught by John Freeman, who has deep research roots in the Bay Area's biotech and computer industries. The course is centered around a real-life startup whose principals agree to work with students on a business plan for the company. Several members of Berkeley's finance faculty can speak with extra authority because they are actively involved in the markets. Hayne Leland is a principal in Leland O'Brien Rubenstein Associates, the firm that created portfolio insurance, a trading strategy that uses stock index futures to protect against a decline in equity prices. You'll find no shortage of outstanding teachers at Berkeley (see the listing at the end of the profile).

Along with UCLA, to which it is constantly compared, Berkeley's tuition for nonresidents is among the lowest of Top 20 B-schools. At less than $7000 for California residents, it's an incredible deal. Getting a top-dollar education for a bargain-basement price prompted one recent grad to co-found a fund-raising program where students pledge to the school 1 percent of their first year's salary. More than 50 percent of Haas School students participated in the first year of the program and 75 percent have signed up in the years since. "We decided to give a little something back to the school, and it instantaneously institutionalized," says the recent grad.

The fact that it did gives you a clue about the sharing culture at the Haas School. "Cooperation may well be the hallmark of Haas," believes a Class of 1992 graduate. "Virtually all major papers were assigned as group projects, and I never personally ran into a classmate who put himself ahead of his teammates. This cooperation also extended to the job search process. If classmates knew of job leads, they usually shared them with others."

That concern for others also translates into a concern for the school and its management. Students take involvement seriously. Through MBA Associates, the student government body, Haas School students make their views known to faculty and administration on such issues as curriculum content, admissions, placement and publications. MBAA serves as the umbrella organization for all extracurricular activities from the Pacific Rim Club and Women in Management to the Graduate Minority Business Association. These clubs promote a functional area of business by preparing résumé directories, organizing events that bring corporate executives and alumni to campus, and sponsoring "days-on-the-job," where students visit a company to learn about its operations. Students also were responsible for having a noncredit core course in communications added to the first year. This replaced an out-of-class oral and written communication requirement. In fact, students are encouraged to create experimental courses and have done so with Business in the Pacific Rim, as well as Business and the Environment, and others.

Eating ethnic is de rigueur at Berkeley: MBAs frequent Plearn for Thai, Blue Nile for Ethiopian, and the New Delhi Junction for Indian cuisine. MBAs don't crowd Berkeley's famed Chez Panisse restaurant every night, but they make a point of visiting it at least once. More typically, they head to Kip's or Bear's Lair for burgers and pizza. Despite the Bay Area's proximity to the wineries of the Napa and Sonoma valleys, local residents and MBAs are also beer and ale connoisseurs. Triple Rock, which serves beer brewed on the premises, is a favorite. Henry's and Raleigh's are also popular MBA hangouts. San Francisco is only 30 minutes away on the Bay Area Rapid Transit system, or BART, so MBAs often take in the night life there.

Rent control in Berkeley just isn't what it used to be. In recent years, the moderates and the courts have controlled the rent board so now it's hard to find any apartment under $500 a month within a mile of the campus. The university only offers a limited amount of MBA housing and it goes fast.

Berkeley MBAs have a penchant for being entrepreneurial. Indeed, a team of researchers from the B-school and the university's Institute of Personality Assessment and Research began a seven-year personality study of 131 Berkeley MBAs in 1985. The findings: Berkeley MBAs were the third most creative group ever assessed by the institute, falling into what it terms the "entrepreneurial category." "The up side to that is the students are flexible, they take initiative, and are willing to try new things," says Charles O'Reilly, co-director of the study. "They are probably slightly less desirable for the corporate environment [because] they're likely to do well in situations that value creativity."

To tap into those interests, the B-school's Partnership for Entrepreneurial Leadership matches MBA students with young, high-growth companies for summer internships, followed by project work for credit in their second year. Entrepreneurs Forums bring participants to the faculty club six or eight times a year for a networking hour with faculty and students. The sessions draw more than 200 venture capitalists, investment bankers, successful and aspiring entrepreneurs, and their lawyers, accountants, and advisors.

Some 150 companies recruited on campus in the year, conducting 2500 interviews. Another 3000 job opportunities were posted via correspondence. The major recruiters of the Class of 1994: Ernst & Young (6); Andersen Consulting (4); Axiom Information (3); Coopers & Lybrand (3); American Airlines (3); Hewlett-Packard (3); Morgan Stanley (2); Silicon Graphics (2); Clorox (2); and Intel (2).

About 10 percent of the class did not have job offers by commencement. Those that had offers averaged about 2.3 each—about average for the 40-plus schools whose graduates are polled by BUSINESS WEEK. Berkeley gets low marks from recruiters at national corporations, many of whom don't even come to Berkeley, partly because grads just don't want to leave the area. About 60 percent of them take jobs in California, while another 25 percent return overseas. They're spoiled by the Bay Area's friendly people, good food, exciting cultural events, and mild—if a bit unpredictable—weather.

No doubt Hasler himself was attracted by the area's allure. Now all he has to do is put the best of Haas together in a new building and build upon it to make the school one of the very best in the world.

Contact: Fran Hill, director of admissions, 415-642-1405
Final application deadline: April 1 for fall

Outstanding Faculty

1. Richard Lyons (****): A recent steal from Columbia University's business school, where he taught international business for six years, Lyons won the teacher of the year award in 1994—his first year at Haas. He's a thirty-something financial genius in the sometimes arcane area of global finance and currency exchange. As one reporter put it after interviewing Lyons for a story: "He could make that stuff understandable to a third grader." Students agree. Raves one: "I never learned so much so fast in all my life."

2. Fareena Sultan (***): After six years at the Harvard Business School, Sultan came to Berkeley and, like Lyons, quickly won a distinguished teaching award for the first-year core marketing course, in 1993. With a background in applied math and operations research, she brings an analytical and quantitative approach to her Harvard-style case discussions. Says Sultan: "It all gets most exciting when instructor and students really dig deep into cases for what they contain, and extract learning from this unruly method of instruction."

3. Robert G. Harris (**): When this business policy professor walks into a class, he immediately reminds himself that there's 120 years of accumulated experience in the room. "I'd be a fool not to use that," Harris says. He does so by challenging students to share their opinions and experiences in lively case discussions. Harris, who earned his Ph.D. in economics at Berkeley, joined the faculty here in 1977. He served as deputy director of the Interstate Commerce Commission in 1980–1981.

4. Sara L. Beckman (**): She spends half her time at Hewlett-Packard where Beckman is "champion" of organizational learning, and the other half at Berkeley as one of its best teachers. Her personal goal: to help U.S. companies regain their status as global competitors through improved product design and manufacturing. An industrial engineer with a doctorate in manufacturing, brainy Beckman began lecturing at Berkeley on manufacturing strategy in 1988 and now directs the school's Management of Technology program. In the classroom, Beckman tries to "engage students in the act of thinking. I want them to leave the class with as many questions as answers."

5. Terry Pearce (*): Would you believe that Pearce gets on this list by virtue of a second-year elective called Speaking as a Leader? A Haas School lecturer since 1989, and author of the book *Finding Your True Voice*, Pearce runs a consulting firm that coaches business and political leaders in how to make their public speeches. His is more than a class in public speaking, however. "One of my students described this as 'a leadership course trapped in the body of a public-speaking course,' " jokes Pearce.

6. Baruch Lev (*): The former dean of an Israeli business school, Lev joined the Berkeley faculty in 1986 to teach accounting and finance. But this popular professor also has an appointment at the Berkeley law school, where he teaches about insider trading and securities law.

Other Best Bets: *David Vogel* (management), *Andrew Rose* (economics), *Fran Van Loo* (nonprofit management), and *Rashi Glazer* (marketing)

Prominent Alumni: M. Anthony Burns, chairman of Ryder System; James A. Cronin III, president of Tiger International; James R. Harvey, chairman of Transamerica Corp.; Paul M. Hazen, president of Wells Fargo Bank; Robert A. Lutz, president of Chrysler Corp.; Robert F. Clarke, chairman of Hawaiian Electric Industries; Alex J. Mandel, chief financial officer of AT&T; Paul H. Stephens, general partner of Robertson Stephens & Co; Akio Tada, managing director of Dai-Ichi Kangyo Bank, Tokyo

Haas MBAs Sound Off

*The program is constantly being fine-tuned to meet the needs and expectations of the students and outside business world. My biggest issue with Berkeley is whether the MBA has any practical application for my chosen field of human resources. I am aware of all the theories driving those areas today, but in terms of day-to-day application of those theories, I am less confident.—**Human Resources Career Path***

*The professors at Haas deserve high praise, not just for their research and teaching skills, but for the effort that they extended inside and outside the classroom. They were very accessible and approachable, and many I consider friends as well as mentors. My fellow students were of high caliber, not only of intellect but of social skills, savvy, and integrity.—**Real Estate Developer***

*For a small program, Haas could avoid some of the bureaucratic pitfalls of its larger, state-run parent, the University of California. Administrative staff did a good job of trying to cut through the red tape, but more autonomy from the university administration would be welcome. Also, a little more emphasis on interpersonal skills could help prepare MBAs for dealing with wider varieties of people with differing backgrounds and education levels.—**Career Path Unknown***

*If you want your education handed to you, this is not the place. If you want to work and play hard outside of the classroom, you will be rewarded handsomely at Haas. Its small size and public status provide outstanding leadership opportunities. The classes, as a whole, are filled with motivated, take-charge people who thrive in an entrepreneurial atmosphere.—**Associate Marketing Manager***

*Although one-fifth of the students are European, the career center doesn't bring any European companies onto campus to recruit. At least half of the companies that come to Berkeley are high-tech firms from Silicon Valley. Surprisingly, Berkeley admits one-third of its class from outside the U.S., but does not help them much to find a job.—**Marketing Career Path***

*After two years, the material learned tends to be a rehash of trendy management concepts without any critical evaluation of their true effectiveness. There is so much emphasis on group work, in the form of papers and presentations in all but finance courses, that writing skills are overlooked as a worthwhile and valuable asset to management success.—**Financial Analyst***

*This was an absolutely fabulous program. The quality of the teaching coupled with the diverse, sharp, and curious student body made learning an exciting, journey-like experience. The work was challenging and stimulating, and the opportunities to shine were everywhere.—**Career Path Unknown***

*Student diversity and internationalism were among the main reasons I came to Berkeley. I've benefited a great deal from my interaction with students from many different nationalities and very diverse backgrounds. The people I met and exchanged ideas with gave this program a value that money cannot pay. It is noteworthy also that while about 30 percent of the students at Berkeley are considered international, the true number is much higher because many Americans here speak more than one language and have spent considerable time abroad. —**Consultant***

Overall, I enjoyed studying here at the Haas School of Business. Most of the professors are very enthusiastic, intelligent, and helpful. The international students are great. They are so smart and have great personalities; I learned so many cultures just by coming to the United States and attending the school. On the other hand, I am a little bit disappointed with the school's American students. They are more laid back, unwilling to study, and less eager to find jobs.
—Assistant Manager

Haas' tradition is to be outstanding in theoretical fields, especially in economics. A business school is not detached from the rest of the campus. Berkeley is arguably one of the Top 10 spots in the world when it comes to intellectual stimulus. I took lots of interdisciplinary courses, including technology management, in cooperation with the School of Engineering. **—Consultant**

The school does everything possible to ensure that we succeed in the program, and afterwards too. But my biggest issue currently is whether the MBA has any practical application for my chosen field in human resources. I feel that I am aware of all the theories driving these areas today. But in terms of day-to-day application of those theories, I am less confident. **—Human Resources Career Path**

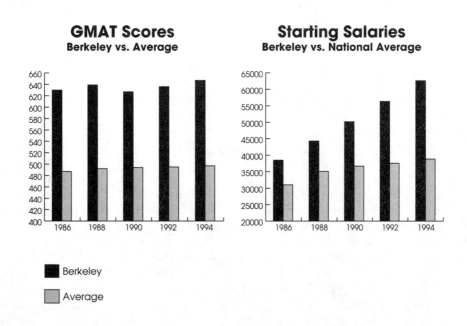

GMAT Scores
Berkeley vs. Average

Starting Salaries
Berkeley vs. National Average

■ Berkeley
▨ Average

20. Purdue University

Krannert Graduate School of Management
West Lafayette, Indiana 47907

Corporate ranking: 10
Enrollment: 195
Women: 31%
Non-U.S.: 28%
Minority: 15%
Part-time: None
Average age: 26
Average years of work exp.: 3
Applicants accepted: 32%
Median starting pay: $53,000

Graduate ranking: 33
Annual tuition: resident—$2884
nonresident—$9556
Room and board: $4500
Average GMAT score: 581
GMAT range: 370 to 740
Average GPA: 3.23
GPA range: 2.37 to 4.0
Accepted applicants enrolled: 55%
Average starting pay: $54,720

Teaching methods: Lecture, 45%   Case method, 45%   Projects, 10%

What MBA program throws more work atop its students than any other? Virginia or Carnegie Mellon? Dartmouth or Berkeley? Wrong. Some of these schools come close to smothering MBAs with excessive workloads, but the business school that seems to top them all is Purdue University's Krannert Graduate School of Management. Some graduates describe the place as a "mental bootcamp" where virtually every minute outside of class is consumed by work.

What makes the toil all the more difficult is that much of it is heavily quantitative. For some, it can be a deadly combination. "Oftentimes we would refer to an exam as being 'multiple guess' because we seem to only see the material and not learn from it," says one recent alum. Complains another grad: "The amount of work is so tremendous that it impedes learning."

Aware of the problem, the school has trimmed back the program's core requirements to offer students more flexibility in choosing electives. But few have seen significant decline in the work. "It's a heavy workload," says Ward D. Snearly, director of admissions. "But in any program of this type the work is heavy. Sometimes it's just a shock to students when they encounter it. But they do get their money's worth."

In spite of all the complaints about heavy workload, Purdue broke into the Top 20 for the first time. However, the B-school's presence on the list is mostly due to overwhelming support from companies. The surprising tenth place corporate poll result is due to the fact that one major industrial company after another considers its graduates the best. The students are less satisfied with the school than recruiters. Purdue received the lowest grades of any Top 20 school in teaching, curriculum, and placement. Indeed, no business school has ever had as low a graduate ranking—in Purdue's case, 33rd—and still made it in the Top 20 overall. Although some students are less than satisfied, it's precisely because of this heavy quant focus that companies pluck Purdue grads.

Applicants get some warning of the heavy workload when the school points out that it does not technically award an MBA. Instead, graduates receive a Master of Science degree in industrial administration, management, or human resources management—a difference that reflects the program's emphasis on technical and analytical training. About 50 percent of the students boast undergraduate degrees in science or engineering. There are major differences between the degrees. The M.S. in industrial administration is granted when you complete Purdue's equivalent of the marathon, a frantically paced run to get a graduate degree in 11 months. (The University of Pittsburgh offers the same type of program.) The M.S. in management and the M.S. in human resources management are the typical two-year programs that permit concentrations in operations, finance, organizational behavior, or other functional areas of management.

The school has completely revamped its two-year program after students responding to BUSINESS WEEK's 1992 surveys ranked their school at or near the bottom in many categories from teaching quality to faculty expertise, from practical knowledge gained in the program to the responsiveness to student concerns shown by the administration. Modeled on Motorola University's Total Quality initiatives (100 Purdue faculty members studied there at the 1992 University TQM Challenge), the new Krannert program is designed to introduce the "softer skills" of quality management into the curriculum.

In an effort to make the curriculum more flexible, Krannert has restructured the way it delivers the program. Students now attend four 8-week modules instead of two semesters yearly. This structural change forced professors to reorganize the content of classes. The first year is still crammed with 15 required courses and 1 elective. MBAs take four courses per quarter in accounting, quantitative methods, operations, economics, finance, communications, organizational behavior, human resources management, marketing, and management of information systems during the first year. You're required to take two modules in each area except for economics, organizational behavior, human resources management, and marketing. In your second year, you'll pick up another quarter of economics and management information systems along with two modules each of strategy and law. So MBAs are free to choose nine electives in the second year and must take six required core courses.

Students still have to pick a major or "option" to gain a degree. They can choose from accounting, finance, marketing, strategic management, operations management, management of information systems, and human resources management. Krannert also offers three new interdisciplinary options: manufacturing management, international management, and general management.

MBAs who choose to take the manufacturing management option take business and engineering courses. So they'll take industrial engineering, computer science, and computer technology courses as well as the traditional accounting, finance, and management courses. Students will not only complete the MBA core curriculum, but also take core courses for this option which focus on manufacturing. For example, students will take a human resources course that focuses on manufacturing and a strategy course that stresses the topic. There is still room for a few free electives which can be taken at Krannert or the engineering school.

MBAs who pick the international option will take courses in international operations, international strategy, marketing in a global economy, and international operations in addition to the core. The general management option is geared toward students with significant work experience who don't want to specialize in a functional area.

Purdue has vastly improved its elective offerings. The school offered 70 electives in 1993–94, a dramatic change from two years ago, when there were only 45. Some new electives: Tools for TQM, Enterprise Integration, Manufacturing Strategy, Teams and Teamwork, and Cross-Functional Teams. However, students still complain about the lack of elective choice the first year, and would like to see the school broaden the scope of its offered electives. More than half the students here also find themselves in one or more consulting experiences with real companies. In case-study courses, half your grade is based on class participation.

Students aren't limited to the B-school for elective choices. They are encouraged to take classes in other schools—many look to the engineering school. An additional 18 courses are offered to students who study operations management—Purdue's major strength. Indeed, some graduates warn applicants to stay away from the school if they aren't interested in manufacturing. Dean Weidenaar is building upon the school's reputation in operations with a relatively new Center for the Management of Manufacturing Enterprises.

Krannert has developed a cohort system in which students are preassigned to teams for eight-week exercises, to help them understand teamwork and to develop problem-solving and team-building skills. During orientation students are given a Meyers-Brigg test and are analyzed to determine strengths and weaknesses in their leadership ability. A second-year mentor is assigned to each group of four or five people.

There are no classes scheduled on Fridays. Instead MBAs must participate in "Forum Days" which are aimed at exploring special topics and experiential activities. For example, all students participate in an outward-bound-type program one Friday. Outside speakers will also visit campus on Fridays and discuss environmental issues or how the latest technology will impact corporations. Plant and company trips are also scheduled on Forum Days. "These things don't fit very neatly into a 90-minute forum so we block out Fridays so we can concentrate on certain topics," says G. Logan Jordan, assistant dean at Krannert.

Despite the traditional gripes about heavy workload, lack of choice and stress on quantitative skills, students from the Class of 1994 were generally satisfied customers. In BUSINESS WEEK's customer satisfaction survey, almost every Krannert MBA gave the school above-average marks for core and elective teaching, a distinct improvement from 1992. "Although the workload is still excessive, the changes they have made have led to a stronger, more interdisciplinary approach," says a 1994 grad.

Purdue offers a big bang for your buck. It is one of the least expensive Top 20 schools. Residents can pick up the degree for about $6000—less than the cost of one semester at a private school. It costs about $20,000 to earn the two-year degree from Krannert if you're not from the state versus the $31,050 it costs to study at Wharton for just one year. The schools say that about 30 percent of the students work for tuition remission in graduate assistantships or residence-hall counselorships. An additional 10 percent receive some form of cash fellowship.

Perhaps the school's best asset is the unpretentious, down-home culture of this small, conservative university town. "You walk down the street and strangers say hello," says Brian Vos, an alum who landed a job with Gallo Winery in California. "You go to the dry cleaner without enough cash and they tell you. 'Don't worry about it. Pay me next time.' People here are so open and trusting."

You can spot the seven-story Krannert Building, named after the founder of Inland Container Corporation, on the southeast edge of the university's stately 1565-acre campus. In a sea of red-brick buildings, it is a massive block of white concrete with narrow strip windows that run up and down. The top floor is packed with computer equipment, while the ground floor is home to a French provincial drawing room that serves as the student lounge. In what is a Krannert ritual, graduate students and some faculty gather in this room at 9:30 a.m. for coffee after the first-period class. The B-school is linked via underground tunnel to a pair of adjacent graduate dorms as well as the Purdue Memorial Union, a popular spot for a quick and cheap lunch. It's also a block away from Chauncy Hill Mall, where grads sometimes meet at the Wabash Yacht Club for drinks or stop in at Garcia's Pan Pizza, Toogies' cookies, and Ben & Jerry's ice cream. Almost a second graduate lounge is Harry's Chocolate Shop, an old, weathered place with scribblings on the walls where students migrate after exams. Many grads live off-campus, where you can get a one-bedroom apartment for as little as $300 a month. You can park in the Grant Street garage just across from the B-school for only $30 a year.

West Lafayette isn't exactly the most exciting place in the world. "There are few distractions here," adds Vos. "You don't have a beach, and you don't have a lot of culture other than what the B-school provides. So your focus is on school." Chicago is 120 miles to the north, while Indianapolis is 70 miles to the south. For biz grads, there's an annual picnic and the softball game on Intramural Field near the Purdue Airport on Groundhog Day, even when there's snow on the ground. Big Ten football and basketball games are *de rigueur.*

But while Lafayette may lack the easygoing charm and dynamic diversity of a Chapel Hill or Austin, it's hardly a wasteland. *Money* magazine, in fact, ranked it 33rd on its list of the Top 300 places to live in 1994. The community has its own civic orchestra and theater as well as a nationally accredited art museum. In the spring, there's the Around-the-Fountain Art Fair next to Lafayette's neoclassical courthouse. In the summer, bluegrass and mountain musicians gravitate to the city for the Indiana Fiddler's Gathering. And in the fall, the Feast of the Hunter's Moon draws thousands of visitors to Fort Ouiatenon where the area's French and Indian history is re-created on the banks of the Wabash River.

Krannert made significant progress bringing companies back to campus to recruit in 1994. Although nowhere near to the 148 companies that recruited on campus in 1990, 72 corporations interviewed MBAs in West Lafayette this year, a 22-firm improvement from 1992. About 83 percent had at least one job offer by graduation. Krannert students on average had 2.1 offers each. The major recruiters included Allied Signal (7); Ernst and Young (5); Andersen Consulting (5); Intel (5); Ford (4); Federal Express (4); Carrier (3); and McKinsey (2).

The school that is the toughest must continue to listen to what its customers are saying.

Contact: Ward D. Snearly, associate director of master's programs. 317-494-4365
Final application deadline: Rolling admissions

Outstanding Faculty

1. Gerald Lynch (****): If Lynch has his way, MBAs who leave his class will think like economists. The dynamic professor also thinks its essential to blend theory and practice and is constantly searching for articles that support the points in his macroeconomics course. Lynch says that because students can get glazed looks on their faces, it's important for them to see that what you're doing in theory will be important to them in practice. "If you're trying to teach someone how to hit a baseball, you can talk about the theory of hitting a baseball, but they're never going to learn how to hit one until they get in a batting cage and take cuts," he says. The delivery of material is also important to Lynch, who likes to break his lectures up into pieces, tell stories, and sometimes use a little humor even though it can sometimes fall flat.

2. John McConnell (****): He's part preppie and part western. This L.L. Bean-type loves to wear cowboy hats. McConnell is demanding and proud of it. His students talk about him the way Vince Lombardi was once described: "He treats us equally, like dogs." However, he points out, alums come back and thank him for what they learned in his classes. McConnell draws upon his extensive consulting experience with numerous law firms, corporations, and government agencies in the classroom.

3. Charlene Sullivan (***): This finance professor has won many teaching accolades from both Krannert and Purdue University. Sullivan juggles single parenting, community service, professional outreach, research, and teaching with ease. She serves on many boards including the Federal Reserve Bank of Chicago. Sullivan's community involvement enables her to bring real-world situations into the classroom.

4. Dan Schendel (***): Many students find him intimidating in class because he doesn't suffer fools gladly. Schendel agrees that he has little patience for students who don't aggressively pursue answers. He takes some responsibility for MBAs' answers: "If you know how to ask the right questions, you've got a better chance of getting the right answers." Schendel takes strategy seriously. The professor is founder and editor of a strategy journal and he is also founding president of the Strategic Management Society. He arrived at Purdue shortly after earning his Ph.D. from Stanford in 1963.

5. Manu Kalwani (**): Dubbed the "king of the case (method)" at Krannert, Kalwani is known for his ability to create an environment where students feel comfortable exploring ideas. The marketing professor won four outstanding teaching awards in the past five years. MBAs admire him for his dedication to teaching and his concern for their career development. Kulwani arrived at Purdue in 1980, after teaching at MIT. He picked up his Ph.D. from Columbia in 1975 and an Industrial Engineering degree from Purdue in 1970.

6. Stephen G. Green (**):   This bird lover can be found in Purdue's courtyard supplying bird feed to students when he's not teaching organizational behavior. Green's known for his wit and sense of humor. Students say he's just "plain likable" even when he's being gruff. He picked up an MBA from the University of Texas in 1968 and a Ph.D. in psychology at the University of Washington in 1976. Green has consulted with firms such as Procter & Gamble, American Cyanamid Company, and the Environmental Protection Agency.

Other Best Bets: *Arnold C. Cooper* (strategy), *Mac Dada* (operations), *Douglas Bowman* (marketing), and *Mark M. Moriarty* (marketing)

Prominent Alumni: W. James Fischer, managing partner of Andersen Consulting; Bruce Flohr, president of RailTex Incorporated; Dave Fuente, chairman of the board and CEO of Office Depot, Inc.; Karl Krapek, president of Pratt & Whitney; Keith Magee, vice president and general manager of the Lincoln Mercury Division of Ford Motor Company; Don Orr, senior vice president of the chemicals group of Air Products & Chemicals; Tom Page, chairman, president, and CEO of San Diego Gas & Electric Company; James Perrella, chairman, president, and CEO of Ingersoll-Rand Company; Cindy Ransom, area manufacturing manager of the international division with the Clorox Company; Donald Rice, president and COO with Teledyne and former Secretary of the Air Force

Krannert MBAs Sound Off

My second year in the program was the first year of Krannert's transition, which included a change to eight-week modules, Friday forum days, and additional emphasis on teams and leadership. The workload in the second year was much more reasonable and integrated across the courses. The number of electives increased, and responsiveness of the faculty and administration to concerns became outstanding. This is a plus for a smaller program, particularly when all parties involved are working toward the same goals of excellence and improvement.—**Marketing Career Path**

The recent changes in the program are an example of the responsiveness of the directors to both market demand and student request. Many more electives will be offered, and students will receive a more interdisciplinary approach to management.—**Finance Career Path**

Although I consider my MBA invaluable for my professional development, I was disappointed by the lack of multicultural awareness of my classmates. Probably because of the location of my school in the Midwest, most of the people with whom I interacted had scarce or no knowledge of other country's cultures. Most of the opinions they hold are based on stereotypes and prejudice. In my opinion, this is unjustifiable in 1994.—**Consulting Career Path**

*Most of the faculty is very conservative. There is a strong emphasis in the economics courses on the value of free markets and private property.—**Financial Analyst***

*The only downfall of Krannert is the excessive workload the first year.—**Business Analyst***

*Purdue is an excellent place to get a top-notch MBA for a reasonable cost. If you were to look at the value added per dollar of tuition, Krannert would be among the top in the country.—**Senior Consultant***

*Another extremely strong aspect of Krannert is that about one-third of all second-year students attend school for free as they receive a quarter-time assistantship. Additionally, about 65 to 70 percent of all students receive substantial financial assistance during the two years.—**Special Projects Manager***

*Going to Purdue University's Krannert School was the best thing I have ever done in my life. It gave my career a boost, and also I gained a lot of leadership skills. Almost all the stuff we did, studied, or worked on was useful for the job. I think I got a lot more at Purdue than I paid for.—**Manager***

*The tuition here makes Krannert a steal. It's almost too good a bargain. It's a great B-school for individuals with undergraduate engineering degrees. The faculty is quite impressive. I doubled my salary in two years—a great return on my investment.—**Finance Manager***

*Many of the best faculty and best students in the program are in the finance department. It is only a matter of time before the corporate world takes more notice. The recent changes in the program are an example of the responsiveness of the administration to both market demand and student requests.—**Finance Career Path***

*I went to Purdue for its program in operations management. I wanted a dual degree in an engineering discipline and an MBA. Although not available, Krannert pursued and implemented a manufacturing management option. The school also changed from 16-week to 8-week sessions to allow more diversity and flexibility in academic programs. These two efforts especially separate such a young business school from many others.—**Operations Manager***

I've been extremely pleased with the education I've received at Krannert. Many doors have opened up for me in terms of career opportunities, and I have had a good increase in salary. The students at Krannert are down-to-earth, work well in teams, and work very hard to fulfill the demanding expectations of the school.

*I've found that professors here go out of their way to help students outside of class, and they take a genuine interest in the student's success.—**Accountant***

*Krannert has made great improvements in the last year, and within two or three years I feel they will have an excellent program. I felt these changes in the program were way overdue. This program should have been revamped several years ago. Krannert's administration was slow in adjusting to changes in the marketplace.—**Manufacturing Career Path***

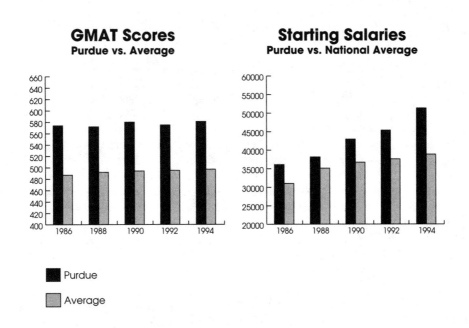

CHAPTER 7

THE RUNNERS-UP

There's a common joke among B-school deans that there are at least 40 schools that claim to be in the Top 20, and as many as 100 that maintain they're among the 50 leading business schools in the United States. Some of these claims are based on little more than marketing bluster, some on less-than-certain standards of excellence such as the number of faculty citations in a handful of scholarly journals.

Truth is, however, that beyond the leading 20 schools that get most of the attention, there's also a slew of excellent institutions that offer the MBA degree. They may lack some of the prestige and clout of the Top 20, but in most cases they deliver the same basic body of knowledge and quality of education you'll find in the more prominent schools. BUSINESS WEEK picked the institutions that are profiled in this chapter as the next best grouping largely on the basis of their standing in our corporate recruiter survey. The magazine also surveyed the graduates of most of these institutions, with only a few exceptions.

You'll discover some familiar names here—schools that have in recent years fallen out of the Top 20 list, such as Yale's School of Management, Rochester's Simon School, and the B-school at Washington University. All three of these institutions have superb reputations and could climb back into Top 20 contention in the future. There are also a host of B-schools—at Emory, Minnesota, Southern California, and Michigan State—that are mounting aggressive campaigns to break into the top tier. And among this runners-up group you'll find two of the most innovative business schools in the world: the B-schools at Case Western and Southern Methodist University.

Some of these institutions are just as selective as their elite counterparts in the Top 20. Some boast better records of placing their students. Others can rightfully claim strengths in niche areas, such as entrepreneurship or ethics, that far surpass what any Top 20 school can offer.

BUSINESS WEEK lists this group without an actual ranking.

American Graduate School of International Management

Thunderbird
15249 North 59th Street
Glendale, Arizona 85306

Enrollment: 1286
Women: 37%
Non-U.S.: 30%
Minority: 8%
Part-time: None
Average age: 26
Applicants accepted: 35%
Accepted applicants enrolled: 56%

Annual tuition & fees: $23,095
Room and board: $6256
Average GMAT score: 570
GMAT range: 450 to 750
Average GPA: 3.3
GPA range: 2.5 to 4.0
Average years of work exp.: 3.5
Average starting pay: $49,660

Teaching methods: Case method, 25% Lecture, 45% Projects, 30%

At graduation every year, the Thunderbird grads do more than don mortarboards and gowns: Many of them carry the flags of their home countries in a colorful parade of bright reds, whites, yellows, and blues. The accents are as varied as the visitors from as many as 60 different countries around the world. "In a lot of ways, this place is like the United Nations," says David A. Ricks, vice president for academic affairs.

Indeed, it is. If you can imagine a business school version of the UN, it might well be the American Graduate School of International Management. The global nature of the school can be seen everywhere on the 160-acre campus. The United Nations flag flys outside the administration building, while a "flag of the day" flaps in the dry Arizona wind in front of Founders Hall.

The uniqueness of the program, of course, goes well beyond these mere symbols. Students here complete not one but three areas of study: culture, language, and business. An internship program offers opportunities to gain experience in multinational corporations and trade agencies. At any one time, a fifth of the enrollment is overseas in internships and exchange or study abroad programs. Every graduate leaves the program with fluency in a foreign language.

Yet, it is not unusual for snobby academics to turn up their noses when you mention Thunderbird to them. Roy Herberger says that some of his academic colleagues expressed surprise when he told them he had agreed in 1989 to become president of the Thunderbird program. They warned him that he would never be able to return to the world of academia.

Phooey on them. Anyone seriously interested in international business cannot fail to consider going to this school for a master's in business. Thunderbird, which takes its nickname from its location on a deactivated army air training base just outside Phoenix, was offering a global slant to business education when most B-school deans never thought it was important. Indeed, for 30 years, the school had the only international business program in the United States. The school was founded by Lt. General Barton Kyle Yount in 1946 to help Americans enter the emerging international business environment.

Now that nearly every executive chatters on about global-this and global-that, Thunderbird is sitting pretty. One recent study proclaimed it the number one international MBA program in the country. Even after increasing tuition by 25 percent in 1990, enrollment zoomed to an all-time high of over 1500. Some students were sitting on the floors in classes. Those growing pains were relieved after President Herberger sank nearly $15 million into four new Southwestern-styled buildings, with red tiled roofs and white stucco trim. In the past two years he has cut ribbons outside a new classroom and lecture hall, a building for his international studies faculty, a world business/administration building, and yet another dormitory to the dozen or so he already had. (The school houses more than 500 students on campus.) In June 1994, Thunderbird opened a new library that offers state-of-the-art electronic retrieval systems. Behind NYU and Harvard, it's now the third largest B-school in the United States.

Thunderbird offers about 45 international business courses and just as many classes in the cultural, political, legal, and religious aspects of countries. Students tend to major in or focus on regions of the world instead of narrow disciplinary functions. "So a student wanting to study Arabic will start with the Arabic language," says Herberger, who left Southern Methodist University's B-school for the presidency at Thunderbird. "Then they'll also, alongside of it, start studying the politics of Islam. They'll look at the cultural influence of the Saudis and royal families. There are a lot of different things that go into the shaping of business practices of an area."

The school offers plenty of flexibility. Students can enter this program at four different points in any year: January, February, June, or September. To graduate, you must be proficient in a foreign language. If you're already fluent in another language when you enter the program, you'll be required to complete 54 hours of coursework in international studies, world business, and electives. If not, you'll have to add nine extra hours of work—mainly in one of 10 modern languages from Arabic to Russian. You can waive out of the core courses in the business basics if you've already covered the material in undergraduate or graduate classes, which can reduce the program to its minimum of 42 semester hours. If you haven't been trained in business and a language, expect to stay at Thunderbird for close to two years.

Among the school's most unusual features is "Winterim" every January. It's a three-week period when the school serves up an unusual menu of courses taught by prominent international experts who travel from around the globe to Arizona to teach. The courses have ranged from Marketing to U.S. Hispanics Seminar to Privatization, and from Countertrade/ Offset to Doing Business in Eastern Europe and Russia. A Winterim CEO seminar in 1994 featured the chairmen and presidents of ARCO International, Harley Davidson, CNN International–Turner Broadcasting, McDonnell Douglas Helicopter, and Honeywell International.

Most business schools offer just a few study-abroad programs. Thunderbird has a slew of them. You can go to the school's own facility in Japan to study a select range of regular courses or regionally specific offerings. You can take a 10-week session in Guadalajara during the summer for courses taught by Thunderbird profs and Mexican scholars. If you're proficient in German, you can take off for the European Business School at Schloss Reichartshausen in Germany, which offers a two-month internship with a German or U.S. multinational corporation. Or you might want to try the 9-week summer program in

France. There are more options in the People's Republic of China, Finland, Norway, and Spain. In early 1993, Thunderbird also opened a campus in Archamps, France, on the outskirts of Geneva, Switzerland, its second satellite after the one established in Tokyo in 1991.

Many students come here to pursue careers outside of the conventional business world. "It's more than a business school," says Ricks. "A lot of the things we are doing in international studies are not offered in regular schools." Foreign ambassadors regularly come to the campus to speak with students, and one of every five graduates goes to work for such not-for-profit places as the CIA, World Health Organization, the Peace Corps, and, of course, the United Nations.

At Thunderbird, only recently accredited by the AACSB, grads earn a MIM (Master in International Management) instead of the MBA. The core curriculum differs from the typical MBA fare. Although the average GMAT scores here have risen by more than 50 points since 1986, they're still on the low side—at 570 for the Class of 1996, they're the lowest of any BUSINESS WEEK runners-up school.

Still, there's no shortage of recruiters wanting the grads. More than 20,000 Thunderbird graduates populate the ranks of such companies as General Motors, American Express, IBM, and General Electric. Thunderbird's top employers are the U.S. Department of State, where 93 alums work; Citibank (88); Chase Manhattan Bank (88); Merrill Lynch (66); Bank of America (64); U.S. Department of Commerce (45); IBM (44); U.S. Agency for International Development (44); Electronic Data Systems (42); Motorola (42); Chemical Bank (37); and Ford Motor (31). Many graduates have foreign postings, or U.S. jobs with international responsibilities. The alumni network is large and strong. On the first Tuesday of every month, alumni gather in local pubs and bars in 157 cities around the world, from Mexico City to Taipei. T-Birds, as they call themselves, live in more than 130 countries and in every state of the United States.

In 1994, 252 companies came to campus to recruit students, conducting 2769 interviews. The major employers: PepsiCo and Cabletron Systems (7 Thunderbird grads); Citibank (6); Deloitte & Touche, Tohmatsu, and Goldman Sachs (5 each); and Federal Express, Federal Mogus, and Nomura International (3 each).

Contact: Brian Bates, director of admissions, 800-848-9084 or 602-978-7210
Final application deadline: January 31 for summer and fall entrance; July 31 for Winterim and spring entrance.

Outstanding Faculty: *Frank Tuzzolino* (***—finance), *James Mills* (***—finance), *Kenneth Ferris* (**—accounting), *Sundaresan Ram* (**—marketing), *M. Edgar Barrett* (**—world business), *Dale Davison* (*—accounting), *Dale Vorderlandwehr* (entrepreneurship), *Peter Bergevin* (accounting), *Allen Morrison* (strategy), *John Zerio* (marketing)

Thunderbird MBAs Sound Off

Thunderbird's good teachers are excellent—the best I've had. However, there are a few professors here who are very bad. Depending upon which section of a class you're in, it can be a great experience or practically a waste of tuition. T-Bird is not a school for those who want to be investment bankers or consultants at the *top consulting firms—they just don't recruit here. But if you're geographically flexible and want an exciting job, T-Bird's got great possibilities. —**Staff Auditor***

*I believe that the school is continuing to accept more and more people who lack work experience. I have found that discussion in class can be somewhat limiting. However, the international diversity and exposure is fantastic. —**Strategic Planner***

*While I feel the school could be more efficient and organized, and I have also heard many fellow classmates bitch about feeling "adrift" and "lost," there is an incredible wealth of experience and knowledge to be gained at Thunderbird if you have the savvy and persistence to go after it, rather than waiting for it to come along on a silver platter. —**Marketing Career Path***

*An important note for any perspective students: If your undergraduate degree is not in business and you wish to attend Thunderbird, try to take your intro business courses before you get to Thunderbird. The "baby" (to use Thunderslang) courses here are weak, and taking them here may prevent you from taking some of the fantastic upper-level seminar courses, unless you can afford to stay for years. —**Management Career Path***

*The school is only starting to formulate strategies for implementing technology for student use. As of now, we do not even have E-mail for students. I find this ridiculous in regards to the school's mission. However, I must add that the school has recruited a prominent I.T. scholar to help remedy the situation, and is also providing additional courses in Information Systems to increase student awareness. —**Global Management Career Path***

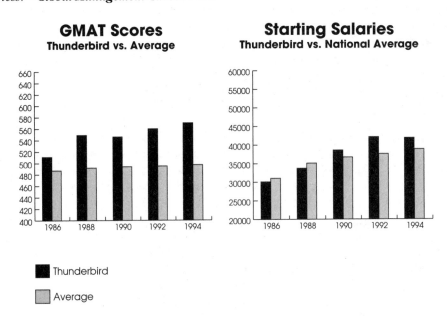

Case Western Reserve University

Weatherhead School of Management
Cleveland, Ohio 44106

Enrollment: 1058
Women: 38%
Non-U.S.: 29%
Minority: 12%
Part-time: 642
Average age: 27
Applicants accepted: 51%
Accepted applicants enrolled: 33%

Annual tuition & fees: $17,600
Room and board: $5200
Average GMAT score: 591
GMAT range: 450 to 740
Average GPA: 3.12
GPA range: 2.4 to 4.0
Average years of work exp.: 4.1
Average starting pay: $57,200

Teaching methods: Lecture, 20%   Case method, 40%   Group projects, 40%

When someone eventually tallies up the foibles and fumbles among the massive efforts by business schools to revitalize their MBA programs, there's one innovative school you're not going to find on the list. It's a school that shunned marketing gimmicks, business fads, and quick fixes. It's a school that pioneered, rather than followed, many of the more meaningful curriculum revisions of the early 1990s. And it's a school in an unlikely locale for a change agent: Cleveland.

But the smallish Weatherhead School at Case Western Reserve University has proven that it's one of the more creative business institutions in America. As Dean Scott S. Cowen puts it, "Innovation in management education isn't really occurring at the Top 20 schools. It's happening at the next level of schools because things like this can rapidly propel you into the Top 20."

It's hard to think of a school that has more dramatically changed its curriculum in more creative ways than Weatherhead, which takes its name from a local entrepreneur. With an entering class of only 150 full-timers, the school promises a small, intimate learning experience and dedicated teachers who use the city's business community as a laboratory for students. It's also promising one of the most distinctive MBA programs. Cowen organizes core courses around broad themes, tying courses overall to skill development, and tailors the MBA program to take best advantage of the strengths and weaknesses of individual students.

First-year MBA candidates will immediately find themselves in a required course dubbed Management Assessment and Development. It has a dull ring to it as many core courses do, but in this class each student will be evaluated for strengths, weaknesses, and personal skills. Professors will test you for leadership potential, for entrepreneurship, and for decision making. You'll take sit-down tests, but your presentations will also be videotaped to see how they can be improved. Then the student, consulting with faculty, will develop a tailor-made learning plan for the remainder of the two-year program.

The approach is getting good reviews. "The Management Assessment and Development program provided me with important feedback on a host of management skills," says Robert L. Kraber, a 1992 alum. "The program forced me to take a hard introspective look at the areas in which I needed the most improvement, and helped shape my graduate studies."

Every course at the school has been audited, not for just the discipline-based knowledge it may impart in such fields as finance or marketing but more importantly for the skills it attempts to develop in students. If you're weak in quantitative methods, you'll be steered to courses that teach those skills better—whether they are in marketing, finance, or operations. If you're weak in communications skills, you'll pick courses that will emphasize that area regardless of their subject matter. It's far more refined than this, of course, since the faculty at Weatherhead has broken down skill development into 72 separate categories, from your ability to sell ideas to your skill in using computer modeling.

That's not all. In the second year, you'll take a pair of what Cowen is calling "perspectives courses" that cover material that transcends the traditional B-school disciplines. Example: Technology and Society, which doesn't really belong in any single department, is team-taught by professors from different disciplines. You'll also become a member of an Executive Action Team of 12 students who will work with a host executive in the area, who will serve as a team mentor. Students will be paired by common interests, weaknesses, and experience. The mentor may bring the team into his or her organization to meet with managers in marketing and production. How does this differ from the typical study group? Team members won't be studying for a particular course. Instead, they'll be sharing their own different learning programs, figuring out how to work together, and exploring the sponsoring organization's way of business life.

Besides these three required courses and the team assignment, you'll have 11 more typical courses. But even here there's a big difference. Weatherhead faculty have been redesigning these core courses to overlay certain intellectual themes. "When you take accounting," says Cowen, "you are not going to just learn accounting, you're going to learn it in the context of several underlying themes." They include: the global economy, understanding the cultural settings in which managers function, social responsibility, and how to adapt to change and technology. With an undergraduate business degree, you could waive 6 of these 11 classes and graduate in 11 months. Otherwise, you typically choose 6 electives from nearly 100 courses offered by a full-time tenure-track faculty of about 80.

A new summer program allows MBA students to earn six credits by combining international management research with a three-week, multi-country study tour in such European countries as England, Belgium, the Czech Republic, Austria, and Germany. In 1975, Weatherhead hopes to expand the Summer Institute to Asia and Latin America. For budding global managers, the school just signed a deal with the well-known Thunderbird school in Arizona to offer a joint MBA/Master of International Management degree. Students can complete their studies at both schools in two years by working through the summer. There's also a Master of Nonprofit Organizations granted through Weatherhead with the university's Mandel Center.

Another Weatherhead strength: its executive mentor program. Like SMU's B-school, Weatherhead matches students with executives from such companies as AT&T, TRW, Eaton, and McKinsey, who serve as mentors throughout the length of the program. And in virtually every course here students are organized to do projects for companies in the

Cleveland area. More than 400 managers and executives annually volunteer their time in class projects, lectures, clubs, or mentorships. The school also boasts student internships tied directly into the MBA program.

What about Cleveland? You obviously won't find an intellectual climate such as in Ann Arbor or Berkeley, or a setting with the dynamics of a Chicago or New York. But Cleveland can surprise. As a Weatherhead professor says on the school's video for applicants: "Cleveland has what every city ought to have, but in more manageable terms." For $10 a seat, students can hear a symphony performed by the first-class Cleveland Orchestra at Severance Hall on campus. For even less, you can sit in the bleachers and watch the Cleveland Indians play at Jacobs' Field, one of the best of the new breed of baseball stadiums to be built in recent years. The B-school took over a new, modern building in 1989 and completely renovated an older facility next door so that the two buildings are linked on the fourth, fifth, and sixth floors. It sits in a park-like campus in Cleveland's University Circle on the eastern edge of the city. Once a rough, high-crime area, it has gone through major gentrification.

University circle is home to the city museums of art and natural history. For drinking and eating, MBAs favor the Greenhouse, a restaurant bar on Murray Hill Drive, just a five-minute walk from campus, and the Euclid Tavern, also within walking distance. Students get together for two school-wide picnics a year and frequent faculty and student softball games. And on the last Thursday afternoon of each month students meet for the latest party in a "survival series" where beer, pizza, and subs help attract a good crowd to the atrium of the building.

Weatherhead obviously isn't on the tip of everyone's tongue. There's little brand-name identity to the program and not much national recognition. In a recessionary year, those disadvantages can clearly be felt by the graduating class. But in 1994, roughly 86 percent of the Class of 1994 had job offers by commencement. Those that did averaged 2.3 offers each, just a tad below the average for the top schools. That's a huge improvement over Weatherhead's recession-plagued stats two years earlier, when 34 percent of the class was without a single offer by graduation and MBAs averaged only 1.4 offers each.

The change occurred because Dean Cowen installed a new placement director and doubled the placement staff to four persons. He also worked overtime to cultivate local corporations. Some 92 companies came to recruit on campus in 1994, conducting 435 interviews. Another 252 job opportunities arrived via the mails. The leading recruiters: Ernst & Young (4) and Andersen Consulting (3). Hiring a pair of Weatherhead MBAs each were A.T. Kearney, KeyCorp/Society Bank, National City Bank, Avery Dennison, Coca-Cola, Cole National, and General Electric.

Contact: Tracey Winland, admissions office, 800-723-0203, 2031
Final Application Deadline: April 15 for four-semester program; April 1 for accelerated program

Outstanding Faculty: *Sam Thomas* (****—finance), *Richard L. Osborne* (****—entrepreneurship), *J. B. Silvers* (***—finance), *Julia E. S. Grant* (**—accounting), *Peter H. Ritchken* (*—operations), *N. Mohan Reddy* (*—marketing), *Robert D. Hisrich* (entrepreneurship), *Scott S. Cowen* (accounting), *Robert T. Kauer* (finance), *Ronald H. Ballou* (operations)

Weatherhead MBAs Sound Off

Almost all classes emphasize teamwork. Student opinion is asked for, and changes, whenever possible, are made. The faculty is available, and very helpful outside class. The curriculum is undergoing some changes, and students are actively involved. **—Marketing Career Path**

Every instructor gives the students his or her home phone number, and I have called many of them at home. They have always been available and helpful to me. **—Information Systems Career Path**

I was thrilled to be a part of the Weatherhead experience. The students are here to learn. The support and cooperation among students is outstanding. You can leave projects and bookbags around the school and come back hours later to find them exactly where you left them. Ask another student for help, and you will get it. **—Health Care Administrator**

A serious drawback I found in the classroom was the lack of work experience among my classmates. Unfortunately, I learned little from them. The benefits of a diverse study body, with a high percentage of Asian students, were rarely achieved due to language barriers. Non-U.S. students rarely spoke in class. I learned next to nothing about Asian management/business practices. **—Venture Capitalist**

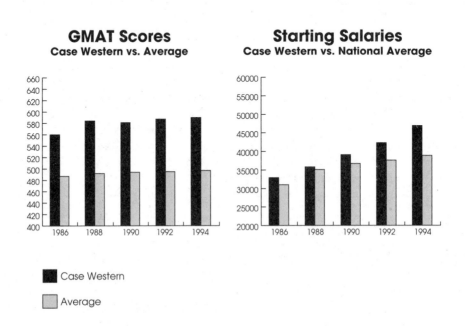

Emory University

Goizueta Business School
Atlanta, Georgia 30322

Enrollment: 443	*Annual tuition:* $18,850
Women: 37%	*Room and board:* $11,000
Non-U.S.: 18%	*Average GMAT score:* 625
Minority: 18%	*GMAT range:* 460 to 760
Part-time: 162	*Average GPA:* 3.2
Average age: 26	*GPA range:* 2.1 to 3.95
Applicants accepted: 36%	*Accepted applicants enrolled:* 48%
Median starting pay: $59,500	*Average starting pay:* $63,830

Teaching methods: Lecture, 30%   Case method, 60%   Projects, 10%

A BUSINESS WEEK magazine cover story called "Clout" told how giant retailers are revolutionizing the way consumer products are bought and sold. But to MBAs at Emory University's Business School the news sounded awfully familiar. More than a year earlier, in fact, the school developed an unusual program with consumer packaging giant Procter & Gamble to deal with the vast changes in the marketplace. The program has been so successful that Coca-Cola, Motorola, and Chubb signed up too.

If anything, the program—dubbed the Customer Business Development Track—demonstrates how responsive this school is to its own customers. The idea of launching the initiative, which includes a summer internship directly tied into the curriculum, came from P&G Chairman Edwin Artzt, who was revamping his company's sales relationships with major retailers such as Wal-Mart and Kroger. Instead of dispatching a single sales rep into the field, the company began to send out teams of staffers from finance, marketing, sales, customer service, and management systems to work more closely with the retailers. Emory's track program puts students shoulder-to-shoulder with P&G managers as intern members of customer development teams.

Once the internship is completed, MBA candidates are run through a Customer Business Development Symposium which features lectures and discussions led by interdisciplinary faculty, corporate officials, and students to further develop the new marketing style. Students not only gain significant practicum experience, but they also experience a classroom environment where the three constituents are equal. It doesn't hurt your job prospects, either.

The University of Texas at Austin has also launched a version of the program with P&G. "In a sense, it's a situation where everyone wins: Students are presented with complex problems and hands-on experience," says Dean Ronald E. Frank. "We benefit from improved curriculum and placement, and companies get curriculum shifts at business schools so they will have better prepared future employees."

That's one reason BUSINESS WEEK agrees with Dean Frank's description of his school as one with upside potential. "It's relatively rare that a local university rises to national attention," says Frank, who quit as dean of Purdue University's Krannert School of Business to come here in 1989. "I can only think of one that has done it in the past 25 years—Stanford. Emory has not accomplished what Stanford has, but it's halfway there. And we're building a first-class business school in that environment."

Like Duke, Emory is known as an excellent liberal arts university with Methodist roots. Emory is now trying to duplicate Duke's success in making a run at the Top 20. "Emory was in a massive state of transition when I arrived," says Andrea Hershatter, who joined Emory's staff seven years ago from Duke's Fuqua School of Business and is associate dean of academic programs. "Fuqua was built gradually," she says. "This was like, 'Let's take a bulldozer through the building.'"

Emory recently renamed its B-school for Roberto Goizueta, CEO of Coca-Cola, without a donation from the executive. The price tag for a B-school naming is usually pretty high—Leonard Stern gave $30 million to NYU in 1988 to bear his name, and J. B. Fuqua handed over $10 million to Duke to cop such an honor. Administrators at Emory may be privately hoping that Goizueta will reach into his deep pockets and pony up a donation. The Woodruff Foundation, named after the family that made Coke what it is today, recently forked over $10 million to help the B-school build a new building. However, the Woodruff name is already all over campus.

No MBA program can aspire to great quality without strong faculty, and Emory has lured teachers from such schools as Harvard, Wharton, MIT, and Northwestern. Three out of four professors are new to the school since 1987—which means that Frank not only recruited new, more qualified people, but also cleaned house. "We've really redefined the faculty in an incredibly short period of time," says Frank.

More importantly, Emory can boast of having some top-notch teaching in its classrooms. The quality of teaching in both the core and the school's elective courses is well above average, according to BUSINESS WEEK's graduate survey of the top 40-plus schools. One of the best is Jeffrey Sonnenfeld, who teaches a fieldwork seminar in Organization and Management that starts off with a video on United Parcel Service. When the lights go up, he saunters into the classroom in a brown UPS uniform. The class turns teams of students into writers of case studies that are used in the school's curriculum.

Sonnenfeld also directs the Center for Leadership and Career Studies which has attracted more than 4000 executives since 1989. The center, which has been dubbed "CEO College," brings CEOs and other top executives together in a noncompetitive atmosphere to attend brief leadership conferences—and provides a great networking opportunity for students. The center also leads to interesting learning opportunities. After attending a seminar at the center, entrepreneurs Ben & Jerry came to talk to second-year MBAs, even supplying ice cream samples for 150 students. The Dean's Speaker Series also brings more than half a dozen senior executives to campus. Some recent guests: former President Jimmy Carter; Warren Buffett; Roberto C. Goizueta, CEO of Coca-Cola; and Stephen Schwartz Sr., an IBM vice president.

The basic Emory program isn't very different from what most B-schools offer. In your first year, there's virtually no flexibility—unless you're able to waive out of some core courses by exam and replace them with electives. Otherwise, 30 out of the 33 credits you're expected to rack up in the first year are in required core courses. After the first-year grind, the program opens up. Some 9 of the 15 credits in your second fall semester are electives and all 15 of the expected credits in the final semester are consumed by courses of your own choosing. Around 20 students will be able to participate in the school's customer development track in 1995, though the school is trying to sign up more corporate sponsors to expand the program.

Emory's small size naturally limits the choice (Emory has about 46 electives), but you can also develop an area of concentration in marketing, finance, accounting, organization and management, and decision and information analysis. Emory MBAs do not receive letter grades; they are evaluated with distinction, high pass, pass, low pass, or they don't receive any credit. Students with undergraduate business backgrounds can complete the program in three semesters. They take an accelerated core in the summer and then jump into class with second-year MBAs.

The dean wants to increase the size of the MBA program, but there isn't enough space to expand. To meet the challenge, Frank opened the school's doors to part-time MBA students for the first time during the summer of 1992. Part-timers have to move through the first half of the three-year program together, just as they would if they were attending full-time. This recent development doesn't mean that he has given up hopes for expanding the day program. With a new building that is scheduled to open in 1997, the program will be able to accommodate 180 new MBAs each year.

A major plus is the school's location in Atlanta, a dynamic community and headquarters to such corporate giants as Coca-Cola, Delta Airlines, and more recently UPS, which just moved into the area from Connecticut. The university campus sits between Virginia Highlands, the artsy, village-like area in mid-town, and Buckhead, a section loaded with clubs and discos. For drinks and conversation, MBAs head toward the Highland Tap or the Euclid Avenue Yacht Club, which serves up extra spicy "nuclear wings." Moe's & Joe's is a favorite for hamburgers.

As with any program on the move, you're apt to find some dissatisfaction with the placement office. Emory's career services office came in for some criticism from the Class of 1994. To be fair, however, graduates felt that the school is trying, but think it will take time before more recruiters recognize it. About 16.4 percent of Emory's graduates failed to have a job offer at commencement. Those who had offers in hand averaged only 1.95 each—nothing much to write home about.

Despite student complaints, many corporate recruiters name Emory as one of the best business schools in the South. "The people who know us think highly of us," Hershatter says, "but a lot of people simply don't think of us, and I want that to change." In 1994, some 82 companies recruited on campus, conducting 1255 interviews with MBA candidates. The leading recruiters were BellSouth (5), Wachovia (5), MCI (4), Ernst & Young (4), Holiday Inn Worldwide (3), Procter & Gamble (2), Smith Barney (2), Hewlett-Packard (2), M/A/R/C Group (2), and Coca-Cola (1).

While most schools these days make all sorts of excuses for their placement efforts, Emory is one of the few that makes it clear it wants to increase the number of companies that come here. "I think we need over 100 companies to come to campus," Hershatter adds. "The ratio should be as close to one company per student as possible. With 140 students, 80 doesn't feel like a huge number." Now that's the kind of customer relationship–building that every MBA applicant would like to hear.

Contact: Julie Barefoot, assistant director of admissions, 404-727-6311
Final application deadline: April 15 for fall

Outstanding Faculty: *Al Hartgraves* (****—accounting), *Jeffrey Sonnenfeld* (****—management), *Jeffrey Rosensweig* (****—finance), *Shehzad Mian* (**—finance), *Jagdish Sheth* (**—marketing), *Benn Konsynski* (*—decision & information analysis), *Hayagreeva Rao* (management), *Rob Kajaizian* (organization), *Consuelo Kertz* (accounting), *Billy Thornton* (finance)

Goizueta MBAs Sound Off

> *I had high expectations when I chose to attend Emory's MBA program. Not only have those expectations been met, they've been far exceeded. Emory offers a flexible structure to their program, which allows students to individually tailor the program to meet their particular needs. I was able to further my interests in consulting by participating in multiple live projects during my time at Emory. I've not only had the opportunity to learn in the classroom from worldclass professors, I've gotten to know them on a personal basis. I also had a chance to go abroad and study at Manchester Business school in England, which proved to be both exciting and career-enhancing.* —**Senior Consultant**

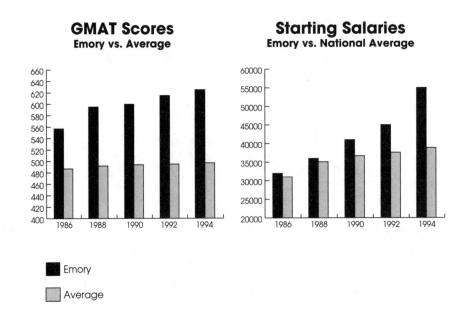

GMAT Scores
Emory vs. Average

Starting Salaries
Emory vs. National Average

■ Emory
▨ Average

Georgetown University

School of Business
Washington, D.C. 20057

Enrollment: 423	*Annual tuition:* $19,584
Women: 40%	*Room and board:* $7210
Non-U.S.: 27%	*Average GMAT score:* 619
Minority: 7%	*GMAT range:* 540 to 700 (mid-80%)
Part-time: None	*Average GPA:* 3.2
Average age: 27	*GPA range:* 2.71 to 3.70 (mid-80%)
Applicants accepted: 40%	*Accepted applicants enrolled:* 40%
Median starting pay: $64,000	*Average starting pay:* $69,830

Teaching methods: Lecture, 40%   Case method, 60%

Little more than a decade ago, Georgetown University's business faculty met every Friday at 7:30 a.m. in "dawn patrol" meetings for six months straight to invent an MBA curriculum. "It was really an exciting time to be here because it was a big deal to launch an MBA program," says William G. Droms, founding director of the program. Even then, sitting in a temporary building on 36th Street, which is now a dorm, the school's objective was to become a national player. "From the beginning, we have taken advantage of what the world thought were Georgetown's strengths, international and government business," he says.

Just 13 years after the first 37 MBA students entered the program and 6 years after the school gained accreditation, Georgetown is already making a name for itself in international business under the leadership of Dean Robert S. Parker, a former McKinsey & Company partner. His mission: to catapult Georgetown to Top 20 stature and carve a niche as the nation's premier school for international management.

He faces tough competition from resource-rich schools with better reputations. But Parker also benefits greatly from the halo effect of an excellent university and from having established high admissions standards. The average GMAT scores here are up 35 points in the past eight years, and the typical first-year student arrives with more than three and one-half years of work experience.

International business is more than just a fad at Georgetown. Each course, whether it's accounting, marketing, or production, is taught from a global perspective. The core curriculum includes Global Environment of Business. One of every four MBAs here is from outside the United States, and nearly three-fourths of students speak a second language or have lived abroad. "We offer a general program that focuses on working with and managing people of all cultures, not just Americans," Parker says. "We don't want anyone without a global perspective."

The urbane dean's focus seems a natural. Georgetown is home of the elite School of Foreign Service that trains diplomats from all over the world. The school offers an International Business Diplomacy Certificate and a joint MBA/MFS degree. MBAs apply for the program during their first year, and need to use all six of their elective classes toward earning the honors certificate. Business types can also earn an areas studies certificate in Russian, German, Latin American, African, Arabian, or Asian studies. Students study the culture, history, and social and economic development of their region. In the regular MBA program, there's one major complaint about the school's international focus: Noncredit languages can be studied, but only on top of the required five courses per semester.

Georgetown's location in the nation's capital obviously provides MBAs with a window on the relationship between business and government—another major theme that runs through the program. Just as NYU students study securities analysis with and under people who do it for a living on Wall Street, Georgetown MBAs have the advantage of learning how government and business interests collide from adjunct faculty working at the U.S. Treasury, the Federal Reserve Board, the Small Business Administration, and the U.S. Senate Banking Committee. "One of the great things about being in Washington is that you can run down to the SEC to do research on a company," says an MBA alum. The constant interaction with these kinds of agencies, the people who work for them, and the visitors that Washington attracts is a major advantage. To promote greater understanding between private and public sector leaders, Georgetown has established a center for Business-Government Relations.

"Quant jocks" need not apply here. About half of the class majored in social sciences as undergrads and another 15 percent have undergraduate degrees in humanities. "The focus is general and not particularly quantitative," says a recent grad. "It's good for liberal arts undergrads." In keeping with the university's liberal arts bent, MBAs are trained as generalists and must take a communications course. Georgetown loads 13 courses into the core, 10 of which are in the first year.

In the second year, students select 6 electives from only around 35 within the business school or from a variety throughout the university. Georgetown recently began offering half-semester elective modules, on topics such as Japanese Management and International Operations. The school is also adding electives taught in French and Spanish. But students complain that there aren't enough electives to choose from within the B-school, and that also limits the number of areas they can specialize in. Although MBAs are not required to concentrate in an area, students do typically develop an area of specialty. The school is adding to its elective offerings each year.

You're also required to take a year-long ethics course that benefits this institution's tradition of emphasizing morals. Like Notre Dame, Georgetown did not jump on the recent ethics bandwagon. "Ethics was a big deal from the first day of this program," says John G. Onto, associate dean of graduate business programs. "For Jesuits, ethics is not a flavor-of-the-month issue." Students are actively involved in tons of community service activities through the MBA Volunteers, a student-run organization that coordinates volunteer projects. MBAs volunteer locally at such places as Joshua House, a halfway house for men. The Volunteers also plan national events like the MBA Ultimate Four Basketball Competition with top U.S. business schools, to benefit the "I Have a Dream" Foundation.

Like the curriculum, Georgetown's extracurricular activities are internationally flavored. With choices like Students for Eastern European Development, Students for Latin American Development, Alliance for Cultural Awareness, and the International Business Forum, it's easy for students to supplement the global focus they receive in the classroom. For instance, Students for Eastern European Development has provided internship opportunities for 50 students since 1992. Graduates can also find opportunities abroad through the MBA Enterprise Corp., a group of schools that sends grads to work in Central European companies for one year.

The building that houses the B-school unites history with modern ideas. Built in 1795, Old North is the oldest surviving university building. "People take great delight in the fact that the youngest school on campus is in the oldest building," says Droms. Old North has a long history of attracting distinguished speakers, including many U.S. presidents. George Washington started the ball rolling when he spoke in 1797. Bill Clinton, the most recent presidential attraction, was preceded by former presidents Andrew Jackson, John Tyler, and Ulysses S. Grant. Old North might be old, but it's certainly not falling apart. The building was renovated several years ago and contains three case-style classrooms and a state-of-the-art computer lab. Students now benefit from a refurbished career management office, which includes a role-playing room with audio, library, and interviewing rooms. Not too long ago company interviews were conducted in faculty offices.

Georgetown itself is a wonderful playground for young adults. Most students live off-campus in townhouses in the cosmopolitan neighborhood filled with trendy bars, foreign restaurants, and tiny boutiques. The private homes are quite expensive, but less luxurious townhouses are shared by groups of students just starting out on the Hill. There are cocktail parties in the MBA lounge in Old North and groups of students often head over to The Tombs for thick, crusty pizza and beer after an exam. There's no shortage of things to do in D.C., which is why students tend not to hang around Old North when classes are over.

Despite the small size of the program, the B-school still splits incoming students into more intimate groups of 40 each. Parker wants to increase the graduating class to 200 during the next few years while at the same time boosting admissions standards. He believes he can do that without sacrificing the personalized attention MBAs get here.

In keeping with the global slant, career management helps find international jobs for U.S. graduates—whether they want to work here or go overseas—as well as for foreign students who want to return to their home countries or work abroad or in the United States for an American corporation. But this is a young program with a tiny alumni base. So far only around 1000 students have received Georgetown MBAs.

In 1994, only 67 organizations came on campus to recruit. Students also had the opportunity to interview with around 100 companies at consortiums. About 12.2 percent of the Class of 1994 graduated without job offers. While the B-school did not attract many companies to its campus, it did manage to lure some top-drawer concerns. Major recruiters included Andersen Consulting (4), Chase Manhattan Bank (3), Citibank (3), Price Waterhouse (3), Coopers & Lybrand (2), Dun & Bradstreet (2), and Ernst & Young (2).

Contact: Nancy D. Moncrief, director of graduate business admissions and services, 202-687-4200
Final application deadline: May 1 for fall

Outstanding Faculty: *John Dealy* (****—management), *Elaine Romanelli* (****—management), *H. Jeff Smith* (****—telecommunications), *Kasra Ferdows* (***—manufacturing), *Thomas Donaldson* (***—ethics), *Annette Shelby* (***—management communications), *Robert Bies* (organizational behavior), *Alan Mayer-Sommer* (accounting), *Bardia Kamrad* (statistics), *Eugene Salorio* (management)

Georgetown MBAs Sound Off

My biggest criticism of Georgetown is the program's hypocritical claim of having such a diverse student body. While 30 percent of my classmates are international students (which is excellent) only 2 percent are African-American or Hispanic-American. If you're going to claim diversity is a strength, it should include both domestic and international diversity. Additionally, this disparity is due to the school's lack of effort in recruiting minority students. **—Marketing Specialist**

I chose Georgetown for its international orientation, and I feel I'm leaving with a Global MBA. Over the past two years, I've interned in D.C., studied and worked in Tokyo, and I'm now bound for Amsterdam after graduation. Georgetown's location, small class size, faculty, and relative youth make it a very special program. **—Consultant**

The faculty's first priority is to teach and develop business leaders. They are very outstanding teachers—conveyors of knowledge and skills. Georgetown may not conduct much "spotlighted" research, but I would match its teaching skills against any other program. **—Marketing Career Path**

The school's current weakness is its youth. The alumni network is relatively weak, and stronger relationships are needed with prestigious employers like General Electric and Microsoft. **—Corporate Finance Career Path**

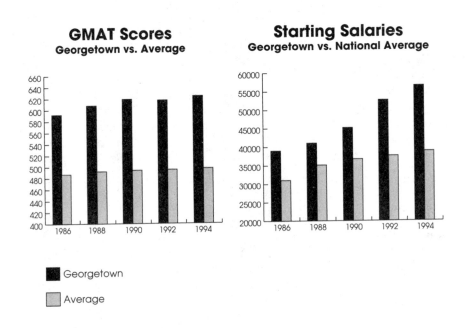

Michigan State University

The Eli Broad Graduate School of Management
215 Eppley Center
East Lansing, Michigan 48824

Enrollment: 250
Women: 32%
Non-U.S.: 31%
Minority: 9%
Part-time: None
Average age: 25.5
Applicants accepted: 37%
Accepted applicants enrolled: 48%

Annual tuition & fees: resident—$8212
nonresident—$16,057
Room and board: $4500
Average GMAT score: 590
GMAT range: 400 to 770
Average GPA: 3.22
GPA range: 2.0 to 4.0
Average starting pay: $41,820

Teaching methods: Lecture, 30% Case study, 35% Other, 35%

Eli Broad remembers Detroit in the 1950s when it was the world's industrial center and when there were few MBAs to go around. "It was sitting on top of the world," the entrepreneur recalls. "The city and the region were dynamic and proud. General Motors was a great company. The Whiz Kids at Ford were part of the aura of invincibility, of might and of genius. Detroit was king."

Broad, who graduated from Michigan State University in 1954 with an accounting degree, left Detroit and eventually began his own home building company. While the auto giants of his hometown stumbled against Japanese competition in the 1970s and 1980s, he was building a highly successful $12 billion financial services concern in California. His fortune and his luck, however, made him look back, both at the region and his alma mater.

What he saw disturbed him. "Somehow, Detroit became insular," Broad says. "After 50 years of success, the region had become self-satisfied. And I saw what was happening at other MBA schools. I saw the best of their graduates going to Wall Street and the commercial banks. What were we producing? Derivatives, hedges, and swaps. But America is not Wall Street. The 1980s became an era of greater greed."

Broad did what few people could do, even if they wanted to: He reached into his pockets and gave $20 million to Michigan State's College of Business. The 1991 gift—the largest ever made by an individual to the business school of a public university—is transforming Michigan State's B-school. It's being used to create a more elite program to produce global MBAs who will make the troubled region think in more international terms. One other thing: It's a program that Broad hopes will produce few finance types anxious to work on Wall Street. He doesn't need to worry. There are as many courses in materials and logistics management here as there are in finance. And one in every four MBAs goes to work in the auto and mechanical equipment business.

Instead of putting Broad's money into bricks and mortar, moreover, $19.5 million is being used to revamp and upgrade the MBA program, with the intention of pushing the newly named Broad Graduate School of Management into the Top 20 B-schools in the country. The treasure chest is being employed to endow scholarships and professorships to entice the best MBA candidates and faculty to Michigan State. Broad is also footing the bill for full-time directors of the MBA program and of MBA placement.

Only $500,000 of Broad's gift went toward a new $21.5 million building that is connected by a covered walkway to Eppley Center, the B-school's old home. The addition was sorely needed. The brick-and-sandstone Eppley Center opened in 1961 to 3000 students and eventually served 8000, until the addition of the new 59,000-square-foot building in October 1993. Until last year, Eppley was crowded and cramped. Several departments of the college and all its people were scattered in six different buildings around campus. The Business College Complex now houses all departments except for economics, and has alleviated the crowding problems.

This is the industrial heartland, and it's in need of revitalization. East Lansing, Michigan, is a short strip of storefronts eight blocks long and one block wide. The main drag, Grand River Avenue, was the old Indian trail from Grand Rapids to Detroit. Neighboring Lansing is the state capital, and home to looming smokestacks and red-brick factories, from tiny tool-and-die shops to GM's expansive Buick-Oldsmobile-Cadillac complex.

Yet, the huge campus is, as *The Chicago Tribune* once described it, "shockingly beautiful." The Red Cedar River flows through the handsomely landscaped and tree-lined grounds. The buildings may be a bit of a hodgepodge, from classic red-clay brick and slate roofs to rectangular slabs of concrete that look like old IBM punch cards. And if the old factory areas can sometimes look shockingly desolate these days, there's lots of activity on the 5000-acre campus that overflows with 40,000 students. More than 24,000 bicycles are registered on campus.

Indeed, incoming MBAs tend to gripe about the difficulty of just knowing how to get around the place in the first few weeks. The MBA program, with fewer than 300 full-time students, is vastly overshadowed by a mammoth undergraduate business program with more than 4500 students. Michigan State has the fifth-largest undergraduate business school in the nation. The program imposes a huge demand upon faculty time, so that some MBAs find it difficult to meet with teachers outside the classroom.

Broad's gift led to numerous changes. The school has phased out its part-time MBA program and has also gotten rid of an abbreviated MBA stint for those with undergraduate degrees in business. These changes are designed to focus more of the school's efforts on a full-time, two-year MBA program launched in the fall of 1992. All MBA candidates must complete at least 54 semester hours of core courses as well as required courses in the environment of business along with an international business component. They also get to pick a field of concentration. Richard J. Lewis no longer leads the transition. After 18 years as dean, Lewis retired. James Henry, former dean of Louisiana State's B-school, took over the helm in July 1994.

So far, these alternations are getting good reviews. "The whole school is going through a very positive transformation," says Duncan Campbell, a 1994 grad. "The caliber of students is improving. It's a school that's on the move, one with direction and purpose."

Entering students are assigned to a cohort group which moves through the core curriculum together, after a brief orientation that in 1994 featured a day of team-building exercises at Camp Highfields. Besides a few obligatory welcome speeches, the program included canoeing on the Red Cedar River, a picnic at Potter Park, and a wine-and-cheese party with the faculty. Some grads have been surprised by the amount of quantitative work in the program, though few have complained that the workload is excessive.

It may especially please Broad that a good number of students here not only haven't given up on American manufacturing but have truly embraced it by getting a master's degree in materials and logistics. The program spans both the management and marketing departments in covering what former Dean Lewis called a "complete systems approach" from procurement of materials to manufacturing and shipment to the final consumer. Some 50 students are signed up for this unusual program, which gets financial support from such companies as IBM, Kellogg, Steelcase, and Procter & Gamble, which offer internships and hire from the program.

As a Big Ten school, Michigan State also offers an all-encompassing campus lifestyle for those who want it. Sure, there's the annual MBA picnic at Lake Lansing Park, and every Thursday afternoon business grads pick a local bar to drink and chat in (the Land Shark on Abbot Road or Olga's downtown are the favorites). Crunchies is great for its $2.25 burger-and-beer special, while Cafe Venecia has become the hangout for MBA fans of expresso drinks. But one of the key social events evolves around the Michigan State Spartans, the school's football squad. For pre-game tailgate parties, MBAs get together across the street from Eppley Center and then walk to Spartan Stadium where they have a block of choice tickets.

More importantly, the Broad gift has also energized the students to become more active in the school. The MBA Association was instrumental in expanding the school's orientation program from one day in 1991 to nearly a full week of group activities in 1992, including the launch of a student mentor system. It has also organized students to serve meals at a local soup kitchen, donate food and clothing to local charities, adopt a highway, and raise money for Big Brothers and Big Sisters. The MBA Association also sponsors an annual international symposium and an Excellence in Business lecture series.

The school's younger graduates (the school still accepts applicants with no job experience, though it prefers more seasoned candidates) make the average starting salaries of Michigan State MBAs look worse than average. The Class of 1994, for instance, pulled down $40,940, over $10,000 below the $54,860 average. The school has one of the lowest average starting salaries of the 40-plus schools surveyed. Still, Broad reports that 93 percent of its class had job offers at graduation, and some 174 companies came to recruit on campus in 1994, conducting 730 interviews. Their offers to start ranged from $23,600 to $62,500. Another 260 jobs were posted by correspondence. The Top 10 hiring firms: Deloitte & Touche (7), Ford Motor Company (6), General Motors Corporation (6), EDS (4), Hewlett-Packard (3), NBD Bank (3), Arthur Andersen/Andersen Consulting (3), Procter & Gamble (2), Kellogg Company (2), and Coopers & Lybrand (2). Quite a lineup, considering that starting salaries are so low. The single largest group of MBAs (26 percent) headed for the automotive and mechanical equipment industries, while 18 percent went into accounting.

Like just about everything else at the school, the placement area is undergoing a renovation. "If you produce a product," says Broad, "and you're not selling it, you can put it in the warehouse for only so long." To better sell Michigan State's product, the school has launched a new MBA placement and career center and hired Michael Agnew away from Wharton's placement operation. Agnew is hoping to expand the school's network of recruiters by tapping into Michigan State's 50,000 alumni around the world (the school has graduated about 5500 MBAs since the program was founded in 1960).

As for Broad and his gift, the entrepreneur intends to closely watch how his money is being spent. "I want to make certain the money just doesn't plug the state deficit," he says. "Detroit will never regain the dominance of manufacturing it had after World War II, but it will become more competitive in the early part of the next century. And we'll see brighter and brighter people go into manufacturing."

Contact: Jennifer Chizuk, assistant director of MBA program, 517-355-7604 or 800-4MSU-MBA
Final application deadlines: April 1 for fall; October 1 for spring

Outstanding Faculty: *Michael Mazzeo* (****—finance), *William McCarthy* (***—accounting), *Dewey Ward* (**—accounting), *John Gilster* (**—finance), *Steven Melnyk* (**—management), *Glenn Omura* (**—marketing), *Shawnee Vickery* (management), *Jack Bain* (communications), *Alison Barber* (management), *Donald Bowersox* (management)

Broad MBAs Sound Off

The program has made significant strides during the two years that I have attended, and it seems poised for even better performance in the future. The faculty have proved to be extremely knowledgeable, and the information provided extremely applicable to my future career. The placement office, as well, has made inroads into an impressive field of companies, and by all indications will continue to secure interview schedules with outstanding firms. Combined with the superb facilities of the new business school building, these attributes have contributed to an excellent MBA experience. —**Marketing Career Path**

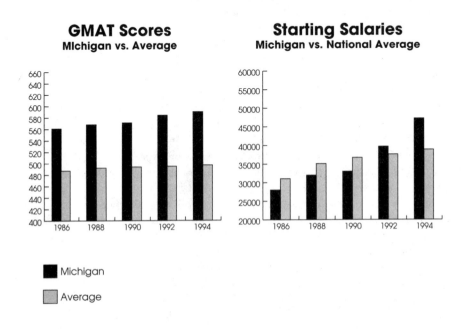

Pennsylvania State University

The Mary Jean and Frank P. Smeal College of Business Administration
106 Business Administration Building
University Park, Pennsylvania 16802

Enrollment: 240
Women: 30%
Non-U.S.: 32%
Minority: 16%
Part-time: None
Average age: 27
Applicants accepted: 19%
Accepted applicants enrolled: 51%

Annual tuition & fees: resident—$5600
                    nonresident—$11,400
Room and board: $8500
Average GMAT score: 580*
GMAT range: 410 to 760*
Average GPA: 3.17
GPA range: 2.05 to 3.97
Average starting pay: $49,120

Teaching methods: Case method, 50% Lecture, 50%

It was a typical entrepreneurial dilemma: Your company comes up with a new product. Should you develop a partnership to more aggressively market the item, or should you make a go of it alone? Either way, exactly how should you proceed? Bruce R. Robinson, a Class of 1993 MBA at Penn State, and four of his classmates had all of 72 hours to come up with the answers. Then the team had to present their ideas to a faculty board and possibly a panel of major company presidents.

Sounds like a bad dream. But the assignment is the culmination of a year-long Managerial Communications course in the first year. Taught by a team of profs, students are assigned to write business memos and letters, and to make individual and group proposals. "After the communications course, making a presentation becomes second nature, and you actually begin to enjoy it," says Robinson.

Penn State's communications program is one of the strongest and oldest in the country. And it's a distinctive feature of the MBA program here that draws raves from students and alums alike. The school has received a similar reaction to the revamped curriculum that it put in place for the 1993 fall semester. "We have thrown away the book that we used to be bound to," says Roger A. Dagen, who directed the MBA Program through the changes.

The book discarded by the school contained the outlines of a highly rigid program with little flexibility or much linkage among courses. For years, Penn State loaded up its core curriculum with so much coursework that MBAs could only enroll in five electives. The new, integrated model rips apart the traditional three-credit courses in 15-week semesters and replaces them with courses of varying length that start and stop at different intervals. Students get their first dose of the capstone course on strategic management, for instance, in the first quarter. Then they pass through two quarters without a single class in the subject, only to pick it up again in the final quarter of the first year. The upshot of all the juggling? Students have to pile up 50 credits to graduate, 4 credits less than before, yet they can select 3 more electives. All told, MBAs now get to pick 8 elective offerings out of the school's menu of 60 per year.

Graduates of the Smeal College of Business Administration welcome the revised program. But many still complain that a palpable tension exists between the student body and the administration. "Dean [J.D.] Hammond does not support the MBA program or its more innovative instructors," says Roger Parker, a member of the class of 1994. "The Dean is not responsive to student concerns."

Several graduates also bemoan the inconsistent teaching in the program. There are obvious exceptions, but BUSINESS WEEK's 1994 customer satisfaction surveys show teaching quality in both the core and elective offerings to be just average. (In fact, the teaching was so bad in one management information systems core class that the school gave students the option of dropping the course [with credit] six weeks into the semester.) That's not too surprising, however, because the school has put far more emphasis on academic research than teaching. More surprising, perhaps, is that some students maintain that some of their colleagues are admitted into the program without significant work experience, even though P.S.U. claims its grads average nearly four years on the job prior to B-school. "It's hard to discuss sexual harassment and discrimination in the workplace with guys fresh out of frat houses," says Danielle R. O'Donohue, a recent alum.

For better or for worse, the small size of the program—no more than 160 in each graduating class—allows just about everyone to know one another. Penn State's MBA program requires total immersion. Students are accepted only in the fall and must spend two academic years in the program. Each incoming class is divided into four sections of 40 (instead of the giant classes of 90 that typify the Harvard experience) which take core courses together. The average class size in elective courses shrinks to about 20. The intimacy such small classes promote creates long, enduring friendships among many of the students.

One thing that hasn't changed since the curriculum's revamping is the school's strength in business logistics—the procurement of raw materials and the distribution of products after they are manufactured. Few other B-schools can beat the course offerings of Penn State in this area. However, students are worried that Penn State's strength in business logistics may erode in the future, because the administration has decided to cut 2 of its 11 logistics positions through attrition over the next two years. (The school has also decided to cut one faculty position in the insurance, real estate, and management information systems departments, respectively, because of declining undergraduate enrollment in Smeal.) Students complain that the dean is trying to direct the program toward a more traditional, Wharton-like philosophy, at the expense of one of its most highly valued areas. "He [Dean Hammond] sees logistics as a blue-collar MBA and decides to cut it, even though [logistics] is what the students want," says Parker. Logistics profs are also peeved about the cutbacks. "I obviously don't agree with it," says John C. Spychaski, chairman of the business logistics department. "It shows a lack of understanding of a strategic strength."

Thanks to the marketing department's Institute for the Study of Business Markets, Smeal also is renowned for its expertise in business-to-business marketing, an area many other schools are only beginning to discover. Penn State has recently taken advantage of the university's strength in engineering by adding a manufacturing option, or major, for MBAs with undergraduate degrees in engineering.

All students live within five miles of the B-school. Penn State likes to say that it is equidistant from everywhere, but it's also in the middle of nowhere. The school is smack in the center of Pennsylvania, off Interstate 80. Pittsburgh is 120 miles west and Philadelphia 150 miles east. Other than Penn State's sprawling 5032-acre University Park campus with 30,000 students, there's nothing much else here.

That means that there are few opportunities for internships or part-time jobs during the school year. It also makes it difficult for students to conduct independent job searches. Indeed, the school's location may deter some recruiters, no matter how good they think the program is. "The problem with Penn State is that they are in the middle of nowhere," says Thomas E. Wagner, director of human resources at Ernst & Young. "That would be a more popular program if it were easier to get to."

Yet, the school's locale isn't a turnoff to everyone. Students give favorable reviews to the lifestyle in what is known as "Happy Valley." The campus, surrounded by mountains, is great for mountain biking, hiking, and other outdoor activities. MBA tailgating parties outside Beaver Stadium feature kegs, hamburgers, and hot dogs every Saturday during the football season. The MBA Association also sponsors a series of get-togethers, from Halloween and Toga parties to semiformal holiday bashes and picnics.

When the MBAA isn't providing students with entertainment, they are good at organizing it themselves. The bulletin board in the MBA lounge, located in "BAB" where students take most of their classes, lists the latest happenings. To unwind, MBAs favor the "G Man," a Houlihans-type bar and restaurant that is a popular hangout on Thursday nights. Also favored is a downright dive, "The Skeller," famous for selling cases of Rolling Rock. Some of the best entertainment in town can be heard at The Saloon, a blues club, and at Tatoo, an alternative dance club.

Like many B-schools, Penn State is attempting to improve its placement efforts. The school added two databases to help MBAs link up with alumni, and changed the name of its placement center to the Office of Professional Development to better manage the expectations of its students. Smeal participates with other Big Ten MBA schools in job fairs held in New York, Atlanta, and Chicago. In addition, P.S.U. offers two career fairs held on campus: the Smeal College Career Fair, open to both graduate and undergraduate business students, and the Minority Center Awareness Days, open to all MBAs.

The number of companies recruiting at P.S.U. has dwindled in recent years. In 1994, 121 corporations visited Penn State, down from 179 two years before. Still, 87 percent of P.S.U. grads reported job offers by graduation, up from 53 percent in 1992. Those with offers averaged 1.7 each. Recruiters luring the most MBAs included Ford Motor (8), GTE (3), Hewlett-Packard (3), Ford Dupont (2), IBM (2), NationsBank (2), TNC Bank (2), and Schneider National (2).

Contact: James Hoy, admissions coordinator, 814-863-0474
Final application deadline: June 1 for fall

Outstanding Faculty: *Chris J. Muscarella* (****—finance), *Stewart Bither* (****—marketing), *David E. Butt* (****—communications), *Terry P. Harrison* (****—management), *Nirmalya Kumar* (****—marketing), *Joseph L. Cavinato* (**—logistics), *Judith Bogert* (communications), *Rocki-Lee Dewitt* (management), *William A. Kracaw* (finance), *Frank Hatheway* (finance)

Smeal MBAs Sound Off

There are some areas of the program that I would like to see improved: (1) more recruiters coming to campus from Philadelphia and Pittsburgh; (2) more electives offered (this is happening now); (3) more networking opportunities; (4) more real-world experiences and interactions; (5) more modern facilities.
—Finance Career Path

Penn State has a weakness, in that the quality of the classes varies considerably. Some of the classes, especially in the core, are poorly designed and poorly taught. Penn State B-school needs to carefully monitor and improve those classes.
—Equity Sales Associate

For those individuals considering Penn State, there are a number of considerations you have to account for; probably the most important is expectations regarding workload. Penn State is a rigorous program, not a two-year vacation! Expect to work, and work hard, for approximately 65 to 80 hours a week.
—Marketing Career Path

The Dean can only turn around this dying MBA program by practicing the innovative, "continuous quality improvement" approach to teaching that the logistics instructors use. —Finance Career Path

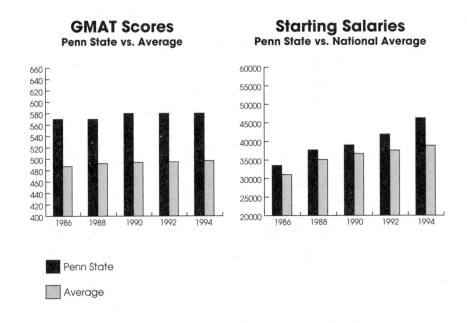

Southern Methodist University

Edwin L. Cox School of Business
Dallas, Texas 75275-0333

Enrollment: 705
Women: 25%
Non-U.S.: 22%
Minority: 8.5%
Part-time: 480
Average age: 26
Applicants accepted: 55%
Median starting pay: $53,500

Annual tuition & fees: $18,034
Room and board: $8500
Average GMAT score: 600
GMAT range: 410 to 790
Average GPA: 3.1
GPA range: 2.2 to 4.0
Accepted applicants enrolled: 54%
Average starting pay: $60,910

Teaching methods: Lecture, 38%   Case study, 37%   Group projects, 25%

Something rather odd occurred at Southern Methodist University's business school in 1992: Not a single MBA graduated. It wasn't because the faculty flunked an entire class of students. It was because the school ditched its compressed one-year MBA stint in favor of a more traditional two-year program launched in the fall of 1991. The upshot: The B-school missed an entire graduating class of MBAs.

Not to worry. The transformation to a two-year program allowed the dean and his faculty the unusual freedom of second-guessing everything the school had ever done. "The calendar change became an excuse for changing the whole program," says David H. Blake, dean of SMU's Cox School of Business. "We opened up everything for change. If we did it any other way, it would have brought out all kinds of resistance here and there. Besides, there wasn't time to engage in the bickering that affects so many faculties."

The result of all that work is one of the most topical and innovative MBA programs in the nation. Blake, who quit as dean at Rutgers University's B-school in 1990 to come to SMU, is aggressively changing the very culture of the school. The differences begin in September, when local managers and executives who agree to mentor MBAs are invited to campus to mingle with first-years and to chat about their occupations and industries. Following the session, MBA candidates submit a list of who, among the 100 or so volunteers, they would prefer as mentors. Soon after, the pairings take place with professionals from such companies as American Airlines, AT&T, Coopers & Lybrand, EDS, Frito Lay, Goldman Sachs, Neiman-Marcus, Texas Instruments, and Xerox. Each manager, executive, entrepreneur, or venture capitalist is matched with as many as five MBA protegés. Throughout the two-year program, mentors meet with MBA candidates, invite them to their organizations for tours and corporate sessions, and share plenty of advice on business and careers.

There's more. All first-year newcomers move through a battery of skill and personality tests to assess their individual strengths and weaknesses. Former supervisors, direct reports, and peers are surveyed—generally nine people in all—to gather a little more insight into each MBA candidate. You're given a report on the results, which become the focus of a four-hour group discussion and an hour's worth of one-on-one counseling. Then, the report offers a host of recommendations to improve your performance. The school's Business Leadership Center sponsors seminars and workshops to cultivate these more subtle skills. After your summer internship, the school puts you through another assessment—an effort to measure the impact of the leadership exercises that occur throughout the first year. A final assessment occurs toward the end of your MBA experience. "I can see us handing our graduates work programs along with their diplomas when they graduate," he says. If a corporation sent you through these leadership activities, it would cost as much as $8000 a person. The only other major B-school that has made assessment a fundamental part of its program is Case Western University.

Also in September, MBAs are required to participate in a day-long community-service project rehabilitating the homes of several Dallas-area low-income elderly minorities. The day merely sets the stage for a series of consulting projects students will undertake with local not-for-profit groups—the best student project wins $7500 in cash from Brown Brothers Harriman & Co., which donates the money to the charity. In the first go-round, student teams did studies for 19 community organizations. One group helped to reorganize the production flow of a local food bank. Another established an executive mentoring program in which managers helped disadvantaged teenagers get and keep jobs.

So what do community service, personal assessment testing, and mentoring have to do with the real world of business? Dean Blake believes these are among the missing elements of traditional MBA education that have led so many schools to produce generations of narrow and insular graduates, quick with a spreadsheet but slow to understand how to motivate and get along with people. The innovations do not end with these new wrinkles. What was once a frenetic 11-month program has been expanded and stretched over 21 months. The 60-hour program features about 33 hours of teaching in core courses. Each required class puts the emphasis on four key issues: international business, ethics, quality management, and workforce diversity. Cox now has four required courses in international business, and every course has been, in the words of Dean Blake, "globalized." "We want all our people to breathe and think in a global context," he says.

Quality Management, the focus of three electives, has also been infused into several core courses. As much as 25 percent of the work in the core organizational behavior class is devoted to cultural diversity. Once you complete your core courses, the remaining hours of classwork can be chosen from an array of some 48 electives in six functional departments, the lion's share offered in finance. Many of these courses are in the evening, combined with the part-time program. Dean Blake teaches a weekly honors integration course that requires students to write a publishable paper in management. Examples: What Leads to Failure in Corporate TQM Efforts? or Why Is Speed a Competitive Advantage? The objective is to synthesize many of the concepts in the core and apply them to topical business problems.

The switch to a two-year schedule also makes it easier to take electives outside the Cox School. Owing to its Texas locale, Cox also boasts a bevy of courses in oil and gas. There are study abroad options with five other business schools as well. The school also offers a more typical joint-degree program in law and business and a less typical program in business and the fine arts with the university's Meadows School. The latter experience is an ideal educational background for an administrative job in the art world. In the program's final semester, you're assigned an internship with a museum, orchestra, or zoo.

Past graduates have flocked to jobs at such places as the Philadelphia Orchestra, the Dallas Symphony, the Fort Worth Opera, and the Bosch in Germany.

The new two-year MBA program has been well received by students. These changes are a key part of an aggressive campaign by the school to gain greater national recognition. The Leadership Center was created after meetings with executives from such companies as J.C. Penney, AT&T, American Airlines, Xerox, and Federal Express—an attempt to better meet the needs of the school's ultimate customers. In the fall of 1994, the Cox School handed out close to $1 million in student scholarships to lure better MBA candidates into the program, four times the scholarship fund of $250,000 in 1991. Over the next two years, Blake expects this kitty to grow to $1.4 million.

When you're not in the classroom, the grassy campus is inviting enough to study outdoors. The university's affiliation with the Methodist Church means that virtually all drinking must be done off campus. That's no problem at all for SMU MBAs, who don't have classes on Fridays. One Thursday evening ritual: margaritas on the patio at OTB—short for On the Border, a Mexican restaurant and bar only a short drive from Cox.

The school's tree-lined, 160-acre campus is set in the middle of University Park, an affluent residential neighborhood five miles from downtown Dallas. The $17 million Cox School is a horseshoe-shaped building, built in 1987, with an open courtyard in the center. Undergraduate and graduate business students have separate wings and dedicated classrooms in the three-story brick building. Few SMU grads live on campus. Most make their homes in "the village," a residential area of apartment complexes about a half-mile away from campus.

One good thing about not having graduated a Class of 1992 is that students didn't have to scramble for jobs in a recession. A year earlier, however, when the school offered only a one-year program, about 98 companies came to campus to interview students. Mostly they were the regional offices of major companies and Dallas-headquartered firms. Another 430 job opportunities were posted by correspondence. About 84 percent of the Class of 1994 had jobs at graduation. Where did grads end up? EDS, IBM, American Airlines, and Andersen Consulting each hired two MBAs from the school. Amerada Hess, American General, Brown Brothers Harriman, Coopers & Lybrand, and Deloitte & Touche each hired one SMU graduate.

Contact: Audrey Randuk, assistant director of admissions, 1-800-472-3622
Final application deadline: May 15 for fall

Outstanding Faculty: *Randolph Beatty* (****—accounting), *Gordon Walker* (****—business policy), *Mike McGill* (***—organizational behavior), *Dileep Hurry* (**—strategy), *Howard Bunsis* (**—accounting), *Roger Kerin* (**—marketing), *Robin Pinkley* (organizational behavior), *Uday Apte* (management information science), *Gopalakrishnan Sharathchandra* (finance), *Dan Howard* (marketing)

Cox MBAs Sound Off

The only two drawbacks of the program were the experience levels of my classmates (roughly half of the class came directly from undergraduate school) and the efforts of the Career Services department. Career Services simply does not have the personnel with the expertise or contacts to pull in companies. The faculty was absolutely superior. The administration was truly concerned with our needs and wants, but due to lack of resources could not always create extra sections of popular classes. Unique opportunities were provided for leadership growth, oral and written communications skill-building, as well as team-building opportunities through the Business Leadership Center. Overall, I highly recommend the program—just be ready to find your own job. **—Health Care Consultant**

The Business Leadership Center is basically a "pop psychology" center headed up by a less-than-adequate director. The programs are just glorified consultants giving short seminars. The overall program is basically a part-time program, with full-time students added on. **—Career Path Unknown**

While I know that SMU has a very strong academic program, faculty, and student body, I also know that SMU's name and reputation continue to primarily be regional. This is the aspect that SMU needs to spend the most time on. SMU needs to develop contacts both in the business and academic communities. I see this happening now through student participation in consortiums in both New York and Atlanta. I also see this improving as SMU produces more alumni who are geographically dispersed. SMU has also been able to attract several highly respected professors to the program in each of the main disciplines. **—Consultant**

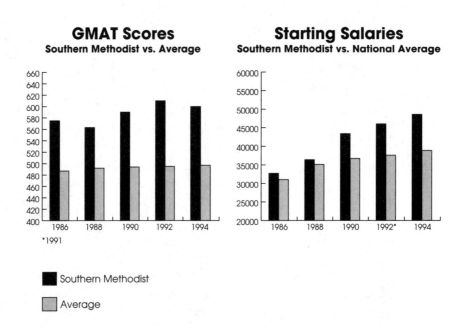

Tulane University

A. B. Freeman School of Business
Goldring/Woldenberg Hall
New Orleans, Louisiana 70118

Enrollment: 381	*Annual tuition & fees:* $19,550
Women: 28%	*Room and board:* $9500
Non-U.S.: 30%	*Average GMAT score:* 600
Minority: 10%	*GMAT range:* 450 to 740
Part-time: 128	*Average GPA:* 3.12
Average age: 26	*GPA range:* 2.2 to 3.91
Average years of work exp.: 3.2	*Accepted applicants enrolled:* 33%
Applicants accepted: 58%	*Average starting pay:* $44,080

Teaching methods: Lecture, 35%   Case study, 55%   Group projects, 10%

The A. B. Freeman School had a reputation as a sleepy business school within a fine university—until Dean Meyer Feldberg came along. He raised $22 million, increased enrollment by 50 percent, hired new faculty, and built a new $7 million home for the school, bringing new life to the dozing institution. So successful was Feldberg that other schools dangled job offers before him, and he left. Now he's dean of Columbia University's School of Business.

What Feldberg left behind in 1986, however, is still a fairly good business school, housed in a modern seven-story building on a pretty 110-acre campus in a residential area of grand Victorian homes in uptown New Orleans. Dean James W. McFarland has built upon that strong foundation with an array of summer-abroad programs for students interested in international business. McFarland is building a worldwide network of outstanding universities and corporations that would trade students, faculty, and internships with Tulane.

Dean McFarland and his faculty, however, have come under criticism from graduates, who think this program fails to deliver the goods. Several Class of 1994 MBAs didn't believe the knowledge they gained was worth the high tuition fees. Some students didn't think the dean was responsive to their concerns. The quality of teaching in both the core and elective courses is well below average, according to BUSINESS WEEK's customer satisfaction survey. And grads were not too keen about the limited job prospects served up by the placement office. "The school improved through the eighties and into the early nineties, but the administration has really lost focus lately," says a 1994 grad.

The business school, all of 80 years old, has followed Kellogg's example in interviewing all domestic applicants to the program. About 30 percent of the class comes from the Southeast. They enter a fairly rigorous program—tougher than many expect in such an enchanting environment. Oak trees stand outside the red-brick building with its three-story atrium. MBAs share the place with 300 undergrads, but there's plenty of room. The new home of the B-school, named after an entrepreneur who owned the state's Coca-Cola distributorship, even boasts a television studio to tape students for a required course in management communications. An elective class in negotiations also puts students on film for evaluation.

Think Freeman and you think small, friendly, diverse, general management, and international, a school whose main competitors tend to be Vanderbilt, Washington University, and Emory. Like those other top private B-schools, this is a program for people who want to study for an MBA with classmates and faculty they all know by name. Cutthroat competition is not on the program.

That's one feature, of course, common to many smallish programs. Indeed, Tulane's full-time program is so small that the university didn't split its admissions and placement offices until 1994. Each year's entering class hovers around 120 (transfers from part-timers tend to bring up the overall full-time enrollment numbers). There are no cohort groups. The class subdivides by itself so that you'll see some classmates in one core class and not in another. On average, a class in the core will have between 30 and 60 students in it.

The focus here is not on a dozen or more specialty areas. Instead, this is a general management program designed to teach people how to manage in an international context. One in three of the full-time students are non-U.S., representing a total of 36 different countries in the Class of 1994 alone. About one-third of the students at Freeman, moreover, participate in study-abroad programs or summer internships overseas.

In 1994, Freeman offered study programs abroad in Europe, Asia, and Mexico—an area with which McFarland hopes to develop far more linkups. The international focus also is evident from a new curriculum installed in the fall of 1992. The revamping injected more international business material throughout the core courseload, but there's also a new required Economic Environment of Global Business course in the first year that now begins with an intensive 12-day "module" that immediately plunges all first-years into the Job of an Executive. The exercise features numerous case studies in which MBA candidates are asked to analyze and debate the role of executives in organizations. They take day trips to visit major corporations and their top execs. There are also computer classes, and a management game that plays up how abusive power can become in an organization.

After the first module, the actual semester begins with a fairly routine group of courses: accounting, economics, communications, statistics, and organizational behavior. The second module, which kicks off in January, explores business issues from regulatory and public policy viewpoints. The six-day course is taught by Helen S. Kohlman, a prominent New Orleans attorney, who covers such things as administrative law, the regulatory process, employee relations, and managing diversity.

Semester two features finance, operations, and marketing, along with the required class in global management or economics and your first free elective. Each module lasts from 6 to 12 days, while each semester stretches from 13 to 15 weeks. Augmenting the traditional courses during the first year are a pair of what Tulane calls "enrichment series." One is strictly pragmatic, emphasizing career development and job-search strategies. Here you'll get the typical stuff on résumé writing, interviewing skills, and networking—some of it taught by outsiders. The other continues to examine the "environment of business" through the use of outside speakers.

In year two, the modules focus on Total Quality Management and leadership. Otherwise, there's only one required course in strategy and policy, and the opportunity to take nine electives. At least one of them must be chosen from a set of six other international courses, which include Global Strategic Management and International Finance. The other requirement is that you choose your electives from four different fields of study with no more than five electives in any one field. Freeman lists accounting and taxation, business law, economic analysis, finance, human resources, management, marketing, and decision information and operations as its "fields of study." The reason for this unusual restriction: the general management focus of the Freeman program.

Tulane boasts one of the oldest MBA programs in the country. Since 1940, when Tulane's MBA program was founded, the business school has churned out more than 3400 MBAs. But it wasn't until a decade or so ago that the university significantly upgraded the quality of the school under Dean Feldberg. "The big change came in the early 1980s, and it was radical," says Walter Burnett, a management professor at the school. "At that time decisions were made to move from being a regional high-quality, teaching business program to a nationally competitive program. Every one of us agrees Feldberg did a marvelous job of laying the groundwork to get it going." That meant putting up a new building and raising money for it.

The campus is just a 20-minute ride by streetcar to New Orlean's French Quarter and, as an MBA student on the school's admissions video gleefully notes, a world of wonderfully spicy cuisine from jambalaya and gumbo to red beans and rice. One stop is certainly Philips' Restaurant and Bar, a popular spot on Cherokee Street. Another popular watering hole is Waldo's bar and grill, which serves up a Greek-Cajun mix of grub on the corner of campus about a block away from the B-school.

Pasquallie's, about two miles from school, is literally a hole in the wall: The joint knocked a hole in the sheetrock that separates the bar from the stage that typically features a live band playing blues well into the wee hours of the night. It's a must for MBA students or any visitor to New Orleans. "There's a heck of a lot to do inexpensively in New Orleans," says Roth Kehoe of the Class of 1994. "The bars offer cheap drinks. And it won't cost you more than a fiver for oysters or shrimp sandwiches. It's easy to get places. Most students walk everywhere." Most students live in and around the campus area in apartments that rent for between $400 to $600 a month.

Thanks to a new placement director, Freeman MBAs had an easier time getting jobs in 1994 than two years earlier, when 39 percent of the class lacked job offers at graduation. Still, for those paying $19,000-plus a year in tuition, it wasn't easy enough. In 1994, 19 percent of the class failed to have a single job offer by commencement. Those that did averaged just 1.65 offers each—below the 2.36 average for the 40-plus schools surveyed by BW. Some 80 companies came here to recruit second-year students in 1994, conducting 341 interviews. Another 1200 job opportunities were posted via correspondence. The major employers in 1994: Andersen Consulting (3), Coopers & Lybrand (2), Deloitte & Touche (2), Texas Commerce Bank (2), Arthur Andersen (1), Bankers Trust (1), Citicorp (1), Robertson Stephens (1), Hewlett-Packard (1), and Federal Express (1).

Contact: John C. Silbernagel, director of admissions, 504-865-5410
Final application deadline: May 1 for fall

Outstanding Faculty: *Russell P. Robins* (****—economics), *James T. Murphy* (****—finance), *Prem C. Jain* (***—accounting), *Chitru Fernando* (**—finance), *Paul A. Spindt* (**—finance), *Arthur P. Brief* (*—organizational behavior), *James Biteman* (management), *Jeffrey A. Barach* (management), *Rodolfo J. Aguilar* (finance), *David W. Harvey* (accounting)

Freeman MBAs Sound Off

For the $18,000 I spent in tuition yearly, I could have chartered a boat, sailed the world, and learned an incredible amount more than I did in this program.
*—**Accounting Career Path***

*The school needs more teachers instead of researchers. They also need to throw out tenure in the school. We're stuck with too many old farts who have lost touch with reality.—**Human Resources Career Path***

The administration doesn't respond to student feedback, and there's been a sharp reduction in quality electives. In fact, in the past two years, four of the top faculty members have left—all to lesser schools, and all due to Dean McFarland.
*—**General Management Career Path***

*Some old tenured faculty members teach poorly. I expect that with the retirement of several old guys and the recruitment of several young Ph.D.s, the school will break into the top tier.—**Financial Analyst***

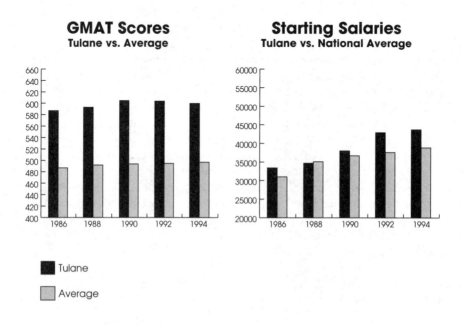

University of Illinois at Urbana-Champaign

College of Commerce and Business Administration
1206 South Sixth Street
Champaign, Illinois 61820

Enrollment: 588
Women: 27%
Non-U.S.: 39%
Minority: 7%
Part-time: None
Average age: 25
Average years of work exp.: 2
Applicants accepted: 62%
Median starting pay: $43,250

Annual tuition: resident—$6748
                 nonresident—$12,628
Room and board: $6000
Average GMAT score: 616
GMAT range: 450 to 750
Average GPA: 4.25 (out of 5.0)
GPA range: 3.0 to 5.0
Accepted applicants enrolled: 54%
Average starting pay: $47,130

Teaching methods: Lecture, 30% Case method, 25% Projects, 45%

When the Chicago Cubs need a steady hand in the bullpen, they bring up a promising young player from the Iowa Cubs in Des Moines. Chicago's business community also has a farm team for MBAs—the University of Illinois. If you've ever wanted to work for Arthur Andersen, Leo Burnett, Kraft, or Price Waterhouse, there's a well-worn path along Interstate 57 from Champaign to Chicago. The only more direct route to a job in the Windy City is to attend The University of Chicago or Northwestern's top-rated Kellogg School of Management in Evanston.

Along with other state universities such as Indiana and North Carolina, Illinois offers a lot of bang for the buck. But in the past Illinois' MBA program has always trailed those other institutions in stature because it was a stepchild to a far larger undergraduate program in business. This has changed with the appointment of Dean Howard Thomas, who views the MBA program as the B-school's flagship program. And Thomas, a management professor who took over the deanship in mid-1992, has been putting the finishing touches on a dramatic overhaul of the program.

The B-school has boosted the size of its student body, faculty, administration, and staff. The changes reflect a desire to become a bigger player on the MBA scene as well as a chance to develop a more innovative curriculum, which will be implemented in the fall of 1995. In the past five years, the program has nearly doubled in size. To help serve the expanded student body, Illinois has hired nine new faculty members and has added to its administrative staff. "Our goal is to create a more flexible MBA program that will position our graduates to better compete in the ever-changing global environment," says Assistant Dean Paul Magelli.

To meet that goal, the school plans on launching a new curriculum in the fall of 1995. MBAs will be required to take eight core business foundations courses in the first year. The courses will be taught by a faculty team to assure integration between finance, economics, marketing, accounting, and other disciplines. MBAs also are required to choose three business environment courses in a variety of topics including leadership styles, environmental issues, international business, and applied management techniques. You'll need to complete seven courses for a specialization to graduate. The changes will make the curriculum more practical, and it will now be standardized so that the focus isn't on individual faculty research.

For now, MBAs will take 12 core courses under four themes: information, integrity, innovation, and internationalization. An underlying theme of the first-year curriculum is teamwork. Students are broken into groups of five to seven, and move through the entire first semester together. The groups are switched around for the second semester, so by the end of the first year MBAs have significant experience within two different groups. "This really fosters an atmosphere of teamwork," says an alum. "The diversity of the students in the groups ensures that each one has a well-rounded assortment of experiences to draw upon."

All but two of the core courses are in the first year of the program. The school also requires two noncredit workshops in the first year, one in computer competency and the other in oral and written communications. In year two, MBAs participate in the MBA cap-stone experience, which is run more like an executive education experience than an MBA class. The three-day retreat to Allerton Park includes panel discussions and speakers. The themes change from year to year. Business Ethics was the focus in 1993. Last year's theme was Creativity and Goal Setting. And Illinois is establishing greater links with nearby companies to supplement the business basics with real-world learning.

Second-year students are required to take 6 out of 95 offered electives. You don't have to declare a major or concentration here. Students can take all their electives in one area or spread them out. Some of the most popular are: Entrepreneurship, Small Business Consulting, Business Ethics, Product Management, and Investments.

MBAs also are encouraged to explore at least another 75 courses available outside the B-school each year. About 13 percent of the students here seek joint degrees with other colleges. Students can pursue degrees with engineering, agriculture, architecture, computer science, journalism, education, law, and medicine. For anyone interested in accounting, a look at Illinois is a must. The school's undergraduate and graduate accounting programs were ranked number one in the country by *The Public Accounting Report* in both 1992 and 1993.

MBA students share space with undergrads in Commerce West and David Kinley Hall. Illinois has set aside tiered classrooms with state-of-the-art technology for MBAs and has scheduled daily coffee breaks that allow grad students to mingle with faculty. "We're trying to send the message that this is a pre-professional program," says Jane Nathan, director of international programs. "We hope the feeling of the MBA program will be closer to an executive workshop than an undergraduate class."

The MBA career services offices came under sharp criticism from MBAs. The school has responded by separating MBA placement from undergraduate services, but graduates are still unsatisfied. In 1994, only 82 companies arrived, conducting 988 interviews with students. Even so, only 23 percent of the Class of 1994 failed to have job offers at commencement. Those that did averaged 2.08 each—below the average for the 40-plus schools whose grads were surveyed by BUSINESS WEEK. The major recruiters were Arthur Andersen (13), Ford Motor (13), Andersen Consulting (11), Ernst & Young (9), Allied Signal (8), Citibank (8), Ford Credit Company (5), Price Waterhouse (5), NBD Bank NA (4), and Continental Bank (3).

Illinois alumni show lots of loyalty to their alma mater, often helping new grads to find jobs. A group of alums at advertising agency Leo Burnett even contributes artwork, photos, and graphics for the alumni magazine, *Commerce,* making it the slickest B-school mag in the country. And an annual event is the MBA trip to Evanston for the Northwestern-Illinois basketball game, an outing that includes sessions with alumni, tours of the Chicago futures and options exchanges, shopping along Michigan Avenue's Miracle Mile, and drinking and dancing at jazz bars and rock clubs until the wee hours. Closer to home, MBAs favor Gully's Riverview Inn for drinks—especially on Thursday nights because no classes are scheduled on Fridays. For the best burgers in town, students go to Murphy's. In between classes, MBAs will often grab a bite at the cafeteria in Newman Hall.

The campus is an oasis of culture surrounded by miles of farmland. The Krannert Center for the Performing Arts pulls in the likes of violinist Itzhak Perlman and rock group Dire Straits. Across from the center is Espresso Royale, which has become an afterconcert institution for coffee lovers. The campus also is home to the World Heritage Museum's extensive collection of ancient art. Even so, you'll find more sports lovers than museum goers. The MBA Association sponsors tailgate barbecues before football games that bring the faithful out to watch the Fightin' Illini and its mascot, Chief Illiniwek, replete with warpaint and feathered headgear. When they can't watch athletic events at Illinois, MBAs vigorously compete in intramural sports. They work on their curve ball in the hopes that next summer they'll be playing on Arthur Andersen's softball team in Chicago's Lincoln Park.

Contact: Paul Magelli, assistant dean of the MBA, 217-244-7602 or 800-MBA-UIUC
Final application deadline: May 1 for fall

Outstanding faculty: *Jay Ritter* (****—finance), *Carol T. Kulik* (***—organizational behavior), *Jose Antonio Rosa* (**—marketing), *Josef Lakonishok* (**—finance), *Paul Lansing* (**—law & ethics), *David Whitford* (**—finance), *Joseph Finnerty* (finance), *Zwi Ritz* (statistics), *Mark E. Roszkowski* (law), *David A. Lins* (finance)

Illinois MBAs Sound Off

I feel one of the best qualities of the Illinois MBA is the opportunities for leadership and student initiative. There are countless opportunities to enhance the skills of students and become involved in the program. Our opinions and input is valued by the administration and faculty. Major developmental activities are organized and facilitated by student teams. Some of these activities include MBA Orientation, Capstone Weekend, Career Focus, the International Group Project, and Ethics Committee and Code of Conduct, to name only a few. It is opportunities such as these that make an MBA program truly well rounded and valuable.
—**Staff Consultant**

The Illinois MBA is the best value in the country. We have good faculty and administrators that are willing to listen to the business world and students. The *program has changed so much in the past two years, and I'm confident the Illinois MBA program will continue to improve. Since the University offers so many ways to finance the MBA program, I will leave with no debt, and the satisfaction of knowing that I paid for my education myself. —**Career Path Unknown***

*Illinois has outstanding faculty in a range of areas, but placement activities could be improved. Also, Illinois accepts many students without work experience, so these students don't have much to offer in terms of "real world" business insight. —**Sales Analyst***

*I enjoyed my experience and learned quite a bit. However, the core classes need to be integrated better. Also, given the relative proximity to Chicago, I was disappointed that more interaction with firms in Chicagoland weren't offered (having speakers come visit, or doing more hands-on projects with firms). I thought the academic background I received was excellent, so overall I was very pleased. —**Sales Management Career Path***

*The lack of constructive interaction between international students and American students was primarily due to the lack of maturity of many students. This aspect also affected class discussion, as many students target grades as opposed to learning. —**Finance Career Path***

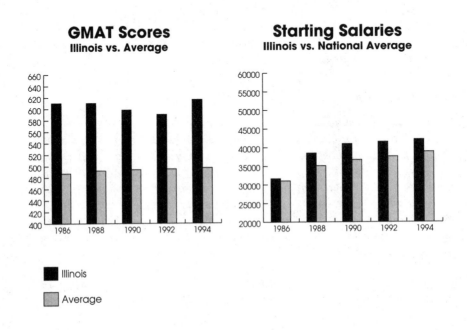

University of Iowa

College of Business Administration
Iowa City, Iowa 52242

Enrollment: 459
Women: 30%
Non-U.S.: 26%
Minority: 5%
Part-time: 240
Average age: 26
Average years of work exp.: 3.2
Applicants accepted: 36%
Median starting pay: $40,250

Annual tuition: resident—$3549
nonresident—$9361
Room and board: $4536
Average GMAT score: 590
GMAT range: 400 to 740
Average GPA: 3.24
GPA range: 2.32 to 4.0
Accepted applicants enrolled: 61%
Average starting pay: $41,620

Teaching methods: Lecture, 85%   Case method, 15%

There's a memorable line in the hit movie *Field of Dreams* that rings true for those who come to the Hawkeye State. At one point in the film, Shoeless Joe Jackson asks, "Is this heaven?" "No," comes the reply, "it's Iowa!" "People make Iowa what it is," says Willis R. Greer, Jr., a B-school professor. "It's a good place to live and a good place to study. The students are straightforward, and the faculty members reflect those values." To the 45 percent of MBAs that come from the state, this kind of down-to-earth approach doesn't seem out of the ordinary. But the sense of community is striking to the out-of-state students.

Think of the word *Iowa* and you're apt to visualize those cornfields that surround the baseball diamond in *Field of Dreams*. For sure, lots of corn gets planted around here. But the state also boasts two outstanding state universities: Iowa State in Ames is known for agriculture and engineering, while the University of Iowa has achieved recognition in medicine and liberal arts. The world-famous Iowa Writers Workshop is held at U of I.

Iowa's B-school has been a well-kept secret except to those who read scholarly journals. The faculty's expertise in finance and economics has led to some influential government appointments. Susan M. Phillips left Iowa in 1992 to serve on the Board of Governors of the Federal Reserve System, and associate dean, William P. Albrecht, recently returned to the school following an appointment to the Commodity Futures Trading Commission.

During the B-school's orientation week, called IMPACT, approximately 120 students spend their time getting acquainted at events like a riverboat cruise on the Mississippi River and a night at a local racquet club. Students are divided into teams of five to seven based on ethnicity, gender, and managerial experience. These diverse groups are then put into cohorts of 60 students, who travel together through the first semester's core courses.

To earn the MBA, students must complete 60 hours of classes. The first year is rigid, with 30 credits of required work. It isn't a lot of fun, either. The quality of teaching in the core courses is decidedly average, according to BUSINESS WEEK's 1994 survey of graduates. With that in mind, you'd probably wish the required basics would be over in the first year. They're not: You have to finish up 6 more credits of core work in the second year just as you begin picking up the remaining 24 hours of electives—where the teaching is only a little better.

Students choose from one of eight concentration tracks, including investment and security analysis, corporate finance, marketing, accounting, human resources management, quality management, production management, and management information systems. If those options don't sound enticing, then you can design your own concentration. A student interested in international business may want to take finance, language, and cultural courses. You can select from the B-school's 48 elective courses, or go outside of the school to choose electives. Iowa is trying to put more electives in its catalog, but don't expect miracles at a state school with limited resources. "The evolution of the program has been somewhat sporadic," says W. Bruce Johnson, associate dean for graduate programs. "But we have essentially opened up the entire second year to electives, and that has encouraged faculty to bring on line classes that develop experience in industry, business, and job functions."

While improving its curriculum, Iowa's B-school has moved into a new facility, the Pappajohn Business Administration Building. The $36 million structure sits right in the heart of campus and houses the entire business school, with a wing dedicated to MBAs. Placement and career advising services are located in the building, along with an impressive library, computer lab, and state-of-the-art "trading room," which is linked by satellite to 30 exchanges around the world.

The big-name CEOs seldom trek to Iowa to address students. But a good number of presidents come here through the school's visiting executive speaker program. The program has drawn executives from Shell Oil, The Bravo Television Network, AT&T, and the San Diego Padres in recent years. The school also draws upon such Iowa-based companies as Amana, Maytag, Winnebago, Deere and Company, and HON Industries for speakers and support.

"We are not a large program, and we don't have plans to become large," says Gary Fethke, the B-school's new dean. "Students here have extraordinary opportunities for participation—in everything from our eastern European consulting program to project opportunities with area businesses." Indeed, there's an MBA student on every one of the school's faculty committees, with the exception of the one on promotion and tenure. That kind of opportunity for student participation is rare at most other B-schools.

Placement has improved considerably since 1992, although most MBAs will tell you that U. of I. still has a long way to go. The placement office convinced 89 corporations to recruit on campus in 1994, a 13-company improvement from 1992. Most of the firms, however, are from the Midwest. "We don't have significant campus contact with the national business community," concedes Johnson, "so our strategy has been to move recruiting off campus, taking students to an additional 176 companies." This extra effort has improved placement numbers. About 86 percent of the Class of 1994 had at least one job offer by graduation, up from 57 percent in '92. Three companies—Andersen Consulting, Kimberly Clark, and Proctor & Gamble—hired two or more grads from the Class of 1994. At least 91 percent of the B-school's first-year students were placed in internships for the summer of 1994.

To some extent, Iowa seems content to live with its regional appeal. As Dean Fethke points out, "We see ourselves as a regionally dominant, nationally visible school. We know that our students are going to be interested primarily in jobs in the extended Midwest." Nevertheless, Fethke feels that Iowa has to broaden its placement focus to match students' career goals with organizations of all sizes across the country. "We can't just sit back and wait for large traditional corporate employers to come to campus," he says.

Unless you've visited Iowa City, it's hard to imagine just how charming this college town is. With a population of 60,000, including 30,000 students, Iowa City is the state's answer to Michigan's Ann Arbor or Wisconsin's Madison. By Iowa standards, housing here is pricey, about $400 for a one-bedroom apartment. Ninety percent of MBAs live off-campus, either in apartment complexes or Victorian homes that have been divided into apartments.

The campus sits on a bluff overlooking the Iowa River and intermingles with the downtown area. During the fall and spring evenings, musicians play guitars and portable keyboards along a downtown pedestrian mall—a favorite place for MBA students to stroll. On Thursday nights, the MBA Association holds parties at Fitzpatrick's, the B-school's unofficial student union. When the weather is warm, students sit at the outdoor bar and eat grilled ribs, burgers, and chicken. Throughout the year, U of I MBAs experience a high quality of life in an environment that is safe, vibrant, down-to-earth, maybe even a little bit hokey. Is it heaven? No, it's Iowa!

Contact: Jeff Emrich, admissions director, 319-335-1042
Final application deadline: April 15 for fall

Outstanding Faculty: *Ken Martin* (****—finance), *Kurt Anstreicher* (****—management), *Doug Foster* (***—finance), *Gary Gaeth* (***—marketing), *Tom Gruca* (**—marketing), *Dan Collins* (*—accounting), *John Delaney* (management), *Charles Klasson* (management), *Poppy McLeod* (management), *Peter Riesz* (marketing)

Iowa MBAs Sound Off

Although there have been aspects that I thought may not be important, especially many of the core courses, the program in total was worthwhile. My goal was to improve my skills and be qualified for jobs that pay in the $30,000 to $40,000 range. I've attained that goal. —**Operations Career Path**

Iowa is a rising star. Equipped with a new business building, a new dean, and a more active faculty, it will certainly begin to turn heads. —**Senior Auditor**

The University of Iowa is a school that is changing. The administration and faculty have assessed the program's strengths and weaknesses and now seek student input. This has given students a rare opportunity to make decisions that will influence the direction of the program. Additionally, the new state-of-the-art

Pappajohn Building offers the best in terms of facilities and computer technology.
—Marketing Career Path

Tremendous opportunities exist for students with entrepreneurial spirits. In the last two years, the University of Iowa has supported students who have initiated a summer international consulting and teaching program (The Emerging Free Market Economies Program). Currently, students are considering incorporating internships into the program. The EFMEP started in the Czech Republic in 1992 and expanded into Russia in 1993. There is continued room for expansion of this program, based on student interests in other countries. **—Finance Director**

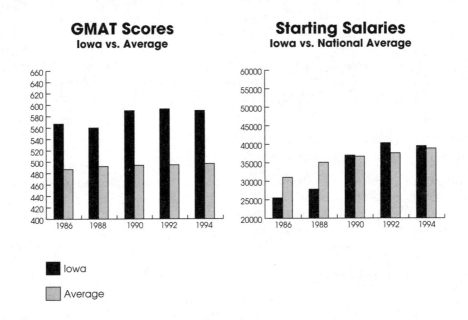

University of Minnesota

Curtis L. Carlson School of Management
271 19th Avenue South
Minneapolis, Minnesota 55455

Enrollment: 1373
Women: 252
Non-U.S.: 20%
Minority: 13%
Part-time: 1085
Average age: 27.5
Average years of work exp.: 4
Applicants accepted: 48%
Median starting pay: $48,000

Annual tuition & fees: resident—$8268
 nonresident—$12,618
Room and board: $4000
Average GMAT score: 600
GMAT range: 410 to 760
Average GPA: 3.2
GPA range: 2.10 to 4.0
Accepted applicants enrolled: 45%
Average starting pay: $48,250

Teaching methods: Lecture, 35%   Case study, 50%   Group projects, 15%

The Carlson School of Management is in the middle of a long-overdue revolution. The latest news from the front: Dean David S. Kidwell is making the badly needed changes here, those that will make this school fully realize its potential to become one of the top five public business schools in the nation. But he still has failed to correct one of the school's major problems: lackluster teaching.

Kidwell, who became the school's ninth dean in September of 1991, has overhauled the curriculum, transplanted innovative ideas into a moribund program, cultivated close ties with the thriving Twin Cities business community, and raised nearly $45 million within seven months for a new business school building to be completed in 1997.

These are vast and welcome improvements at the Carlson school. Indeed, the only area in which Kidwell's rhetoric has failed to match reality is teaching quality. For all of his talk about putting teaching more into balance with the research priorities of the faculty, there's been shamefully little, if any, enhancement in the quality of instruction at Minnesota. In both core and elective courses, the teaching quality is well below average for a top school, according to BUSINESS WEEK's graduate survey.

Indeed, Minnesota's overall teaching grades over BW's past three polls—from 1990 to 1994—show that it ranks 40th out of the leading 41 U.S. schools. Only Iowa has lower scores in teaching quality. These results are even more remarkable when you consider the small size of this program: core classes average only 50 students, while elective courses average about 35. (Smaller classes generally are easier to teach.) If Minnesota is ever to become a Top 20 school, this will have to change.

Perhaps Kidwell's single greatest accomplishment is the way he has jolted a leaderless school out of the limbo it had been stuck in. The new MBA curriculum—which debuted in the fall of 1993—features an integrated approach to coursework, with extensive involvement with the local business community. The first year of this program is broken into three sections. The fall quarter features four foundational core courses, in data analysis, managerial economics, behavioral science, and financial accounting. The winter quarter is focused around the "functions of the firm," including marketing, finance, human resources, operations, and information systems. And the spring and final quarter of the first year is devoted to leadership and the exploration of such topics as managing change, ethics, international business, and quality.

The school has lumped all the core courses, with the exception of its innovative and well-received 14-week field project for local corporations, into the first year. That frees up virtually the entire second year of study for nothing but electives. Carlson offers 79 electives in any given academic year, but MBAs can take up to 12 credits outside the business school.

A workshop series, dubbed "Nexus: Research Meets the Real World," has been continued. Launched in 1992, it gives students the chance to discuss with faculty current research projects and how they link up with the practice of management. A new mentoring program that matches every four students with a local business executive also got off the ground in 1992. A new self-assessment program also has been launched to determine student skills in teamwork, computing, and communications.

The school is named for local entrepreneur Curtis L. Carlson, who in 1986 kicked in $25 million (of which $18 million was allocated to the B-school) to launch a major university fund-raising effort. The three-year campaign eventually raised about $365 million, with the Carlson School share of the bounty a whopping $40 million. Carlson himself has handed over a total $28 million. The university claims this makes Carlson the nation's third largest contributor to a single business school. This impressive total includes a recent $10 million gift to the already successful campaign, to build a new state-of-the-art building. The groundbreaking is set for the spring of 1995.

Typical of urban schools, Carlson MBAs are scattered around the Twin Cities area and tend to have their own lives away from school. Outside of classes and MBA Association events, the only time MBAs regularly get together is on Thursday nights at Bullwinkle's, a bar about two blocks from campus. A winter in Minneapolis-St. Paul can sometimes make you feel like the Abominable Snowman. It gets cold here—*really* cold. But even the parking garages are heated so cars don't freeze, and virtually all the campus buildings are linked by tunnels and skyways.

Twin Cities' corporations recruit heavily here, accounting for many of the 87 companies that interviewed MBAs for jobs in 1994. To give Carlson students greater exposure to more employers, the school is taking students to companies rather than waiting for recruiters to come to Minneapolis. An additional 33 companies interviewed MBAs at career fairs in Chicago, San Francisco, and Atlanta.

It's already clear, however, that Kidwell has dramatically improved the school's career placement operations. About 9.8 percent of the Class of 1994 did not have a single job offer at graduation. Two years earlier, about 32 percent of the graduating students failed to have an offer. True, those with job opportunities at commencement averaged two each, just a bit below the 2.36 average for the top 40-plus schools. Yet, that number also is better than the 1992 stats, when MBAs averaged 1.5 offers. The top hirers: Northwest Airlines, Norwest Bank, A.C. Nielson, Deloitte & Touche, Cargill, Cardiac Pacemakers, Ecolab, Pillsbury, US West, and Kimberly Clark.

Now Kidder has to whip his faculty into shape. Somehow, teaching needs to become a priority at this school.

Contact: Sandra Kelzenberg, MBA office, 612-624-0006
Final application deadline: April 1 for fall

Outstanding Faculty: *Bruce Erickson* (****—management), *Ken Roering* (****—marketing), *James Gahlon* (***—finance), *Mike Stutzer* (**—finance), *Norman Chervany* (**—decision sciences), *Arthur Hill* (*—operations), *George John* (marketing), *Sal March* (decision sciences), *Akshay Rao* (marketing), *Bob Schmidt* (operations)

Carlson MBAs Sound Off

Overall, it was a great learning experience. But the professors seem to teach to the lower levels of the class at times. This pulled the good students down, and failed to weed out the few that should not have been in the school in the first place. **—Finance Career Path**

Our greatest strength and weakness are the students themselves. They are always willing to cooperate and function as teams. However, they also are too apathetic. I expected to work until 2 a.m., five nights a week, to keep up; to be constantly challenged by my peers; to have informal case discussion groups outside of class. Many of my classmates didn't. I think the school can reduce the apathy by making courses more challenging and by getting rid of grade inflation. If a third of the students were going to get C grades, they would be more motivated to work harder. **—Financial Analyst**

The program is very personalized. Professors and administrators know most students by their first names. With only 150 new students admitted each year, students have a chance to get to know a lot of people. It is a very tight-knit community that I believe serves as a strong support system for students. **—Marketing Assistant**

There were too many night classes where we were combined with night students. This caused some problems in scheduling group meetings, etc. **—Financial Analyst**

Professors never moved classes in the direction of a brainstorming session, as to how one might fix problems that were identified in case studies. In fact, no direction was given on how to spot problems that weren't so obvious a high school student could identify them. I paid over $25,000 for a piece of paper, but will learn all the practical information I thought I would learn in graduate school on the job. **—Marketing Career Path**

I am most unhappy with the quality of the Carlson School faculty members. For the most part, they are so mediocre! They surely could have been better.
—Marketing Manager

The administration and professors are very open to feedback and suggestions to improve the program and individual classes. The greatest aspects of the school are the students and the school's relationship with the business community. By and large, the students are cooperative and have a lot of great ideas. As far as the Twin Cities business community, it is very easy to use area businesses for class projects. **—Financial Analyst**

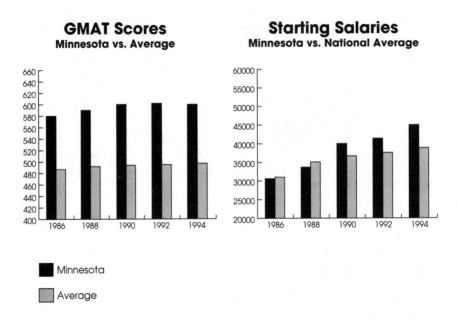

University of Notre Dame

College of Business Administration
109 Hurley Center, Room 109
Notre Dame, Indiana 46556

Enrollment: 283
Women: 26%
Non-U.S.: 25%
Minority: 8%
Part-time: None
Average age: 25
Applicants accepted: 63%
Accepted applicants enrolled: 44%

Annual tuition & fees: $17,430
Room and board: $5000
Average GMAT score: 578
GMAT range: 420 to 730
Average GPA: 3.02
GPA range: 2.01 to 3.95
Average years of work exp.: 2.3
Average starting pay: $49,230

Teaching methods: Case method, 35%   Lecture, 65%

Most people wouldn't even want to imagine themselves within the 40-foot concrete walls of Indiana State Prison. Not Notre Dame's MBAs. They toured death row, interviewed inmates, and took turns sitting in the electric chair. Notre Dame's effort to prevent white-collar crime? Not at all. The visit to the state's forbidding maximum security prison was just one aspect of Notre Dame's annual Urban Plunge program, which also includes visits to South Bend's Welfare Center and its Homeless Shelter.

Notre Dame's interest in the community is one result of its Catholic heritage. Founded by the congregation of the Holy Cross in 1842, Notre Dame still retains its religious identity. That doesn't mean that MBAs are required to start their days with Mass, but you're not apt to forget you're attending a Roman Catholic university. There is a chapel in every dorm. Murals cover the walls and ceilings of the university's elaborate cathedral, which is situated in the center of the campus. Adjacent to the church is Notre Dame's administration building, with its huge, golden dome topped by a statue of the Virgin Mary.

Amidst this environment, you'll find a fairly nuts-and-bolts MBA that comes in two flavors: a regular two-year program and a three-semester version for students with under-graduate degrees in business. The abbreviated MBA program consists of 44 credits and begins with the summer semester. Two-year MBAs are required to take 12 core courses and 10 free electives for a total of 62 credits, with admission only during the fall semester.

There are no "modules," integrated theme courses, or experiential projects in the core curriculum—just the plain, old-fashioned business basics. One concession: In the fall of 1993 the school added an international business class in the first year in addition to a currently required second-year course. A pair of one-credit Management Communication classes also have been introduced. Designed to show students the importance of effective communication, one class focuses on speaking, the other on writing.

In year two, MBAs will find some pretty basic electives, too. The small size of the school prevents it from offering more than 44 choices in any given year. By taking 3 to 5 courses in one of six areas, you can gain a specialization, such as finance or marketing, but it is not required. One of the most popular electives at Notre Dame is Entrepreneurship, taught by a consultant who works with small businesses in the South Bend area. In the course, students are divided into groups of five and assigned to solve a business problem for a local business with sales of about $1 million to $20 million a year.

Given the basic structure and limits of this program, Notre Dame attempts to differentiate itself on the basis of its ethics slant. The B-school's ethics program is one of the oldest in the country. Second-year MBAs examine such things as labor relations, environmental issues, and equal opportunity for women and minorities in the required Business-Government-Society class. Taught by Rev. Oliver F. Williams and John W. Houck, the approach to these issues is not always conventional. Houck emphasizes classics to examine social behavior, and ties that into the modern business community. The school also plans to better integrate ethics throughout the core by getting professors to pinpoint ethical dilemmas in marketing, finance, accounting, and other functional areas.

But as the trip to a prison suggests, ethics and community service are critical elements in the school's overall culture. "Urban Plunge really opens students' minds to other people's lot in life, especially for the stereotypical MBA who is all caught up in wealth," says Paul Kucera, 1992 president of the MBA Association. While Urban Plunge is aimed at broadening the minds of MBAs, it is Christmas in April that provides students with the opportunity to actually get out there and do something. The annual university-wide event brings teams of students together to rehabilitate run-down houses in South Bend. Students aren't the only ones repairing dilapidated houses. Notre Dame's tradition of community service is carried on even after MBAs receive their degrees. The Michigan chapter of the Notre Dame Alumni Association went to downtown Detroit to participate in "Paint the Town." That is not surprising to Larry Ballinger, director of Notre Dame's MBA program. "It is inherent in the Notre Dame tradition to look toward other individuals who may not be as fortunate as we are," he says.

The school's small size provides a family-like atmosphere—with the exception of the dean, whom students have criticized for being aloof and unavailable. MBA students number 260, including 80 in the three-semester program, and about 43 of the 91 B-school faculty members teach MBAs regularly. That assures an intimate learning experience. Classes are so small that when MBAs walk into the Huddle, the campus food court where students often study in small teams, it would be rare not to see a group of familiar faces. "It is the type of school where a professor sees you in the hall and says, 'Hello Gail, how are your studies going?'" says Gail Boyden, a recent alum.

While many students find Notre Dame a welcoming environment, some still take advantage of the school's London Program, which is located in its own Law/MBA Centre in the heart of London's financial district. A Notre Dame professor acts as resident director, teaching one course for the semester-abroad experience. The remainder of the coursework is taught by professors from British schools. Through academics and field trips, MBAs get a feel for the European Economic Community. A similar program in Santiago, Chile, began in the fall of 1993.

Located 90 miles east of Chicago, South Bend's population is about 110,000. The campus is located on the northern edge of the town, and students tend not to stray too far. There's a slew of school-sponsored gatherings, ranging from the annual Halloween Costume Party to the Spring Formal, where students mix with faculty and administrators. The stadium parking lot bar run by the alumni association is a hangout on Thursday nights for both students and faculty. Popular spots include Coach's and The Linebacker, just a few blocks off campus. Coaches, for pizza and beer, boasts a pair of big-screened TVs and is crammed with jocks and other fans. A block away, the Linebacker is tiny, jam-packed, and smoke-filled.

With names like Coaches and The Linebacker, it's easy to guess that football is popular here. What an understatement! "You never miss a football game at Notre Dame," says Rachelle Carrier, of the Class of 1993. "When you walk into that stadium, you're in awe." In addition to going as a group to tailgate and watch the Fightin' Irish play football, MBAs participate in several intramural sports. Some MBAs spend the whole year practicing for "bookstore basketball," a tournament held on courts outside the bookstore.

While Notre Dame's size provides many benefits, it also means resources are somewhat slim. That will change when a new $22 million management center opens in the fall of 1995. The four-story building will house both MBA and executive development classes, faculty, and a new Office of Career Development. Until fall of 1992, MBAs used the university's centralized office. Joyce Manthay, director of career development, thinks it is important to teach MBAs the skills necessary to find a job at any time in their careers. This kind of individualized attention was not possible in the university placement center, which concerned itself only with placing bodies into jobs.

In 1992, 86 companies came to recruit MBAs here—not so bad for a graduating class of 160 students. Most of the firms, however, are from the Midwest. The B-school counts on local alumni associations to help MBAs get interviews with companies in California, Texas, and Florida. The strong sense of loyalty alums feel toward their alma mater is definitely a plus. The big hirers of the Class of 1994: AT&T, IBM, Arthur Andersen, and Whirlpool all hired 2 NDMBAs, Ford (5), Andersen Consulting (4), General Motors (4), and Deloitte & Touche (3).

Contact: Lee Cunningham, MBA admissions coordinator, 219-237-8671
Final application deadline: May 1 for fall

Outstanding Faculty: *James Schrager* (****—entrepreneurship), *Frank Reilly* (****—finance), *Stephen Dee* (**—marketing), *James Davis* (**—strategy), *James O'Rourke* (**—management communications), *Neil Beckwith* (*—marketing), *Lee Tavis* (finance), *Jim Wittenbach* (accounting), *Donald Fehrs* (finance), *Raphael Tenorio* (economics)

Notre Dame MBAs Sound Off

As far as the professors are concerned, the majority really care and want you to succeed. Sometimes, however, I felt like the grading system was too generous. The teachers realize students need a 3.0 to graduate, and therefore scale their grades from straight B (3) to straight A (4). I don't think that helps people. It only punishes the ones who really achieved. **—Corporate Finance Career Path**

The overall level of the class was very impressive, but the bottom ten percent were unqualified and should not have been admitted. **—Career Path Unknown**

269

The school needs direction—there is no strong leader for the MBA program. Twenty-five percent of the students have no work experience, and therefore have virtually nothing to contribute in class. This causes companies to avoid ND when recruiting. Why should we pay so much for an MBA when we could have gotten the same experience for less money? Notre Dame is filling seats with poor-quality students at the expense of those students who gave up careers for higher learning. Obviously, the program is going for money rather than quality! **—Marketing Career Path**

The large number of international students adds a great deal to the learning process. Unfortunately, too many students are accepted who are not fluent in English. This really distracts from learning, in terms of class lectures and group projects. **—Marketing Career Path**

The key to ND's MBA program is that it is smaller than most, which fosters better and more sincere relationships among students. In fact, during my summer internship I worked with two Wharton interns who had never met each other during the whole school year. That just wouldn't happen at Notre Dame. The school is also committed to the international development of the student body. A good chunk of the students go abroad, and bring many new and different angles back to the classroom. **—Commercial Lender**

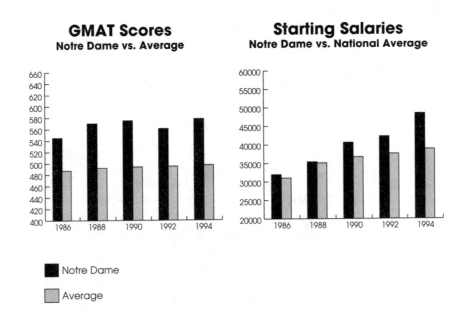

GMAT Scores
Notre Dame vs. Average

Starting Salaries
Notre Dame vs. National Average

■ Notre Dame

▨ Average

University of Pittsburgh

The Joseph M. Katz Graduate School of Business
276 Mervis Hall
Pittsburgh, Pennsylvania 15260

Enrollment: 986
Women: 30%
Non-U.S.: 30%
Minority: 10%
Part-time: 506
Average age: 26
Applicants accepted: 47%
Accepted applicants enrolled: 50%

Annual tuition: resident—$13,476
　　　　　　　　　 nonresident—$22,734
Room and board: $11,000
Average GMAT score: 603
GMAT range: 450 to 750
Average GPA: 3.2
GPA range: 2.4 to 3.9
Average starting pay: $46,070

Teaching methods:　Lecture, 50%　Case method, 40%　Projects, 10%

From the outside, the Katz School of Business looks more like the contemporary head-quarters of a high-tech corporation than an educational institution. The only ivy around this striking glass and steel building hangs from the nearby centerfield wall of the old Forbes Field, once home to the Pittsburgh Pirates and Steelers. Dean H. J. Zoffer jokes that he should exchange his building with PPG Industries in town, because the company's structure looks more like a university building than his own.

But that's not the only surprise for students who come to "Pitt." Katz offers a first-rate MBA in a unique 11-month program. That's right. A virtual two years of study crammed into 11 tortuous months. When AT&T Chairman Robert E. Allen once came to campus to deliver the graduation address, he called the program "the intellectual equivalent of swimming the English Channel underwater."

At times, that's exactly how students feel. Potential students should think carefully before attending, warns a 1992 alum, because "the intensity and the pace are not for everyone." While your friends are still on the beach, you're showing up at Katz for five days' worth of orientation at the beginning of August. The first of six 7-week terms begins about August 15. The last one doesn't end until June 16.

Twice a week at 7:30 a.m., small groups of students gather on the third floor of Mervis Hall for the breakfast with the dean. "In the first term, they complain about the pressure and the difficulty of managing their time," says Zoffer, Pitt's dean for 25 years. "By the third module, they're still wondering what they committed themselves to. In the last module, the complaints turn to placement or whatever." Scheduling is a common gripe among students. They complain that it's easy to get blocked out of popular electives. Because they only have 11 months of classes, it's common for students to leave without taking the more popular classes they badly wanted.

The school revised its curriculum in the fall of 1994. Instead of 14-week courses tucked into three terms, Katz now offers 7-week courses split up into six different modules. This should allow students more options to pursue their interests. Packed into those six modules is a whirlwind of activity: 14 required courses in the core curriculum, and 14 electives.

The main drawback to the program is that you lose the opportunity of a summer internship. For the career switcher or someone with little work experience, that is a considerable negative. If you're trying to convince H. J. Heinz to hire you for a marketing job despite your financial background, a summer job at Procter & Gamble makes the task a lot easier.

What you gain, in turn, is the chance to participate in what Zoffer calls a "living laboratory." More than most B-school deans, Zoffer has been adept at luring corporate executives to his 10-year-old building to sit and chat with students. Two or three times each month, Zoffer hosts an Executive Briefing, in which CEOs from major Pittsburgh corporations talk for 40 minutes on the challenges and frustrations of the job and then field student questions. After each session, a handful of students heads for the University Club for a private lunch with the chairman of Westinghouse Electric Corp., Bell Atlantic, or Alcoa.

Each spring, over a dozen corporate executives also come to campus for the American Assembly Dialogue. Pitt MBAs set the agenda for the off-the-record discussions that have attracted the likes of a varied group of big-time chieftains from Ted Turner of Turner Broadcasting System Inc. to Richard A. Zimmerman, chairman of Hershey Foods Corporation. The real-world thoughts of visiting CEOs provide a good balance to all the learning in Pitt's tiered, horseshoe-shaped classrooms. Katz offers students about 100 electives, the most popular of which is Short-Term Finance. A key part of the program is its emphasis on how to use information as a strategic resource. Katz boasts an impressive computer lab filled with $6 million worth of hardware and software. Electives in management information systems outnumber those in finance, marketing, human resources, and international business. Students can also take Japanese, French, German, and Spanish for credit in the business school.

Some of the most rewarding electives are "project courses" that allow students to consult with corporations on actual problems. Pitt MBAs have helped to forecast trends in entertainment behavior for Eastman Kodak Company and helped to build a computer-simulated model of an operating room for a local hospital. Special programs? If you're really an academic masochist, Pitt offers the MBA in double-degree programs with a master's in the management of information systems (21 months), international business (two years), international affairs (21 months), area studies (21 months), or health administration (two years), and even a Master of Divinity with the Pittsburgh Theological Seminary. "We are using a second year to add a more specialized focus for those students who want it," says Zoffer.

Most students, of course, find one 11-month degree program tough enough to handle. The B-school doesn't schedule classes on Fridays. Pitt loads up that day with optional workshops and executive briefings. There's also a Significant Film Series, in which such famous flicks as *All Quiet on the Western Front* and *Caine Mutiny* are shown to students on Friday afternoons. Each film comes with a lecture on how the movie portrays relevant business issues.

Although Katz's average student boasts four years of work experience, many grads fault the school for admitting too many students with little or no experience. The upshot: Class discussions aren't always as dynamic as they should be. Student evaluations of teachers are now made public at Pitt, so you can do some homework on whom you should avoid. That's important, because graduates polled by BUSINESS WEEK rate the quality of teaching below the average of the 40-plus schools surveyed. One very major exception: Kenneth Lehn, the former chief economist of the Securities and Exchange Commission, who recently joined the school's faculty. Praises one fan: "He was challenging and demanding, and single-handedly made my MBA experience worthwhile."

Students gravitate to the basement of Mervis Hall for lunch at Clara's Cafe. As you might have guessed, Clara runs the joint, even reprimanding the dean for grabbing too big a piece of cake for lunch. For drinks, the MBAs favor Zelda's, which serves up pizza and is only one block from the school, and Doc's Place, the yuppie watering hole in Shadyside some two miles away. Most students choose private housing near campus, in the culturally diverse Oakland section of Pittsburgh.

Some 98 companies came to Pitt in 1994 to conduct 1000 interviews. The major recruiters included Ford Motor Co. (8); Arthur Andersen (8), PNC Financial Corp. (5), Price Waterhouse (4), Ernst & Young (4), Intel (3), Deloitte & Touche (3), Johnson & Johnson International (3), Andersen Consulting (2), and Avery Dennison (2). About 17 percent of the Class of 1994 did not have a job offer by commencement, although the lucky ones had about 2.1 offers each—below average for the top 40-plus schools whose graduates were surveyed by BUSINESS WEEK.

Contact: Kathleen Riehle Valentine, director of admissions, 412-648-1700
Final application deadxline: May 1 for fall

Outstanding Faculty: *Ken Lehn* (****—finance), *Robert Atkin* (***—human resources), *Dan Smith* (***—marketing), *Yuhchang Hwang* (**—accounting), *Madeleine Carlin* (**—accounting), *Thomas Satty* (*—operations), *John Grant* (strategic planning), *Tim Heath* (marketing), *Robert Nachtmann* (finance)

Katz MBAs Sound Off

I am extremely pleased with my educational experience at the Katz Graduate School of Business. The quality of the program, faculty, facilities, and support services is excellent. The ability to earn an MBA in one year makes KGSB well worth consideration for any student, but particularly for a student with significant work experience who can afford to give up a summer internship.
—Consultant

The outstanding feature of the program at Katz is the fact that it takes only 11 months to complete. However, this is probably not the attribute a top-tier business school wishes to "hang its hat on." A Katz MBA does not appear to "travel" well, or open many doors except in a few areas. **—Career Path Unknown**

Too much work in too little time created a whirlwind of information which had little time to settle in. The speed greatly inhibited my ability to find time for a job search. **—Marketing Career Path**

Students need to be self-motivated for their career search, because there is not an overabundance of top firms interviewing at Katz. If you look and work hard enough, the job you want will appear. **—Corporate Management Trainee**

The dean gets an impressive list of local executives in to speak to the students; unfortunately, most of the companies these people represent don't recruit.
—Finance Career Path

Overall, I believe Katz offers an excellent program. However, the frenzied pace of an intense one-year program sometimes impedes learning subjects of interest in depth. There literally is no time to dig deep. Nonetheless, the material taught, the faculty, and the practical application opportunities are excellent. **—Marketing Career Path**

I feel that the concept of teamwork is often misapplied. Often, the members of a team are required to evaluate each other for grade percentages. This promotes individualism, and decreases harmony within the team. **—Production Manager**

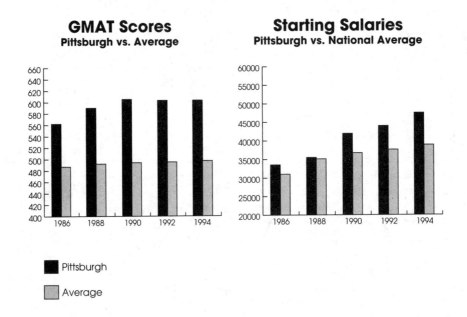

University of Rochester

William E. Simon Graduate School of Business Administration
Rochester, New York 14627

Enrollment: 702
Women: 242
Non-U.S.: 44%
Minority: 12%
Part-time: 302
Average age: 26
Applicants accepted: 38%
Median starting pay: $56,750

Annual tuition & fees: $19,080
Room and board: $4950
Average GMAT score: 612
GMAT range: 480 to 740
Average GPA: 3.22
GPA range: 2.38 to 4.0
Accepted applicants enrolled: 38%
Average starting pay: $60,670

Teaching methods: Lecture, 60%   Case study, 40%

When students pour through the doors of Schlegel Hall, they can glimpse him at the end of the long corridor. He's still there when they leave in the afternoon or trek to the library. He always wears a business suit, and he likes to hang a jacket over his shoulder.

The real William E. Simon doesn't spend all his time in Schlegel—it's only the cast-iron statue of the former Treasury Secretary that never leaves. But Simon's spirit and ideas are ubiquitous at the University of Rochester's business school. His notion that free markets provide the best solutions to business problems is taught as gospel here.

When Simon's figure first went up in Dewey Hall—now reserved for the B-school faculty and administrative offices—students used to carry the statue around, sometimes plopping him in the elevator or positioning him so as to stare at a nearby bulletin board. But ever since Simon and the students moved to the 64,000-square-foot, state-of-the-art Schlegel Hall, he has been bolted to the floor.

So has his philosophy. The belief that virtually every business decision, whether it concerns finance, marketing, organizational behavior, or operations, can be explained in terms of microeconomics, permeates the school's curriculum. "All the courses here are taught from a common framework of economics," says Dean Charles I. Plosser.

With the exception of the University of Chicago, there isn't another B-school more strongly committed to the free-market or price-theory approach than Simon. Combine that with a coterie of brilliant scholars, the intimacy of a small program, and one of the best B-school facilities around, and you get a rather unique business school experience. Not that Rochester hasn't had its problems.

The school went through a difficult period in 1992, when a new dean resigned within eight months of taking the job because of a funding dispute with the university president. The crisis, however, mobilized both the faculty and students to work together to improve the program. Plosser, a longtime professor at the school, took over as dean to contain the damage. And a new, more supportive university president arrived.

Among the initiatives that came out of the trouble is the school's Vision Program, a newly required leadership component of the curriculum modeled after Chicago's successful LEAD program. Backed by such corporate sponsors as AT&T, Procter & Gamble, Bausch & Lomb, Wells Fargo, and Xerox, it is a series of seminars, group exercises, team-building raft trips and simulations that address the "soft" aspects of management long overlooked by this school. For each of the 18 modules there's a student leader, a faculty advisor, and one or more executives from the corporate sponsors. The school itself invests nearly $200,000 in the program each year.

Vision kicks off the MBA experience as part of the orientation program in mid-September. Entering students are assigned to the Blue, Gold, Green, or Purple cohort of 40 MBAs each. During the first three quarters, each cohort takes all the 10 required courses and the management communication sequence together. Students also are assigned to study teams of four of five members, for group projects throughout the first year. Simon's initial core courses tend to be more theoretical than those at many other business schools in the 1990s. But the small size of the faculty, and the student cohorts, also allow for far more integration of coursework across functions.

In the second year, all students take at least one "integrative course," in a subject such as business policy or competitive strategy, which serves as a capstone experience. They also must complete at least one of 11 concentrations in such areas as public accounting or entrepreneurship. Simon offers students less program flexibility and fewer choices than many other larger business schools. As Plosser readily admits, "We're small, and we cannot be all things to all people. We have to carve out our market niche."

Yet for a small school, there's a remarkable degree of diversity here. Indeed, 44 percent of the Class of 1996 is international—a record for Simon, and the highest percentage of any major business school in the U.S. (Some international students complain that the U.S. students get preferential treatment when it comes to scholarship and fellowship money, but 60 percent of the school's applicant pool is now non-U.S.) The largest single contingent of non-U.S. students is from Japan, represented by 15 admits in 1994. Simon gets roughly 180 applications from Japan each year, though students hail from more than 30 countries. "Just when you think you've seen every transcript possible, you get one from Poland," says Priscilla Gumina, assistant dean for MBA programs.

The school makes good use of this mix. Besides the mandatory teams that mix cultures and backgrounds, students initiated a "Broaden Your Horizons" seminar series that features lunchtime presentations by students from countries around the world. MBAs from Argentina, Australia, Brazil, Hong Kong, India, and other nations will conduct sessions on the economics, culture, politics, and business protocol of their home countries. Simon students also publish *Simon International,* the only journal of global business written by MBAs for MBAs. An executive seminar series, meantime, attempts to lure senior executives to campus, from the CEOs of Bethlehem Steel to Saatchi and Saatchi. Of course the real Bill Simon—not the statue—is a frequent guest.

Simon's faculty are a powerful and entrenched group at the school. They boast great brainpower in finance and economics, and Simon profs edit several top academic journals—the *Journal of Financial Economics, Journal of Monetary Economics,* and the *Journal of Accounting and Economics*—all virtually unreadable scholarly tracts. Even so, Plosser is happy to remind visitors that recent studies of research productivity have ranked Simon's faculty among the top five in the U.S. Perhaps because of the small size of the school, the faculty's pursuit of its research agenda hasn't destroyed its ability to deliver quality teaching rates, above average for the top 40-plus schools.

Like Cornell's Johnson School, Simon is located in upstate New York, which has more in common with the Midwest than with New York City. In many ways Rochester is a company town, home to Eastman Kodak, Xerox Corp., and Bausch & Lomb—three major supporters of the school and of the arts. And when it comes to the arts, Rochester can boast of the university's world-renowned Eastman School of Music, the Rochester Philharmonic Orchestra, and the International Museum of Photography.

Simon is part of the university's main or River Campus, located on the banks of the Genesee River about three miles from downtown. Most of the MBA action now centers around the attractive Schlegel Hall, a modern four-story building that opened in the fall of 1991. The faculty resides in Dewey Hall, one of four stately, columned buildings on the Eastman Quad. There's no undergraduate business program at Rochester, so most of the resources here can be lavished on the MBAs and the school's Doctor of Philosophy program. The management library on the third floor of the university's Rush Rhees Library, located at the head of the Eastman Quad, is one of the quietest places on campus.

So how do Simon MBAs fare in the job market? In 1994, roughly 21 percent of the class failed to have a job offer at commencement. Those that did averaged only 1.81 offers—below the 2.36 average for the 40-plus schools surveyed by BW. Some 92 companies came to campus to recruit second-years, doing 1582 interviews. Obviously, this is an area in need of improvement. Luckily, the dean hired a new career services director, Lee A. Junkans from Duke University's Fuqua School, who should make a difference. The major 1994 employers: Bausch & Lomb (4), General Motors (4), Bank of Nova Scotia (3), Bear Stearns (2), Coopers & Lybrand (2), First Empire State (2), Procter & Gamble (2), Quantitative Financial Strategies (2), Xerox (2), and AIG (2).

Of course, some companies find Rochester a bit too out of the way to make Simon a regular stop on their recruiting tours. And some stay away because Rochester winters are harsh, a fact of life that makes some students wonder why they ventured so far north for an MBA. Humor serves as the best antidote to the cabin fever known to set in after many frigid nights. Students can no longer move William E. Simon around, but that hasn't stopped them from putting a Halloween mask on his face, or slipping a pair of white boxer shorts with little red hearts around his middle.

Contact: Priscilla E. Gumina, assistant dean for MBA programs, 716-275-3533
Final application deadline: June 1 for fall

Outstanding Faculty: *Michael Barclay* (****—corporate finance); *Ronald Schmidt* (****—economics & organizations); *Clifford W. Smith, Jr.* (****—finance); *Gregg A. Jarrell* (***—applied economics); *Neil Pearson* (**—finance); *Ronald Yeaple* (*—marketing); *Abraham Seidmann* (information systems); *Thomas F. Cooley* (economics); *Ray Ball* (marketing); *Gerald Zimmerman* (accounting)

Simon MBAs Sound Off

Simon boasts a superstar finance faculty. All the courses are coherently integrated. Simon MBAs feel ready, both conceptually and analytically, to face any challenge in their careers. Worth every penny I paid. —**Research Assistant**

Almost without exception, the teaching is first-class: the professors seem very interested in the subjects they teach. The facilities are first-rate, and the administration is almost always quick in responding to any problem. The winter weather is naturally very cold, but shuttle buses and tunnels between buildings make life easier. Unlike the faculty, administration, or the facilities, the students are not uniformly excellent: there is quite a wide disparity, from very bright students to those who really don't belong in the program. **—Finance Career Path**

The Simon School is a finance school, is a finance school, is a finance school. The marketing department needs focus and depth. **—Product Marketing**

The school's reputation in the corporate world lags behind its excellent reputation in finance and accounting academia. Still, I think Simon has an enormous amount of potential. **—Finance Associate**

My Simon experience far exceeded my expectations. I am now on a first-name basis with professors at the cutting edge of their respective disciplines, and would feel quite comfortable calling any of them for counsel. I got a top-level education and an extensive international network which I will use for the rest of my life. **—Consultant**

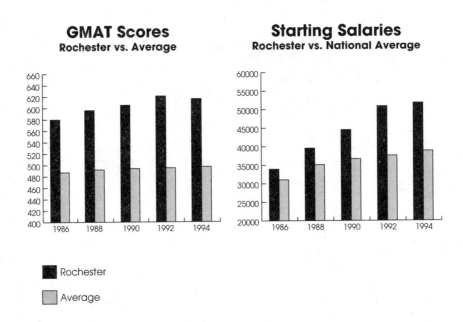

University of Southern California

Graduate School of Business Administration
University Park
Los Angeles, California 90089

Enrollment: 1120
Women: 27%
Non-U.S.: 16%
Minority: 15%
Part-time: 750
Average age: 27.6
Applicants accepted: 33%
Median starting pay: $53,000

Annual tuition & fees: $17,230
Room and board: $10,000
Average GMAT score: 610
GMAT range: 500 to 740
Average GPA: 3.1
GPA range: 2.0 to 3.96
Accepted applicants enrolled: 48%
Average starting pay: $52,030

Teaching methods: Lecture, 40% Case study, 40% Group projects, 20%

First, you hear the rather uplifting classical music. Then, you see the strolling students and teaching teachers on a sun-drenched California campus. High-tech spinning graphics overlay the scenes of energized classrooms and spreadsheets on computer screens. Before long, leadership guru Warren Bennis is staring at you with his Mediterranean blue eyes. "The future," he intones in a rich voice, "is in our bones."

Welcome to the video version of the University of Southern California's business school. The feel-good promo, produced by USC MBAs and dispatched to the school's applicants, cues you into the school's famous faculty and its programs in entrepreneurship and international business. It also makes sure you're aware of the Thursday beer bash, the campus that's only 20 minutes from the roaring surf and two hours from the ski slopes. Proclaims one of the B-school's top teachers: "Accounting can be cool."

So how does this infomercial stand up to reality? What you see is generally what you get. Sure, you're not going to hear what MBAs here typically complain about: Lackluster teaching by adjunct professors in evening classes often taken by full-timers in their second year, a less-than-aggressive career services office that makes it tougher to land a good job, or the competitiveness of some students. But you'll get a good sense of the strengths of this program and the culture of the school.

For years, it has been home to some of the sharpest and most articulate management thinkers in America. Bennis, one the world's best-known B-school profs for his work on leadership, leads the pack. He's among great company of the likes of Edward Lawler, who runs the school's Center for Effective Organizations, and Morgan McCall, who has developed some of the leading management simulation exercises on the market today.

The strength of the school's organizational behavior (OB) group, among the best two or three in the world, had often overwhelmed other departments, making recruiters believe that USC was a "soft" school. But in recent years the school has picked off superior teachers in finance, accounting, and marketing from Wharton, Michigan, Harvard, and Northwestern. One of those master teachers, Randolph W. Westerfield, the former chairman of Wharton's finance department, is now dean of USC's B-school.

The school revamped its MBA program in the fall of 1991 to emphasize fundamental skills in business economics, statistics, accounting, finance, and communication in the first semester, a cross-functional approach to process innovation in the second, and the freedom to pursue a concentration of one's own making in year two. The program kicks off with a two-and-a-half-day retreat, aimed at teaching the skills needed for working in project teams and at building a collaborative learning environment. The entire first year is taught by a dedicated faculty team featuring some of the school's best professors. No wonder the quality of the teaching in the core courses is well above average, according to BUSINESS WEEK's surveys of graduates at the top 40-plus schools. An interesting down side to this strategy is that many electives are taught by weaker faculty—a reason why the teacher ratings for electives are considered to be significantly below average.

Integration of the core courses is accomplished through a "key cases" program, in which groups of faculty share a single classroom to present business cases from different perspectives. MBA candidates take a required business presentations and writing class, taught in small groups, and are graded for their communication skill in every first-year class. Case competitions with executive judges, business simulations, and field-study projects keep the focus on real-world application throughout year one.

The school's contingent of 171 full-time profs offer students many options. You can gain a concentration in one or two areas by taking at least four courses in a given topic. Of the nearly 170 electives offered to MBAs, the lion's share is in accounting (49). Finance and business economics offer 34 advanced courses: management and organization, 21; marketing, 20; information and operations management, 19. Another 10 courses each are taught in the school's programs in entrepreneurship and real estate—two of the school's major areas of strength. And MBAs can also take courses outside the B-school in law, cinema-television, public administration, urban planning, music, communications, and international relations.

A good number of these elective courses are offered only at night, requiring full-time students to enroll in them with USC's 650 part-timers. Most of the complaints about the quality of teaching seem directed at these night courses. To encourage better teaching, the school has set up a Teaching Excellence Center, established mentoring relationships among faculty, and now makes public student evaluations of teachers for the first time.

Located on a 150-acre campus, the B-school occupies three buildings, including the I. M. Pei–designed Hoffman Hall. Currently in the midst of a capital campaign, the school plans to add a new $18 million building to its existing facilities by 1997. The reason: MBAs are packed in with some 2000 business undergraduates. To make life a little more comfortable, the school opened a dedicated MBA lounge and information center, as well as a 20-unit Macintosh computer lab in 1992. "It is important that both the undergraduate as well as the graduate programs have their own separate facilities to further enhance the learning experience, because each group has different needs," says Dean Westerfield.

The campus, about two and a half miles from L.A.'s central business district, is next to Exposition Park, site of the 1984 Olympics and home to the L.A. Raiders and the L.A. Clippers. It's not the greatest of neighborhoods, although many students rent nearby apartments because they come cheaper than the more desirable spots closer to Santa

Monica beach. A limited number of on-campus dorms are available, but you have to apply early to get in.

Getting out of this program with a job has been a bit of a sore point here. In 1994, some 113 companies came to campus to recruit students for permanent jobs, conducting 1475 interviews. Another 520 job opportunities came over the transom via correspondence. The major recruiters: Ernst & Young (6), Price Waterhouse (6), Arthur Andersen (4), Deloitte & Touche (4), Kenneth Levanthal (3), Andersen Consulting (3), Standard Chartered Bank (3), Mattel (3), Allied Signal (3), and Citibank (3).

About 14.8 percent of the Class of 1994 failed to have a job offer at commencement. Though a bit high, it's at least nowhere near the 28 percent level of two years earlier. Class of 1994 grads here averaged only 1.83 offers each, below the average 2.36 of the 40-plus schools in the BUSINESS WEEK sample, and well below the 2.72 average at nearby UCLA. Now that's one elusive fact that didn't make it onto the video. . . .

Contact: Annette Loschert, assistant dean of admissions, 213-740-0669
Final application deadline: March 15 for fall

Outstanding Faculty: *Randolph W. Westerfield* (****—finance), *Dennis Draper* (****— commodities), *Ken Merchant* (**—accounting), *Walt Blacconiere* (**—accounting), *Mark Defond* (**—accounting), *Richard Eastin* (**—managerial economics), *Dennis Rook* (marketing), *Mark Zupan* (managerial economics), *Harry DeAngelo* (finance), *Mark Weinstein* (finance)

Southern California MBAs Sound Off

USC's first-year core program is an extremely rigorous and challenging experience. The workload borders on excessive, but provides a thorough grounding in basic business concepts. The core is stacked with the elite professors at the school, all of whom bring the most current issues into the classroom to integrate the "real world" with the world of academia. The second year is much less structured and somewhat less challenging. While the quality of the faculty is superb, the elective instructors are somewhat less dynamic than the core professors.
—Finance Career Path

The cooperation and teamwork among students, and the close relationship of faculty and students, is a highlight of the USC experience. In talking to students of other Western U.S. B-schools, the closeness of USC students was the most distinguishing characteristic of the school mentioned. **—Consultant**

A major drawback during the second year is that the evening MBA students take classes with the full-time students. They tend to bring extensive experience into the classroom, but it is clear their priorities are work first, school second. This

makes it difficult to work effectively in groups, because of conflicts of interest.
—Finance Career Path

The administration is committed to constantly upgrade the program. I truly felt like a customer: the administration made every effort to meet all my needs. To better understand student desires, focus groups on various topics were conducted throughout the semester. The administration was very responsive to our input. **—Finance Career Path**

This school is a complete sham. I am no more employable than I was when I came here. The school nickels-and-dimes students to death over little $25 to $35 charges, and wonders why you don't want to contribute as alumni. The teaching is awful—half the faculty don't speak English well enough to teach grade school, and most are so wrapped up in their own petty research—which they teach as gospel—that they have no time for teaching things that are important. **—Finance Career Path**

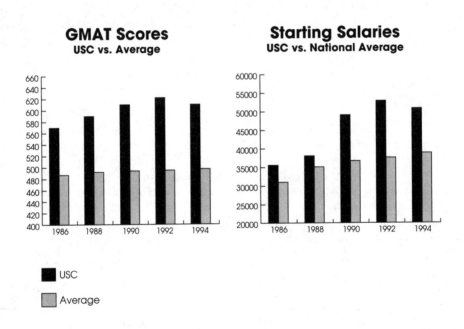

University of Washington

Graduate School of Business Administration
110 Mackenzie Hall
Seattle, Washington 98195

Enrollment: 350
Women: 34%
Non-U.S.: 19%
Minority: 5%
Part-time: 50
Average age: 28
Average years of work exp.: 4.6
Applicants accepted: 42%
Median starting pay: $43,000

Annual tuition & fees: resident—$4566
nonresident—$11,436
Room and board: $9350
Average GMAT score: 617
GMAT range: 400 to 740
Average GPA: 3.25
GPA range: 1.7 to 4.0
Accepted applicants enrolled: 65%
Average starting pay: $44,140

Teaching methods: Lecture, 30%   Case method, 50%   Seminar, 20%

Call it the "Rainier Factor." Put this business school into almost any other region of the country and it wouldn't be nearly as good as it is. The natural beauty of Seattle and its environs is a powerful draw. Mount Rainier and other nearby recreational spots allow for a lifestyle that lures quality students and faculty. "Most of us are recreation nuts, and within one hour of this place you have skiing, biking, and kayaking," says Ann Harris, director of the University of Washington's MBA program.

No wonder this school attracts an outdoorsy, rather diverse and mature crowd for a runner-up school. The average age of newcomers is 28, a full four years older than MBAs at the University of Illinois and two years older than Wisconsin's students. And the Class of 1994 ranges in age from a youthful 21 to a middle-aged 49. "Our students include everyone from a director of development from the San Francisco Ballet to the more traditional marketing manager from Microsoft," adds Harris.

The faculty here is a pretty good group, too. Many can boast of training from some of the world's leaders in business education, including Northwestern, Stanford, Chicago, Michigan, Columbia, Berkeley, and Rochester. Former Dean Robert S. Leventhal deserves credit for luring talented faculty to Seattle. During his five years as dean, Leventhal replaced about one of every four of the 100 full-time tenure-track teachers at the school. He retired in the summer of 1994, and the school is searching for a new dean.

Leventhal also left behind a revamped MBA curriculum, which began in the fall of 1993. The first-year core integrates the different disciplines of business, and places a greater emphasis on international business and ethics. Students are assigned to multidisciplinary teams which are used throughout the curriculum. MBAs also attend several sessions on professional skills, many taught by consultants who specialize in business training. Executives come to campus to share their expertise with students through Washington's new Conversations with Executives program.

In the second year, MBAs design their own program. In addition to the typical specialties, new programs include Environmental Management, International Management,

Entrepreneurship and Innovation, and Manufacturing Management. The Environmental Management Program has attracted the most attention and the most students—just what you'd expect from a business school in environmentally conscious Washington State.

In the first year, expect to be in class roughly four hours a day, Monday through Friday. Grads say you need to do about two hours of prep work before a class, plus another two hours of homework after it. Students are grouped into cores of 45 each and attend the required courses together. Washington uses a mix of lecture, case study, and seminars to deliver the business basics. The teaching quality in the core courses is nicely above the average, but it falls down a bit in the elective offerings, according to BUSINESS WEEK's survey of graduates of the top 40-plus schools. Most of the workload in the first year falls on the individual, while the second year tends to be dominated by group work. The school offers a menu of 90 electives, including some 25 offerings in accounting alone and about one dozen in marketing.

Washington claims that its environmental program, begun in 1991, is the first of its kind in the country. The program gives MBAs the chance to gain a certificate in environmental management by taking a sequence of three core courses in the subject as well as a pair of environmental or natural resource electives from the B-school and other university programs. Students work in small groups on actual management consulting projects dealing with environmental issues.

The international management fellows program provides students the chance to combine an MBA degree with advanced language study, indepth area study, and an overseas business internship. The school requires a minimum of two years of college-level instruction in Chinese, German, Japanese, or Spanish for applicants. After admission to the 24-month program, you'll show up for a brief orientation in June, then travel abroad for a crash language course covering business terms. Fellows return to Washington in the fall to begin the full-time MBA program. The summer and fall quarters of the second year are devoted to the overseas internship and study at a foreign university.

That's only for students who can tear themselves away from this beautiful locale. The University of Washington itself is in a park-like setting with a combination of classic old buildings and nicely styled new ones. Everywhere it's green. In the spring, cherry trees bloom along the main campus corridor. Around the east perimeter of the grounds are the shores of Lake Washington, the residence of the graduate sailing club. Looming in the background are the majestic Olympic and Cascade Mountains. Balmer Hall, a four-story stucco building housing the library and classrooms, and Mackenzie Hall, the faculty and administrative center, form the focus of the B-school on the upper campus. Lewis Hall, one of the two oldest historic buildings, houses the MBA career center. The school plans to break ground for a new building in 1995.

Outdoor activities are a major attraction. MBAs hike through the rain forest on the Olympic Peninsula or climb Mount Rainier. A fixture of MBA life here is the salmon bake—an event that has seen just 100 grads wolf down 40 pounds of fresh salmon barbecued on grills off the shores of Lake Washington. The Thursday evening ritual, dubbed TGIT (Thank God It's Thursday), sees most MBAs pick one of the several microbreweries in town in which to swill such tavern-brewed beers as Ballard Bitter, Pyramid, and Red

Hook. Nearly as popular as the local brew is the local espresso. MBAs like the outdoor porch of the Burke Museum for its potent coffee drinks. They also like to travel into Vancouver, British Columbia, for weekends, or to Portland. When in Seattle, you might live in the university's graduate housing, but most students reside off campus.

MBAs created what they call a Business Diagnostic Center in 1991 to volunteer their services to local businesses. Student teams solicit proposals from small companies and nonprofit organizations in and around Seattle, roll up their sleeves, and go to work. An example: MBAs drafted a new marketing plan for a nearby resort. It's been so successful that students can't meet the demand for their services, and in the fall of 1992 the school incorporated the center into the MBA program with credit and faculty supervision. One surprise outcome: Many internships and jobs are now coming out of what was once a voluntary initiative.

About 17 percent of the graduating class did not have a single job offer by commencement. The pickings were indeed slim: Those who had offers averaged only 1.44 each—the lowest of any of the 40-plus schools in the sample with the exception of Thunderbird.

In 1994, only 38 companies came to recruit on campus. To help offset the decline, Washington brought students to job fairs in Chicago and Los Angeles, where an additional 57 companies interviewed MBAs. "Companies would like to see a diverse group of students, but can no longer afford to go to a whole bunch of schools," says JoAnne Starr, a former Wharton staffer who now directs Washington's career business center. Major recruiters included Deloitte & Touche (10), Andersen Consulting (5), Hewlett-Packard (4), Intel (4), Ore-Ida Foods (3), Microsoft (2), and Weyerhaeuser (2).

Up to 65 percent of the students (about 40 percent enter the program from the area) stay here once they are handed their MBA degrees. And who can blame them? Chalk it up to the Rainier Factor.

Contact: Leighanne Harris, director of MBA program, 206-543-4660
Final application deadline: International: February 1, 1995; Domestic: March 1, 1995

Outstanding Faculty: *Robert C. Higgins* (****—finance), *Stepan E. Sefcik* (****—accounting), *David A. Gautschi* (***—marketing), *Charles Hill* (***—management), *Karma G. Hadjimichalakis* (**—finance), *Alan C. Hess* (**—finance), *Jennifer Lynch Koski* (finance), *Cecil H. Bell, Jr.* (management), *Anne Ilinitch* (management), *Pamela Ashley Posey* (strategy)

Washington MBAs Sound Off

Some of the best students and teachers come here because they want to be in Seattle. The problems are mostly related to facilities (not enough computers, classrooms, lounge space), but construction on a new building starts this summer. Also there are problems related to UW as a state school—the MBA program is great but other services can be a mixed bag, especially the financial aid office. The range of caliber of students and teachers is fairly wide—some of the very best and some not so good. —Consultant

The program provided a solid base in core business skills, but it lacked strong marketing classes. Students gained marketing skills through internships and their own initiatives. This school has great potential. The location, faculty, and students are outstanding, but it's impeded by the administration. We expect major changes with the new dean. —**Product Manager**

I was a member of the last class with a less integrated core. The class of 1995 has a much improved first year, with extensive integration and more focus on ethics, international business, and strategy. The most beneficial and surprising element of my experience was the cooperation and teamwork with other students.
—**Information Systems Career Path**

UW is a bargain, especially for Washington residents. Since many people come to the program to stay in the Northwest, UW has a reputation for being a tough place for national recruiters to come to. This is true to a certain extent, but it would help UW to attract better firms for recruiting. —**Accounting Career Path**

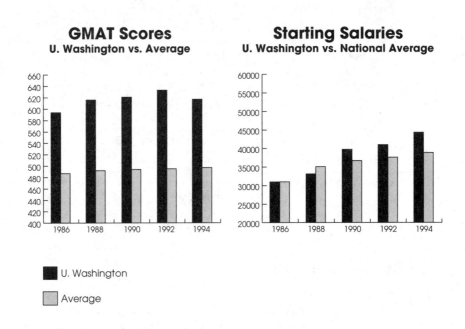

University of Wisconsin—Madison

School of Business
Grainger Hall
975 University Avenue
Madison, Wisconsin 53706

Enrollment: 544
Women: 34%
Non-U.S.: 26%
Minority: 17%
Part-time: None
Average age: 25
Average years of work exp.: 2.7
Applicants accepted: 50%
Median starting pay: $46,750

Annual tuition: resident—$4659
                  nonresident—$12,505
Room and board: $4810
Average GMAT score: 603
GMAT range: 420 to 730
Average GPA: 3.4
GPA range: 2.5 to 4.0
Accepted applicants enrolled: 45%
Average starting pay: $49,700

Teaching methods: Lecture, 65%   Case method, 30%   Projects, 5%

Here's a business school that moved into a new $40 million facility in the fall of 1993. Grainger Hall doubled the capacity of the B-school's computer labs, tripled the size of its library, and vastly expanded the public areas where students socialize and study. So why is this school the incredible shrinking MBA factory?

The University of Wisconsin's B-school has reduced the size of its MBA population by 25 percent, to 550 students from 800 in 1988—at the same time that many rival schools have gone in the opposite direction. Wisconsin adopted a different strategy in a bid to vastly increase the quality of its students and program. "To just hand out degrees when corporations are cutting back isn't right," says Dean Andrew J. Policano. "Business schools need to react to that by having a smaller number of students. The quality of education increases and the flexibility of innovation increases."

The strategy seems to be working. The average GMAT scores here have jumped by nearly 40 points since 1986, finally surpassing the 600 mark in 1992. Seven years ago, moreover, the whole admission process was far less personal. Wisconsin demanded no essays or résumés and did few interviews with applicants. These days a third of all potential MBA candidates are interviewed, and every one of them must write a well-organized essay describing why they want the degree and what they're able to bring to the program.

Policano arrived here as dean in 1991, raising the eyebrows of some because, at an annual salary of $165,000, he reportedly makes more money than the state's governor. A former economics professor who had been a dean at State University of New York at Stony Brook, he wants to make Wisconsin one of the top five public university business schools in the country. That won't be easy by BUSINESS WEEK's standards. He'll have to compete with the likes of UCLA, Berkeley, and the B-schools at the universities of Washington, Minnesota, and Texas at Austin. No wonder Policano is defining success by the fuzzy standards of "scholarly research, high-quality state-of-the-art educational programs, and service to the business, government, and not-for-profit communities."

Still, you have to give him credit for trying. Already, he's attempting to forge better ties with the local business community and become more responsive to their needs. Policano even led a team of faculty and administrators to Procter & Gamble to study the company's Total Quality Management initiatives. His local business contacts have led to what the dean calls "niche programs" in such areas as distribution management, logistics, manufacturing systems, and marketing channels. About half of Wisconsin's students are involved in these specialized programs, which equip MBAs with overall business skills combined with a high level of expertise in specific areas. Because these programs are small, students connected with them get lavish amounts of personal attention, career advice, and networking opportunities.

Like many other deans, he's also allocating more attention to international business. The school already had a required course in the subject taught by a faculty team, but now it is "globalizing" the entire curriculum. Wisconsin offers half a dozen electives on international issues. MBAs can also sign up for foreign language and culture classes outside the B-school. Each summer, MBAs can take advantage of a three-week intensive course abroad sponsored by the school's real estate department. In 1992, students trekked to Japan, Korea, and Hong Kong for lectures and study on real estate in the Pacific Rim. A year earlier, MBAs traveled to London and Paris. In 1993, they went to Latin America to visit with real estate developers, policymakers, and local academics and business leaders. There's also a summer-abroad program at a university in France.

You need 54 credits to gain the Wisconsin MBA, 39 of them consumed by required core courses. In half the courses, students are asked to work together in groups. "Teams can range from analyzing a case study to actually developing a new product," says Policano. A revamped core curriculum features four newly created courses that reflect the challenges of managing the twenty-first-century corporation: International Perspectives; Decision Information Systems; Political, Legal, and Ethical Environments and Innovation; and Technology Management. "In order for the United States to remain competitive, we are going to have to produce a different kind of manager," says Jack Nevin, former chairman of the marketing department. "Our new MBA program is a major change in that direction."

After completing the core, you'll have only 15 credits for advanced coursework unless you've been able to waive out of some classes. If you select a concentration in 1 of 11 areas of study, you could find yourself left with only two remaining electives. One out of every five MBAs majors in finance, while 17 percent of them enroll in a marketing concentration. The research orientation of the school's faculty hasn't helped the quality of teaching in either the core or the elective offerings. Of the 40-plus schools whose graduates were surveyed by BUSINESS WEEK, Wisconsin ranks below average in teaching quality.

Like its rival—Ann Arbor, Michigan—Madison is a liberal, cosmopolitan community. But there's no denying that Wisconsin is the land of beer, brats, and Badgers (the name of the school's sports teams). A popular MBA hangout is the Kollege Klub. When the weather warms, MBAs trek to the Memorial Union to drink beer and wine on the terrace overlooking Lake Mendota, a favorite spot for canoeing. Wisconsin is no UCLA, but a resort mentality prevails here during late spring and summer when temperatures climb to the eighties and nineties.

About 19 percent of the Class of 1994 failed to have a single job offer at commencement. And even the lucky ones weren't all that lucky: They averaged only 2 offers each—against an average of about 2.36 for the 40-plus schools whose graduates were surveyed by BUSINESS WEEK. Underlying these numbers, however, is a shift in recruiting practices by many brand-name corporations that has been especially felt by runners-up schools. "Today, employers are hiring just-in-time to fill positions that open up," says Karen Stauffacher, director of career services. "In the past, they hired in advance. MBA jobs were served on a silver platter."

Although some 115 companies came to campus in 1994 and tallied up 1078 interviews with MBA candidates, not many recruiters brought their silver platters with them. Only nine companies hired more than a single graduate of the school in 1992. They were Arthur Andersen & Co. (8), Oscar Mayer (5), Price Waterhouse (5), Andersen Consulting (4), Ford (3), KPMG Peat Marwick (3), Alexander & Alexander (2), Dane County (2); and UW—Madison (2). Rather than wait for companies to come to Wisconsin, Stauffacher is trying to bring more MBAs to them. The school annually brings students to job fairs in Chicago, New York, Atlanta, and San Francisco. But 52 percent of the graduating class remains in Wisconsin.

Policano doesn't expect any more cutbacks in the student population at Wisconsin. But his remaining students have found lots more room in his fancy new building.

Contact: Richard Miller, assistant dean of master's programs, 608-262-1555
Final application deadline: June 1 for fall

Outstanding Faculty: *Denis Collins* (***—ethics), *Peter Knez* (***—finance), *Robert Pricer* (***—entrepreneurship), *Peter Dacin* (**—marketing), *Anne Miner* (**—management), *J. Paul Peter* (**—marketing), *Joan Schmit* (risk management), *Dan Anderson* (risk management), *Mark Fedenia* (finance), *Alan Filley* (entrepreneurship)

Madison MBAs Sound Off

A key strength of the UW-Graduate B-school is the niche programs it offers. These programs include channels of distribution, real estate development, marketing research, applied finance (investments), fine arts administration, and health-care management. Courses in these areas are open to MBA students, in addition to students enrolled in the niche programs. The opportunity to tailor my MBA education to include courses in these areas provided me with a very broad business education that will serve me well in my future career. —**Assistant Brand Manager**

There is legitimate effort at diversity here; however, too much lip service and not enough results. I do not care for the teaching style here at all, because a lot of relevant information is thrown at you, not allowing for adequate time to properly absorb it. —**Staff Consultant**

*The admission criteria appear to be way too easy, based upon the intellectual level and seriousness of many of my classmates. The faculty and administration are not very concerned about improving the core MBA program. Instead they seem to give undue importance to niche programs, such as real estate and risk management. —**Health Care Consultant***

*The University of Wisconsin—Madison is a good school overall. The facilities in our new building are state-of-the-art. However, the university does not offer a great deal of hands-on experience. I think the theories taught are presented as best they could be by the professors; however, it would be nice to actually try to apply them in a real-world setting and not an academic one. I don't believe the mix between people with work experience and people without is very good here. Too many students come directly out of undergrad, and as a result are on a different level than the rest. I think for the cost of the education (as a resident of WI) it offers a lot, and for students right out of an undergraduate program it is a good school. But if money is not a problem and someone has work experience, it may make sense to go elsewhere. —**Senior Consultant***

*Career services is trying to improve their assistance to students—they provide better services for private searches. The companies that came on campus were not completely appealing. —**Financial Analyst***

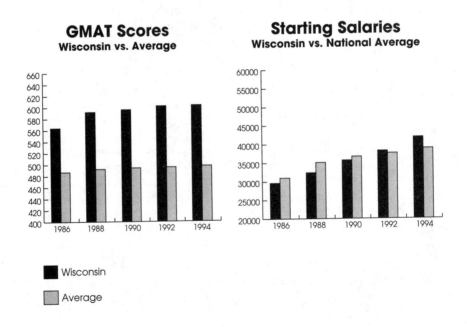

Vanderbilt University

Owen Graduate School of Management
401 Twenty-First Avenue South
Nashville, Tennessee 37203

Enrollment: 388
Women: 27%
Non-U.S.: 20%
Minority: 5%
Part-time: None
Average age: 26
Applicants accepted: 48%
Median starting pay: $52,500

Annual tuition & fees: $19,851
Room and board: $6950
Average GMAT score: 610
GMAT range: 420 to 750
Average GPA: 3.15
GPA range: 2.2 to 4.0
Accepted applicants enrolled: 44%
Average starting pay: $54,310

Teaching methods: Lecture, 60% Case study, 35% Group projects, 5%

Schools hovering near the bottom of BUSINESS WEEK's Top 20 ranking face a tough reality: They must continually improve just to stay still, or they will quickly tumble off the elite list. Sadly, Vanderbilt University's Owen School—which broke into the Top 20 for the first time in 1992, when it was ranked 19th—lost ground two years later.

The Class of 1994 was nearly caustic in its criticism of Dean Martin S. Geisel, a big, hulking academic with a Ph.D. from Chicago. Many MBAs believed he had failed to adequately manage a student scandal that erupted in 1994, when a student government officer allegedly embezzled about $3000 out of the treasury. Some grads thought Geisel should have either suspended the individual or withheld his degree. Instead the student was required to return the money and complete 100 hours of community service before gaining his degree.

To be fair, Geisel says his hands were somewhat tied by university policy and a need to keep the specifics of the case confidential. "My first reaction was, 'What a dumb thing to have done,'" says Dean Geisel. "But I also was disappointed in why the students couldn't place their trust in the university's established procedures to deal with this. Some students got highly agitated about it and thought the guy wasn't being punished at all." Add to those problems the fact that Owen received less support from the corporate sector in 1994. No wonder the school fell out of the Top 20.

Still, Geisel has brought the school national prominence since coming on-board in 1987. He hired 20 new faculty members, recruiting tenured profs with endowed chairs from several universities and real-world practitioners from admired companies such as Hewlett-Packard and Northern Telecom.

In the basic curriculum, he's also placed greater emphasis on communication skills and international business. No less interesting, the school has launched an entire sequence of courses in environmental management, customer service, service quality measurement, and response time and quality management—relatively new areas where management thinking is rapidly changing.

Owen only recently reached adulthood in the B-school world, having celebrated its twenty-first birthday in 1990. It is a school with a quirky history. The school was founded by local businessmen who wanted a quality regional school to keep Southerners at home and away from Harvard. The school is named after Ralph Owen, a star quarterback at Vanderbilt in the late 1920s and founder of Equitable Securities Corp. In the 1970s, the school became a victim of the counterculture, a place where encounter sessions and sensitivity training assumed more importance than basic accounting and finance. At that time, when international enrollment at B-schools was minuscule, up to 40 percent of the students were foreign. The university's Board of Trust came within one vote of shutting it down in 1975. Instead, Owen found a new dean who began to build a more middle-of-the-road business school. Dean Geisel, who once taught economics at Carnegie Mellon and the University of Rochester, installed his changes on top of what had become a rather basic, but quality MBA program.

He had a lot going for him. One pleasant surprise is the lack of undergraduate students. The full-time MBA program is not only the flagship program, it's basically the only program, other than an Executive MBA. There are no business undergrads and no part-time students at Owen. So MBAs don't have to share or fight with others for quality time with the faculty or the staff in the computing lab or the library. The 10-to-1 student-faculty ratio, one of the lowest among the top B-schools, assures lots of attention anyway. Everything occurs in Management Hall, a modern red-brick and plate-glass building merged with Old Mechanical, one of the oldest structures on the 300-acre campus.

Owen starts you off in late August with a five-day orientation period, which includes sessions on career planning and an Outward Bound-like group problem-solving and team-building experience. The groups used during orientation are deliberately formed to maximize diversity, and students remain in these groups for various purposes through the first year of the program. First-years are divided into three sections, though the typical cohort system at larger MBA factories does not apply here. The small size of the school does not require it.

The school will march you through 12 core courses, including a required three-credit communications class that stretches over the first two semesters. The course features self-assessment tests, then aims to build a communications program to help address a student's weak points. Owen made the class a requirement after alumni urged the school during a curriculum review to put more emphasis on oral and written presentations and negotiation skills. You can waive out of the lecture-dominated core classes, but must substitute electives in their place. You can pick up to five graduate courses outside the business school, including study of a foreign language. A total of 21 courses are required to graduate.

It's telling that the areas of marketing and operations management boast as many or more electives as finance and accounting—the mainstays of every business school. Some grads grouse that Owen's finance classes tend to lack enough real-world application. Far stronger, they say, are the school's offerings in both marketing and operations. Owen probably offers the most extensive curriculum in service quality at any MBA program. Among its 15 marketing electives is a mini-sequence in services that begins with Customer Service and the Customer Orientation, taught by Roland Rust. Organized around the Baldrige Award criteria, the course is an intro to service quality and relationship management. The second course is a Services Internship in which students complete work projects for such companies as AT&T, Northern Telecom, Federal Express, NationsBank, and others for academic credit. That's followed by Service Quality Measurement, a seminar-like course taught by Rich Oliver. The course teaches MBAs the nuts and bolts of how to measure service quality and the psychology of customer satisfaction.

Among the 75 or so elective standouts is the Seminar on Trade and Industrial Competitiveness. The course kicks off with six weeks of classes, then students are divided into teams which go off to a foreign locale during the spring vacation to study some aspect of international business. Over the years, students have trekked to Japan, Europe, Mexico, and Latin America. In 1994, the group toured São Paulo, Brazil, and Buenos Aires, Argentina. Other than pocket change, students don't have to pay for these excursions because the costs are underwritten by sponsoring companies. Owen has also recently launched a new international elective on Global Competitiveness taught by the retired CEO of Northern Telecom, Edmund Fitzgerald, and another on current U.S.—Japan Relations.

Just about everyone—students and faculty alike—lives within a five-mile radius of the school. Most graduate students share off-campus apartments that can be rented for $600 a month. The San Antonio Taco Co., across the street from the B-school, is the number-one hangout for MBAs, who go there for buckets of beer on ice and Mexican fare. Only one block away, students converge on Granite Falls, a well-known meeting place for hamburgers, salads, and singles. The campus itself is on the fringe of the inner city, about two and a half miles from downtown Nashville. Of course there's Opryland USA and Graceland, which everyone visits once. A more regular event is the "Keg in the Courtyard" on Thursdays at 5 p.m. after which it's time for the "Larry Tate Society," a diehard group which moves to a local bar once the keg is drained. The "society" takes its name from the advertising exec on the TV show *Bewitched*. Thank goodness there are no classes on Friday.

Students, including those from abroad, find Nashville a welcoming locale. In the home of country music you don't have to look hard to find anything, from home-cooked Southern meals to gourmet dining, or from hole-in-the-wall bluegrass joints to slightly pretentious supper clubs. Though the city is hardly a corporate center, it is home base to a few national companies, including Hospital Corporation of America, Genesco, and Aladdin Industries.

As a newcomer among the top schools, however, Vanderbilt's program is still in an improving mode. The alumni base is thin. (Indeed the notes describing the doings of grads cover only four or five pages in *The Owen Manager,* even though the alumni magazine is published only twice a year.) The small size of the school also prevents it from offering a truly broad selection of electives. More importantly, Owen students tend to be on the young side, with less full-time experience.

Like most second-tier business schools, which get less traffic from the high-paying consulting and investment banking firms, Vanderbilt's placement record isn't going to make any headlines. About 12.3 percent of the Class of 1994 failed to have a single job offer at graduation. Those that did walked away with only 1.78 job offers each, under the 2.36 average for the top 40-plus schools in BUSINESS WEEK's survey.

Owen claims that 144 companies recruited second-year students on campus in 1994, conducting 2350 interviews. Another 160 jobs were posted via correspondence. The major employers: Deloitte & Touche (4), Northern Telecom (4), Morgan Keegan Investment

Bank (4), Goldman Sachs (3), M&M/Mars (3), Andersen Consulting (3), RJR/Nabisco (2), Bankers Trust (2), Boston Consulting Group (2), and Price Waterhouse (2).

To get the school back on track, Dean Geisel will have to gain ground with the corporate recruiting community and pay more attention to his students.

Contact: Joel Covington, director of MBA program, 615-322-4076
Final application deadline: June 1 for fall

Outstanding Faculty: *William G. Christie* (****—finance), *Craig M. Lewis* (***—finance), *Anthony Zahorik* (***—marketing), *Nancy Lea Hyer* (**—operations), *Joseph D. Blackburn, Jr.* (**—operations), *Richard L. Oliver* (**—marketing), *Ronald W. Masulis* (finance), *David Rados* (marketing), *Hans R. Stoll* (finance), *Richard L. Daft* (management)

Owen MBAs Sound Off

Owen would step to the next level if the school had an effective dean. Our current dean has absolutely no concept of student desires. He strictly manages by committee, without the involvement of students. **—Entrepreneur**

The school suffers from being a great regional school but unknown elsewhere. For those of us who do not want to work in the Southeast, recruiting is a big problem. **—Marketing Career Path**

Placement could do more to attract recruiters from all over the country. Other negatives include a sometime bureaucratic administration, a questionable tenure policy, and a somewhat elitist finance staff outlook. **—Marketing Career Path**

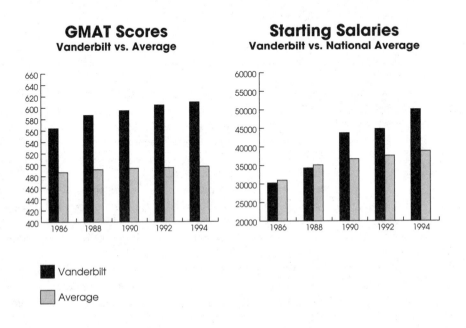

GMAT Scores
Vanderbilt vs. Average

Starting Salaries
Vanderbilt vs. National Average

■ Vanderbilt
▨ Average

Washington University

John M. Olin School of Business
Campus Box 1133
One Brookings Drive
St. Louis, Missouri 63130

Enrollment: 647
Women: 27%
Non-U.S.: 16%
Minority: 12%
Part-time: 348
Average age: 26
Applicants accepted: 482
Median starting pay: $50,000

Annual tuition & fees: $18,350
Room and board: $9000
Average GMAT score: 608
GMAT range: 420 to 760
Average GPA: 3.14
GPA range: 2.25 to 4.0
Accepted applicants enrolled: 37%
Average starting pay: $53,400

Teaching methods: Lecture, 55%   Case study, 30%   Group projects, 15%

Only a few years ago, BUSINESS WEEK likened Washington University's Olin School of Business to a hit record listed on the Billboard charts with a bullet. Then, in 1992, the school climbed into the Top 20 for the first time ever. Olin failed to maintain the momentum, however, and slipped out of the golden list in 1994.

The school has effectively been without a full-time, active dean since March of 1992, when Robert L. Virgil left the job to become the university's executive vice-chancellor. Virgil, who built this school into a top-ranked contender over his 16 years as dean, has since left the university entirely. His absence from Olin, as well as the university's failure to name a permanent successor, has dealt a serious setback to this B-school's reputation.

For one thing, the Class of 1994 was highly critical of the school's decision not to tenure several of its best professors—including two of Olin's top three teachers, or three out of the best ten. That's just about the worst retention record of best profs of any of the major schools in the past two years. It's also an unforgivable detraction from the quality of the program, in a day when most schools are paying far more attention to teaching quality than ever before. Without a permanent dean to promote the school and its students, Olin also lost significant ground to competitors in BUSINESS WEEK's corporate recruiter survey.

No wonder Olin lost its Top 20 status. However, this school still has a lot going for it. It remains a vastly improved, albeit lacking, MBA program, backed by a hefty endowment raised by former Dean Virgil. The most visible sign of the school's success is its home. Built in 1986, the modern $13.5 million John E. Simon Hall is the largest single building on Wash U's Hilltop campus. Inspired by the architecture of the universities of Oxford and Cambridge, the school is housed in a slate-roofed building of red granite trimmed with limestone. The first-floor classrooms look out on an enclosed courtyard, a favorite gathering area. It's a far cry from the old B-school home in Prince Hall, originally built as a dormitory for the Olympic athletes for the 1904 track and field games. Its halls were so narrow that students often had to walk through them sideways.

Even though Virgil has long gone, the school hasn't been completely without a leader. Acting Dean Lyn Pankoff, a grandfatherly statistics professor, has overseen what the school calls a "substantially reorganized curriculum" in the fall of 1994. The changes increased the emphasis on organizational behavior and strategy, human behavior, management, and the politics and power in organizations. While many schools have dropped macroeconomics from their core curriculums, Olin improved the required course by adding more material on international trades and capital flows. In addition, students can now select an elective course in the spring semester of their first year.

In the first year, incoming MBA candidates are divided into two sections of about 70 students each. The business basics are taught in classes that generally meet between 8:30 a.m. and 1 p.m. on Monday and Wednesday or Tuesday and Thursday. On afternoons, students study alone or in groups, participate in clubs, and attend the career management series held by the placement folks. Fridays are free. In class, you'll find yourself moving through what Olin calls a "modular schedule." Translation: Different core classes vary in length, a central feature of most B-school curriculum overhauls. You can waive some of these classes by exam, and you can also take evening courses designed for part-timers if you prefer.

Unlike the first year, which is fairly rigid, students pick eight classes of their choice during the second year. The school offers 46 electives in an average academic year, though you can take up to 25 percent of your total workload at other university departments. Indeed, you can even study a foreign language outside the B-school for credit as long as it's at the graduate level. A central feature of the second-year curriculum is the "Tycoon Game" played in the first semester in conjunction with Olin's strategy course. It's the same management simulation game played out by Dartmouth MBAs (see the profile on the Amos Tuck School for more details). Another major annual event is the John M. Olin Cup Competition, in which student teams make presentations to local and national business leaders on a topic of importance to American business.

Among the most popular electives is a "practicum" in which four-student teams work as consultants with a faculty supervisor on a problem facing a sponsoring company. Students gain three credits and up to $750 for their work. The sponsoring organizations, which have included Apple Computer, Ford Motor, and Monsanto, pay a fee of $10,000 to ensure their interest in working with students and implementing their solutions. "The goal is to affect an organization, not to just do a study," says Russell Roberts, a young, gung-ho prof who directs Olin's Management Center. In 1994, Olin students did a regional market analysis of the Probe and Mustang cars for Ford Motor Co., to determine if the new Mustang would harm the sales of its sporty and successful Probe model.

The Management Center, which administers this and other programs, is a key part of the Olin School's strategy to put more "experiential learning" into the MBA program. The Practicum, which was launched in 1991–1992 with only 10 projects, is expected to become a critical element in the changes. Roberts, a self-styled "educational entrepreneur," hopes to have 40 of them a year with as many as 160 students involved in teams. But he's also in charge of a spate of nontraditional programs to make the Olin experience more real-world. Another example: Roberts, recruited from UCLA, put together a nonprofit consulting program in which student teams work with local nonprofit agencies from the Catholic Charities to the St. Louis Food Bank. For the latter, MBA students reorganized warehouse operations, improving among other things the timing and delivery of trucks carrying food. The 10-day project at the end of the first year MBA program is a one-credit elective.

There's also the "Close Encounter" and the "Friday Free-for-All." The former brings together business leaders and students for informal but substantive discussions. Each session is limited to 20 students, chosen on the basis of questions they submit about the speaker or the speaker's company. Encounters have brought the chief executives or chief financial officers of Procter & Gamble, NEC Corp., Motorola, and Pet Inc. to campus. "Free-for-Alls," meantime, are meant to provoke informal debates among students and faculty on topical business issues. Roberts hands out a small packet of readings to students in advance of the meetings and then sparks the discussion. They've covered such topics as: Quality—Who Is This Deming Guy? and Why Does Business Provide Health Care Benefits? The Social Responsibility of Business Is to Make Profits!

These are important additions to the school's MBA program and its overall ambience. Like most smaller programs, Olin can't provide the breadth of course offerings that larger institutions routinely offer. The school has only 9 finance electives, for example, compared to more than 40 at New York University. And even though finance is almost always the strongest area at most business schools, several graduates at Olin have been disappointed with both the quality and quantity of the school's finance professors and courses.

There's an informality and friendliness here that's hard to find at large or urban schools. Even though MBAs share the facilities with undergrads and a larger part-time program, full-timers describe the atmosphere as small and close-knit. Every Friday, the FAC (Friday Afternoon Club) brings together MBAs and faculty for a keg party to swap stories and jokes. "It's a great chance to sit down and have a beer with one of your favorite teachers," says one graduate.

MBAs hang out at Krueger's because of its amiable bartenders, and Murphy's, where the beer is cheap. There are no dorms or graduate housing, so all the students live within four or five miles of the campus in apartments and shared homes throughout the metropolitan St. Louis area.

What about the placement situation? About 11.6 percent of the Class of 1994 failed to have job offers at graduation. The lucky ones reported 2.6 offers each, much better than the 1.5 average in 1992 although just a tad above the current 2.37 for the top 40-plus schools. Olin reports that 90 companies came on campus to recruit second-year students, doing 1500 interviews. Another 746 job opportunities came through the mail. The major employers: Ernst & Young (7); Emerson Electric (5); Procter & Gamble (4); Deloitte & Touche (3); Andersen Consulting (2); Barnes-Jewish-Christian (2); Exxon (2); National Starch & Chemical (2); Ralston Purina (2); and Spectrum Group (2).

Contact: Ron Van Fleet, director of admissions, 314-935-7301
Final application deadline: March 30 for fall

Outstanding Faculty: *Dean H. Kropp* (****—operations), *Russell Roberts* (****—economics), *Marcia K. Armstrong* (***—marketing), *Mahendra Gupta* (***—accounting),

Nicholas Baloff (*—organizational behavior), *Chung-Lun Li* (*—management science), *William P. Bottom* (organizational behavior), *Srinivasan Maheswaran* (finance), *Martin K. Sneider* (marketing), *Siddhartha Chib* (economics)

Olin MBAs Sound Off

The school is struggling to determine where it should go. A dean needs to be found soon, and many students are upset with decisions not to tenure two former teachers of the year. —**Consultant**

Like many other students I have been frustrated with the apathy of the administration, as evidenced by its lack of response to student concerns. Moreover, I have found the incentive system for teachers here to be unduly complex. Tenure is granted here "only if the faculty member could be tenured at the University of Chicago." Unfortunately, the inevitable outcome of such a policy is a faculty with low morale that generally cannot devote more than cursory attention to students. In sum, Olin often leaves me with the impression that it is long on pretensions and short on substance. —**Finance Career Path**

An appropriate tenure system must be put in place. If Matt Pincus, Chris Lamoureaux, Steve Lawrence, and Jim Hess were still going to teach at the Olin School, my marks on the survey for teaching quality would have been all 10's. —**Consultant**

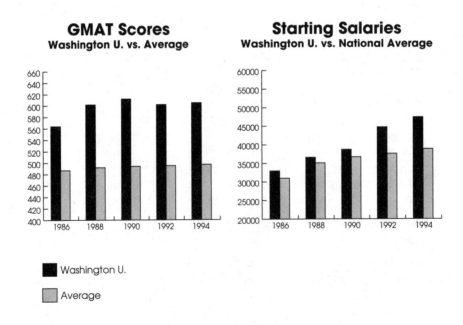

GMAT Scores
Washington U. vs. Average

Starting Salaries
Washington U. vs. National Average

■ Washington U.

▨ Average

Yale University

School of Organization and Management
Box 1A
New Haven, Connecticut 06520

Enrollment: 445
Women: 33%
Non-U.S.: 34%
Minority: 12%
Part-time: None
Average age: 27.5
Applicants accepted: 36%
Median starting pay: $70,000

Annual tuition & fees: $20,990
Room and board: $7560
Average GMAT score: 656
GMAT range: 530 to 790
Average GPA: 3.3
GPA range: 2.3 to 4.0
Accepted applicants enrolled: 51%
Average starting pay: $74,030

Teaching methods: Lecture, 60%   Case study, 30%   Group projects, 10%

A little joke has been simmering in conversations around the Yale campus. It goes something like this: If the Yale School of Management ran itself as well as it manages the SOM dining hall, Yale would be ranked closer to Harvard than the University of Hartford's B-school. Indeed, SOM operates the most efficient food system on campus, complete with full-service grill, sandwich shop, and drink stand. The offerings are so diverse, in fact, that many undergraduates make the 15-minute trek up Prospect Street for lunch.

Unfortunately the school does not, and has rarely, run itself as smoothly and efficiently as its dining hall. Although SOM has survived what administrators call "The Time of Troubles," which lasted from 1989 to 1991, the school still sits at a crossroads. Applications, which hit a peak of 1622 in 1989, fell to a 15-year low of 1134 for the Class of 1995, forcing SOM to accept a surprisingly high 42 percent of applicants. Even worse, more than half of the candidates given acceptances turned Yale down, preferring to go elsewhere. The school says this downward trend was finally reversed in 1994, though the numbers hardly give cause for celebration.

While most top business schools typically outperform their universities in national rankings, SOM is a classic underachiever. Though Yale generally ranks among the top three national universities with Harvard and Princeton, its business school has failed to make our Top 20 list since 1988, largely because graduates were unhappy about a change in the program's focus and because the school lacks much corporate support. Embarrassingly, one of the university's own economics professors ranked SOM 63rd out of 63 schools studied, in a novel B-school ranking published in 1994. The study—dubbed "nonsense" by Dean Paul MacAvoy—rated schools by the value they add to students' earning power.

More importantly, however, the university has failed to find a replacement for MacAvoy, whose two-year interim stint expired in June of 1994. One of the school's original founders, MacAvoy has promised to stay on until a successor is named, but he admits that it could take a long time to find a new dean. "What are the chances of convincing [someone] to be dean when the long-term prospects are bleak?" asks MacAvoy.

Bleak? By MacAvoy's reckoning, SOM severely lacks the resources to become a major B-school player. One of the few schools without revenue-producing executive programs, Yale has two times less endowment money per student than other 1960s and 1970s B-school startups such as Duke, Cornell, and Georgetown. "Yale's completely on the cheap in its capital allocation to SOM," says MacAvoy. "We need another $75 to $100 million to survive long-term." That kind of money isn't likely to come from the university, which is suffering a $12 million budget shortfall of its own for 1994–95.

The upshot: SOM has been unable to increase the size of its 42-member faculty and 210-member classes. "We can't continue to operate with 13 full-time professors [who teach only at SOM] at a rate of 200-plus students per year," says MacAvoy. "That ratio doesn't work." Overburdened with heavy workloads, professors tend to agree with the dean. "We have too small, too lean a faculty," says finance professor Stephen Ross, a 15-year SOM veteran. "We need to grow to a size that makes us more comparable to the great schools."

MacAvoy hopes that a rich donor who went to Yale College and then continued at an older, richer MBA program will earmark hundreds of millions of dollars in funds from the current university campaign for SOM. With such support, the school could "bring an executive education program to New York" and "double the size of its faculty," says MacAvoy. "I believe Yale will do it [make the program into a national powerhouse] in spite of itself."

That seems a long shot. Yet the cloudy long-term picture is unfortunate, because SOM has put together a pretty good program. The school continues to draw some of the most qualified MBA candidates in the country. And their average GMAT score—656 for the class of 1996—is among the highest of the Top 20 schools. What they now find when they come to campus is a more traditional B-school program with a heavy emphasis on economics and finance—the still-controversial legacy of former Dean Michael Levine, who gutted large parts of the organizational faculty in the late eighties and early nineties. In 1994, MacAvoy pulled off a major coup by luring finance guru Ken French from Dartmouth's Amos Tuck School. To get French aboard, however, the dean had to give him an especially sweet deal, requiring French to teach only two classes his first year. MacAvoy retorts that French will carry a full teaching load in his second year, be on campus three to four times a week, and launch a new finance center at Yale.

Despite the change in focus, Yale has not forgotten its dual public-private mission. SOM graduates still receive a Master's in Public and Private Management, not an MBA. In almost every class, students gain perspectives in both areas: 5 of the 13 case studies in one marketing class are from the public or nonprofit sector. At most schools, you'd get one or two public-sector cases in a class, at best. In the mid-to-late 1980s, roughly 50 percent of the students came from public or nonprofit jobs, with little or no business training or experience. These candidates have fallen to about a third of the student population today. Still, SOM boasts a substantial internship fund, to encourage students to forgo lucrative summer job opportunities in investment banking and consulting for work in Third World countries and charities. SOM grads who accept more traditional internships donate a fixed amount, or 3 percent, of their summer earnings to support these classmates.

MacAvoy also hasn't tampered with the noncompetitive culture of the school. Grading is pass/fail, and almost nobody flunks out. There's no grading curve, no rank in class, and no honors grade. The curriculum remains true to SOM's vision of melding private business training with broader views of the public and nonprofit sectors to groom leaders who can move comfortably from Wall Street to Washington and back. In the first year, students take eight core courses, along with a two-semester sequence entitled "Perspectives on Organization and Management." The course brings in business executives, consultants, and others as guests, to spur real-world discussion and debate on the more theoretical foundation laid down in the core courses.

In the second year, SOM grads choose from six to eight team-taught sessions of a course called Analysis of Institutions that examines such issues as health care, control systems, and bargaining relationships. Each class of no more than 35 students is taught by two teachers from different disciplines—an early format of Yale's program that had been set aside. In the recent past they have studied varied topics, such as Managing the AIDS Epidemic, Corporate Governance, and the Market for Corporate Control. To finish out their requirements, students choose at least seven electives, including two from the same area of management.

Business Week's most recent B-school surveys show that the class of 1994 is a satisfied bunch—a dramatic departure from two years ago, when grads trashed the school and speculated about its closing. Yale grads say that the finance, nonprofit, and consulting strategies professors are top-notch. They are much less enthusiastic about profs in the other departments—especially marketing, which failed to place a single teacher among the Top 10 at the school (see "Outstanding Faculty" listing).

The students are a diverse lot, an odd mix of smart, slightly offbeat types. Four out of five SOM students live in Yale's "graduate student ghetto," a square-mile enclave of lovely old Victorian homes broken into apartments. The neighborhood is a 15-minute walk from the cluster of low-rise buildings of metal and glass—dubbed Pizza Huts—that dot the landscape across from Science Hill. Most foreign students end up in university dorms during their first year in the program. The bars of choice are Humphrey's, Bar, and Toads. Many students spend Thursday nights at the Gypsy, an on-campus graduate student bar and notorious pick-up place. The weekends begin early at Yale, because there are no classes on Friday.

A constant concern is the placement operation. In 1994, only 41 companies came on campus to recruit Yale's second-year students. Roughly 95 percent of the class boasted job offers by graduation, much lower than peer institutions although a big improvement from 1993, when only 55 percent had offers. Who hired the largest number? CS First Boston (7), Booz Allen & Hamilton (6), McKinsey (4), and Arthur D. Little (3) topped the list in 1994.

Nonetheless, if the school is to run as smoothly as its popular dining hall, SOM needs to name a new dean who can revitalize this program and assure its long-term viability. The job of turning around this troubled institution is far from over.

Contact: Richard Silverman, director of admissions, 203-432-5932
Final application deadline: March 30 for fall

Outstanding Faculty: *Sharon Oster* (****—management & entrepreneurship), *Arthur Swersey* (****—operations research), *Roger Ibbotson* (***—finance), *Ed Kaplan* (***—public management), *Victor Vroom* (**—organizational behavior), *Jonathan E. Ingersoll, Jr.* (**—finance), *Steven Ross* (economics & finance), *Richard R. Lindsey* (finance), *Barry Nalebuff* (management science), *Jonathan Feinstein* (economics)

Yale MBAs Sound Off

*The major complaint I have about the school concerns the career development office. I received more helpful information and contacts from alumni and friends than I did from career development. —**Finance Career Path***

*If you come to Yale wanting to study M.I.S., operations management, or entrepreneurship, you're going to be disappointed. People come to Yale for finance, consulting, and nonprofit programs. SOM is too small to be all things for all people. —**Consultant***

*The noncompetitive grading system not only fosters teamwork but also encourages you to take the classes (the ones in which you really need to improve) without worrying about grade-point averages. —**Consultant***

*Although I believe our Career Development Office needs considerable work, its task in bringing companies to campus that appeal to our broad student body is a difficult one. We simply do not have the critical mass of students that the other schools can offer. —**Consultant***

*SOM has its problems. Particularly because of the turbulence surrounding the Levine years, the school is still hammering out its identity; still tinkering with the curriculum and its mission. —**Career Path Unknown***

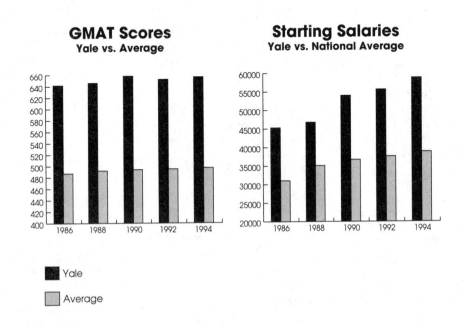

CHAPTER **8**

THE BEST BUSINESS SCHOOLS OUTSIDE THE UNITED STATES

It's hard to have a chat with either a senior executive or a business school dean these days without at least a mention of *the* word: *global.* We routinely speak about the global economy and the global corporation. What about the global business school? Is an international gloss on an MBA an asset or a liability with corporate recruiters?

American business schools are feverishly pumping more "international" material into their programs, creating more opportunities for students and faculty to study abroad. But they also face growing competition from non-U.S. institutions that are aggressively expanding as interest in all things international widens. Many of these B-schools located abroad are truly global, with a more diverse mix of cultures and nationalities among faculty and students. As a prospective business school student shopping for the right place to collect the MBA, you might ask: Should I go to a business school outside of the United States?

Already, some of these institutions are attracting foreign MBA students who in an earlier era flocked to the United States. And some observers believe that they could begin to grab their fair share of quality American MBA applicants. If you're interested in getting an MBA outside the United States, there's a staggering range of business schools from which to choose. The programs they offer vary as greatly as their geographic locations. You can get an advanced degree in business at schools in Nigeria, Thailand, or Bangladesh. At INSEAD, based in Fontainebleau, France, you can pick up an MBA in just 10 and a half months at what is the best non-U.S. business school in the world. At England's classy Cambridge University, it would take you as long as three years.

All told, as many as 250 institutions outside the United States offer a master's degree in business. In Canada alone, more than two dozen institutions compete with Ontario's Western Business School and the University of Toronto's B-school for the honors of offering the best in that country. About 24 MBA factories have sprouted up in Australia, while another two dozen are scattered throughout Asia. They include Tokyo's International University of Japan, the National University of Singapore, or Bangkok's SASIN Graduate Institute of Business Administration in Thailand. A number have also blossomed where communism has failed in Budapest, Warsaw, and Prague.

By far, however, Europe boasts the greatest concentration of business schools outside the United States. For many years, the American MBA degree had been derided as crass in Europe. In recent years, a shift in attitude has rippled through the European continent: Management education has become respected as a way to train managers and accelerate careers. The supply of MBAs stamped in Europe has more than doubled since 1987 to about 7000 annually. Though that's only one-tenth of the MBAs produced by the United States, the increase in the past five years demonstrates how popular the degree has become.

To satisfy the high demand, European schools have been opening up the gates of enrollment. INSEAD, for example, has boosted enrollment by more than 40 percent, to 460 students in the past five years. London Business School plans to up its enrollment by nearly 45 percent, to 600 MBA candidates by 1995. And new business schools have been popping up all over the world at both world-famous universities and obscure institutes. The number of MBA programs in the United Kingdom has doubled in five years. Cambridge University's three-year MBA program only debuted in October 1991. Oxford University plans to get into the game with a traditional two-year MBA in 1995. That elitist Oxbridge would choose to launch MBA programs is perhaps the best testament to the degree's cachet. "We're delighted with Oxford and Cambridge," says Jean-Pierre Salzmann, an official at INSEAD. "They're adding to the image of an MBA education."

Ironically, American business schools are contributing to the boom abroad. The deans of many U.S. B-schools have been jetting around the world, inking cooperative pacts to help fledgling institutions get off the ground. They've also been anxious to sign agreements to allow for faculty and student exchanges. Indeed, such exchange deals have been touted by many American deans as proof that they are working hard to internationalize their MBA programs. New York University's Stern School of Business now boasts exchange programs with 21 non-U.S. schools, 14 in Europe. London Business School alone has exchange agreements with 27 institutions, many of them in the United States.

U.S. B-Schools versus European B-Schools

Besides the obvious differences in location and culture, there are less obvious disparities between the American pioneers in business education and their relatively new upstarts overseas. U.S. business schools, for example, have traditionally been stronger in nuts-and-bolts technical skills, while their European counterparts have tended to emphasize softer skills. "The European curriculum has never been as quantitative as North America," says George Bain, principal of the London Business School.

That's certainly true from the students' point of view. Stefanie Lynn Smith, a Wharton MBA who went to LBS for a term on an exchange program, says that London paid far more attention to strategic issues than technical skills. She also believed that London devoted more class time to integrating the various business disciplines, from accounting to marketing. "It was perfectly normal to discuss management issues during a marketing class or operational issues during a class on international corporations," says Smith, who now works as a consultant at Grant Thornton in New York.

Another key difference: European schools have long had close ties with business. Lacking the huge endowments of many American institutions, the Europeans were forced to put greater emphasis on executive education. "We had to be much closer to our customer," Bain insists. Because senior executives are likely to be more demanding than MBA students, he also believes that European schools had to put more weight on teaching excellence than most U.S. schools. Still, the vast number of curriculum overhauls in the United States is narrowing such differences. These days, one U.S. business school after another is emphasizing softer skills at the same time that many European schools are urging their faculties to do more academic research.

Some even argue that INSEAD may very well be the ideal model of a modern business school, on the verge of replacing the best American institutions at the cutting edge. "That bodes ill for U.S. schools," says Terry Williams, senior partner and former director of recruiting at McKinsey & Co., the world's most prestigious management consulting firm. He notes that from his firm's perspective, European business schools are highly competitive with American ones. The "dirty little secret" of business schools, adds Williams, is that their quality depends more on the students than the faculty. "Harvard Business School has proven able to attract very good students, and INSEAD is attracting the best and brightest in Europe. I see no difference in the quality of students at these two institutions."

Things to Consider Before Applying Abroad

So what are the pros and cons for prospective MBA students? If you live in the United States and strongly desire an international experience, then schooling abroad is the right choice. The chance to fully immerse yourself in another culture is the chief advantage. No American business school, no matter what it contends in a marketing brochure about being global or international, can duplicate the wonderful experience of living in a different country where Americans are a minority. It enhances your ability to handle cultural differences, a soft skill that may be useful in management. It broadens your perspective in ways that will make you more mature and more experienced. It will significantly add to your ability to speak a different language. And it will give you an appreciation for all things different and foreign. As Bain of the London Business School puts it, "You get two learning experiences: business and culture. The second is almost free. It's something you experience. It's always a useful experience to do one or two degrees in your own country and to go do another degree elsewhere."

If you badly want to work abroad, a non-U.S. school again may be the right choice. Even though there are no guarantees, an MBA from a prestigious school located abroad will enhance your opportunities to get hired by a foreign company or one of the overseas outposts of an American multinational. At INSEAD, 36 percent of its MBA graduates get a job in a country different from the one they worked in before joining the school. Some 32 percent work in a country other than their nation of origin. But non-European Community members must remember that their employers have to get them work permits before they can work in any country in Europe. In some cases, that can pose a formidable barrier.

From an American perspective, the allure of a non-U.S. degree may have a down side. You'll probably pay more for the MBA. Your job search will be far more complicated. And if you return to the United States, you'll likely find that the degree could lose much of its cachet. After all, how many American companies have heard about the International Institute for Management Development in Lausanne, Switzerland? Yet, it's one of the more established, prestige institutions granting the MBA. Alumni networks at most of these schools are limited at best. You're not going to find too many alums from the Copenhagen Business School in Chicago or L.A.

Choosing a foreign setting for your degree may also be quite a luxury. The cost of tuition, room and board, and travel is likely to be substantially higher than in the United States. Fewer loans and other financial aid are available. Just 10 months at INSEAD runs more than $24,000, not including the sizable expense of living in Fontainebleau, France, or the airplane tickets to get you there and back a couple of times. You can get a two-year MBA from Northwestern University's Kellogg School for $13,000 more.

What you gain in the "international" diversity of the student population at a non-U.S. business school is often lost by the paucity of minority students in these schools. Many of the prestige foreign institutions are far more class-conscious and overtly elitist than their U.S. rivals. Some of them don't even grasp the concept of minority representation. And what's truly international to some, of course, isn't terribly global to others. By many standards, some of the top American business schools are far more international than they are given credit for. Consider MIT's Sloan School: Roughly one-third of the 105 full-time faculty hails from abroad, and 35 percent of the students are non-U.S., from 47 different countries. By either faculty or student standards, that's far more global than you'd get at the London Business School, where 7 out of every 10 professors are British and 1 out of every 4 students is from Great Britain alone. The American Graduate School of International Management, known simply as Thunderbird, in a suburb of Phoenix, Arizona, has established a strong reputation as a global school. In any given class, you'll find students from more than 60 countries, and every graduate of the school must be proficient in a second language.

Yet Another Option for an International Experience

Another option tries to capture the best of both worlds: Go to an American business school that offers exchange programs with foreign institutions. This route can get you the clout of an American MBA while giving you a taste of living abroad. You won't get the chance to really soak up a foreign culture in a single semester, but you also won't need to scramble feverishly for a job. And few people in the United States or elsewhere will question your decision to get an MBA from Northwestern, Chicago, Michigan, or Wharton.

Smith, who went to LBS for 10 weeks while pursuing her Wharton MBA, has no regrets about her decision. Indeed, she enjoyed her experience so much that she thought, "Maybe I should have gone here the whole time." Wharton seemed more obvious, however. She was 24 years old with public-sector experience when she enrolled at the University of Pennsylvania's B-school. "I went to business school to learn about business," says Smith. "If I had worked in an American corporation for six years, I would have gone abroad."

With the sole exception of the Harvard Business School, every Top 20 B-school in the United States has at least one exchange program. New York University leads the pack with 20 options, while Stanford offers only one—its own program in Kyoto at the Center for Technology and Innovation in Japan. The latter offering for the spring term of second-year students is followed by a summer internship with a Japanese firm. Georgetown University boasts six semester-abroad programs, as well as a trio of summer-study-abroad opportunities with Oxford University, Japan's Waseda University in Tokyo, and France's Benjamin Franklin Program in Paris. These options will increase the cost of your degree, but not nearly as much as a full program abroad.

There's also another route you could select if you decide to link up with a U.S. B-school. Many of the best schools now offer joint-degree programs in both business and Asian or European studies. One of the best is Wharton's Joseph H. Lauder Institute. An alliance between the business school and the university's School of Arts and Sciences, the 24-month program is an innovative way to capture an international experience. After spending the month of May on the Philadelphia campus, students ship overseas to countries in which their chosen foreign language is spoken. (A second language is required for admission to the program.) While there, they tour the facilities of a dozen corporations and take in lots of cultural activities. Students return for the traditional start of the school year in September, only to go back for 12-week internships with both foreign companies and the overseas affiliates of U.S. firms. They then return to campus to complete their studies.

Despite the program's quality, Laura Lee Garner of London Business School's Class of 1993 says she turned down a place at Wharton's Lauder Institute for the opportunity to study full-time abroad. Looking for an international experience, Garner concluded that "Europe seemed to offer more" than an American MBA program could. At LBS, Garner believes she has learned as much from her fellow students from all over the world as she did from her professors. She recalled a classroom debate on the South American debt crisis. Brazilians, Chileans, Venezuelans, Americans, Britons, and Europeans were going at it with a vigor that wouldn't be found in a predominantly American classroom.

If you do decide to take the plunge, full-time or through an exchange option, the next question is: Which school? Factors to consider include the language requirements, the additional cost, and the program's length, in addition to the overall quality of the institution. INSEAD requires three languages in its 10-month program. IESE in Barcelona demands two languages by graduation from their two-year curriculums. IMD's one-year stint requires English only, although a second language is recommended as being attractive to recruiters.

Whatever your choice, your experience will certainly be memorable. You'll learn as much about business as you will about another country and culture. You'll make very different friends with different people. And you'll probably return a different person yourself. As Garner puts it, "You'll break down barriers you may not realize you have, especially for an American. We come in with frameworks. It takes a challenge to recognize that."

Leading Institutions Offering Exchange Programs with Top 20 B-Schools*

School	Location	Language of instruction	Top 20 alliances
Europe			
Katholieke Universiteit Leuven	Leuven, Belgium	English	3
Copenhagen Business School	Copenhagen, Denmark	English	4
London Business School	London, England	English	11
Manchester Business School	Manchester, England	English	8
ESSEC Graduate School of Management	Cergy-Pontoise, France	French	5
l'Ecole des Hautes Etudes	Paris, France	French/English	3
Institut Superieur des Affaires, Groupe HEC	Jouy-en-Josas, France	French/English	6
Koblenz School of Corporate Management	Vallendar, Germany	German	3
Scuola do Direzione Aziendale dell' Universita Luigi Bocconi	Milan, Italy	Italian/English	8
Rotterdam School of Management, Erasmus University	Rotterdam, The Netherlands	English	10
Norwegian School of Economics and Business Administration	Bergen-Sandviken, Norway	Norwegian/English	2
IESE Instituto de Estudios Superiores de la Empresa	Barcelona, Spain	English/Spanish	7
Stockholm School of Administration	Stockholm, Sweden	English	5
St. Gallen University	St. Gallen, Switzerland	German	5
Asia			
The Chinese University of Hong Kong	Hong Kong	English	4
International University of Japan	Niigata, Japan	English	3
Keio University	Yokohama, Japan	Japanese	2
SASIN Graduate Institute of Business Administration	Bangkok, Thailand	English	2
Australia			
Australian Graduate School of Management, University of New South Wales	Sydney, Australia	English	2
University of Sydney	Sydney, Australia	English	4

*Institutions with the most exchange partnerships with Top 20 U.S. B-schools in 1992. About 12 non-U.S. schools have exchange programs with two of the Top 20. (The four listed were chosen on the basis of the prestige of their U.S. partners.)

The European Institute of Business Administration (INSEAD)

Boulevard de Constance
77305 Fontainebleau Cedex
France

Enrollment: 460
Women: 24%
Non-French: 85%
Minority: NA
Part-time: None
Average age: 28
Average years of work exp.: 4.5
Applicants accepted: 27%

Annual tuition & fees: $25,000
Room and board: $17,000
Average GMAT score: 650
GMAT range: 540 to 790
Average GPA: NA
GPA range: NA
Accepted applicants enrolled: 78%
Average starting pay: $90,410

Teaching methods: Lecture, 30%   Case study, 50%   Projects, 20%

Located on what was once the private hunting grounds of French kings, INSEAD is Europe's preeminent business school. In the picturesque town of Fontainebleau, at the edge of the Fontainebleau forest, the school is just a 40-minute drive from Paris. But faculty and students here would cringe if you called the Institut Européen d'Administration des Affaires a French business school. Rather, they insist on calling the school "international," emphasizing its diversity and the global character of the many case studies they dissect and debate. "INSEAD isn't even European," claims Lawrence Freedman, a Class of 1993 student from Ithaca, New York. "It has its own culture."

Founded in 1959, INSEAD has long enjoyed a reputation as the best graduate school of business in Europe. Even though its program is only 10 and a half months long, many companies believe an MBA from INSEAD is as prestigious as one from Northwestern or Harvard. Privately funded and not affiliated with any university, the school underwent a major expansion in 1986 that led to a 40 percent rise in enrollment, to 460 MBA students a year. Increasing interest in global affairs allowed the school the luxury of expanding without lowering its admissions standards. "Demand grew by leaps and bounds and we tried to meet it," says Jean-Pierre Salzmann, director of public affairs.

The increase also allowed INSEAD to support another goal: enlarging the faculty and the amount of research generated by the school. The number of professors more than doubled, to 82. Hailing from 22 nationalities, the faculty is "highly individualistic," Salzmann says. There is "no INSEAD mold in the faculty." Many of the new faculty recruits, moreover, are research-oriented professors, reflecting the school's efforts to improve its reputation among academics. MBA Director Herwig Langohr, a finance professor from Belgium, views academic research as relevant to actual business operations. "Nothing is so good for practice as a good theory," he says. However, Langohr envisions the school moving toward more project work in the long run. The combination of research and practical experience should lead to a "more insight-oriented" program.

Although 6 of every 10 students at INSEAD are European (compared to only 47 percent at the London Business School), Langohr believes his school is "international in all dimensions." The largest single group of students, 17 percent, come from France, while 16 percent of the students hail from the United Kingdom. Roughly one in every four students here is from some other European country. North Americans account for about 13 percent of the student population, outnumbering those from Asia (6 percent) and the Middle East (4 percent). "No one nationality or culture dominates," says Herwig.

The interaction among diverse students and faculty creates a mindset that is impossible to duplicate in a program dominated by one nationality. To successfully avoid cultural clashes, Americans must learn "a style, a grace" in working with others, says Kristin Allen, a U.S. student in the Class of 1993. The differences are readily apparent in the classroom, where an array of accents and languages are spoken. For one thing, students here must speak both French and English to gain entrance to the program. Allen says she met the French requirement by taking a two-month, $3000 intensive French course before the school year began. By the time they graduate, students must be able to at least maintain a business conversation in a third language. INSEAD offers German and Spanish for four and a half hours a week for 30 weeks, which is added to the regular MBA courseload.

The program runs at two different times of the year: from August to June and from January to December, with a six-week break in the summer. The odd schedule may make it difficult for some students to land summer internships, but many still gain summer employment to tack onto their résumés. The program is divided into five eight-week periods, the first pair of which is crammed with the business basics of the core curriculum.

The workload is heavy. "Time pressure is pretty hairy here," Freedman says, citing days from 7 a.m. to 2 a.m. as typical. Although he prefers eight hours of sleep a night, he says "I get six if I'm lucky." But it's also not as highly competitive as some U.S. schools. With class participation accounting for only 10 to 30 percent of your grade in any given course, class discussions tend to be more constructive.

The school's blend of hard work and play seems to pay off: Top recruiters, including McKinsey, Boston Consulting Group, Citicorp, and IBM routinely make on-campus rounds here to woo grads. In 1993, 182 organizations recruited on campus, conducting 5251 interviews. Another 602 job opportunities arrived via correspondence. One in three graduates heads for the consulting business. In 1994, only 1.7 percent of grads didn't have a job offer at commencement.

The school's exalted reputation tends to be larger than its actual influence in business. That's because INSEAD has produced a smallish alumni base, especially compared to any of the major U.S. business schools. Its presence in the United States is minimal: Only 460 of its MBAs now work in the United States. Some 408 alums are American, though more than half of them live outside the country. INSEAD boasts 25 alumni clubs around the world, each in a different country. Most are in Europe, but there are also groups in Hong Kong, India, Japan, and Singapore. The school also has a North American office in New York City.

Contact: Helen Henderson, director of admissions, 33 1-60 72 4000.
Final application deadlines: April for August start; August for January start

International Graduate School of Management (IESE)

Avda. Pearson, 21
08034 Barcelona
Spain

Enrollment: 400
Women: 20%
Non-Spanish: 38%
Minority: NA
Part-time: None
Average age: 27
Average years of work exp.: 3
Applicants accepted: 30%

Annual tuition & fees: $14,700
Room and board: $10,000
Average GMAT score: 600
GMAT range: 490 to 730
Average GPA: 3.0
GPA range: 2.6 to 3.9
Accepted applicants enrolled: 65%
Average starting pay: $45,000

Teaching methods: Lecture, 15%   Case study, 85%

In his quest for a second language and an international MBA, Anthony Dunaif found the answer in the Barcelona-based IESE. The 29-year-old from New York, who had been in advertising, jumped at the chance to take part in the school's bilingual MBA program and perfect his Spanish, what he calls "the second most useful language in the world."

The International Graduate School of Management, in Spain's second largest city, is the only choice for someone seeking a two-year MBA in Spanish and English. But those aren't its only distinctions. IESE also has links to Harvard Business School and Opus Dei, a Catholic organization of laymen and priests who strive for a Christian way of life. Both influences can be felt on the lovely palm-tree-dotted Barcelona campus.

Harvard's influence is found in IESE's reliance on case studies as the primary means of teaching. And the school boasts a forced grading curve, not unlike the one imposed at the famous Boston school. That's no surprise, because Harvard profs advised the school when it created its MBA program in 1963. The ties between the two institutions are kept strong through annual meetings among faculty and administrators. And the influence of Opus Dei, which helped start the school in 1958, is found in its emphasis on ethics and social responsibility.

Many schools are now emphasizing ethics, but IESE has been doing so "long before the scandals" of the 1980s on Wall Street. Not only is there a course on the subject in the first-year core, but discussions involving ethical dilemmas often crop up in many of the MBA courses here. The school also has a trio of professors in ethics and theology. "Ethics are an essential part of any business decision," says Dean Carlos Cavalle. "Managers are more and more aware of the impact of decisions on the environment." One result: More than 100 students help the elderly and handicapped for one day in Project Reach Out and Help.

But don't get the impression that the serious study of business isn't going on. Students are putting in 80- or 90-hour weeks during their first year on nuts-and-bolts courses like finance, accounting, and marketing. The class of about 195 students is divided into three cohorts of 65 MBA candidates each. Two of the sections take their classes in Spanish, while the third cohort—composed of students from 30 countries—gets its courses in English. Each section moves through all the first-year classes together in the same classroom.

Although the workload lightens a bit during the second year, students are still slogging their way through electives like Competitive Decision Analysis and Information Systems and Technologies. Students choose from about 50 offerings, most taught in Spanish, including Social Doctrine of the Church, and another 7 or 8 electives in English.

Interest in entrepreneurial activities isn't confined to the United States these days. One of the most popular electives here is New Business Ventures, taught in both languages. In it, MBAs hammer out the traditional business plans for starting their own companies. The best proposals are then presented to businesspersons who sometimes carry them out. The school says that a third of its graduates run their own businesses by the age of 33, reflecting the entrepreneurial spirit of the school.

A different possibility during the second year is study at another business school. About 12 percent of the students here sign up for the exchange programs with Northwestern, Wharton, the London Business School, and Keio University in Japan. The school requires proficiency in both English and Spanish by the end of the program. Language study, plus working in Spain during the summer break, makes fluency possible for Americans who start with English only. Dunaif achieved fluency after his summer stint as the head of transportation for the 1992 Summer Olympics in Barcelona. The program requires 10 weeks of work in the summer.

The Spanish requirement was "the biggest plus" of IESE for 24-year-old Bonnie Duhart of Santa Barbara, California. Duhart, who worked for an Italian marble company before starting at IESE, chose the school because of its unique Spanish/English program. Another plus: the small size of the sections and the supportive atmosphere. Duhart says students will lower their hands in class to give shy students a chance. "There's a unity," she says. The Spanish sections, by contrast, are very competitive.

Cooperation is also encouraged within the 10-person groups that meet daily during the first year to prepare for class discussion and to ready papers. Students openly share information despite a forced grading curve (the top 10 percent get A's and the bottom 10 percent get C's). Students who collect more than four C's a year are placed on probation.

About 190 companies recruit IESE grads, including such big U.S. MBA hirers as A.T. Kearney, Andersen Consulting, Boston Consulting Co., Booz Allen & Hamilton, Chemical Bank, Hewlett-Packard, Johnson & Johnson, McKinsey & Co., Pepsi-Cola International, and Procter & Gamble. The largest single group of graduates in 1993 went into manufacturing (31 percent), followed by service industries (22 percent). Consulting and banking and finance grabbed 17 percent of the class, while consumer goods lured 13 percent.

The school, however, reports only 105 alumni in the United States—not much of a network to provide any kind of job security in the United States. A loosely organized alumni association has met twice, in Boston and New York, in the past six years.

Contact: Paul McDonough, director of the MBA admissions office, 343-204-4288
Final application deadline: May 15 for fall

International Institute for Management Development (IMD)

Chemin de Bellerive 23, P.O. Box 915, CH-1001
Lausanne, Switzerland

Enrollment: 82
Women: 11%
Non-Swiss: 95%
Minority: NA
Part-time: None
Average years of work exp.: 6.5
Average age: 30
Applicants accepted: 12%

Annual tuition & fees: $25,330
Room and board: $23,330
Average GMAT score: 620
GMAT range: 490 to 780
Average GPA: NA
GPA range: NA
Accepted applicants enrolled: 80%
Average starting pay: $106,890

Teaching methods: Lecture, 15%   Case study, 85%

Surrounded by a pristine Swiss landscape along the shores of Lake Geneva, the attractiveness of the International Institute for Management Development's (IMD) physical locale in Lausanne is nearly matched by its MBA program. This European school has the distinction of offering the most intimate and selective MBA program in the world. The school's total enrollment of only 80 students is less than the size of a single class section at Harvard. Only 12 percent of the applicants gain entrance to the program, making IMD nearly as choosy as Stanford, the most selective U.S. school.

With a small class size and an integrative approach, the institute is a good bet for the slightly older student seeking an intense, multicultural experience. "Being small is our starting advantage," says Xavier Gilbert, acting director general of IMD. Gilbert, a business policy expert, views the teaching process as similar to making handicrafts: Both require time and attention on a few items rather than mass production.

The slight increase in enrollment will give the school a rare and exceptional student-to-teacher ratio of little more than 3-to-1. Twenty-five of the 42 faculty members here teach in this 50-week-long MBA program, allowing for plenty of interaction with students. "You get to know professors," says Arlene Ashton, a 35-year-old attorney from Philadelphia in the Class of 1993. "You can't hide. You aren't screaming for attention."

You also get to intimately know your classmates in ways that just aren't possible in most MBA programs. All students attend the same classes in the same auditorium. Seats are rearranged every month to increase your exposure to other students who typically hail from more than 30 nations. In fact, no more than eight students from any given nationality are usually enrolled.

Another distinctive characteristic of the students is their average age: 30, a full 3 years older than Northwestern's students and 4 years older than Harvard's. They come to school averaging 6.5 years of full-time work experience each. That's a selling point for older potential applicants, according to 30-year-old Kate Bolger from Boston. Praising the quality of her classmates, Bolger says IMD students are "second to none in years of experience, variety of experience, and international experience." That reflects admissions' emphasis on maturity and professional background.

Despite its international atmosphere, English is the only required language at IMD (though you can study other languages while you're here by arrangement with local schools). The school not only offers the smallest elite program, it's also the most rigid and inflexible. There are few electives in the 50-week course, which runs from January to December. Instead, all the learning is packed into eight issues-oriented "modules." Each module is interdisciplinary and builds on knowledge learned in previous modules. For example, in the first module, Managers as Decisionmakers, students use accounting, quantitative analysis, communication, human resources, and marketing in learning decision making within an organization. The first five modules focus on management skills; the following four emphasize developing judgment. The final outcome: managers who have not only skills but also vision and can act as "agents of transformation," believes Gilbert. "We go out of our way to avoid focusing on one topic."

Consulting projects are another key aspect to the curriculum, taking 50 percent of the time during the second half of the program. Student teams work on business problems assigned by the top management of client companies. The projects follow four phases: industry analysis, company analysis, issue analysis, and finally implementation. The companies pay the school an average of $16,000 for each project. The students recommend how that money should be used, such as for advising a Czech steel company on how to enter European markets.

IMD is the product of a merger between two well-respected Swiss management schools, formerly Geneva-based IMI (International Management Institute) and IMEDE (International Management Development Institute), which took effect in January 1990. The MBA program at IMEDE, which was founded by Nestlé with support from Harvard Business School, began in 1972. That explains why learning here is so heavily based on case studies in the Harvard tradition. Indeed, the school claims that it's the biggest producer of teaching materials outside North America, generating 50 to 70 case studies a year. IMI, founded by Alcan Aluminum of Canada, began its MBA program in 1984. The total number of graduates from both MBA programs is 1500.

Graduates of the program post among the highest starting pay packages in the world—partly because they are older and more experienced. About 40 companies recruit on campus, including such well-known U.S. organizations as McKinsey, Price Waterhouse, Citibank, General Motors, Ford, and Eli Lilly. The school maintains that students average three offers each. In 1994, about 93.5 percent of the class had jobs by graduation.

There's one obvious drawback to IMD: its relatively puny alumni base. Although about 1400 North American managers have attended the school's executive education programs, only 230 of the school's MBA graduates live in North America. That's not much more than the annual output of the smallest Top 20 school. Still, it's a function of the school's greatest advantage: its elite intimacy in a stunning locale.

Contact: Marianne Wheeler, MBA admissions office, 41-21-618-02-98
Final application deadline: August 31

London Business School

Sussex Place
Regent's Park
London NW1 4SA
United Kingdom

Enrollment: 240
Women: 25%
Non-British: 75%
Minority: NA
Part-time: 60
Average age: 28.5
Average years of work exp.: 5
Applicants accepted: 40%

Annual tuition & fees: $19,600
Room and board: $14,400
Average GMAT score: 620
GMAT range: 470 to 770
Average GPA: NA
GPA range: NA
Accepted applicants enrolled: 70%
Average starting pay: $79,100

Teaching methods: Lecture, 25% Case study, 50% Group projects, 25%

Set upon the lovely green grounds of Regent's Park, the Sussex Building of London Business School is a magnificent greeting to a new student. Inside the grand Georgian walls, you can sip tea while gazing through huge windows at swans and geese gliding on a lake. Once a week, the Queen's Calvary parades across the park. The scene is postcard-perfect England.

These days, it's a postcard that includes greater numbers of American MBAs than ever before. Calling the school "a bridge between North America and Europe," Principal George Bain recommends that North Americans ease their way into careers in continental Europe by picking up their MBAs in England first. "I see us as an aircraft carrier off the coast of Europe," he says, "a place where students can perfect a language and get sensitized to a new culture. After that immersion, students can 'take off' from the carrier to land anywhere in Europe."

True enough, London is a welcoming place, particularly for Americans who don't have to overcome a language barrier to get around the country or the school. Unlike INSEAD, which requires applicants to speak both English and French and graduates to pick up a third language, London Business School only requires English. Proficiency in another language isn't required until you graduate. Students can take French, Spanish, German, or Japanese through language courses offered at London University.

Like other European business schools, cultural sensitization is inevitable in an environment where no one nationality dominates the student body. In the Class of 1993, one in five students hail from North America (the highest of any non-U.S. school). Still, an equal number are non-British European, while 19 percent are Asian, 7 percent are from Australia and New Zealand, and about 4 percent are from South and Central America. The largest single chunk of the class is British, accounting for 26 percent of the enrollment.

That truly international mix leads to stimulating discussions in and out of the classroom. You not only debate the substantive issues of business and economics, you feel the passion and the heat those issues often stir. Laura Lee Garner, an American in the Class of

1993, recalls how on one occasion tempers flared when Japanese and American students debated trade barriers between their home countries. When the word *rice* was mentioned, "the room just exploded," says Garner.

The 21-month course for full-time students adopts an American-style approach, with the core courses set up front and all the electives in the back. The program is divided into six terms, with the basics of business hogging the first three terms. At year's end, students must pass a two-day qualifying exam, each a grueling four hours long. Then, in the second year, the school piles on the electives. You can choose from among 60 different courses that range from New Venture Development, the most popular course, to Managing East European Operations.

Each year and in the summer, students also complete a team project generated by corporate sponsors who ante up cash for each student in return for the work. The opportunity to work on real business problems attracts many students. "It is the reason why I came to LBS," says William E. Northfield Jr., a 28-year-old from Boston in the Class of 1993. The projects range from an analysis of the pharmaceutical industry in both the United Kingdom and the United States to a feasibility study for a luxury Spanish restaurant.

London's longer full-time program, two years versus the one-year length at either INSEAD or IMD, allows for both a summer internship and a semester abroad in what may well be the largest MBA exchange program offered by any business school in the world. London boasts exchange pacts with 25 other schools, many of them in the United States (American students, of course, cannot spend a semester abroad in a U.S. program).

The first-year workload, just as it is at most U.S. schools, is tough: 12- to 16-hour days are typical. But Northfield says he manages to get 7 hours of sleep per night and to take off one weekend evening for fun. The Windsor Castle Pub, attached to the school, is a convenient stop for pints and also serves up traditional English pub grub from bangers and mash (sausages and potatoes) to cottage pie (ground beef layered under mashed potatoes). The school also boasts numerous clubs, including wine and performing arts societies.

London, of course, offers many diversions and historical sites that are easily accessible from centrally located Regents Park. A small museum, Sherlock Holmes' home, is a mere three-minute walk away. The financial district, called The City, is about 15 minutes away on the subway. Students themselves live throughout London and get to campus by bus or subway (the school is just a block from the Baker Street underground stop). Study bedrooms on campus are reserved for executive education programs and for international exchange students.

LBS's Career Management Centre says that in recent years more American companies are recruiting for their head European offices. German companies have also increased their recruiting at LBS for non-German managers. In total, 103 companies recruit at LBS each year, conducting about 1264 interviews in 1994. The big hirers: Gemini Consulting (8), CSC Index (4), Andersen Consulting (3), Bankers Trust (3), Fidelity International (3), and Merrill Lynch (3). The school counts just 367 American MBA graduates and boasts an alumni office in New York City. Overall, about 500 LBS alums live in the United States.

Contact: Nandee Sugarman, North American admissions officer, 44 71-262-5050
Final application deadline: May 1 for fall

SDA Bocconi

Via F. Bocconi, 16/18
20136 Milano
Italy

Enrollment: 130
Women: 25%
Non-Italian: 50%
Minority: NA
Part-time: None
Average age: 29
Average years of work exp.: 3.5
Applicants accepted: 25%

Annual tuition & fees: $17,700
Room and board: $12,000
Average GMAT score: 590*
GMAT range: NA
Average GPA: NA
GPA range: NA
Accepted applicants enrolled: 70%*
Average starting pay: $54,000*

Teaching methods: Lecture, 20%   Case study, 40%   Group projects, 40%

Set in Milan, Italy's nitty-gritty industrial center, yet merely an hour and a half drive from skiing in the Alps or swimming in the Mediterranean, SDA Bocconi's Italian locale adds zest to the pursuit of an MBA.

It's why 1992 American graduate Mario Recchia chose the school, the first to offer the MBA degree in Italy. "I wanted to work in Europe, particularly Italy," he says, after spending five years at a regional bank in the United States.

The program's bilingual curriculum was another draw. Although English is the only required language, students can take Italian language courses and attend classes taught in Italian. Most students succeed in learning Italian by graduation—although fluency in the language is not a requirement for the degree. Like bilingual IESE in Barcelona, students can take their core courses in English and can then choose from a selection of electives taught in either English or Italian.

MBA Program Director Pamela Adams says Bocconi's emphasis on classroom-oriented learning makes it distinctive. Students are in class six hours a day, five days a week, for the first 10 weeks. "They are learning how to work in groups," she says. "The interaction is a very important part of the program." And it helps to bring together a diverse group of cultures and people. Students hail from 26 nations (50 percent are Italian, 28 percent are other Europeans, and 22 percent are from elsewhere). Eight out of the 127 members of the Class of 1994 are Americans.

The composition of the class reflects the school's efforts to become more international. When the MBA program began in 1974, only 5 percent of its students were non-Italians; in 1989, 20 percent were. The start of the school's bilingual program in 1990 and the creation of its English section has boosted its diversity so that every other MBA student now enrolled at the school isn't from Italy.

Like IMD in Switzerland, Bocconi's primary focus is its executive education programs, which account for 75 percent of the school's annual revenues. That makes its MBA program purposely small, with an enrollment of only 130 students. The school says there's lots of interaction between MBA candidates and the executives who come to Bocconi for advanced training. The school also offers a Master's in International Economics and Management, a 12-month program for students with more work experience.

There are few bells and whistles in the regular MBA program. At 16 months, it is slightly shorter than most American programs and does not allow for a summer internship. Students get a rather traditional set of core courses in the business basics in Part One of the program, which lasts from September to May. Part Two, June through December, focuses on integrating those basic skills. It includes intensive electives, taught in either English or Italian. This is total immersion, as each elective lasts just one week long. You take one elective in the morning for 4 hours per day and one in the afternoon, for a total of 40 hours of classtime per week. Often, professors from other business schools, including Harvard and New York University, fly in to teach the courses—perhaps that's why Bocconi crams everything into a single week. Given the small size of the program, you'll find only 28 electives here—one of the smallest selections of any business school.

During the second half of the program, students also take part in company projects in Italian or English. Adams says these exercises provide an experience superior to a summer internship, which students do not get to do, because Bocconi ensures the projects are integrated with the curriculum. The B-school also assures client companies, which may pay up to $25,000 each, that the work performed will be of high quality.

But the workload here is not excessive. Recchia, for example, says his weekends are virtually free, save for a couple hours of study per day. He estimates about nine hours of classes and homework per day, Monday through Friday. "It's intense, but it's also fun," he says. The Italian students, however, are especially studious because they tend to be among the best and brightest young people Italy has to offer. That's why the school has the reputation, deserved or not, of being "the Harvard of Italy."

Along with its modern bustle, Milan offers the romance of historic buildings and art collections that rival those in Rome and Florence. The grandoise, white marble Piazza del Duomo, constructed from 1386 until the late 19th century, lies at the city's center. The school itself obviously doesn't rival that architectural wonder, but in early 1993 it moved into a newly renovated pale yellow, 1930s Milanese-style, concrete building constructed at a cost of $4 million. Most students end up sharing two-bedroom, furnished apartments with two or three people for about $900 a month.

For any non-Italian student, recruiting is pretty skimpy. Bocconi doesn't have the pull of either INSEAD, IMD, or the London Business School. Most of the 115 recruiting companies are Italian-based firms hiring for the local market. A few U.S. companies do visit: Procter & Gamble, Eli Lilly, Merrill Lynch, and Goldman Sachs. But as one American student put it: "If you don't want to be in Italy, you're stuck out in the cold." The school maintains that 98 percent of students land a job six months after graduation.

Not surprisingly, you'd be hard pressed to find much of an alumni network outside of Italy. There are no alumni clubs in the United States and not many elsewhere in the world. The school estimates that 53 of its MBA graduates live in the United States, only 33 of whom are American.

Contact: Gabriela Alliatis, admissions officer, 392-5836-3286
Final application deadline: April for fall

Western Business School

The University of Western Ontario
London, Ontario
Canada, N6A 3K7

Enrollment: 450
Women: 24%
Non-Canadian: 10%
Minority: 25%
Part-time: None
Average age: 28
Average years of work exp.: 4
Work exp. range: 1 to 15 yrs
Applicants accepted: 30%

Annual tuition & fees: resident—$3300
                                    nonresident—$14,000
Room and board: $4000
Average GMAT score: 630
GMAT range: 560 to 790
Average GPA: 3.4
GPA range: 2.7 to 4.0
Accepted applicants enrolled: 59%
Average starting pay: $60,000

Teaching methods: Lecture, 10%   Case study, 70%   Group projects, 20%

If you're looking for value with cachet in your MBA program search, then Western Business School in London, Ontario, may be an unusual answer. With annual tuition of about $14,000 for non-Canadians, the two-year degree is substantially cheaper than many American programs, including some offered by public universities. And as one of Canada's top business schools, it offers quality with clout. Of the more than two dozen graduate schools of business in Canada, Western is held in high esteem by corporate recruiters, executives, and deans, who have repeatedly ranked it No. 1 in the country, according to *Canadian Business* magazine.

"The value I'm getting for my education is really second to none," believes Tony Cianca, a 25 year old from Nashville who's in the Class of 1994. Formerly a college textbook salesman, Cianca chose WBS over American schools like Vanderbilt in part because the price was right. "Vanderbilt is $25,000 a year. Here it's maybe a third of that."

But that isn't the only reason why he and many others are selecting the school. The quality of the teaching faculty is another draw. Many of the professors in Western's classrooms got their educational credentials stamped at Harvard and Stanford. So they bring high expectations and high-level experience to their courses. They're also known for their close contact with students. Cianca, for instance, recalls that on Thanksgiving, which Canadians do not celebrate, one professor awarded him a ham and some cranberry sauce, recognizing him as the section's only American. "It really made me feel good. It's a personal type thing." And unlike the dominating emphasis on esoteric research at many U.S. schools, often to the detriment of good teaching, Western has put more focus on the quality of instruction in class. As Dean Adrian Ryans puts it, the school "rewards good teaching through promotion and tenure and places less emphasis on research and publication." What research it does do tends to be directed toward the development of case studies. The school claims to be the second largest producer of cases after Harvard.

There are other strong business schools in Canada, including the programs at Queen's University, McGill University, the University of Toronto, and the University of British

Columbia. But none of the Canadian B-schools makes much of a showing in BUSINESS WEEK's surveys of corporate recruiters, with the exception of Western Business School.

For U.S. students, time spent at Western is bound to be less of an international experience than one could gain in Europe or Asia. Americans face no language barriers in Canada, and you'd be hard pressed to find colleagues who are more like Americans than the typical Canadians in a Western classroom. Only 10 percent of the students here are not from Canada—making Western less "international" in some ways than most of the better B-schools in the United States. Indeed, Cianca doesn't really feel he is in a foreign culture. "As an American, it's not any big deal to adjust to Canada," he says. Yet the American MBA candidate believes he's getting a more global perspective on business by attending the school.

The hub of Western's efforts to think globally lies in the Center for International Business Studies, which supports research and other international programs. WBS's international elements include an active exchange program with business schools in Europe and Asia, under which students can study in Italy, Spain, Sweden, Britain, Japan, or Hong Kong for a four-month term. The exchange program, in turn, also brings foreign students on-campus, which helps to diversify the student body. WBS deliberately does not conduct any exchanges with American schools, to encourage exposure to more foreign cultures.

Each MBA class of about 200 students is divided into three sections. All of the program's first-year classes are required, and they focus on nine basic building block areas. In the second year, only one course is required: Business Policy. Then you're finally free to select from an array of electives that range from The Operating Manager to Creative Business Leadership. The former requires students to approach problems from the perspective of a young manager who must lead and operate effectively in an environment that is not under his or her control. The latter explores how business leaders can instill a stronger sense of mission in employees.

WBS is housed in a two-story, sandstone, fortress-like building that is one of the oldest on campus. Two gardens outside the building provide the settings for 500-person garden parties. Although the school offers some on-campus housing, nearly all students live off-campus in nearby apartments in and around London—a two-hour drive to Detroit or Toronto and a two-hour flight to New York.

Some 83, mostly Canadian, firms recruit at WBS. But the lineup also includes such prestigious organizations as McKinsey, Citibank, Merrill Lynch, First Boston, Bank of Switzerland, Goldman Sachs—all of which recruit for their Canadian outposts and U.S. operations. The placement office reports that 84 percent of students find jobs within six months, with the average student getting three offers. In 1994, about 11 graduates landed jobs in the United States, while 14 went to Europe and Asia. The school lacks an alumni association in the United States, where about 6 percent, or 417, of its alumni make their living.

Contact: Larysa Gamula, admissions director, 519-661-3212
Final application deadline: For North American applicants, May 15 for fall

CHAPTER 9

MBAS FOR BARGAIN HUNTERS

Let's face it. Not everyone pursuing an MBA can get through the doors of a Top 20 contender—or even wants to. Some highly talented people find it difficult to overcome the admission hurdles. Others simply can't scrape up the mountain of cash necessary to attend an elite graduate school.

Take Brent A. Berthy. Accepted at the University of Pennsylvania's Wharton School of Business, he chose to go to the University of Florida. It was a logical choice. He wanted to remain in the state and launch his own business. The clincher for him was the out-of-pocket costs. "Why should I pay $20,000 a year for a private school, when I can go to Florida for $4000?" he asks. After gaining his MBA in 1992, Berthy put together an agricultural biotechnology startup—and has no regrets about his decision.

A lot of Whartonites, of course, think their money is well spent. But MBA seekers can find good educational values among the more than 750 institutions that grant the degree. And as MBAs from even brand-name schools find it tougher to get high-paying jobs out of the gate, it may make more sense than ever to shop around.

To help in that search, BUSINESS WEEK selected 15 quality business schools that offer consumers the most bang for the buck (see table). The impossible-to-beat bargains are the business schools at Indiana, North Carolina, and Texas at Austin. These schools, though, are so good they already make our Top 20 or runners-up lists. The business schools we're highlighting in this section provide solid foundations in the business basics, and some are even on the leading edge of management education. They are not necessarily, however, the next best bunch of schools—in overall quality, you're apt to do better at private institutions, such as Boston University or Babson College.

To assure a basic level of quality, BUSINESS WEEK looked at schools which accepted applicants whose scores on the Graduate Management Admission Test averaged no lower than 575 out of a possible 800. Some B-schools, such as those at the University of Georgia or Rice University, boast averages well into the 600s. Others, such as the University of Kansas, just meet the threshold.

Then we compared each school's total tuition bill to the starting salaries of its graduates to determine which gave the most value. Public schools, not surprisingly, dominate the list. For $11,750 in nonresident tuition, students can graduate from Bernard Baruch College of the City University of New York, with average starting salaries of about $40,000 in 1994.

BUSINESS WEEK's **Best Buys**

School	Full tuition*	Average starting pay	Average GMAT	Applicants accepted
Alabama (Manderson) Tuscaloosa	$11,280	$35,600	585	45%
Arizona State Tempe	15,000	41,403	605	34
Baruch New York	11,750	39,747	589	55
Brigham Young (Marriott) Provo	12,000	49,000	601	52
Buffalo Buffalo	14,632	40,942	586	49
Florida Gainesville	17,384	44,826	610	25
Georgia (Terry) Athens	12,300	46,121	626	27
Georgia Tech Atlanta	13,866	46,600	626	34
Kansas Lawrence	13,848	36,183	584	47
Kentucky Lexington	15,060	35,750	598	36
Maryland College Park	19,990	45,950	625	20
Ohio State Columbus	24,000	44,000	612	34
Rice (Jones) Houston	22,600	47,000	622	46
Tennessee Knoxville	12,384	46,500	601	31
Texas A&M College Station	13,200	41,990	607	52

*Tuition is for out-of-state residents.

What state schools lack in snob appeal, they often make up in affordability—especially for state residents. A Georgian, for instance, can get a degree from the University of Georgia for a total of $4704. That's less than the extra fees alone required of every Harvard MBA, never mind the $42,000 tuition bill. In some states, nonresidents can often qualify for lower resident fees in their second year of study, putting some of the tuition estimates in the accompanying table on the high side.

The upshot: MBAs from these schools seldom graduate heavily in hock. That's quite a different matter for grads of the elite schools. The huge tuitions demanded by most Top 20 institutions force MBAs from those programs to graduate with an average of $30,540 in debt hanging over their heads. Load those numbers into a calculator and the cost-benefit analysis alone makes BUSINESS WEEK's list of bargains look even better. "If cost isn't an issue, get into the best school you can and have a good life," advises William E. Mayer, former dean of the University of Rochester's Simon School, who now heads up the business school at the University of Maryland. "But if money is an issue, I can give students a first-rate education at an affordable price in a setting that has a lot going for it."

Besides, an MBA from an elite school, the so-called "golden passport," is looking a little less golden these days. Many companies refuse to pay the high premiums commanded by Top 20 graduates. Some even prefer graduates from less prestigious schools. "We have found that it is the second-tier schools that produce the really hard workers, who are willing to roll up their sleeves and prove themselves," says Joe S. Disbennett, director of executive development at FHP Health Care. He maintains that the health care company values the effectiveness of the individual people over the prestige of the institutions they attend.

Some major recruiters of MBAs are also slowly beginning to recognize the lesser-known schools that have long been in the shadow of the brand-names. Tom Wagner, director of human resources for Ernst & Young's management consulting practice, believes the cream of the graduates from second-tier schools is just as good as those he lures from the top institutions. That's why most of these schools boast lists of recruiters from many brand-name corporations.

What may surprise many observers is that some of the bargain schools are pioneers in management education, too. Consider the University of Tennessee in Knoxville, which has cleverly carved out a niche in the Total Quality Management field. In the fall of 1991, the school launched a revolutionary curriculum: Its students don't take the traditional core courses, with each discipline taught separately by one specialist in the area. Instead, a first-year student takes only one class each semester which combines all of the functional areas, from finance to marketing. The class is team-taught by 14 core faculty members. Some days 4 or 5 of them will lead the class; on others, only 1 or 2 are at the helm.

The underlying theme of the entire curriculum is aimed at creating customer value. "Not only are the students learning about customer value, they are getting it as well," says Warren Neel, dean of Tennessee's College of Business Administration. "If your program is going to be premised upon the idea of customer value, then look at it and make sure that students see the cost as a major advantage in coming," he says.

The down side of a second-tier degree? Graduates often discover that their degrees don't travel well. They tend to hold more value in local or regional markets, where the school has a better following, than outside them. Three out of every four graduates of the University of Tennessee's B-school, for example, stay in the Southeast. About 65 percent of the University of Maryland's MBA output is placed in Virginia and Maryland. That can make it far more difficult to land a job with a prestigious national company, though some deans maintain it's not impossible. "Those are not doors that are closed to our graduates," insists A. Benton Cocanougher, dean of the College of Business at Texas A&M. "They may just have to knock a little harder."

Richard T. Ney Jr., a 1992 graduate of the University of Florida, certainly had to pound hard to get his job as a research assistant at a prominent Wall Street firm. Although Ney thinks he got a pretty good education for the dollar, he wasn't thrilled with the placement program. "They did not have any connections here, I don't even think they know where New York City is," he says. While Ney got the job he wanted, if he had it to do over, he says: "I would probably go to NYU."

For students intent on a job with a large national company, attending a Top 20 school might still be the easiest route. After all, more big-name corporations recruit at the elite schools whose alumni networks keep them coming back for more. Many of these bargain institutions have either small or young programs with far less alumni support. That means you'll have to take more responsibility for your job search. BUSINESS WEEK's survey of graduates, for example, found that even at some of the runners-up schools there was a significant dropoff in the ability of MBAs to quickly land jobs by graduation. About 30 percent of Thunderbird's Class of 1994 graduated without a single job offer.

On the other hand, schools located near "hot spots" of economic activity can be well positioned to provide graduates with plenty of job opportunities. Take Brigham Young University in Provo, Utah. The B-school has a strong relationship with the local business community, a hotbed of software startups. Ronald R. Burke, director of career services at Brigham Young, believes the school's location makes it a prime hunting ground for MBA opportunities that arise in the area. In fact, approximately 25 percent of the school's internships are with the emerging companies of "Software Valley" in the towns of Orem and Provo. "As far as the regional setting, it has a great advantage for jobs that are created in this area," he says.

An MBA from these schools also makes good sense for would-be entrepreneurs such as Berthy. Plenty of schools can teach the basics of writing a business plan, lining up venture capital, and making a go of a startup. If you're intent on launching your own business, why pay for a school's name or for its skill in attracting a slew of big-name recruiters? It may make more sense to buy less of a credential and more of an education.

There are tradeoffs, to be sure. But if money is a little tight, if your GMAT scores are a little too low, or if your ambition is more localized, the schools on this list provide an excellent opportunity to get a solid education at a great price.

Arizona State University

College of Business
Tempe, Arizona 85287

Enrollment: 690
Women: 38%
Non-U.S.: 12%
Minority: 2.4%
Part-time: 390
Average age: 27
Applicants accepted: 34%
Accepted applicants enrolled: 53%

Annual tuition: resident—$1894
 nonresident—$7500
Room and board: $3515
Average GMAT score: 605
GMAT range: 500 to 750
Average GPA: 3.3
GPA range: 2.8 to 4.0
Average starting salary: $41,403

Teaching methods: Case method, 40% Lecture, 50% Projects, 10%

Wanted: Sun worshippers, outdoorsy individuals who want a solid MBA education at a great price.

If you fit the description, you might consider this growing program in Arizona's "Valley of the Sun." Located in the Phoenix suburb of Tempe, Arizona State boasts a sun-drenched, 600-acre campus complete with subtropical landscaping and modern architecture.

What you'll find at the B-school is a vastly improving MBA program that tends to be overwhelmed by part-timers who outnumber the full-time students four to one. The school claims that the average GMAT scores of its Class of 1994 hit an impressive 605, up from only 560 for 1990 admits, and starting salaries jumped to nearly $41,000 in 1992, from about $32,000 two years earlier.

That's a good trend line. In the fall of 1993, the program's first year switched from semesters to trimesters in an effort to consolidate the core curriculum. Students will still be required to complete the same 36 hours of core and 12 hours of electives, but all of the core classes are now piled into year one. That leaves four electives for the entire second year.

A breeze? Maybe. It's possible for more students to get the degree in a year and a half. But administrators are encouraging students to use the extra time to pursue other opportunities, including a career track program which allows students to take a group of specialized seminars given by 11 B-school departments to better prepare them in their respective fields of interest. MBAs can also sign up for coursework throughout the university or from other institutions, including the highly respected Thunderbird, only 45 minutes away.

If they're interested in landing a good job, of course, students should load up on every option this program can offer—especially since MBA candidates must compete with 43,000 students for attention at the central placement office. In 1994, about 89 companies came to campus to recruit MBAs, including Applied Materials, US West, Wells Fargo, Frito Lay, Hewlett-Packard, Honeywell, Deloitte & Touche, KPMG, and Intel. The situation should improve when MBAs are assigned their own placement director in the fall of 1994.

Contact: Judith K. Heilala, director of graduate programs, 602-965-3332
Final application deadline: May 1 for fall

Baruch College

The City University of New York
17 Lexington Avenue
New York, New York 10010

Enrollment: 2489
Women: 25%
Non-U.S.: 25%
Minority: 13%
Part-time: 1853
Average age: 28
Applicants accepted: 55%
Accepted applicants enrolled: 47%

Annual tuition: resident—$3375
nonresident—$5875
Room and board: $11,600
Average GMAT score: 589
GMAT range: 470 to 790
Average GPA: 3.26
GPA range: 2.4 to 4.0
Average starting salary: $39,747

Teaching methods: Lecture, 75%   Case method, 25%

With more than 15,000 students, Baruch College is the largest school of business in the world. The New York City institution—named after the famous financier and industrialist, Bernard M. Baruch—is teeming with 13,000 undergraduates, nearly 2500 MBAs and over 200 full-time professors.

Like a well-stocked supermarket, the school offers more variety than many people can absorb: You can choose from 155 elective courses in a single academic year; you can specialize in any one of six different marketing majors. You can even concentrate in such topics as industrial psychology or operations research. And Baruch can make the unusual boast that it's one of the few B-schools to have a Nobel Prize winner on its staff—Dr. Harry M. Markowitz, a professor of economics and finance.

What's surprising given the size of the school is that the core classes in the full-time MBA program average fewer than 60 students each, while elective courses hold about 30 each. Still, the urban campus setting in Gramercy Park and the predominately part-time nature of the MBA program make it difficult for full-timers to bond and network. The school is hoping to cultivate more student unity through extracurricular events and social gatherings. In the fall of 1994, for instance, full-time MBAs started attending core classes in cohort groups.

Like most of these "value" schools on BUSINESS WEEK's list, Baruch has been increasing the quality of its students in recent years. The average GMAT of matriculated students is now 585, up from 510 in 1984. Starting salaries for Baruch graduates, meantime, have jumped to nearly $40,000 a year from just under $32,000 in 1986.

Baruch now requires 54 credits (down from 66 two years ago) to obtain a degree. Students take 27 credits of core, 9 credits of electives, and 18 in an area of specialization. The school has also added a "General MBA" option, for students who want to choose their own combination of advanced courses.

Baruch's location in New York makes it an easier place than most to find jobs. In fact, the school maintains that 88 percent of its Class of 1994 had jobs by graduation. The B-school attracted some 379 companies to campus in 1994.

Contact: Francis J. Connelly, dean of school of business, 212-447-3280
Final application deadline: June 1 for fall

Brigham Young University

Marriott School of Management
640 Tanner Building
Provo, Utah 84602

Enrollment: 250
Women: 17%
Non-U.S.: 24%
Minority: 3%
Part-time: None
Average age: 26
Applicants accepted: 52%
Accepted applicants enrolled: 73%

Annual tuition: LDS member—$4400
                     nonmember—$6600
Room and board: $5000
Average GMAT score: 601
GMAT range: 450 to 780
Average GPA: 3.5
GPA range: 2.47 to 3.95
Average starting salary: $49,000

Teaching methods: Case method, 60%   Lecture, 30%   Projects, 10%

The students at Brigham Young University quip that the Tanner Building, where Marriott students take classes, was the box that the famous Mormon Temple in Salt Lake City was shipped in. Its business school building is a huge granite-and-glass rectangle that looks like a boxy corporate headquarters.

While obviously a joke, the connection between the business school and the Church of Jesus Christ of Latter Day Saints is very real. The school, named after the Mormon founder of Marriott Corp., boasts a strong honor code. Students aren't supposed to drink coffee, tea, or alcohol, and they're advised against viewing R-rated movies. More than 90 percent of the students are Mormons, who get a tuition break to come to this campus at the foot of picturesque Mount Timpanogas.

The religious affiliation, however, isn't the only thing that makes the Marriott School unique. Eighty-five percent of its students are bilingual, and most have spent two years in foreign countries serving as Mormon missionaries. Six-person study groups are also assembled around foreign-language competence, including Spanish, Portuguese, Japanese, French, German, and Korean. Foreign languages are also being taught at the business school, with an emphasis on business vocabulary and current events.

Another unusual aspect of the two-year program is a team-taught course that brings together the MBA basics for strategic decision making. There is a high level of integration between the functional courses. When the class recently took apart a marketing case study, for example, faculty from four disciplines (economics, quantitative methods, strategic planning, and marketing) were all involved.

In 1994, 95 companies came to campus to recruit MBA students. Bill Brady, the placement director, is seeking to lure a larger group of companies here in the future. Among the leading recruiters are Intel, Ford Motor, Chrysler, Pizza Hut, Arthur Andersen, Procter & Gamble, Otis Elevator, and Payless Shoe Source.

Contact: Gary F. McKinnon, director of MBA program, 801-378-3500
Final application deadline: March 1 for fall

Georgia Institute of Technology

212 School of Management
Atlanta, Georgia 30332

Enrollment: 220
Women: 30%
Non-U.S.: 27%
Minority: 15%
Part-time: None
Average age: 26
Applicants accepted: 40%
Accepted applicants enrolled: 51%

Annual tuition: resident—$2343
　　　　　　　　　nonresident—$6933
Room and board: $2700
Average GMAT score: 626
GMAT range: 420 to 760
Average GPA: 3.2
GPA range: 2.3 to 4.0
Average starting salary: $46,600

Teaching methods: Case method, 33% Lecture, 33% Projects, 33%

After a five-year wait, Georgia Tech finally got its act together and hired a new dean, Arthur Kraft, from the Rutgers University School of Business. With Dean Kraft at the helm, the school—which has long attracted some exceptional students—will try to make significant changes to integrate the disparate parts of its program. Georgia Tech's major goal—to revamp the core curriculum so that it better reflects the school's philosophy of using quantitative methods to solve management problems—will not be in place until the fall of 1995 at the earliest.

Whatever the future has in store for this program, what won't change is the science-math culture that permeates the school, explainable both by the type of students who come here (37 percent boast engineering backgrounds) and the heavily quantitative curriculum the school offers. Georgia Tech doesn't hand out the typical MBA. Its diplomas are stamped with the initials MSM, Master of Science in Management.

In the first year of the current rigorous six-quarter program, every one of your 14 courses is required as part of the core curriculum. There are even separate computer lab courses: In the first quarter you work on the Macintoshes; in the second, on IBMs. In Classroom 2000, where accounting, finance, and other courses are taught, professors can take control of students' computers and project their screens for the entire class to review. The 1994-95 curriculum is pretty flexible. Although many students use the nine required electives toward a concentration, you don't have to specialize.

Georgia Tech, a campus spread over 330 acres and 143 buildings near midtown Atlanta, also has an aggressive reputation for getting its B-school students summer internships with such firms as UPS, Federal Express, NCR, and AT&T Global Information Systems. The school claims a 90 percent placement rate for its internship program. By virtue of the school's technology bent, about one out of every two graduates here takes a job in information systems or operations management. More than a quarter of the students become management consultants, often with more technical firms. Only 30 percent of the class land jobs outside of the Southeast.

Contact: Ann Johnson Scott, director of the MSM Program, 404-894-2604
Final application deadline: June 1 for fall, April 1 for assistantships

Ohio State University

Fisher School of Business
1775 College Road
Columbus, Ohio 43210

Enrollment: 414
Women: 34%
Non-U.S.: 25%
Minority: 11%
Part-time: 138
Average age: 26
Applicants accepted: 34%
Accepted applicants enrolled: 35%

Annual tuition: resident—$4842
    nonresident—$12,000
Room and board: $4257
Average GMAT score: 612
GMAT range: 370 to 750
Average GPA: 3.16
GPA range: 2.29 to 3.98
Average starting salary: $44,000

Teaching methods: Case method, 60% Lecture, 40%

Ohio State has so much trust in its MBA students that it turned over $5 million of endowment money for them to invest. The risk has produced big profits for the university and hands-on investing experience for students. During the past two and a half years, students participating in the Student Investment Management Program (SIM) have achieved nearly $2.5 million in portfolio growth, and have even bested the performance of Standard & Poor's 500 index.

With all the success in portfolio management, it's not surprising that finance and accounting are the B-school's strongest departments. Ohio State is also one of the nation's top schools in operations and logistics management, and it believes that the marketing and real estate departments are other areas of strength.

The required 16 core classes and 9 electives can be completed in six quarters. The school has added two new requirements in the past year: a management communications sequence, in which MBAs practice and try to improve their written and oral presentation skills, and a yearlong teamwork and leadership laboratory, which focuses on management style. More than 80 percent of the students also participate in summer foreign exchanges or internships.

For a campus with 55,000 students, the MBA class size is minuscule—about 138 full-timers graduate each year. While the small number helps to provide an intimate learning experience, it also hurts Ohio State in the placement area. Some companies are not willing to make the trip to Columbus because they can't fill more than a day of interviews. The B-school wants to increase the size of the program to 240 students a year, but the Hagerty Hall facilities are already overcrowded. The school has just raised $65 million for a five-building, state-of-the-art complex to house undergrad, graduate, and executive education. However, it won't open until 1997, so there are limits to the B-school's growth.

Ohio State attracts some 106 companies to recruit at its campus. The biggest recruiters: Ford Motor Co., Andersen Consulting, and Deloitte & Touche.

Contact: Susie Cinadr, coordinator of admissions, 614-292-8511
Final application deadline: April 1 for fall, February 1 for fellowships

Rice University

Jesse H. Jones Graduate School of Administration
P.O. Box 1892
Houston, Texas 77251

Enrollment: 234
Women: 26%
Non-U.S.: 16%
Minority: 4%
Part-time: None
Average age: 26.7
Applicants accepted: 46%
Accepted applicants enrolled: 37%

Annual tuition: $11,300
Room and board: $8700
Average GMAT score: 622
GMAT range: 520 to 750
Average GPA: 3.24
GPA Range: 2.16 to 4.0
Average Years of work exp.: 3.5
Average starting salary: $47,000

Teaching methods: Case method, 50%   Lecture, 50%

It would be easy to mistake Rice University's B-school for a modern museum. Nestled in a grove of oak trees, the red brick and white limestone building is topped by terra cotta roof tiles. Its sleek design is worthy of the pages of top architectural reviews. In fact, Herring Hall, the home of Jesse H. Jones Graduate School of Administration, *has* been featured in *Progressive Architecture* and *Domus* of Milan.

A museum, however, it is not. The B-school, named after a Houston entrepreneur and financier, offers one of the best MBA programs in the Southwest. By design the classes are small and personal. Of the 1300 graduate students on this 300-acre campus in a Houston residential area, roughly 15 percent go to the business school. And the academic standards are high. That's why the school is commanding greater attention these days.

One odd fact about Jones: It lacks official accreditation because of an undergraduate "managerial studies" major that the school does not control. The AACSB believes it should run the program. Another sticking point could be that the part-time faculty of about 30 teachers outnumbers the 27 full-time professors on the tenure track. Still, it doesn't seem to bother the recruiters or the students, many of whom could easily get into far more prestigious programs.

The core curriculum is a real grind, just as it often is at most other top B-schools—you need 64 credits to earn a degree. The most unusual feature of the core is a yearlong study of "legal and governmental processes" that explores the government's impact on business. The course reflects the program's early roots in initially granting not an MBA but a Master of Business and Public Management degree, like Yale University's B-school. Jones' diplomas are now stamped with the MBA.

This is a very small program. The advantages are obvious in the low student-faculty ratio and the intimacy of the program. With only 56 electives, however, there are far fewer courses from which to pick and choose. And because many of these are taught by adjuncts, it's not always easy to arrange time to see professors outside of class.

In 1994, 63 companies recruited on campus, including Compaq, Chase Manhattan, Paine Webber, American Airlines, Booz Allen & Hamilton, and Exxon.

Contact: D. Richard Trask, director of admissions, 713-527-4918
Final application deadline: March 1 for fall

Texas A&M University

College of Business Administration and
Graduate School of Business
331 Blocker Building
College Station, Texas 77843

Enrollment: 520
Women: 31%
Non-U.S.: 23%
Minority: 8%
Part-time: None
Average age: 25
Applicants accepted: 52%
Accepted applicants enrolled: 51%

Annual tuition: resident—$2200
nonresident—$6600
Room and board: $3150
Average GMAT score: 607
GMAT range: 480 to 730
Average GPA: 3.26
GPA range: 2.74 to 4.0
Average starting salary: $41,990

Teaching methods: Case method, 50% Lecture, 50%

You wouldn't expect to find anything but a rather ordinary MBA program at the adolescent business school at Texas A&M University. But you'd be dead wrong. While most new MBA candidates are climbing ropes and juggling five courses, incoming students at A&M spend their first week in an intensive course called The MBA Challenge. The class explores the foundations of business behavior and its interactions with such key stakeholders as customers and suppliers. It also simulates a business environment by requiring students to make decisions under stress.

The unusual course provides the framework for the entire MBA program. Then, first-years roll up their sleeves for three "highly integrated" classes in accounting, info systems, and quantitative methods. In the second semester, Texas A&M splits the program into a pair of seven-and-a-half-week terms, putting MBAs through only two core courses at a time. To reach the second year, students must also complete a mandatory cross-discipline project and attend executive skills development workshops held every Friday. While your colleagues at other schools may head for the beach in the early summer months, A&M encourages you to pick up a pair of electives. You can do this by studying abroad, taking a corporate internship, or signing up for the school's Washington, D.C., campus program. You also must take a course in international business.

In the second year, students plunge into the capstone course on Corporate Strategies and Public Policy as well as two remaining core courses. That doesn't leave much flexibility to choose many electives. In fact, if you picked up a pair over the summer, you only need 4 more from among a broad range of 146. Finance and accounting are the school's strongest departments. All told, students have to tally up 53 hours' worth of work: 35 hours of the new core curriculum and 18 through six elective courses.

College Station, about an hour and a half drive from Houston, is a comfy, inexpensive place to spend a couple of years. The B-school and all of its students—including a rather overwhelming 5600 undergrads—is housed in a modern, six-story building. About 70 companies recruited on campus in 1994.

Contact: Susan L. Robertson, director of masters programs, 409-845-4714
Final application deadline: February 1 for fall

University of Alabama

Manderson Graduate School of Business
P.O. Box 870223
Tuscaloosa, Alabama 35487

Enrollment: 181

Women: 21%

Non-U.S.: 13%

Minority: 9%

Part-time: None

Average age: 23

Applicants accepted: 45%

Accepted applicants enrolled: 58%

Annual tuition: resident—$2260
  nonresident—$5640

Room and board: $3500

Average GMAT score: 585

GMAT range: 490 to 720

Average GPA: 3.2

GPA range: 2.5 to 4.0

Average starting salary: $35,600

Teaching methods: Case method, 33% Lecture, 33% Other, 33%

Alabama's best MBA school is as quintessentially Southern as a mint julep or a Goo-Goo Cluster. Six of every 10 students at the B-school hail from either the state or the Southeast, and typically they end up there. And like those two famous products of the South, the school has a long way to go to build a national reputation. Yet it's hardly short on ambition. As Robert J. Allen, MBA program director, puts it: "We are a regional school, but we aim to be recognized nationally."

Allen has made several changes to attract more qualified applicants from outside the South. His first step was to diversify and upgrade the quality of the student body (GMAT scores have risen 45 points, from 540 in 1986.) His second step was to build a new $40 million facility, which opened in the fall of 1993. The three-building complex, connected by skyway walkways, houses updated classrooms and a new business library. While the additions are new, the architecture remains traditional, featuring massive white columns and winding staircases.

Allen also is hoping that a recently restructured curriculum will lure more out-of-state students to the Tuscaloosa campus. While many B-schools have added to the MBA workload, Alabama actually decreased the number of hours needed to graduate to 49 from 60 in 1992. The school—named after Lewis Manderson, who made his fortune in billboard advertising—squeezed what had been six courses in accounting, marketing, and economics into one in each field. So now students only take four classes a semester, instead of the original five. The idea is to free up more time for students to pursue other interests, such as undergraduate language courses.

You'll get a fairly standard MBA from Alabama, even though its program has been revamped of late. The first year is crammed with basic requirements, 24 out of the 33 core credits. The remainder of the basics, plus 5 electives, make up the second year. MBAs can choose from among six concentrations by piling up 3 to 4 electives in one area.

Around 100 companies come to campus to recruit MBAs. In recession-troubled 1994, the school maintains that 68 percent of its graduates had jobs by commencement.

Contact: Jim Johnson, coordinator of graduate recruiting, 800-365-8583
Final application deadline: July 1 for fall

University at Buffalo, State University of New York

School of Management
206 Jacobs Management Center
Buffalo, New York 14260

Enrollment: 730	*Annual tuition:* resident—$4300
Women: 36%	nonresident—$7316
Non-U.S.: 16%	*Room and board:* $5593
Minority: 7%	*Average GMAT score:* 586
Part-time: 406	*GMAT range:* 370 to 750
Average age: 24	*Average GPA:* 3.29
Applicants accepted: 49%	*GPA range:* 2.25 to 3.96
Accepted applicants enrolled: 48%	*Average starting salary:* $40,942

Teaching methods: Case method, 30%   Lecture, 65%   Projects, 5%

In the early 1980s, Buffalo became a symbol of the decline of industrial America as Bethlehem Steel and other major corporations shuttered their factories in and around the aging city. These days, the news about Buffalo is decidedly more upbeat. Companies based in Toronto are setting up shop in Buffalo because of its strategic location on the shores of Lake Erie. That may be one reason why one of every four MBA students here is international—an extraordinarily high percentage for a "value" school.

For anyone attending the B-school at the University of Buffalo, the comeback of the city is certainly good news. The school, part of the State University of New York system, encourages a high level of student involvement with the community, and the flexibility of the curriculum allows it. You'll have to put together 60 credits of coursework to get an MBA here. That translates into 13 core classes that eat up 36 credits, and 8 electives that account for the rest. MBAs can use some electives to specialize in one of 11 areas that include health care systems management and management information systems. A new dean, Frederick W. Winter who headed up the University of Illinois' business department, took over last year.

The manufacturing and operations management option includes a paid, semester-long internship worth six credits with a cooperating firm, such as General Motors or Motorola. MBAs also can gain real-world experience through The Center for Industrial Effectiveness, a joint venture between the business and engineering schools. The center dispenses technical and managerial advice to struggling local companies and claims to have saved thousands of jobs.

Buffalo is attracting its share of quality students, too, with GMAT scores now averaging 586, up more than 50 points since 1986. That has helped the school in placing its students with a slew of well-known companies. The school says that 65 percent of the Class of 1992 had jobs by commencement. In that year, some 87 companies came to campus to recruit Buffalo MBAs.

Contact: Arlene Bergwall, assistant dean, 716-645-3204
Final application deadline: July 1 for fall

University of Florida

MBA Program
134 Bryan Hall
Gainesville, Florida 32611

Enrollment: 350
Women: 33%
Non-U.S.: 24%
Minority: 11%
Part-time: None
Average age: 26
Applicants accepted: 25%
Accepted applicants enrolled: 65%

Annual tuition: resident—$2658
nonresident—$8692
Room and board: $9000
Average GMAT score: 610
GMAT range: 470 to 750
Average GPA: 3.28
GPA range: 2.7 to 4.0
Average starting salary: $44,826

Teaching methods: Case method, 40%   Lecture, 40%   Projects, 20%

Immediately after donning cap and gown at Florida's B-school two years ago, Brent A. Berthy turned entrepreneur and launched his own company. But he wouldn't have been able to pull it off without his MBA. No one ever said that a B-school degree is a prerequisite for taking the entrepreneurial route. But Florida's unusual entrepreneurship program, in which Berthy sketched out the planning for his startup, is aimed at students who plan to form companies or work as venture capitalists. The program trains students to write business plans for their own new ventures, and it also teaches them the skills necessary to manage those companies effectively.

After completing a semester of core requirements, students can enter the certificate program in the spring of their first year. They begin with a preliminary industry analysis and use the summer for an internship with a startup or venture capital firm. In year two, students develop their own business plans while completing the regular courseload. Entrepreneurs give students constant feedback and guidance, and just before graduation MBAs go head-to-head in a business plan competition.

The school has tried to upgrade the quality of its student body in recent years (average GMAT scores rose 12 points for the most recently admitted class). Florida claims its traditional strengths are in marketing, finance, and health care. Students are expected to take 16 classes to graduate—10 core and 6 electives. In the first semester of your second year, you can study in England, France, or Italy. The one-year program in Nijenrode, the Netherlands School of Business, allows students to earn a Master of International Business Administration degree in addition to their MBA.

Among other things, the B-school moved into the expanded Bryan Hall in 1992. The larger building houses new placement facilities. The expanded placement operation attracted 83 companies to campus in 1994, up by 6 from 1992. Sixty-nine percent of the Class of 1994 had job offers by graduation. More than 80 percent were placed in the Southeast, where the job market is healthy.

Contact: Robert Williams, director of admissions and student services, 904-392-7992
Final application deadline: April 1 for fall

University of Georgia

Terry College of Business Administration
Brooks Hall
Athens, Georgia 30602

Enrollment: 15%
Women: 30%
Non-U.S.: 21%
Minority: 9%
Part-time: None
Average age: 26
Applicants accepted: 27%
Accepted applicants enrolled: 55%

Annual tuition: resident—$2352
  nonresident—$6150
Room and board: $3225
Average GMAT score: 626
GMAT range: 400 to 740
Average GPA: 3.19
GPA range: 2.23 to 3.96
Average starting salary: $46,121

Teaching methods: Lecture, 70% Case method, 30%

The old South meets the new at the University of Georgia's B-school. On a campus that could have been the setting for *Gone with the Wind,* MBAs study finance, accounting, insurance, real estate, and management information systems—all growth areas in Georgia's dynamic service-based economy. Rhett and Scarlett would feel right at home on UGA's 532-acre campus, with its antebellum architecture, tree-lined walkways, and fiery-colored azalea bushes.

Located 70 miles northeast of Atlanta, Athens calls itself Georgia's Classic City—and with good reason. People joke that there are probably more Greek columns here than any place else except the original Athens. One thing Georgia's Athens has that the Greek one doesn't is a progressive music scene: REM and The B52's originated here.

Georgia offers two versions of its MBA: a two-year program for students without undergraduate business degrees, and a one-year program for those who have undergraduate degrees from AACSB-accredited schools. The two-year students are expected to complete 50 credit hours of core in the three quarters of the first year. Georgia's faculty has recently revised the core curriculum. The changes, including a new course in negotiation and a required international class, will be in place by the fall of 1995.

In addition to the core curriculum, students are required to pick 2 "sequences" out of a possible 21 to follow in many differing fields. You can pursue investment management in the finance department or strategic management of innovation in the management group. You can also pick one of three novel paths offered by other areas of the university: media organization management, textile management, or pharmacy care administration.

Accounting, finance, and management are among the strongest departments at Georgia in terms of faculty research. But the innovation and entrepreneurship, insurance, and real estate areas attract strong student followings. About half of the students admitted in 1992 received assistantships. In return for two years' worth of tuition, students work around 13 hours a week for a professor. Some 65 companies recruited in Athens last year.

Contact: Don Perry, director of MBA admissions, 706-542-5671
Final application deadline: March 15 for fall

University of Kansas at Lawrence

Graduate Advising Center
206 Summerfield Hall
Lawrence, Kansas 66045

Enrollment: 428
Women: 30%
Non-U.S.: 27%
Minority: 2%
Part-time: 261
Average age: 25
Applicants accepted: 47%
Accepted applicants enrolled: 75%

Annual tuition: resident—$2366
nonresident—$6924
Room and board: $3384
Average GMAT score: 584
GMAT range: 430 to 710
Average GPA: 3.3
GPA range: 2.16 to 4.0
Average starting salary: $36,183

Teaching methods: Lecture, 60%   Case method, 40%

You know the famous line in *The Wizard of Oz,* when Dorothy finally returns home to Kansas. "Auntie Em," she intones, "there's no place like home." Even MBA students who hail from the Sunflower State share her sentiments: More than half of the B-school's MBAs are Kansans who typically end up working in the region as well.

Founded in 1924, 15 years before the famous movie made its debut, the business school has taken the unusual route of shrinking the size of its MBA program by 16 percent in the mid-1980s at the height of the MBA boom. The reason: It could become more selective and increase the quality of its students. That strategy worked well, with average GMAT scores rising to 580, from a rather lackluster 516 a decade earlier. The best B-school in Kansas still hasn't been able to gain much of a reputation outside the region.

Yet, the present or former chieftains of three big accounting firms, KPMG Marwick, Ernst & Young, and Deloitte & Touche all received bachelor degrees from the school. As Dean Joseph Bauman says, the program is based upon the belief that the person who knows how will always have a job, and the person who knows why will always be their boss. The school attempts to create future bosses by laying on what it calls an MBA Foundation Skills course loaded with leadership exercises. A total of 56 hours are needed to earn the degree. Of the required 44 core credits, 29 are taken in the first year. The second year is filled with 5 more classes in the core and only 4 electives. Students can use their electives toward a concentration, but a major isn't required. A pair of electives can be taken outside the B-school. Many MBAs use this flexibility to bone up on foreign languages while studying abroad.

Unlike most other institutions, Kansas's business school is not departmentalized. The school believes this is a hidden asset, because professors are more likely to cooperate with each other across the different disciplines—a goal of many curriculum revision efforts these days. While the core classes are not integrated, the interdisciplinary background of the professors helps to bring continuity into the classroom. In 1994, 72 companies came on-campus to interview MBAs.

Contact: David O. Collins, associate director of masters programs, 913-864-4254
Final application deadline: May 1 for fall

University of Kentucky

College of Business and Economics
Lexington, Kentucky 40506

Enrollment: 248
Women: 11%
Non-U.S.: 16%
Minority: 1%
Part-time: 123
Average age: 24
Applicants accepted: 36%
Accepted applicants enrolled: 71%

Annual tuition: resident—$2730
                    nonresident—$7530
Room and board: $6068
Average GMAT score: 598
GMAT range: 460 to 730
Average GPA: 3.28
GPA range: 2.5 to 4.0
Average starting salary: $35,750

Teaching methods: Case method, 50%   Lecture, 50%

All of BUSINESS WEEK's "value" schools—which are primarily public institutions—offer a good education at a reasonable price. But many of them are feeling the effects of the budget squeeze hitting higher education. That's certainly true at the University of Kentucky, where the B-school already has had to whittle down the number of electives offered MBAs. Indeed, Kentucky seems to be fighting an uphill battle: trying to improve the quality of its program with fewer and fewer resources.

That's too bad, because the B-school recently moved into a new $10 million building with a modern library, student study areas, and computer-linked classrooms. The facility is shared with more than 2500 undergraduates and 400 graduate students. Moreover, the school has been able to increase its average GMAT scores to 597, up from only 500 a decade earlier. Future cuts in the school's budget, however, threaten to undermine the quality of education that Kentucky can deliver.

UK recently reorganized its MBA curriculum. The school offers two options: one for former undergraduate business majors, and one for those who lack the business basics. Both tracks are now 36-hour programs. All students take the same core courses in their first semester. During the second semester they split into the two tracks, with the experienced students taking one core course and three other courses in a specific concentration, while the nonbusiness students take four additional core courses. In the third semester, the business-track students take two core courses, an additional course in a concentration, plus an elective, while the nonbusiness-track students take three core courses and one elective. The specific concentrations offered for the business-track students include finance and banking, management information systems, and marketing and distribution. Electives for both tracks are given in such areas as health care, total quality management, and international business. New courses have been added to the core of both tracks, Global Business Management and Top Management Leadership in Contemporary Societies. Students may also participate in internships with local companies and/or study abroad in Asia or Europe.

During the past two years a placement office has been added to the MBA program. In 1994, about 80 companies recruited MBA students.

Contact: Donald J. Mullineaux, associate dean for academic affairs, 606-257-3592
Final application deadline: July 24 for fall

University of Maryland at College Park

College of Business and Management
College Park, Maryland 20742

Enrollment: 500
Women: 33%
Non-U.S.: 33%
Minority: 28%
Part-time: 200
Average age: 26
Applicants accepted: 20%
Accepted applicants enrolled: 57%

Annual tuition: resident—$6287
  nonresident—$9995
Room and board: $7500
Average GMAT score: 625
GMAT range: 550 to 770
Average GPA: 3.25
GPA range: 2.7 to 4.0
Average starting salary: $45,950

Teaching methods: Case method, 55% Lecture, 45%

William E. Mayer, the Wall Street whiz kid and former CEO of First Boston, has made his return to the University of Maryland's business school campus in College Park. This time, he's not an MBA student. He's the dean. Recruited in late 1992, Mayer is heading up an all-out attempt to vastly improve the quality of Maryland's MBA program. Even while the overall university faces budget cutbacks, the new dean extracted a pledge of future support from the president, who sorely wants the school to achieve national recognition. The upshot: While many public B-schools are cutting back, Mayer has been given authority to hire 10 new teachers to increase the size of his faculty to at least 84 professors.

He also moved the school into a new four-story building in early 1993—the handsome structure features a huge skylighted roof that floods the building's cherry-wood interior with sunlight. It's equipped with state-of-the-art classrooms and labs, as well as more comfortable interviewing rooms for the extra recruiters Mayer hopes to entice to the campus. More importantly, the new plant houses an overhauled MBA program. The school's new academic program incorporates seven required mini-courses, called Experiential Learning Modules (ELMs), into the core curriculum. The ELMs have been designed to introduce the "softer skills" of management to students. For example, in one ELM, called The Washington Experience, Maryland grads learn the importance of government and public policy to the business community. The group meets with Capitol Hill staffers, participates in practice committee hearings, and questions lobbyists at a mock Ways and Means Committee hearing. They also attend EPA and SEC briefings and hear from lobbyists who represent business associations and labor unions. Other features of the revised curriculum include a mandatory group field project and a required course in business communications.

In an academic year, students select from up to 74 elective courses. Maryland has increased the proportion of elective versus required courses. Electives now constitute 21 of 54 credit hours, enabling students to pursue their own individual interests.

One area in which Maryland needs to show improvement is the placement office. Only 71 percent of Maryland's class of 1994 had jobs at graduation, and more than 5 out of 10 were placed in the Baltimore-Washington area.

Contact: Mark Wellman, director of master's program, 301-405-2279
Final application deadline: May 1 for fall

University of Tennessee at Knoxville

College of Business Administration
722 Stokely Management Center
Knoxville, Tennessee 37996

Enrollment: 160
Women: 30%
Non-U.S.: 8%
Minority: 5%
Part-time: None
Average age: 28
Applicants accepted: 31%
Accepted applicants enrolled: 52%

Annual tuition: resident—$2412
                      nonresident—$6192
Room and board: $5000
Average GMAT score: 601
GMAT range: 490 to 720
Average GPA: 3.3
GPA range: 2.6 to 4.0
Average starting salary: $46,500

Teaching methods: Case method, 50% Lecture, 50%

When it comes to teaching business, most MBA programs come in two flavors. There are the case-study champions led by Harvard, and there are the quant schools led by MIT. Then there's the University of Tennessee.

Who? Relatively unknown until recently, this innovative B-school has made a name for itself by embracing one of the most influential movements in contemporary business: Total Quality Management. It did so largely in the executive education arena. Now it's trying to pull off a similar feat by overhauling its MBA curriculum.

By many accounts, little Tennessee is among the B-school pioneers in developing a program for the 1990s. First-years no longer take the traditional core courses, with marketing, finance, and other disciplines taught separately by one specialist in each area. Instead, students are thrown into just one class each semester combining all of the functional areas. They're divided into five-to-seven-person teams, taught by groups of faculty, and sometimes awarded team grades. The entire first year of work is based on a complex case written by the core faculty. Memos are sent to the students via mailboxes or e-mail, notifying them of their grandfather's death and their subsequent inheritance of his vegetable manufacturing company, Volunteer Vegetables. The fictional company is managed by MBAs who face a series of problems called "milestones," which build throughout the year to include new-product launches and international expansion.

Moreover, the class is team-taught by 14 core faculty members. Some days four or five of them will lead the class, while on the other days only one or two are at the helm. Not only do the core professors teach together, they all prepare test questions and agree on a final semester grade for each of the 80 first-year students. MBAs are given only one grade at the end of each semester, but they receive extensive comments on their work throughout. The second year of the program is more traditional, and pretty flexible. Students have to complete 24 credits of electives. A minimum of three classes (9 credits) are needed for a concentration.

MBAs had trouble finding jobs in 1994. The school reported that only 50 percent of them had offers by graduation, most placed in the Southeast.

Contact: Donna Potts, director of MBA admissions, 615-974-5033
Final application deadline: April 1 for fall

APPENDIX

Every two years, BUSINESS WEEK names the Top 20 graduate schools of business in a fall edition of the magazine. Since 1988, when BUSINESS WEEK first combined the views of MBA graduates and recruiters into a new ranking system, we have chosen the best institutions on the basis of customer satisfaction: how the schools determine and satisfy the needs of both graduates and the corporations that hire them.

Like previous rankings, the latest contained in this book are based largely on a composite of two separate polls conducted by the magazine during the spring and summer of 1994. One poll surveyed the Class of 1994 at 44 top graduate business schools—selected on the basis of their standing in our corporate recruiter survey. The 36-question survey asked graduates to assess the quality of the institutions that stamped their diplomas. All of the questions, as well as raw results, are reproduced in Chapter 4. Another poll surveyed the leading organizations and corporations that actively recruit MBAs. This questionnaire asked recruiters their opinions regarding the schools of which they have knowledge and experience.

Through three separate polls of the graduating class at top schools in 1990, 1992, and 1994, BUSINESS WEEK has built a longitudinal set of data to capture the opinions and views of 12,984 MBAs. A larger number of independent observations in such a study lends greater reliability to the results. It also helps to smooth the impact of short-term ups and downs in any one year. That's why BUSINESS WEEK uses three years' worth of longitudinal data to compose its graduate rankings, giving the greatest weight to the latest survey. The corporate ranking remains based solely on the most recent poll of recruiters, because the sample of companies surveyed has remained virtually identical to previous studies.

To assist BUSINESS WEEK with the polls, the magazine employed an expert in survey design and statistical methods as a consultant. Matthew Goldstein, president of the Research Foundation in New York, consulted with BW on all aspects of the polling process. A well-published academic in the field, Goldstein also has co-authored four books on statistical methods and has served as a consultant to pollster Louis Harris Associates, AT&T Co., and General Foods. His description of the methodology follows:

The Graduate Survey

Sample Design

The 1994 BUSINESS WEEK study of a predetermined group of 44 MBA programs is based upon data provided from a sample of their 1994 graduates, as well as data for the 1990 and 1992 cohorts. Since fewer MBA programs were surveyed in 1992, and still fewer in 1990, data are not available for every school for the three study years.

A sample of 6353 graduates were allocated among the four strata proportional to the size each represented in the population. A total of 4608 usable questionnaires were returned from the graduate cohort (a response rate of 73 percent).

Graduates were asked to answer most questions on a scale of 1 to 10. One example: "How would you judge the school's performance in providing you with numerous ways of thinking or approaching problems that will serve you well over the long haul?" If a graduate thought the school did an "outstanding" job, he or she would answer "10"; graduates who believed the school's performance was "poor" would answer "1." The responses were weighted to account for how closely they related to overall satisfaction.

The 1994 graduate survey instrument is largely identical to what was used in 1992 with the exception of two additional questions asking for satisfaction ratings on the areas of diversity and information technology. Several other questions, including one in which respondents were asked to name the two best teachers in their program, were not included in the ranking process.

Using some refinements of the weighting scheme employed in the 1992 graduate component of the study associated with item variability and item association with overall satisfaction, standardized scores were obtained for each of the programs. Using a weight of 50 percent with 1994 results and weights of 25 percent for both the 1990 and 1992 graduate standardized scores, an overall set of scores was derived. The graduate ranking, then, is the result of 4608 responses in 1994, 4712 graduates from 1992, and 3664 responses from the 1990 poll. Subsequent studies will seek to use a longitudinal set of three years' worth of data by culling the oldest set of responses and giving greater weight to the most recent data. This process allows for data smoothing, permitting, for example, gradual patterns resulting from the perceived changes in the direction or management of programs to be better understood and time tested.

The Recruiters' Survey

In addition to the data from graduates, responses from recruiters representing companies having familiarity or experience with the programs were obtained. While building on previous classes of graduates to arrive at a richer pool for study is compelling since, among other things, it allows for some smoothing and variance dampening, only the current data from recruiters were used in the 1994 study. The decision to restrict analysis to the most recent observations was made primarily because the recruiter sample has much in common with the two previous studies.

1994 Surveyed Schools and Graduate Poll Response Rates

School	Total replies	Response rate
California, Berkeley	124	82.67%
Carnegie Mellon	86	88.66
Case Western Reserve	64	76.19
Chicago	191	71.00
Columbia	205	71.68
Cornell	125	69.83
Dartmouth	86	86.00
Duke	153	74.27
Emory	64	76.19
Florida	42	61.76
Georgetown	54	65.06
Harvard	228	64.04
Illinois	94	63.95
IMD	51	65.38
Indiana	121	81.21
INSEAD	127	59.35
Iowa	27	56.25
London Business School	107	67.72
Michigan	162	70.74
Michigan State	31	63.27
Minnesota	53	71.62
MIT	129	72.47
New York University	140	67.31
North Carolina	60	83.33
Northwestern	231	77.26
Notre Dame	75	75.76
Penn State	47	67.14
Pittsburgh	95	65.97
Purdue	49	75.38
Rochester	80	80.00
Southern California	67	77.91
Southern Methodist	67	79.76
Stanford	169	80.48
Texas	178	77.39
Thunderbird	126	58.60
Tulane	52	72.22
UCLA	155	84.24
Vanderbilt	83	83.00
Virginia	131	87.92
Washington (Seattle)	41	58.57
Washington Univ. (Olin)	74	74.00
Wharton	254	70.56
Wisconsin	33	66.00
Yale	77	77.00
Grand Total	**4608**	**72.53%**

A set of 354 organizations with established histories of recruiting at business schools was selected and asked to provide an officer in charge of the company's recruiting efforts who would respond to a mailed questionnaire. Respondents were assured that their individual answers to the survey would be confidential. Recruiter replies totaled 254 out of 354 surveyed (a response rate of 72 percent).

For those schools the company in question has knowledge of, or involvement with, the recruiter was asked to indicate overall preference, taking into account such things as the school's quality and his or her company's success rate with its graduates. Each recruiter was allowed 10 schools to evaluate, hierarchically ranking them on a scale of 1 to 10. A school named No. 1 received 10 points, while a school ranked No. 10 received 1 point. The total score for a school was then divided by the number of responding companies that recruited MBAs from the school.

All other things remaining equal, it is fair to assume that fewer recruiters will visit the smaller programs as opposed to those programs with larger classes. Mindful of this, the standardized scores for the recruiters' component of the study were weighed up to create a more logical basis for comparison. As a result, 11 of the Top 20 schools had adjusted scores. Once accomplished, the standardized scores for the two data sets were joined to generate the overall ranking.

Recruiter opinion naturally looms larger in the overall ranking because there's a wider spread between the top and the bottom in that survey. In the graduate survey, for example, the difference between No. 1 Stanford and the University of Iowa, ranked 44, was about 39 percent. The difference in the corporate poll between No. 1 Wharton and Case Western Reserve, which ranked last out of 44 schools, was about 382 percent.

BUSINESS WEEK - 1994 B-SCHOOL SURVEY

All your responses to the following questions are strictly confidential.

Name _____

Address _____

Phone number _____ Age _____ Sex _____

Undergraduate institution _____

Degree_____ Year _____ Major _____

Current/expected employer _____

Title _____ Career path (e.g. marketing) _____

First-year starting salary _____

Signing bonus _____

Other first-year compensation _____

Would you be available for a telephone interview by a Business Week reporter? Yes No

The survey is based on a numerical scale of 1 to 10. On most questions, though not all, you should circle 1 if your satisfaction level was poor (bottom third) or 7 if it was excellent (top 15%). A score of 10 would indicate an unusually outstanding level of performance (top 2%).

1. To what extent did your MBA experience fulfill or fail to meet your expectations of what a good program should be?

Failed expectations		Barely met		Fully met		Surpassed		Vastly exceeded	
1	2	3	4	5	6	7	8	9	10

2. Do you believe your MBA was worth its cost in time, tuition and lost earnings?

Return was 0%				50% Return				100% Return	
1	2	3	4	5	6	7	8	9	10

3. How would you rate the quality of the teaching in core courses?

Poor		Average		Good		Excellent		Outstanding	
1	2	3	4	5	6	7	8	9	10

4. How would you rate the quality of the teaching in elective courses?

Poor		Average		Good		Excellent		Outstanding	
1	2	3	4	5	6	7	8	9	10

5. Overall, how did the quality of the teachers compare with others you have had in the past?

Poorly		Similar		Better		Much Better		Superbly	
1	2	3	4	5	6	7	8	9	10

6. Were your teachers at the leading edge of knowledge in their fields?

Never		Sometimes		Usually		Often		Always	
1	2	3	4	5	6	7	8	9	10

7. Were the faculty available for informal discussion when classes were not in session?

Never		Sometimes		Usually		Often		Always	
1	2	3	4	5	6	7	8	9	10

8. To what extent were faculty aware of the material other faculty members would cover?

Never		Sometimes		Usually		Often		Always	
1	2	3	4	5	6	7	8	9	10

9. To what extent was the coursework integrated as opposed to being taught as a cluster of loosely-related topics?

Never		Sometimes		Usually		Often			Always
1	2	3	4	5	6	7	8	9	10

10. How current was the material/research presented in class for discussion and review?

Never		Sometimes		Usually		Often			Always
1	2	3	4	5	6	7	8	9	10

11. Do you believe the faculty compromised teaching in order to pursue their own research?

Never		Sometimes		Usually		Often			Always
1	2	3	4	5	6	7	8	9	10

12. Did you receive practical information during the program that will be usable on the job?

Never		Sometimes		Usually		Often			Always
1	2	3	4	5	6	7	8	9	10

13. Was the amount of assigned work and reading so excessive that it impeded learning?

Not enough				Just right					Excessive
1	2	3	4	5	6	7	8	9	10

14. To what extent were analytical skills stressed in the curriculum?

Too little				Just right					Excessive
1	2	3	4	5	6	7	8	9	10

15. To what extent were interpersonal skills stressed in the curriculum?

Too little				Just right					Excessive
1	2	3	4	5	6	7	8	9	10

16. As a result of the program, how would you judge your ability to deal with computers and other analytical tools that affect your ability to manage?

Poor		Average		Good		Excellent			Outstanding
1	2	3	4	5	6	7	8	9	10

17. How would you judge the school's performance in providing you with numerous ways of thinking or approaching problems that will serve you well over the long haul?

Poor		Average		Good		Excellent			Outstanding
1	2	3	4	5	6	7	8	9	10

18. Do you feel your classmates emphasized individual achievement at the expense of teamwork?

Never		Sometimes		Usually		Often			Always
1	2	3	4	5	6	7	8	9	10

19. Did the caliber of your classmates impede or enhance the learning process?

Mostly impede				Enhance				Greatly enhance	
1	2	3	4	5	6	7	8	9	10

20. Would you urge friends or colleagues to take the same MBA program at the school?

Never		Maybe		Usually		Often			Always
1	2	3	4	5	6	7	8	9	10

21. How would you judge the responsiveness of the faculty and administration to students' concerns and opinions?

Poor		Average			Good		Excellent		Outstanding
1	2	3	4	5	6	7	8	9	10

22. How would you assess the responsiveness of the school in meeting the demand for popular electives?

Poor		Average			Good		Excellent		Outstanding
1	2	3	4	5	6	7	8	9	10

23. How would you judge the opportunities given to you--either in class or in extracurricular activities--to nurture and improve your skills in leading others?

Poor		Average			Good		Excellent		Outstanding
1	2	3	4	5	6	7	8	9	10

24. How would you appraise your school's efforts to bring you into contact with practicing professionals in the business community?

Too Little				Just Right					Excessive
1	2	3	4	5	6	7	8	9	10

25. How would you judge the school's network and connections that can help you throughout your career?

Poor		Average			Good		Excellent		Outstanding
1	2	3	4	5	6	7	8	9	10

26. How would you judge the aggressiveness of the school in helping you with summer job placement or a summer internship?

Poor		Average			Good		Excellent		Outstanding
1	2	3	4	5	6	7	8	9	10

27. How would you characterize the school's performance in helping you find a job before graduation?

Poor		Average			Good		Excellent		Outstanding
1	2	3	4	5	6	7	8	9	10

28. How would you characterize the number and quality of firms recruiting on your campus?

Poor		Average			Good		Excellent		Outstanding
1	2	3	4	5	6	7	8	9	10

29. If the organizations you targeted for employment did not recruit on campus, how would you assess your school's assistance in supporting your independent search for a job?

Poor		Average			Good		Excellent		Outstanding
1	2	3	4	5	6	7	8	9	10

30. How would you appraise the placement office's help with matters such as interview training, negotiating strategy, resumes, etc. ?

Poor		Average			Good		Excellent		Outstanding
1	2	3	4	5	6	7	8	9	10

Appendix

Please name two members of the faculty who you consider to be the best teachers at the school:

_____   _____

Please name your two most favorite elective courses:

_____   _____

Based on your level of satisfaction, please appraise your school's efforts in the following areas:

	Outstanding (Top 2%)	Superior (Top 5%)	Excellent (Top 15%)	Good (Top Third)	Average (Middle Third)	Poor (Bottom Third)
International Business						
Ethics						
Leadership						
Quality Concepts						
Diversity						
Information Technology						

What's the size of your outstanding educational loan due to your MBA? _____

How many job offers, if any, did you have at the time of graduation? _____

What was your approximate pay in the year before business school? _____

Additional comments (Please feel free to comment on any aspect of your MBA experience)

INDEX

American Graduate School of International Management (Thunderbird), 29–32, 34, 36–41, 43–45, 48–60, 223–226, 305, 324, 343
Arizona State University, 322, 325
Australian Graduate School of Management, University of New South Wales, 308

Babson College, 5, 321
Benjamin Franklin Program, 307
Bernard Baruch College of the City University of New York, 321, 322, 326
Boston University, 321
Brigham Young University (Marriott), 322, 324, 327

Cambridge University, 303, 304
Carnegie Mellon University, 5, 9, 14–16, 23, 26, 27, 29, 31–41, 43–45, 48–60, 166–173, 343
Case Western Reserve University (Weatherhead), 29, 34–38, 41, 43, 44, 48–60, 227–230, 343, 344
Chinese University of Hong Kong, The, 308
Columbia University, 6, 8, 14–16, 26, 27, 29–31, 33–41, 43–45, 48–60, 118–125, 343
Copenhagen Business School, 305, 308
Cornell University (Johnson), 14–16, 26, 27, 30–32, 34, 35, 37, 39, 40, 43, 44, 48–60, 174–181, 343

Dartmouth College (Amos Tuck), 8, 9, 14–16, 26, 27, 30–41, 43, 44, 48–60, 158–165, 343
Duke University (Fuqua), 8, 11, 12, 14–18, 22, 23, 26, 27, 33, 35–41, 43–45, 48–60, 142–149, 343

Emory University (Goizueta), 29, 32, 33, 35, 41, 44, 45, 48–60, 222, 231–234, 343
ESSEC Graduate School of Management, 308

European Institute of Business Administration (INSEAD), 303–305, 307, 309–310, 343

Georgetown University, 30–37, 41, 43–45, 48–60, 235–238, 307, 343
Georgia Institute of Technology, 322, 328

Harvard University, 5, 6, 8, 9, 14–16, 23, 25–27, 30–32, 35–41, 43, 45, 48–60, 94–101, 307, 343

Indiana University, 8, 14–16, 26, 29–36, 39–41, 43–45, 48–60, 110–117, 321, 343
Institut Superieur des Affaires, Groupe HEC, 308
International Graduate School of Management (IESE), 307, 308, 311–312
International Institute for Management Development (IMD), 305, 313–314, 343
International University of Japan, 303, 308

Katholieke Universiteit Leuven, 308
Keio University, 308
Koblenz School of Corporate Management, 192, 308

l'Ecole des Hautes Etudes, 308
London Business School, 304–308, 315–316, 343
Lyon Graduate School of Business, 192

Manchester Business School, 308
Massachusetts Institute of Technology (Sloan), 6, 9, 14–16, 23, 26, 27, 29–33, 35–39, 41, 44, 45, 48–60, 134–141, 305, 343

Michigan State University (Eli Broad), 29–41, 43–45, 48–60, 222, 239–242, 343
Monterrey Tech, 191

National University of Singapore, 303
New York University (Leonard N. Stern), 14–16, 23, 26, 27, 32, 34, 35, 37, 40, 44, 48–60, 182–189, 304, 307, 324, 343
Northwestern University (J. L. Kellogg), 4, 8, 9, 14–17, 21–23, 25–27, 29, 34–41, 43–45, 48–60, 70–77, 305, 343
Norwegian School of Economics and Business Administration, 308

Ohio State University (Fisher), 322, 329
Oklahoma State University, 27
Oxford University, 304, 307

Pennsylvania State University (Mary Jean and Frank P. Smeal), 31–36, 38–41, 44, 45, 48–60, 243–246, 343
Purdue University (Krannert), 9, 26, 30, 31, 35–37, 40, 43, 44, 48–60, 214–221, 343

Rice University (Jesse H. Jones), 321, 322, 330
Rotterdam School of Management, Erasmus University, 308

St. Gallen University, 308
SASIN Graduate Institute of Business Administration, 303, 308
Scuola do Direxione Aziendale dell' Universita Luigi Bocconi, 308, 317–318
Southern Methodist University (Edwin L. Cox), 30, 32–36, 40, 41, 43–45, 48–60, 247–250, 343
Stanford University, 8, 11, 13–17, 25–27, 29–38, 40–41, 43–45, 48–60, 86–93, 307, 343, 344
Stockholm School of Administration, 308

Texas A&M University, 322, 323, 331
Tulane University (A. B. Freeman), 29–31, 33–41, 43–45, 48–60, 251–254, 343

University at Buffalo, State University of New York, 322, 333

University of Alabama (Manderson), 322, 332
University of California, Los Angeles (John E. Anderson), 5, 14–16, 22, 26, 27, 29–41, 43–45, 48–60, 126–133, 343
University of California at Berkeley (Walter A. Haas), 14–16, 26, 27, 29, 31, 34–40, 43, 44, 48–60, 206–213, 343
University of Chicago, 8, 14–16, 18, 22, 26, 27, 29–31, 33–38, 41, 45, 48–60, 78–85, 343
University of Florida, 22–23, 29–34, 36–41, 43–45, 321, 322, 324, 334, 343
University of Georgia (Terry), 321, 322, 335
University of Illinois at Urbana-Champaign, 29–34, 36–41, 43–45, 48–60, 255–258, 343
University of Iowa, 29–41, 43–45, 48–60, 259–262, 343, 344
University of Kansas at Lawrence, 321, 322, 336
University of Kentucky, 322, 337
University of Maryland at College Park, 322, 323, 338
University of Michigan, 6, 8, 9, 14–16, 18, 21, 22, 26, 27, 29–34, 36–41, 43–45, 48–60, 102–109, 343
University of Minnesota (Curtis L. Carlson), 29–41, 43–45, 48–60, 222, 263–266, 343
University of New Mexico, 27
University of North Carolina at Chapel Hill (Kenan-Flagler), 14–16, 26, 27, 29, 30, 32–39, 41, 44, 48–60, 198–205, 321, 343
University of Notre Dame, 23, 29–31, 33, 34, 36–39, 41, 43–45, 48–60, 267–270, 343
University of Pennsylvania (Wharton School), 6, 8, 9, 14–17, 21, 22, 25–27, 30, 31, 33, 34, 36–41, 43–45, 48–60, 62–69, 70, 306–307, 321, 343, 344
University of Pittsburgh (Joseph M. Katz), 23, 29, 31, 32, 34–38, 40–41, 44, 45, 48–60, 271–274, 343
University of Rochester (William E. Simon), 14–16, 30–33, 35, 36, 40, 41, 48–60, 222, 275–278, 343
University of Southern California, 5, 27, 30, 31, 34, 35, 39, 40, 43, 45, 48–60, 222, 279–282, 343
University of Sydney, 308
Univeristy of Tennessee at Knoxville, 322, 323, 339
University of Texas at Austin, 14, 15, 26, 27, 29, 32, 33, 35, 36, 48–60, 190–197, 321, 343
University of Toronto, 303
University of Virginia (Darden), 8, 14–17, 26, 27, 29–33, 35, 37, 44, 45, 48–60, 150–157, 343
University of Washington, 29–34, 36–41, 43, 45, 48–60, 283–286, 343

University of Wisconsin—Madison, 29–41, 43–45, 48–60, 287–290, 343

Vanderbilt University (Owen), 29, 30, 32–35, 37–41, 44, 45, 48–60, 291–294, 343

Wake Forest University, 27

Waseda University, 307
Washington University (John M. Olin), 32, 34–36, 39–41, 43, 45, 48–60, 222, 295–298, 343
Western Business School, 303, 319–320

Yale University, 14–16, 18, 27, 29–40, 44, 45, 48–60, 222, 299–302, 343

About the Author

John A. Byrne is a senior writer at BUSINESS WEEK. With a team of BUSINESS WEEK editors, Mr. Byrne has prepared and written *The Best Business Schools,* Fourth Edition. He has followed the business school scene for many years, and writes BUSINESS WEEK's semiannual cover stories surveying the top schools. Mr. Byrne is also the author of *The Headhunters* and *The Whiz Kids: Ten Founding Fathers of American Business—and the Legacy They Left Us.*